"My China –
Living Inside the Dragon"

Jeremy Bazley

authorHOUSE®

AuthorHouse™ UK
1663 Liberty Drive
Bloomington, IN 47403 USA
www.authorhouse.co.uk
Phone: UK TFN: 0800 0148641 (Toll Free inside the UK)
*   UK Local: (02) 0369 56322 (+44 20 3695 6322 from outside the UK)*

Published by AuthorHouse 07/19/2022

ISBN: 978-1-7283-7431-4 (sc)
ISBN: 978-1-7283-7430-7 (hc)
ISBN: 978-1-7283-7432-1 (e)

Library of Congress Control Number: 2022913475

Print information available on the last page.

Synopsis

My China – Living inside the Dragon is a compelling memoir that details the author's fifteen years of living, working, and travelling in China at a pivotal time in the country's development. Readers will find this work to be as insightful as it is entertaining.

Living in China away from large expatriate communities, both through business activities, in private life and supplemented by travel around much of the country, the author was exposed to the wide-ranging variety of Chinese culture and its differing geographical influences. These included the ways and the lifestyle of the Chinese people, with those personal observations and opinions reflected in this book.

This critique is widely varied in content from daily routines to a view on the more sophisticated aspects of society with all its complexities, seen through the eyes of a foreigner. Containing credible personal views including extracts from detailed personal diary notes written during this extraordinary period of China's truly historic growth and evolution. This transformation period during the early part of this century (2002-2017) laid the foundations for its current wealth, successes, and a platform for its continual drive towards achieving its future ambitions.

The Author

Jeremy Bazley

Jeremy Bazley was born in England, later studying in Aberdeen, Scotland, and London Business School. A former national league basketball player, he entered the paper industry and progressed to senior executive positions in the UK industry, working for international companies serving global speciality markets. As such he has traveled to nearly fifty countries.

In 2002 he went to work in China on behalf of a UK based entrepreneur managing a joint venture with a state-controlled company making high quality cigarette paper for the huge Chinese market. His responsibilities were to be expanded to include directorships in a variety of companies in four different Provinces.

These activities brought him in contact with all aspects of life from the brushes with corridors of power in the Great Hall of the People in Beijing, local government powerbases, the modern mega cities and to the starkly comparatively less affluent rural countryside.

He was awarded China's Friendship Gold Medal in 2005, *"the highest award that China was able to bestow upon a foreigner"* for *"outstanding contribution to China"* in the presence of Premier Wen Jia Bao.

He was to remain living and working in China until early 2017 when he returned to the UK to live.

Contents

Part 3 The Travel Experiences

Foreword

April 2020 and I found myself like so many others, at home, self-isolating in rural southwest England due to the coronavirus lockdown. Out of the blue I received a package from China, a box of face masks to protect me and my family against contracting the virus. This came with a letter from an old friend in local government expressing care, appreciation, and support, this being three years after I left those shores. It was a truly kind gesture during extremely troubling times in recognition of my past contributions and was indicative of the Chinese approach to life through 'friendship'.

This virus started in Wuhan, Hubei province, China, and it was apparent that this virus was not only having a major effect upon the world, with its associated natural cull, but consequently the associated effects upon the global economies that it will most likely change the future for so many of us in so many ways. The short term was scarily uncertain for all! This is effectively the pseudo "war" of my generation and the two subsequent generations given the impact that yet is to fully unfold. It was a global shock and wakeup call that will result in future re-alignments in attitudes and the way that things are done.

China almost inevitably, was coming under criticism, both from the politically motivated media in the West and for other reasons directly related to the handling of the virus, transparency, and credibility of the statistics relative to number of coronavirus cases and deaths being recorded there. Global scrutiny is on the rise and conspiracy theories as to the virus's origins and motivation abounded.

I found myself staring out from my study over the rural countryside reflecting upon my prior life in China, truly a world apart. I went there in May 2002 to live and work for a UK based company managing a joint venture manufacturing company in the city of Jiaxing in Zhejiang province, in eastern China. Its location was 80 kilometres from the vast and dynamic metropolis of Shanghai, one of the most exciting cities on the planet. Born in Britain I had not lived and worked abroad before, although through travel I was not naive when it comes to overseas cultural differences having visited forty-eight countries, flown 1.63 million miles, on 826 flights through different 175 airports to date.

Wind back to January 2002, forty-four years old, and I was looking for a job having parted ways with my American employer some nine months earlier. Until then I had enjoyed a career as a senior executive in the international speciality paper industry, working within corporations from a relatively early age. The opportunity arose to work in China and the lure of witnessing China first-hand during an historic moment in the world's development was too much to refuse, a life changing and cultural experience for my family and me. After some serious family soul-searching I decided that I would go alone, my three children remaining at school in the UK.

I accepted the job without a prior visit, although there was a quick verification visit in April that year, just prior to starting full time in May. My intention was to work two years there after a six-month trial, and consider it from there onwards, a career steppingstone. In the event my experience lasted fifteen years, despite deciding to come home after four years. Indeed, I resigned, but persuaded to stay, and that decision was to change my life in more ways than was potentially imaginable.

During that time China morphed itself into the second largest economy in the World and chasing down the number one spot, re-inventing so much of its lifestyle. It developed at an incredible pace in front of one's eyes, and the world started to see the impact of 'China's Century,' after the prior century which undoubtedly belonged to the USA and the century or two before that belonged to Britain. Even now I do not believe that most of the world is ready for or understands the extent of what is happening in China despite extensive coverage globally, some of it emotive and alarming in nature.

The personal consequences were not all good, resulting in the painful break-up of my first marriage and this of course was never a part of my plan, nor to live at distance from my family long term. I was later remarried, to a wonderfully delightful Chinese lady and subsequently had another two wonderful daughters later in life; that was the positive outcome.

The pain though along the way, both from my domestic situation and the extreme challenges of business took their toll. The experiences along the way though were incredible for a boy from down in Devon, England.

The current focus upon China and its global impact brought back so many memories, some good, indeed exceptionally good, and some frankly not so good. Some of the commentaries included are serious observations, some are lighter in nature, but always these are intended to be factual as I understood them and non-judgmental of the environment that I was living in.

I should declare up front that during my time I was presented with various awards of recognition through the all-important 'Friendship', from the Jiaxing city and Zhejiang provincial governments in China, but also at the pinnacle in the autumn of 2005 I received the 'Chinese Friendship Gold Medal', awarded for *'Outstanding Contribution to the development of Chinese culture, economy, technology, science and education'* in The Great Hall of the People in Beijing, held in the presence of the then Premier, Wen Jia Bao, and culminated in attending the National Holiday's State Banquet dinner in the Great Hall hosted by President Hu Jin Tao and the Politburo. The reason for this personal award and recognition, *the 'highest award that China can make to foreigners',* was basically a combination of our company's progressive investment activities, my personal relationships with local government officials, and as always in life being fortunate enough to be in the right place at the right time. Based in Jiaxing at a time when its rapid upward trajectory was just really starting and was becoming recognized on the national landscape.

These recognitions were business related, but all along the way the government insisted that these were personal awards for my personal friendship, diplomacy, a solution orientated approach and cooperation with the local joint venture partner and Chinese government at various levels. This therefore differentiated my prior such pinnacle event of being greeted by Her Majesty Queen Elizabeth II of England and HRH the Duke of Edinburgh a decade or so earlier at an award ceremony within Buckingham Palace, London, for the Queen's Award for Technological Achievement. It is fair to say that the first few years in China went well and for a while so did my career!

I was later to revisit the Great Hall of the People as a part of UK Prime Minister Gordon Brown's delegation to Beijing in 2008, representing my company as a long-term investor in China, the most notable British delegation attendee present from the business world being Sir Richard Branson.

Jiaxing had not initially develop at the rate that many neighbouring cities did in the 1990's, but it held a special place in the national psyche as this is where the declaration of the formation of the Chinese Communist Party was signed in 1921, on the Red Boat by the island at the city's South Lake. As such, being positioned geographically between the magnificent cities of Hangzhou and Shanghai, it became a place of pilgrimage for 'Party' members from all parts of China as well as regular tourists as it tapped into the increasingly impressive transportation infrastructures that developed.

The fact that I received this award should not identify me automatically as a sympathizer or promoter of all things Chinese, nor conversely a critic. I was though able to recognize the issues, factors and way of life that prevailed in China and was in a good place to make balanced views and observations on life, factually and unemotionally. My feelings are not intended to offend either individuals or the government of China in any way, but if they do, I apologize right now. My views though reflect what I lived through, saw, heard, smelt, and witnessed, the considerable frustrations, from what I saw and endured. My personal politics are not Communist or Socialist, but that does not mean that one cannot learn from the positive things in such an environment.

This book includes documented personal diary entries, often focused on the human side. Not a straight political critique of the Chinese system or the politics, but the experiences that come from being immersed in a culture and the system. Living for the most in 'Chinese China' in relative isolation as an expatriate, not in internationally populated cities like Shanghai, not in an expatriate compound with foreigners and foreign entertainment around.

I intend to stay away from my direct business experiences, but there were moments in my life, indeed it was all embracing, when business and personal circumstances overlapped and so inter-twined that references will appear. I should declare that the business side of my adventure was not as successful as one may have wished, for a diverse range of reasons, extraordinarily challenging in the face of the loaded dices dealt, and its best left at that for now.

I do though feel extremely privileged to have lived through China's rapid growth during these extraordinary times. I made friends and was warmly and generously welcomed in the most and for that I am eternally grateful. China has an immense ancient history and traditional culture to go with an enormous population. I have no doubt that given its size and power, its ambition, its pride, education, discipline, and motivation, that it will grow further towards global domination through its trade and relationships over the coming decades. It is unfettered by some of the weaknesses, limitations and restrictions that prevail throughout Western society, which influence their government's ability to govern and manage their countries as effectively as the public would wish. One can interpret this as one may wish to do so politically, but that must be the reality unless something monumental happens to stem the developments; it is about sheer population numbers, wealth, strength, pure ambition, and 'face'!

China's historic culture is incredible, but as a Westerner that provides its own challenges. As a rule of thumb I was to learn that any subject raised will be responded to by an approach from 180 degrees in the opposite direction compared to Western thinking, assuming of course that it was translated properly in the first place. This point, literal and cultural interpretation of the same words to differing meanings, presented its own challenges. The agenda was always different!

Every race and creed also have their own cultural influences, one can't ignore that however one may wish, it's one of those facts of life even in our all-inclusive, globalized world we now live in. We Brits have our own quirks, mindsets and ways and so do others. It is possible that some of my observations, as a well-travelled Brit, may be interpreted by those who may wish to do so, as generalist racial stereo-typing or racist. This is not the intent and I ask that such instances should not be viewed in that way but considered constructively without the need to criticize for the sake of it.

I spent 25 per cent of my life living in China, in what was a non-expatriate city. Indeed in 2012 I was presented with a ten-year residency green card for China, eradicating the need for a standard visa, and making my passage in and out of China much easier. The issuing of such cards remains tightly restricted in China with immigration controls tighter than most of the Western world. There is no real opportunity for a foreigner to get a Chinese passport should they wish unless an expatriate of recent Chinese descent.

I feel that given my combination of experiences of life in China, outside of the traditional diplomatic, intelligencia in the comfort of the expatriate communities, that I am uniquely placed to comment. I note from various exchanges and meetings that much of the major city-based expatriate community was not aware of many of the ways of the China at large. The views shared though are purely my own observations and at times I may have misunderstood things, but that was the life that I had led and what I saw, understood, and interpreted at the time.

China continues to learn from the rest of the world developing at an incredible pace and the rest of the world can learn things from China. I will never forget the words of Premier Wen Jia Bao when addressing us in late 2005. He stated to the effect that 'China whilst having made great strides in recent years, was still a developing economy and will continue to need the world's help to as it seeks to reduce and eliminate poverty and increase the development of its middle classes.' Since that time China has made unbelievable progress!

So, it was a question of *'going east young man'*. I did not make my fortune but developed a new life and had experiences that are indelible to me of the extraordinary and complex society that China is.

You will see me referring throughout the book to 'foreigners,' not Westerners, not identifying by their specific nationality, but 'foreigners,' as that typically is how China generically refers to those of us who are not Chinese; 'Lao Wai' as everyone of us gets to hear spontaneously when spotted.

What follows are my experiences and associated observations, the human side, about life in China during a truly historical period 2002-2017; *"My China – Living Inside the Dragon"*.

PART 1

My Introduction
and Early Days

Chapter 1

My China

I had only planned to stay in China for two years, four years maximum, as my family stayed at home in the UK due to schooling commitments. Life's events took over and I stayed another year, then another, and consequently, I did not return to live in the UK until April 2017, nearly fifteen years. My first and prime job in China was as general manager of a joint venture with one of the top state-owned paper factories specializing in making cigarette paper. This needs more explanation to recognize the context.

China was the world's largest cigarette market and is still the largest producer and consumer of tobacco products. Since 1984 China's tobacco industry has been controlled rigidly by the State Tobacco Monopoly Administration (STMA) - yes, a state-owned monopoly. On a routine basis the industry is controlled by the China National Tobacco Corporation (CNTC), the regulatory body that was all a part of the STMA. In 1984 34.5 per cent of all Chinese smoked, over one third of the population. By the time I have arrived this had declined slightly to 31.4 per cent (noting the offsetting increase in population over time to the percentage drop) and by 2015 this was down to 27.7 per cent, still a substantial proportion of the population. Worth noting that about 70 per cent of the Chinese population were estimated to be exposed to secondary smoking effects. Smoking was so prevalent that it reminded me of the old UK trade union-management meetings of the late 1970s and early 1980s with smoke filled rooms and yellowing office ceilings, teeth, and fingers. At dinner or lunch, the first courtesy was to offer and then throw cigarettes around the table to others to catch for their consumption prior, during and after the meal. Large packs or bundles of cigarettes were typically given as respected gifts at seasonal holidays, especially the Chinese New Year, or to visitors.

It is worth noting that I have never been a cigarette smoker. I was partial to the occasional after dinner cigar, which was not a big thing in China in my early years. I did find that over dinners with customers it was important I smoked as a sign of goodwill and friendship, but I never felt the need to do it outside of this environment and circumstance.

In the period just prior to my arrival (1996-2000), China had invested ¥4.2 billion into the entire tobacco distribution system to modernize and develop it. Exchange rates vary but call it around £480 million at current exchange rates ($660 million). The industry modernized, consolidated by closing or merging inefficient factories, rationalizing brands and established a world-class manufacturing supply chain to a keenly well-promoted brand-lead market.

Officially, the STMA directly controlled 40 per cent of the industry profits. In 1997 the Chinese State collected ¥90 billion in direct taxes (£10.25 billion or $14.07 billion at current exchange rates). This represented direct tax income of 11 per cent of China's total tax revenue income at that time, not counting indirect income. My deputy at work during my introduction provided numbers that suggested with indirect income the tobacco industry's contribution to the state was closer to 25-30 per cent although I never saw the specific facts to support -- but let's go with the fact that it was a significant proportion of the country's GDP.

This was a powerful industry staffed by powerful people entwined with government at national, provincial and city levels, collectively with all the aspirations that goes with it. What did impress me was that at every stage they talked about the need for high quality product, a rigid target that was not a universal thought elsewhere in China at that time. This industry had set itself upon modernizing --- tobacco technology, paper and filter technology, spectacular branding, new designs, and world-leading paper and cigarette manufacturing processes and efficiency. They demanded the highest quality, in a country that is traditionally noted for the lapses in quality of goods. The irony being perhaps that this talk of quality was in the cigarette industry and all the obviously negative issues which go with that. Their narrative that new equipment alone resulted in best quality was not entirely appropriate in these circumstances, but the focus was there.

Since that time production has reduced by over a third, driven by

President Xi Jin Ping's smoking curbs and greater middle-class awareness of the dangers of smoking, but it is still significant.

I arrived at a sensitive time when our state controlled joint venture partner had, without agreement, set up another brand-new large paper production process which was effectively in competition to its own joint venture and hence with our company. They were able to do this after having acquired the technical knowhow as a part of the process and investing in a world class production line imported from Europe, with more expansion to follow paid for by the joint venture's profits. It was a question of *contractual interpretation* that had enabled them to do this with a sense of legality and government approval accordingly!

The consequence of this was that our joint venture lost highly profitable and prestigious business to our joint venture partner's new line's products, whilst also losing key volumes of sales that were damaging with reduced operational efficiency and lower profit margins; hence, the joint venture was forecasting hugely reduced profits and potential losses - obviously not an acceptable situation for our majority shareholder.

This was the scenario that I walked into when taking the job, one of competition with our own joint venture partner on the same production site (in direct conflict with the strategic paths of the CNTC), falling volumes, falling profits, and falling reputation in the Chinese tobacco market since our products were sold into this market by the same joint venture sales managers employed by our joint venture partners and it was clear where their allegiances were. At that stage there was uncertainty whether the joint venture would survive at all despite being only seven years into a contractual twenty-five-year joint venture life. All the key services and supplies were provided by the joint venture partner as well as the land of the joint venture site, which I later discovered had never been transferred legally to the joint venture's ownership. This was a contractual and investor shock of significant magnitude, a contractual sleight of hand and interpretation of the translation. This was a classic Chinese State-owned company move -- establish a joint venture with an overseas partner, preferably a leading one, be the minority partner with minimal cash investment, provide land and acquire the technical intellectual property, understand the optimized manufacturing processes and techniques, improve product quality, and get outside investment to fund it. Then the high level of profits as a result are used for reinvestment initially in a modern, more competitive, and larger volume production line with very supportive banking arrangements. Then enjoy the benefits of long-term profitability and all that it entails including the additional income from funds because of a Shanghai Stock Exchange floatation.

This was my challenge, to ensure initially that we had a viable business at all, maximize profits in an extremely difficult and highly sensitive political situation at many levels, and to do so for the longer term. Business management school situations could not make up the scenarios that were encountered with the largest industrial partner in the city!

So my plan had to involve recovering sales volumes and margins, improving production efficiency, which we did, enhancing product design and quality and developing further our own support services. All done effectively and diplomatically trying to gain the credibility of our joint venture partner, the CNTC and our customers who at that time were 100 per cent within China (we were prevented at that time from exporting under monopoly rules as part of counterfeiting prevention measures). Additionally I had to be active to re-assure an increasingly depressed workforce that the joint venture had a future. The workforce was very plugged in to the joint venture partner's narrative as they were primarily all the ex-factory employees of the state-owned partner. They had work ethic and mindset baggage that goes with this and living together in the same community.

Due to my job, initially with a Chinese customer base and combined with my relative novelty in those days as a *'Lao wai' (foreigner)*, I had to embark on a programme of getting out and meeting the industry and our customers. This also suited our joint venture partners, to a point, who were still keen to promote the benefits of overseas partners technically but became less comfortable with my promotions of our joint venture, our parent company contributions and brand. As one employee once told me a couple of years into my stay, *'They thought that they could control you, Jeremy, but learnt that they couldn't which challenged them, but you also earned their respect'.*

I was therefore to have the privilege to travel pretty much all over China on business noting the country's vast diversity and the immense size of the country, which is not dissimilar to that of the USA, but with a far greater population. Each province has similarities, but so many localized differences as well. With a few notable exceptions I travelled to:

> Nineteen of China's twenty-seven provinces -- Anhui, Fujian, Gansu, Guangxi, Guangdong, Hainan, Hebei, Heilongjiang, Henan, Hubei, Hunan, Jiangsu, Liaoning, Shandong, Shaanxi, Sichuan, Xinjiang, Yunnan, and Zhejiang.

> Both of China's SAR's (Special Economic Regions) -- Hong Kong and Macao.

> Three of China's four independently governed regions -- Beijing Shi, Chong Qing Shi, and Shanghai Shi.

In total I visited twenty-four out of thirty-three regions, covering 73 per cent by region in all geographic areas of China.

Many of these areas were visited on numerous occasions in some cases more times that I can recall.

The nine provinces and regions that I did not get to included Guizhou, Inner Mongolia (an omission, should have made time), Jiangxi, Jilin, Ningxia, Qinghai, Shanxi, Tianjin Shi, and Tibet (another omission). I would like to have visited them all.

I came to learn that *business travel* during the early part of the century was regarded in China as an opportunity for something of an associated holiday – several days travel for what in the West may have been just a flight and overnight stay. This included banquet dinners at the best local restaurants, staying in the best hotels, entertainment – wide and varied in nature, visiting key local tourist destinations was a must, hosted by the ever courteous and proud local contacts. In my case, on many occasions it included meeting with senior local government officials at many levels. This was the given norm for business travel at that time and I was truly privileged at the experiences it afforded me due to our State-controlled joint venture partner's leadership and a showcase of the Western influence upon their company. This was all part of the *guanxi*.

Through circumstance I found myself living a life for the most in *Chinese China*, with few fellow expatriates around especially in the early years. Indeed only two other foreigners working full time in urban Jiaxing city, a fluent Chinese speaking German who lived in Shanghai and a German engineer who was initially kept separate from me as he was providing alternative competitive technology for the new papermaking process. Therefore I was away from the more isolated chattering classes, intelligencia and professional communities of the larger cities, building a life in a country where I didn't speak the language, in the early days, but also benefiting from the privileges that went with the job position.

I also visited several key countries immediately surrounding China and was able to note the Chinese influences, connections and indeed attitudes that prevailed at times through the so-called *Bamboo* network. These included Taiwan (Which China has publicly declared that it wants under Chinese control and is a somewhat more than a sensitive matter – Reclaiming Taiwan is an absolute and non-negotiable objective of China, and which is does not regard as a separate country); Vietnam, Malaysia, Thailand, Indonesia, Japan, South Korea, the Philippines, India, and Russia. Many with established, wealthy, and influential expatriate Chinese populations which was truly an eye opener. These connections should not be underestimated as a key part of China's growth and were key to its Asian regional exports and commercial development often supported by huge investment funds provided out of Hong Kong.

From 2004 onwards our UK based business principal went on an entrepreneurial investment spree that resulted in more travel around China and included investment in a new paper manufacturing business manufacturing tea bag paper (with the same original joint venture partner), which was primarily export orientated. Also another cigarette paper joint venture, a tea plantation, a plastics business, land and premises, packaging lines, and an automotive filtration paper manufacturer.

The growth in every aspect of life had been astronomical since China started opening in the 1980's. Maybe it was a slow and cautious start, but by the time I arrived on those shores this was rapidly gaining momentum and that growth was to explode exponentially over the coming years. This was truly the 'wild East' as centralized government policies were locally interpreted in a pseudo capitalistic way and adapted to create both localized and immense personal wealth for some! China is now vying with the USA as the largest economy in the World.

The absolute ambition is extreme at all levels, from the government through to individual families and the *"Tiger Mums"*. The West has become comparatively comfortable in life, fat and lazy, some may say, decadent certainly, with breakdowns of traditional values and folks consumed by their next holidays, personal freedoms, rights and drinking too much alcohol, China sees everything with a genuine hunger and wants everything, especially money, not surprising perhaps given its not so distant history. China like India has a huge population, a growing globally migrant population with second and third generation overseas diaspora and nationalistic pride and ambition. China has the advantage over India in terms of its government's centrally controlled policies and the absolute power it must make things happen quickly and control the agenda!

The Chinese development strategy has been well documented and clear, although perhaps still not fully recognized by the majority. My summary observations of this would be:

> Become the 'factory for the world', creating trade, creating much needed jobs, increasing the skills of the populace, and developing wealth, bringing in cashflows of the much-coveted US$.

> Start by making standard, low quality, easy to make, cost driven products, and then improve quality over time, trading up towards to making newer more scientific products with high quality. The targets being the higher technology markets which are cleaner, can yield greater value and control. Ultimately the goal is to ensure the World becomes dependent upon China for its products as it closes its factories and relocates manufacturing to China, effectively reducing competition and locking in the international markets. It is a long-term game.

> Draw in huge overseas investment, which was a crucial aspect, with overseas funds effectively funding the re-construction of its manufacturing base and the closures of its old inefficient and polluting factories.

Get hold of as much *intellectual property* as possible from investing companies or service contracts. This is key to the strategy and at any costs, with notable exploitation of IP taking place.

Gain understanding the World markets, knowhow, working methods, quality expectations, its culture, and requirements through a policy of sending out its political and commercial leaders to gain experience, understanding and to modernize thought processes. This includes education of its middle-class children overseas, something that Party families have been quietly arranging for decades. With increased wealth and success, overseas holidays for the burgeoning middle classes have expanded this process as the masses participate in the global experience.

Effectively colonizing areas of the globe through trade. Huge investment funds support local Asian commercial development. Parts of Africa is being effectively colonized in many parts in a way that no Western country could do, as indeed with others such as Pakistan, providing massive infrastructure and housing as encouragement and repayment for raw materials. Overseas corporations, including Western ones, are being acquired or have significant Chinese shareholdings. Investing in overseas housing is now seemingly a cultural pastime!

Develop China's own internal markets rapidly, tapping into the huge population of 1.4 billion people that are rapidly getting wealthier as the urbanization draws people out of the countryside fields into the mega cities to participate in the manufacturing and commercial experience that prevails. Key to this is the building of new apartments in huge quantities, creating individual security through ownership. These markets have grown hugely, demanding high quality goods and international fashions. This strategy has effectively reduced the dependency upon income from overseas markets having de-risked the exposure somewhat in recent years, albeit the overseas markets remain very important.

Developing the cities structures for the future, improving lifestyles and all importantly the connecting infrastructure to support trade, travel, and growth. Huge networks of toll road motorways, high speed rail systems, new planes with spanking new vast airports and all that goes with modern newly planned high rise-based cities. Everything is specified for the future and projected expansions.

Keeping control of its population as best it can, maintaining security in a way that few Westernized countries are able to and most importantly maintaining *social stability*, crucial with so such a large population and memories of the Mao lead revolution not so long ago. Whatever the political views, most Western leaders must look on with envy at the power, control, and lack of overt domestic criticism that their Chinese counterparts enjoy. China carefully controls its immigration policies, thereby protecting its culture from outside influences.

Developing the country's military might, as quietly as possible but with very visible exposures when it suits. The priority is global development via trade, but as per the USA's and British models before-hand, military might, and dominance is key in negotiations and expansion progress. The most obvious signs of this being building an infrastructure in the seas close to home in Asia which appears to be spreading.

Exporting its people. Sensitive subject perhaps. When we look around so many parts of the World have rapidly growing Chinese communities, contributed to, like me through the social contact that inevitably develops through increased exposure, some through the commercial opportunities that go with that, some through the opportunity of an overseas education and sometimes a presence that perhaps was not so legally achieved. The Chinese are generally hard working with strong communities, and as with so many immigrant populations they must work harder to establish themselves. In general, they add value where they go. As model examples look at western Canada and its Chinese demographic spread, Australia, and New Zealand for example where the demographics have overtly changed so rapidly, but in truth it is happening in most places. This in time will influence voting policies and elected leaderships.... all a part of the process and long-term game, not necessarily controlled but a consequence. Government and individual ambitions coincidently converge as a part of this process.

Encourage foreigners to work in China, for tourist income and sales of their goods, yes, but on the business side to acquire knowledge and expertise through its 'foreign expert schemes'. The numbers of those working there will be controlled ongoing and minimized over time to reduce costs (foreigners are traditionally very expensive, but also considered not needed when skills have been acquired). Foreigners are tolerated for the most and there are interesting dynamics involved as nationalist traits are balanced by relationships, interactions, and income. Deng Xiao Ping was quoted as once saying 'when you open the windows the flies come in', in response to compatriots complaining about the methods and lifestyles of foreigners and the consequences of it. Tolerance is the understood word.

Having acquired the know-how and educated its populace, to build on these technologies and take proactive leadership roles in the lucrative global markets.

The wealth of the masses – another quote from Deng Xiao Ping in the 1980's 'It is okay to get rich'! At that stage the gloves were off!

All done through 'relationships' which can mean many different things. One thing I was to learn quickly was that you cannot get anything done in China without a *friend* to assist!

This is obviously not absolute but is indicative of my interpretation of China's strategy and this will be expanded elsewhere in this book.

This is the background, environment, and circumstances to my time in China that was to dominate my life.

Chapter 2

Around China

For context relative to this book, the first thing to recognize is that China is huge, a vast country, the third largest land area of all countries on earth at 3,705,407 square miles (9,596,961 square kilometres) behind Russia and Canada and *notably given the global economic leadership race, similar although slightly bigger than the USA which was 3,677,649 square miles (9,525,067 square kilometres).*

    I show the top ten countries by size in comparison.

Position	Country	Total Size in Square Miles
1	Russia	6,601,670
2	Canada	3,855,100
3	**China**	**3,705,407**
4	United States	3,677,649
5	Brazil	3,287,956
6	Australia	2,969,907
7	India	1,269,219
8	Argentina	1,073,500
9	Kazakhstan	1,052,100
10	Algeria	919,595

Data from the United Nations Statistics Division/Wikipedia

    Given it vastness, much of my travel was by airplane, but increasingly by train, especially the high-speed rail links. A four-hour car journey was deemed a *short trip* usually driven by a full-time driver, although the use of taxis for these trips was not unusual either in remote provinces.

See below a map of China showing its provinces, key cities, and divisions as well as the comparative sizes of the provinces relative to the immediate surrounding countries in the area.

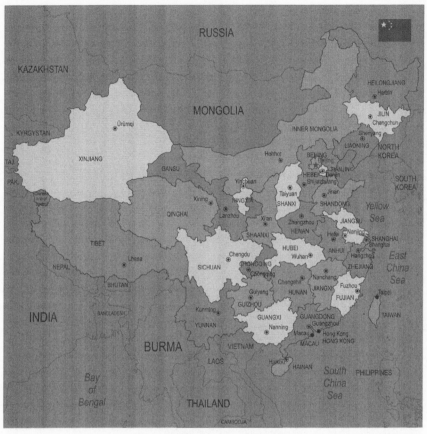

Map of China and its Provinces

China's population based on 2019 statistics is 1.433 billion people, the largest globally representing 18.6 per cent of the total population. I show this to indicate the scale of the massive population that China has, put another way, approximately one person in five is Chinese. I knew there were a lot of people in China, but nothing prepared me for the impact of the sheer numbers everywhere, although slightly less so towards the west of the country.

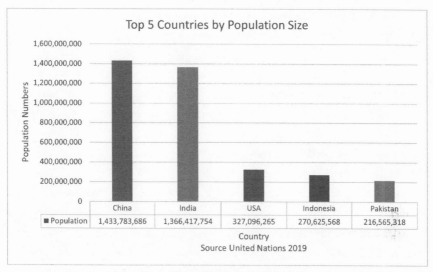

Top 5 Countries by Population

There are thirty-three provinces and special administrative regions and cities, which divide into twenty-seven provinces, two SAR's (Hong Kong and Macao being 'special economic regions') and four special administrative cities, the "Shi's" (Beijing, Tianjin, Chong Qing, Shanghai). This is how China has divided itself up on a comparable basis to the USA's fifty States.

Most of the population is based in the northeast, east, south, and central and this thins out as one goes west and north to Tibet (thirty-two out of thirty-three provinces by population), Xinjiang (twenty-four), Qinghai (thirty-one), Gansu (twenty-two) and Inner Mongolia (twenty-three), although these still have sizeable populations.

My *home province* of Zhejiang was tenth in population size and has over fifty-four million people, virtually the same size as that of England (fifty-six million), which on a personal level put my Zhejiang provincial friendship gold medal award into perspective for me. The nearby city of Shanghai has twenty-three million people registered there, noting these figures are topped-up by migrant labour, a figure of several million more I gather. Guangzhou in the South, over the border from Hong Kong, has the largest provincial population with one hundred and four million, followed by Shandong in the north with one hundred million and Henan with ninety-four million.

This is staggering given that the comparative population of the entire UK, at sixty-eight million, would rank it only seventh in size China's provincial system.

Most of China's population excluding the western provinces are predominantly Han Chinese, with Muslim populations dominating in the western part of the country. The most populous province for Muslims is Xinjiang with thirteen and a half million representing 61 per cent of the population, followed by Ningxia with two and a half million representing 40 per cent of that provincial population.

Taiwan is obviously very separate, although China has openly stated its intent to reclaim these islands at some stage in the future, managed in a comparable way to the reintegrated Hong Kong and Macao, managed as a special region within the country under a separate set of rules that converge over time. China is unyielding in this ambition. I have been to Taiwan, where Chiang Kai-Shek, the leader of the Chinese Kuomintang party, fled to after the Chinese civil war against the communists, and thereafter became heavily subsidized by the USA. Seriously emotional subject though at many levels, both Chinese and Taiwanese, and best avoided as there is no quick or easy solution. I recall my secretary in 2003, unexpectedly and which took me aback at that time, stating that she supported China going to war to recover Taiwan, something that was being widely reported at that time. Be sure, China does NOT recognize Taiwan as a separate country. Extremely sensitive currently especially following Russia's recent invasion of Ukraine. China had special departments and policies related to Taiwan.

China's provinces are increasingly linked by the most impressive infrastructure of modern airports, high speed train systems and modern toll motorways. Many of the places that I visited were before the main development of this infrastructure, which remains an ongoing project.

It was a pleasure to visit twenty-four of these regions experiencing so much of what they had to offer, tasting the foods and wines, local tourist attractions, the phenomenal geographic differences, varying architectures, seeing first-hand the people and their culture, an absolute privilege. Sadly, so many of the memories are in my mind alone as these visits were before the advent of phone cameras and my prime focus was upon business. For the most, with notable exceptions, the venues that I went to were usually far off the tourist destinations and quite often where there had been few or no foreigners there. At 6'2" in height and being a Westerner, I was readily noticed and any self-conscious inhibitions I ever had about being stared at quickly dissipated.

I was welcomed and treated extremely well on my business travels, but I quickly became weary of the many traditional tea ceremonies reflecting a 2,000-year-old tea drinking culture, which seemed to take forever. Likewise the Buddhist temples, often with impressive differing styles of modern Buddhas on show for one-upmanship – the tallest, the longest lying down, the biggest sitting down, fattest, and so on. The temples always with the residual scents from the josh sticks but I found that I could only take so much of this hospitality and even the translators got bored translated the rafts of facts presented on tours.

Along the way I travelled to seventy-five cities through thirty-nine airports in China. At times Shanghai's two airports at Pudong (primarily international) and Hong Qiao (primarily domestic) felt like second homes given I spent so much time travelling through them.

I was aware from the start that as a part of the development plan that China was investing heavily in its infrastructure to open the country economically and to facilitate the affordable and efficient movement of the masses for migrant infrastructure jobs including the massive programme of urbanization that saw the building of mega cities. The mass movement of people from the countryside into urban cities was fundamental as was the emergence of the domestic tourism industry. The plan seemed a wise and successful one.

I had been to some impressive airports internationally but was increasingly impressed by the huge new airports that were developed around the country, for the most located far outside of the built-up city areas leaving room for expansion, but also for safety and noise reasons, usually replacing crumbling old military airports. These were modern and cavernous in nature, great designs, the most obvious being the developments of the Shanghai Pudong airport on lowlands near the coast, but also the Beijing airport in readiness for the 2008 Olympics. Such projects were being mirrored all around the country albeit on a lightly less immense scale and supported by brand new plane fleets. Unfortunately, internal flights were often delayed, with often no adequate explanation, although rumoured to be deferential to the travel of political leaders and military activity. I noted that when I first started going to and from and around China that there were no Chinese travelling in business class, a situation that has reversed in more recent years given the increase in wealth and mindsets.

The motorways are wide and impressive, crossing the country, land, and sea, over some of the world's newest and longest bridges and through networks of tunnels. Notably they are virtually all toll roads, pay roads that contribute to funding, but also add the additional dimension of security and control. These toll booths, invariably with a police station in nearby proximity, and like the small police stations on all the main arteries in and out of cities, enable China to monitor and control people movements when needed. A notable example to me was when SARS broke out and the military's medical corps descended to be based at the toll booths to oversee completed health declaration forms but also to check everyone's temperature, a great method of control that would be beneficial in any lockdown situation. These roads are increasing monitored by speed cameras, photographing the car number plates of those breaking speed limits. The result is that at the next toll booth, there is a big electronic sign with the list of number plates of the offenders' vehicles, which are duly pulled over by police, the drivers fined, and points deductions implemented through centralized computer systems, instant Karma! I recall a few times when checks were implemented including when the police were trying to track down a suspected murderer.

The railways have developed rapidly through high-speed rail links across the country along with their impressive railway stations. Unlike the UK, these are quite cheap in comparison and very efficient, learning from the likes of the world's leading train systems such as the Japanese bullet-trains, with one hundred per cent computerized personal seat and carriage number allocations. These are fast and comfortable; indeed I found the Beijing run from Shanghai more reliable than the plane option given the inherent plane delays. These lines are not as fast as the Maglev train from Shanghai Pudong to Shanghai centre, a short run, which reaches speeds of 431 km/hour, which was the highlight trainline in Shanghai and a tourist must see, but were much less costly than the unjustifiably expensive Maglev.

The cities developed rapidly with families relocating from rural countryside homes that lacked amenities and appropriate sanitation in many cases, into the cities with its modern apartments, city life activity, job opportunities, medical amenities, wider food availability, and life choices. All quite different from the isolation, boredom, and relative poverty of the countryside. The consequence was the need for a huge building programme of apartments and associated infrastructure and amenities, not just the creation of the well documented mega cities with miles and miles of high-rise tower blocks, but the associated cultural and enhanced educational changes as well as control. I assume that this is the greatest mass migration in global history given the sheer numbers involved and inherently must have shaken up future gene pools further.

Across the country substantial numbers of hotels were built, from the Western joint ventures in the big cities to domestic investments, often state-owned related, often so impressive and increasing opulent catering for international tourism and business but also the increasing expectations of the ever-growing middle classes.

Chapter 3

My Chinese Adventure Starts

My job and *home* was in the city of Jiaxing, Zhejiang province in eastern China.

Before starting, having accepted the role, I was afforded a short orientation trip to China four weeks prior to view the situation firsthand. This was something of a jetlagged blur to another world, flying via Frankfurt and returning via Munich with spent mainly in Jiaxing, with some time spent at the end of the week in Shanghai. Apart from my first phenomenal impression of landing at Shanghai's then very new Pudong airport terminal one, my first memorable moment was driving out on wide new three lane motorway leaving the airport in the fast lane despite no other traffic and suddenly the driver unexpectedly swerving evasively. Immediately looking back out of the rear window to see the cause I noted that there was a garden wheelbarrow left parked right in the middle of the fast lane by a countryside worker sporting an Asian conical hat, who was cutting the immaculate bushes that filled the central reservation with shears resembling large scissors. This was an example of old and new in one snapshot. Welcome to China!

I recall the Sunshine hotel in Jiaxing, which was the most modern and international in the city at that time. I remember sitting in the corridor outside of the joint venture's board meeting, for hours awaiting a call to attend, a meeting whereby my appointment as general manager was supposedly being ratified and then I was to have been called in to participate The call never came, due to the tensions that existed between parties and which no one wanted to expose me to. In the event someone was kind enough to appear and suggest that I went back to my hotel room to rest and would be called later. I waited hour after hour, all day until just before dinner with all sorts of scenarios playing out in my mind in this odd situation; had I got the job? Was this some sort of omen? I remember eventual introductions that evening to my new senior company colleagues, and the joint venture partner leaders, warm, but the tensions obvious. I got the job, but.......... Then next day a factory tour of what in many respects was a less than impressive old factory premises with some new equipment and good processes inside. Then there were the team introductions to take on board.

I remember a late-night meeting, unsolicited, in my hotel room, a discrete and private visit by a European fellow who had attended the board meeting, and who approached me in confidence, familiar with proceedings and situation, who came with genuine good intent and confidentially advised me in the strongest possible terms not to take the appointment as it would end in disaster very quickly; *'everything is a disaster'*. I listened to the serious points that he made, as well as what I had observed, and weighed them into life's decision-making equations. Jiaxing the city was grey and overcast, but fine, I decided there and then to just do this – I liked a challenge and there was no doubt from the start that this would be one.

Shanghai, despite torrential rain and low cloud was evidently very different, even though I was not to see the best of it in the conditions that prevailed but became immediately aware of the counterfeited goods available around the streets of the Nanjing Road at low prices if one negotiated well. My first job was as a bag carrier for our principal, trying to keep the cheap contents of numerous carrier bags dry. The high point of the trip or consolation depending upon viewpoints, was buying some cheap branded silk ties.

My thoughts were of course mixed, floating between *'what have I got myself into here'* and the obvious attractions of a challenging job in this incredibly dynamic economy that was only really getting started still.

I travelled back to the UK with immediate thoughts as to how I could add value quickly, but aware there was the potential that this job wouldn't last long. Not the ideal circumstances, but the UK investor seemed committed in adversity, indeed resolute, and that was good enough for me.

For this Chapter I defer almost entirely to extracts from my diary notes from my early weeks in China documenting my initial observations, reactions, and activities in real time.

5th May 2002 - I arrived Saturday morning, my second trip to China, and was picked up at the new and impressive Shanghai Pudong airport by my translator and driver in 'my car' a black GM Shanghai Buick.

Had dinner tonight with the only other Brit in town and family. Nice spot, a revolving restaurant on the twenty-sixth story of the Diamond hotel. Good way to see the city and two hours to revolve all the way round. Food great, even the fried snake course that was his favourite. Jiaxing has 350,000 people living in the centre, but three million in outlying districts he said, most of them on bikes seemingly and with comparatively few cars – must be the world's worst drivers at first glance, not negotiable.

Sunday, jetlagged, was up early shopping at the new RT Mart supermarket. Very smart, got all sorts of stuff and basics for the apartment. Good news is that there is good Chinese red wine at three £ per bottle (Joint ventured with a French producer twenty years ago)! Realized afterwards that I had forgotten to buy all sorts of stuff as well, like a bottle opener! Tried to cook – deep fat fried stir dry with noodles which I welded together and mushrooms that could pass as bullets. In between I am reading Wild Swans, a recent gift from a friend that is a magnificent insight into Chinese modern history, and of course banned out here I gather.

First day at work on Monday went well, except that the new leather sofa that I had ordered with chairs and coffee table to match my nice brown desk and brown leather desk chair turned up in light vivid blue/turquoise leather with stainless steel legs – I've just gone art décor! Growing on me as the week goes on and matches the same light blue on all the computer chairs in other offices, suggesting a job lot.

Our business I have found has all sorts of issues with the joint venture partners and market changes since China entered the WTO, but I wouldn't want it easy, would I? The mill is shut for most of first week due to May-Day holidays.

People were very friendly and genuinely hospitable! The country is westernizing unbelievably quickly – everyone in this part of China wants to modernize. Quickly discovered that I seem to feel about twice the height and three times the weight of the average local. There is a massive tree planting campaign with and new bushes and shrubs everywhere. Very fertile and immaculately kept with park areas being planted all around the city. Plenty of new tower apartment blocks being constructed.

Tuesday was getting kitted out with bank accounts, photographs, filling in forms, receiving my new laptop – a 'Legend' brand, but I'm impressed, a new state of the art Motorola telephone – I'm now a techie learning all sorts of things and have full unrestricted internet access from home as well as work. Everything is very bureaucratic – forms in triplicate and I have my own personalized seal (there are few signatures – a seal is used, a personalized ink stamp used as standard on all documentation) and my business cards with my name written in Chinese.

Wednesday dealt with problems in our markets, mild and brief case of depression, opened the first bottle of wine of the week, but restricted myself to one full mug (No glasses in apartment yet!) after pacing the streets late to find a bottle opener. Cooking still a bit dodgy, but my wok skills are improving! Tried Chinese dumplings for breakfast but binned them after welding them together in the pan, then incinerated sausages that were apparently meant to be steamed not fried.

Thursday, had to go to Hangzhou about one and a half hours' drive away for a medical for my working visa. City centre very built up, but the West Lake is simply wonderful, very peaceful, and picturesque. Had to wait four hours after my medical for results and certificate, so we went out in a small rowboat on the lake, had wonderful lunch overlooking the lake ('Beggars' chicken, bamboo, fish, fish soup) – excellent. Went up to the nearby green tea plantations and tea shops, then walked up an historic thirteen story ancient wooden pagoda. Medical results fine and got full bill of good health and stamped certificate to say so.

Found out today that I am invited for dinner tomorrow night with the chairman of the joint venture partner, a state-controlled stock exchange listed company, and his cronies. He is also chairman of the city's largest factory Communist Party (Jiaxing is the 'home of communism'). Am informed that this will require eating a wonderful banquet, smiling, saying nice things and drinking a shed load of red wine! Just also discovered that he lives in an comparatively opulent apartment in the same street just opposite me, although you wouldn't believe so from the outside. Have also discovered that my number two is a deputy in the local factory communist party – I suspect they are watching me somehow but remind myself that this is the system!

My apartment is pleasant enough and to Western-ish standards of furnishing, although the quality is lower and not built for permanence. It is right in the centre of the city in a white tiled building that was built in 1998 *and aging rapidly. Since superseded by nicer looking buildings. Entrance is very Council block style, but once inside the outer heavy metal 'safe' outer door it's fine when things work. There are permanent un-uniformed 'watchers' staffing the entrance, low level security if you like.*

Arrived home to no hot water, no cold water in bathroom taps and kitchen. Some of the skirting boards are badly stained, fused all the lights because I turned on the bathroom extractor fan and the wallpaper is coming off because it was decorated too quickly when new before the plaster had dried. And oh yes, I broke one of the three security lock keys off in the front door on the second day. Have had workers here all week trying to sort these things and others I have found, but hopefully it will be decorated by mid-June, and I will have furnished it with some more basics. Beds, leather couch, dining room set, very large television etc are good. Took me until today to realize that I have satellite TV and can get Star Sports – thus I will be able to watch the impending soccer World Cup in English! In summary though it is nice – large lounge area open to a large eight chair dining area, two double bedrooms (one ensuite) and one large twin room, kitchen with glass table for four, bathroom, utility room, plenty of cupboard space and eight air conditioners that I am told I will need in a couple of months' time. DVD shop nearby with excellent up to date replicas available for less than £1 each, need to buy a DVD player, a good one will cost circa £80.

When I walk outside, I am something of a curiosity, which is slightly discomforting to a sensitive Englishman. Security and personal safety seem good.

w/c 10ᵗʰ May 2002 - Friday went generally well. I had my first management meeting, which although the team generally speak reasonable English, is still best conducted in Chinese via a translator. Pace is very frustratingly slow as a result. Meeting though was a success, with everybody agreeing that this 'new concept' was actually a good idea. Also my employment permit arrived so I'm now 'legal'! Discovered that the scratching above my office was mice, so we had the place fumigated. Also found birds nest in the cupboard by the safe but was promptly informed that this was a good luck sign in Chinese – which I translate to myself as Chinese for bullshit!

Had dinner for ten in a private banquet suite at a local city centre restaurant last night. The others were all key people from the joint venture partner, the local Party chairman who I took a liking to and my senior colleagues. An unqualified initial success, although I had to toast everyone around the table, twice, which involved saying 'ganbei', smiling at someone, lining up glasses and then downing the drink in one! We were on red wine, the good news that they were small glasses and only partially filled each time. There will be fun and games with this mob in future though workwise I suspect, but step by step. Found out halfway through the meal that the first dish was marinated snakes skin sliced – okay, glad I found out afterwards though.

Afterwards a couple of my new colleagues came back to my spartan apartment to drink some more wine. Had to stop and buy this and wine glasses on the way back, or else we would have been sharing one mug three ways!

Saturday, I started scrubbing the apartment clean with toothbrush; kept me going. Dinner Saturday night was with my Brit neighbour and his family at a local hotel. His son at nearly three years old is something of a local celebrity (half Western, he is the only one in town and has appeared on TV and several covers of children's' magazines).

Found out that Jiaxing has three revolving restaurants in the city centre although only one still actually rotating! On the way home I was advised by my colleague to have a head massage at a local hairdresser. This was wonderful and lasted over an hour, including having my scalp massaged with oils, face and general head, arms, hands, neck, and back massage – very relaxing and therapeutic, but hard work for the hair stylist!

The unfortunate bit is that my Brit pal had resigned shortly prior to my arrival and is leaving Jiaxing at the end of May. I will then be the only Westerner around when he departs and probably end up dragging out another expatriate at some stage. I seem to be okay with him – as a sanity check apparently and the only person to understand his dry sarcastic British humour. That's a good point, one makes a dry comment to my new Chinese acquaintances and nothing.........................! Everyone looks at each other for explanation or looks totally blank. My secretary/interpreter is starting to catch on a bit, but it will take time.

Shopped on Sunday in the city centre for more apartment essentials. Went with my colleague to KFC for lunch. I am also starting to be aware of a high number of child and adult beggars around on the streets. There are referred to *as 'out of towners' from elsewhere in China, to me looking more 'Mongolian' in nature than pure Han Chinese. The adults are a pain, but the children are heart breaking and disarmingly persistent, despite ignoring them. Apparently, there are 'Fagin' type organizations that round up disabled kids and take them to a city to make money on the streets – all very sad! My new home safe was delivered by two burly characters, absolutely knackered (I live on the fifth floor). It is not bolted down, but there is scant likelihood of anyone running off with it as it is so heavy! The DVD player enables me to go out now and buy some counterfeit DVDs (in English). The city centre is surprisingly modern with two very large apartment stores among others where you can buy virtually anything. The city continues to grow on me – old (re: drab) and new (E.g.: Neon lighted shops). Bad news is that the combination they gave me for the safe only unlocks the safe once in ten attempts!*

Sunday night was initially my most frustrating experience to date in China. I was recommended by my translator to go for a coffee at a Western style restaurant with an English translated menu! I thought that it was time to branch out on my own, put my lack of natural lack of self-confidence to one side to get fed by myself. Getting through the door was easy, sitting down, window seat all very comfortable and plush. Menu put in front of me – and the waitress is immediately trying to sell me ice cream with coffee. I ordered fried rice, fish soup and a beef dish with apple tea, but she does not want me to order this, politely, but insistently pushing me to have another dish – steak, including salad, soup, and bread – she had obviously decided that as she had a live foreigner there that I was going to have Western food! Cancel the fried rice, cancel the fish soup, change the chopsticks to knife and fork. Ten minutes later I had discovered that they sell beer in cans, albeit small ones, but I needed one. Salad appeared, small but okay followed by a delicious soup with bread topping, followed by a sizzling dish with a lid that when removed meant that none of us could get closer to it than three feet for a few minutes. When the sizzling stopped, I found steak, a large shrimp cooked in a crepe, shells, and all still on, and a fried egg which should have been called the 'thousand pieces' fried egg as that's how many pieces it came off the sizzler in – they even supplied tomato ketchup – actually very good and I got a coffee eventually (with some spirit in it) – also the first time that I used a knife and fork over here. This though was a very expensive meal in local terms (£14.90). In the meantime many passers-by stopped to stare at this strange guy sat in the window and at what he was eating, all very zoo like. One little girl, maybe three years old, who came up to touch me to see that I was real and then ran away to everyone's entertainment!

I also had my first trip on a pedal tricycle taxi today – poor cyclist looked almost disheartened to see this large Westerner approaching armed with ironing board and loads of other heavy shopping. The effort nearly killed him, but he eventually got me home to the main entrance pedaling hard on what appeared to be a bike with limited gears befitting the flat landscape.

The apartment is also starting to grow on me and becoming increasingly habitable despite its three different types of electric plug sockets. Chinese as standard somehow have two different types and then there was another design from somewhere and you have a third variation. Upshot is that all the stuff that I bought to date does not plug into any of the wall sockets that I want, so I will have to get more adaptors. The electrics generally worry me to death, sometimes with flashes coming from the sockets when I plug in.

Also I started washing – need to get clothes ready for the end of the week when I am flying to Beijing for the Government State Tobacco Exhibition. I am honoured, as I will be the only foreigner at this huge exhibition as it is officially closed to outsiders, the first ever I am told, but I have special permission as I have a work permit managing a foreign joint venture within the industry. Great opportunity for me to meet key customers and to make some high-level contacts. Beijing is a two-and-a-half-hour flight from Shanghai's domestic airport. It is a shock to my translator, she hasn't been much further than Hangzhou, one and a half hours by car.

Monday to Thursday were very frustrating as my translator was seconded to a four-day training course to become eligible to become a member of the Communist Party – typical, the timing is lousy, and I have suddenly lost both my mouth and ears! I quickly realize that I am a baby without her – helpless at many levels and totally dependent. All a bit suspicious and puts me on my guard going forward.

Monday, I had dinner at the local Chinese equivalent of a fast-food place – bright colour pictures of food to point at and order, bit variable as pictures can be deceiving, but all for £1.10! Also kept the buying habit going – CDs of the Beatles, Scorpions, John Denver, Enya double album, U2 double album, Moulin Rouge sound effects, Linkin Park, and Nirvana all for about £6 total! Had first go at washing – very good except the waste pipe blew out and covered the place in muck; floor drains in the utility room saved the day though. Important bit was that the whites came out white, but unable to work out why the machine did not consume its softener. Spin cycle must have woken everyone in the district. Monday is the first time we had any wind followed by warm light rain, spoiled the evening outdoor market though.

Tuesday its still raining hard. Got paid in cash at work mid-month, which was a slight variation on the norm – I haven't been handed my salary in my hand in cash since 1977. My Chinese credit card turns out to be a debit card, but at least I have one. Lunch at work today was not good and discovered that everyone at work knew what my salary was. Lunch was the usual rice, but the meat for the first time was truly awful, this was not helped when they told me that it was sliced pigs' tongue, but I am unsure how the bone and gristle related to it.

Had an excellent meeting with the joint venture partner sales director today. I didn't have to get nasty and indeed he seems like a good guy, especially as he promised to keep our plant's capacity full for the coming year. Brother in-law of the chairman I gather; an early illustration of how things work. Immaculate offices he had, upmarket, the JV partner is one of the biggest employers in the area, employing 5,000 people after recent slimming down. Like all paper companies, they claim not to be making any money, but the more that they invest, their share price goes up. Much more positive as we have an immediate future.

Failed miserably at cooking the second five sausages in the packet. This time I tried them in the rice boiler, but still couldn't cook them. Thoroughly fed up I had another head massage to calm me down. Decided to clean the rice boiler from the aborted sausages only to discover that I hadn't removed the paper liners that came with the unit – burnt paper everywhere, hell of a mess!

Wednesday lunchtime I went with my translator for a lunch at a small place just by the factory simply called the 'noodle restaurant', which is a loose description of this dirty garage that we ate in (not untypical). Managed to splash soup noodles all down the front of my clean shirt and looked a mess for the rest of the day. Cost me around £0.35 for what was a bowl of excellent beef spicy noodles, which would have cost me more than £10 back home, however I wouldn't come down at home with any illness that I suspect that I may come down with out here! Wednesday night is a time to relax. Invited around to my Brit pal's for dinner then he is going to take me around the town. Both drank beer at a couple of local bars. I understand why his wife doesn't like him drinking. A local bar just opened has a local live band playing some western music and Chinese pop.

Thursday was preparation for the Beijing trip. This could be hard work trying to convince China genuinely that my 'old paper mill' (only six years old) is world class. Meeting the head of the Chinese State National Tobacco Company I am told, which is conveniently a Monopoly. Potential future leader apparently. Serious power though! The word 'power' keeps getting used I note.

Still not started learning Chinese, but I am at least starting to get some sort of feel for the pronunciations of certain words. I have two words that I won't have a go at writing.

My Chinese name turns out to be misleading. My credit card came stamped translated back from Chinese into Pinyin (The Westernized interim language between English and Chinese) as 'Bei Zi Lei', which is a truer translation than the British pronunciation of Bazley of one thinks about it. Later found out that this card must go back and be changed as it is a confusing contradiction to my written passport name.

A few other things that I have noticed:

> *Two boys/men walking down the road holding hands doesn't mean the same thing that it does in the UK!*

> *If they are cuddling, it still doesn't necessarily mean what you think it may mean!*

> *It is the wedding season. Families take over modern hotels with many friends and relatives, brides wearing very impressive western white wedding dresses, restaurant floors and tables suddenly look like war zones at the reception meals given the discarded food and drink and other.*

> *There is a rapidly expanding and developing affluent middle class in Jiaxing.*

> *Some of the police go around on motorbikes or in sidecars, the types that we last saw in the UK back in the 1960s and 1970s.*

Everyone – cars, lorries, pedestrians, cyclists, children, animals, ignore red lights on the roads. They cross the roads any time, night, or day, anywhere, crossings or no crossings. Don't get fooled by zebra crossings and feel quite free to stop for a chat at anytime, anywhere on the road when crossing.

Counterfeit American Chinese computer software is troublesome. Unable to get more technical than that at this stage but seem to be some initial operating issues. This is unlicensed and its use endemic throughout the user population. An issue for the computer companies to control indeed and leaves companies exposed, but cheap!

My driver is excellent, but evidently thinks that it is funny that I see that I feel the need to put my seat belt on! Through translation he explains later that he is a safe driver and there is no need to do this, reflecting thought processes and health and safety awareness levels.

Receipts are on universally standardized pro-forma forms wherever you buy things from, details handwritten, and they must be very precisely having the exact name of the individual or company to whom they must be addressed, together with seller's official stamp. One small error, deliberate or not, and the company cannot claim back against tax. In large stores payments are through separate payment booths for security.

Standards of workmanship are very different. The wooden fittings of my replacement skirting boards are good; trouble is that they are totally the wrong colour and not matching. Unlike my apartment floorboards where the standard of replacement fitting is truly awful, although the colour match closer.

There is no monetary tipping in China at this time, almost seen as disrespectful. I am sure that will change once they catch on, not missing an opportunity to make money, but for now, a no-no.

Everybody wants to say 'hello' to me, when I respond they are totally lost for words having used up their entire vocabulary of the English language, although there is the occasional 'sorry' as follow up.

China is obviously on course to become an immense superpower and it has evidently been developing for a long time in readiness.

I feel very safe! I am told that anyone touching a foreigner would probably be executed, an obvious deterrent. I find this strangely consoling!

There are several modern building sites that are already starting to change the city landscape quickly.

Guilin, as seen on the tourist films about China on TV, looks fabulous. Must go there, seems like one of the most mystical places on earth.

Counterfeiting here is a huge business, all black money – cigarettes, CDs, DVDs and is apparently run by heavily developed organized crime gangs elsewhere in China.

Lunchtimes start at 11.30 hours daily and are one and a half hours in length. Employees usually get to sleep their offices after a quick meal (often eaten prior to 11.30 hours at their desks or restrooms as standard). This week I couldn't enter the locked Boardroom at lunchtime, which had the lights turned out at 12.55 hours, I was to find out that the 'ladies were asleep in there; a daily ritual'! Time discipline is evidently an issue.

Stocks and shares are taking off big time here – passed a rolling stock exchange transaction building this week – all up to date shares you can buy. Some Communist society this is!

Virtually everyone seems to smoke, mainly the male population, but not exclusively. I come home smelling like an ashtray and will have to handle this situation delicately, given what I know about health effects, but also the fact that we are making paper for the cigarette market. My deputy went into apoplexy when I floated the idea of no smoking signs and restricted smoking areas.

The government in China did a joint venture with VW many years ago – the result is that virtually every other car seems to be a VW Santana model, 1980 something style. All the taxis in Jiaxing are painted the identical maroon red. The few plusher cars in the city are an Audi A4, GM Shanghai and the odd Honda, all of which are black.

When you are given money, cash, don't feel embarrassed about counting it, there and then, note by note, in front of the giver, indeed it is expected and the accepted norm.

Neon type bright lights are certainly in evidence everywhere including inside of apartments on ceilings – and so ornate - very typically Asian, perhaps something to do with the flies, no, probably just a liking for bright lights.

I have never seen so many newly planting shrubs and trees anywhere else, lining roads, willows lining canals, just everywhere and immaculately kept. Market gardening would seem to have a great business here.

w/c 16ᵗʰ May 2002 - *My translator took her Communist Party provisional entrance exams, so I get her back from tomorrow and can therefore start functioning again. I now call her Chairman, which she sees the funny side of despite her apparent declaration of open love and devotion to Mao. She doesn't believe a word of international views that Mao liked young girls and had a secret concubine. Better be careful what I say.*

In a good mood today. Have announced that we will be having an interdepartmental 'housekeeping' competition at work in two weeks' time in a desperate attempt to get some of the grime, dirt and rubbish out of the factory and to set new standards befitting a modern factory. The place is taking it very seriously and people starting to run around everywhere. I am gradually getting my office to how I want it, starting to fall in love with my turquoise leather couch and chairs. Files getting sorted out, as are the mass of dust collecting cables. The software on my computer is all but loaded except for the new XP software, which knowing my history with such things will probably knacker it. As it is the portable laptop PC is starting to have wobbly moments.

Also found out that I must pay a lower tax rate out here (legally) than I had previously assumed at 25 per cent, which is wonderful, as I had thought that it was going to be 35 per cent. My bonus is also pinned down to monthly payments spread evenly. I have also convinced my accountant that it is a good idea to pay my salary directly into my bank account. I am starting to melt now ever so slowly in the increasing heat, and my office air conditioning is nicely set at fridge temperature, as is my car and apartment. Also got my Chinese work card along with my 'Z' Visa that permits me unlimited entry to China for the next twelve months.

My Brit pal's wife showed me how to cook tonight, set up the iron to the right setting and she had previously been back to the 'safe' shop to find out why we couldn't open my new safe. Apparently, it's all in the key action (I was putting the in 0.5mm too far after dialing the codes), I now apparently have a workable safe, although remain skeptical about this declaration and get the feeling of being fobbed off. The food is good – meatballs, egg, and tomato omelet ish mixture, cold chopped mixed vegetables, and boiled rice. All very nice.

Whilst packing I note that several lights are on in the apartments opposite, it dawns on me that they all seem to have turquoise couches! Badminton on TV, it is big out here. Everybody goes nuts – players, coaching staff, supporting players, crowd.

Friday, off to Beijing, my first visit. Advised by my deputy that I had to take ¥10,000 in cash (£900). I'm not too thrilled about carrying that amount of cash around with me but am assured that this 'is normal' a phrase that I keep hearing.

Having travelled to over 110 airports around the world to date, airplane travel is not really a problem for me. However, it suddenly hits me that China has lost two passenger liners within the last month with about 300 killed in total.

Not sure how to break it to my translator that the orange plimsols with large white rubber frontages and thick soles are not exactly what I was expecting for business meetings, especially as we think we are going for three days and she has turned up with one little soft bag slung over her shoulder, capacity for about three handkerchiefs.

Beijing was quite an amazing place, the scale of which was hard to come to terms with. Beautifully landscaped, tree lined grove roads, very wide roads, and large buildings; what I saw, including Tiananmen Square, Mao's Mausoleum, Forbidden City, Great Hall of the People were very impressive, with red silk fluttering flags, tall Liberation Army Officers (no longer called the Revolutionary Red Army) parading. You will not convince me that this is not a capitalist city though. The places where the politburo used to watch over the parading tanks and marching guards brings back memories and a few hairs stand up on my neck, but one must be impressed by the scale of it all. The Tiananmen Square massacre was not to be mentioned. I suddenly found myself being slightly overwhelmed by the emotion of it all, special moment in life; I was indeed lucky to be here.

Outside of the Forbidden City, Beijing, 2002, just
of Tiananmen Square. My first visit

Very hot and clear sunshine. Advanced, bigger shops and more choice than many in the West. Shops were an amazing array of down market, sophisticated super department stores and seriously upmarket brands reminding me of Tokyo, e.g. the choice of shoes for example is amazing, but who the hell wears shoes that look like that? People look taller and wider as standard up here, with some even quite fat, a different look, many looking like they have had too many McDonalds and KFCs. Pictures, posters, and advertisements of David Beckham everywhere – is there a bigger star in the World today given Michael Jordan's retirement? There are a fair few westerners around, who are generally Americans and generally loud and overweight, making me feel better until one tourist tout asks me if I am American. I don't feel unduly uncomfortable, just a tourist target. Had dinner at a famous Beijing Duck speciality restaurant off the 'Walking Street' (Pedestrian). Slight variation on the crispy duck that we get at home in the UK, but I think this was rather special, although unsure about the cold duck's gizzards which came as a separate course. Traffic habits far more disciplined than Jiaxing.

The day was spoiled by the fact that we had our fourth customer quality complaint of the week for paper manufactured in April, the month before I started – and I had been previously told there wasn't a quality problem! Intend to use my newest Chinese proverb 'Failure is the mother of Success' line on the customer to turn this into a positive future scenario. There is a creditable suggestion that our JV partner is making these complaints up in conjunction with the customers to enable paper supply to be switched from our JV to the JV partners new production line, bringing an uncomfortable feeling.

Saturday: Just call me pink face! The strength of the Beijing sun yesterday afternoon has lined me up to meet customers resembling a New England Lobster.

Stepped into the bath-shower, stood straight up, and brought down five panels and three alloy rods from the suspended ceiling – brilliant start to the day. These folks are a tad smaller than me generally.

WOW! Just Wow! Move over Beckham! Sadly, I did not get to meet the new director of the CNTC, as compensation I got to meet just about everyone else at the exhibition. One of the advantages of being the only Westerner allowed by special permit into a packed Chinese domestic only exhibition is that everyone wants to meet me or be seen with me. This exhibition was for tobacco companies from all over China, with many never having seen a real foreigner in the flesh. I must have been photographed probably 200 times on the first morning alone, as well as being followed by video cameras and TV Cameras. Life is hard sometimes, but every stand appeared to want their glamourous models in their smart and colourful regional dresses to be photographed with the tall westerner on their display stands for their own promotional motives.

These models could genuinely be described as beautiful and looked about twice the height of the average Chinese woman. I even had one photograph taken with a mock diamond tiara on my head, stood next to the model who had lent it to me.

I will probably look hot and sticky in most of the photos due to the baking hot Beijing weather. Photos with company chairmen were a little bit more serious. My team has informally changed my job title to 'special promotions director'. Even managed to get myself photographed with a cigarette in my hand in a mock smoking pose. Also managed to acquire forty-seven large specimen brand packets of cigarettes as gifts, unfortunately no one gave me any classic cigars though. I will raffle these cigarettes off back at work. My translator is privately pleased, as she appeared in many of the photos. Eventually deduced that I and my deputy were the only two in a cast of thousands at the exhibition wearing a jacket, and he only did because I was, accordingly, looked as if we had a sauna together given the heat – what a pair of pillocks!

Later it dawned on me that I had probably been promoting many brands with paper from my competitors. Reflecting though – it was at this stage that I realized that this is going to be a very different gig to any that I had undertaken before. A big part of all of this was going to be about star power and personal presence in the face of a lot of people! This was a light switch moment for me; I am different here and I must figure out how best to use this to the advantage of the company.

Afterwards, we headed back into central Beijing for some more sightseeing. We went to the Forbidden City (The former Imperial Palace); out of this World (and apparently actually was isolated for a long time). Reportedly, the Emperors of the Ming and Qing Dynasties were allowed up to 3,000 wives each, but apparently Communism brought an end to this practice and concubines generally. Plenty of chances to use my newly acquired Chinese queuing skills, which I am starting to enjoy, as most of the competition don't wish to mix it with sixteen stones of anything. The main sign at the second palace turns out to be sponsored by American Express – this is not a communist country, at least as I thought I knew it.

At dinner everyone is basking in the light of the amount of attention our company received today at a national level. Good company and they are getting good at picking excellent food that appeals to my tastes. Nothing too exotic, but good and the vegetables were excellent. Over dinner it was casually mentioned by my deputy that tomorrow there are not going to be any of our key customers at the Exhibition, so he has already booked me on a trip to the Great Wall and that I will be flying back to Shanghai tomorrow night – 'it is normal', Chinese hospitality, and its offensive to refuse, so I chose not to, but suspect that he wants me out of the way, which I will have to watch for in future. Going forward the hospitality is going to have to stop as there is work to be done.

Sunday is another early start to the Great Wall tour bus. I find that I'm on a bus tour of the Wall and other places, which were not expected. My translator is strangely subdued and in no mood to translate. Later she confided that after dinner last night she had caught up with an old university boyfriend who now lives in Beijing. I choose not to pursue the matter further.

Enjoying my first visit to the Great Wall of China at Badaling 2002

First stop was at a jade shop. Which is all very impressive if you like that sort of thing. Second stop was an ex-Emperor's tomb from the Ming Dynasty; again this was impressive, set in one of the loveliest county settings imaginable and reminded me a bit of parts of Tuscany, with large hills all around and fertile fruit groves growing in the valleys; should really be a wine growing region, but a beautiful place to be laid to rest.

Next stop was the famous 'China Academy of Traditional Chinese Medicine Imperial Family Chang Ping Traditional Medicine Specialist Department of Ton Ren Pharmacy' (genuine title) Chinese medical centre. There was a lecture by an eminent doctor who was clapped into the room as we stood and my translator has come around now, so I get to find out what it's all about. Apparently, Hilary Clinton went there for a problem, as did the President of Indonesia when he went blind but can see again now. I was feeling the best that I have done for years when I went in, but part of the process was a checkup ancient Chinese style. One look at my tongue told the doctor that he needed to prescribe me various stuff to proactively bring me back to full health and I was duly ripped off. I now had two lots of traditional Chinese medicines that I will have to take three or four times a day. Even these medical guys are serious capitalists! Funny, but doctors tend to look the same anywhere in the world.

On the way I discover that my translator is related to my deputy, a cousin, who is also the senior joint venture Communist Party representative. The plot thickens!

The great Wall at Badaling was mightily impressive; problem was that on a Sunday afternoon, half of China turned up at the same time. Good exercise and its some Wall, amazing, but not enough time to fully enjoy it and was over commercialized at this spot, which removed just a little of the sense of occasion. My translator nearly passed out in the heat going into her dying swan act, not liking anything physically challenging. Coming down from the Wall I was parched and pleased to see the sign saying, 'Beer Garden'. Sadly, it turned out to be a 'Bear Garden' with darned great live black bears in a pit and big at that! Bless. Several Americans here again and they are starting to annoy me – loud, overweight, and arrogant, so sad; it's amazing how you notice these things in a different cultural environment, they just stand out.

Travelling back my translator feels sick and by the time she's on the plane she is throwing up everywhere. Landed at Shanghai with her still camped in the plane's loo. Returning to Jiaxing the contrast to Beijing was stark; Jiaxing is a long way behind Beijing in its development at this stage.

Monday - Nothing eventful planned this week, except for a visit to see a company bank president and an insurance company general manager. Production quality is not where it needs to be either yet. Lots of feedback from the exhibition to ponder over as there is a consistent narrative, a tad too consistent.

I arrived at work and managed to fall over some pallets outside the main entrance doorway that I had been telling my Brit pal should not be there for two weeks. Grazed my shin badly and lost my temper for the first time. I think that there will not be any pallets left within 100 yards of this position in future. Workwise getting things done in China is not always as easy as it first seems, frustrating. First signs of blood pressure rising. Things will change!

To cap it all the new safe at home still won't open. Whilst out shopping I got spat upon. Poor fellow really didn't mean to, he just loudly cleared his throat, as one does in China, and turned without seeing me coming in the fast lane and gobbed over me. This is the first time that I have seen genuine Chinese apologies, even thought he was going to kiss my feet at one stage, filled up with emotion; maybe he thought that I may hit him, or even worse report him. All whilst being scolded by seemingly all the other Chinese within fifty yards, who seemed genuinely annoyed at him! I did what all us Brits would do, smiled, and calmly walked off around the corner indicating no bother – Bad words came to my mind, speculating as to whether I may need another rabies jab, or more pertinently perhaps, hepatitis.

A few more observations from the week:

> *Chinese exams: I am told that somehow, they know all the questions and all the answers before they start; noting they still must remember them.*

> *The Chinese are very nosey direct people; they get straight in there if they are curious. They think nothing of putting their heads in between two people having an argument so that they can find out up close what is going on and just listen. What's more the people arguing don't seem to mind at all. I would be tempted to plant the interloper. I have noticed this happen a few times already.*

> *The Chinese don't queue. If you see a place you need to get to, don't pause, just go for it, no matter how many you trample on route. I noticed that if you don't it is distinctly possible when waiting for a bus that even if you were at the front of the queue, you may not get on. I notice that my translator is very good at this, I must educate her at the*

airport, where at check in she walked straight to the front of the check in queue and tried to jump in, albeit without success.

Lot of North Korean restaurants in Beijing, the waitresses dressed in traditional dress attire (colourful and odd looking, but that is what they traditionally wore in Korea I am told, although suspect that is not the reality anymore).

Bargain as hard as you can. Divide initial offer price by four as a starting point. Argue, then walk off, they follow, stop, and argue again, walk off, they follow you again, argue and haggle, make obscene faces, apparently insult each other, argue again, spit, throw your arms around, world about to end expressions and end up getting the item for about one third of the original stated price. Then its smiles all round and all best friends – this is the way it is done. No problem! Large stores are less flexible, generally about 8.5 per cent discount in Jiaxing.

Hotels haven't yet learned to leave spare loo rolls in the bathrooms, no matter how small the roll in use is. Embarrassing phoning up the translator to order new loo rolls from reception. The reason is of course that all spare rolls are stolen for use elsewhere.

Chinese don't clean anything properly, due partly to a lack of cleaning chemicals and knowledge of their use. They love new things, must have new, but struggle to keep them that way. The new bit is driven by the country's leaders to modernize and is now in the collective psyche.

Labels are always left on purchases, including material one's such as sofas, including the price.

Chinese put the corner of the cloth napkins at a dinner table under the plate that you are eating from. Accordingly, I suggest that it is not a good idea to tuck the opposite corner into one's belt as you are bound to forget and when standing there will be food everywhere as the bowl flips over and spills the drinks glass. Don't even think about tucking it into your collar, noodles, or no noodles!

In Jiaxing you still see the occasional tradition 'coolie' hat (more correctly, Asian conical hats) worn by countryside workers e.g. sweeping roads, but baseball caps are taking over. I note that the only other folk wearing 'coolie' hats are Americans at tourist spots!

Chinese clear their throats anywhere and anytime as loudly as they can, which I assume means that it is not too impolite. My team tell me that this is the countryside people, but I witness this habit differently. Whilst I'm on such subjects, slurping your soup or soup noodles as loudly as possible seems to be the norm.

All the pavements are catering excellently in the big cities by having ridged walkway strips for the blind as standard – very impressive and wheelchair access seems to be universal in new buildings and centres. Hard to walk on though and subsequent changes often lead these blind straight pathways into newly planted trees, signposts, or lampposts; it's just the way it is.

As a rule of thumb, it seems to me that there are too many people employed for each job; this is partly how the country creates jobs for its 1.3 billion people, inefficient, but the county must deliver employment of the masses.

The city roads are spotless, being cleaned every night, puts most western cities to shame in comparison. That said the practices for litter here are dreadful, just that the system recognizes this and arranges it to be picked up every night, by dedicated road sweepers.

In China surnames come before Christian names. I notice this on my Z Visa where I see that my name is Bazley Jeremy.

Washing – hang your washing outside of the apartment window, select the most unfashionable, oldest, most worn, and private pieces of clothing and then put these at the front for everyone to see.

21ˢᵗ May 2002 - Tuesday was another strange day. Torrential rain all over China. Everyone in the factory has started the cleaning process, but I have this feeling that it isn't going to get us to where we need to be, although a major step in the right direction. I keep dropping hints that the standards could be better, the result is that there are fewer smiling faces and indeed several frowning faces. Otherwise it was just a day learning for me about the business and getting organized.

Would you believe that we don't seem to be able to find anyone to teach me Chinese? My translator may fill in a little but is unsure about this. 1.3 billion people in China and no one to teach me Chinese. This is frustrating. It's in the back of my mind that some folk may not want me understanding what is going on.

Wednesday was a day of fatigue. Dinner at my Brit pal's made up for it. We had dumplings – that's it, Chinese dumplings, lots, and lots of them. Some steamed and some fried, which were delicious, even more so as it was my first meal for twenty-four hours.

Thursday was the day of my visit to the bank for introduction. It is the biggest in China by a long way. Nice buildings at first look, i.e. board room on twelfth floor, but wallpaper coming off the walls. Glass chandelier in reception was very impressive, but black with dirt, suggesting that it had not been cleaned since it was hung up. Lifts didn't seem to work very well. This seven-year-old building managed to look very old and worn – this is typically Chinese I am learning, but it is strange as they are very proud and conscientious people. I suggest that this neglect (a 'blind spot') will change in coming years. The positive side was that we had a good meeting. Again I got photographed everywhere I went on the tour of the bank, although the poor photographer was publicly chastised for being late. Particularly impressive was the new 'foreign exchange' data on a screen where you could view currency rates against each other updated every minute – the wonders of modern innovation just astound you sometimes. I didn't like to dampen their enthusiasm about their newly formed department, but the international time clocks on the international trading wall (London, Frankfurt, New York) were all an hour out and I was immediately embarrassed when I pointed this out. Can't cash travelers' cheques though! Apparently, our company is a very big customer and the only one with a triple AAA credit rating in Jiaxing. Got invited to a banquet dinner tomorrow night and tentatively to a Sunday meeting with fifteen other foreign senior people in Shanghai June. I am in unsure on several counts as they haven't given me much detail about it. Opera; that would be special, the Opera here is world famous, and everybody knows how much into Opera I am!

Later found out that tomorrow night we are eating at the new entertainment centre at the TV Broadcasting Station. Now sometimes, I am a bit dim! Although the location seemed a bit odd, I am advised that it is a very special place. Later it was suggested by a colleague that I had better prepare myself for an impromptu five minutes on TV. It's a maybe, maybe not situation – let's just hope there is lots of important international news tomorrow.

I have discovered that sometimes when I ask for things, they get done with extreme efficiency and commitment. They are taking my good housekeeping competition very seriously suddenly! First, I noticed a funny smell in the offices, upon investigating I literally fell over the Finance Manager who was scrubbing the floor of his office on his hands and knees! I've started something here. Further investigation reveals that everyone in the offices is cleaning everything in sight, the smell was from the cleaning fluids. Unbelievable, it's like a picture from a cartoon with little folk scrubbing every nook and cranny. I can honestly say that I have never witnessed such response to a request. Real Power I muse! I am informed that the cleaner is getting the sack for unacceptable performance – and I thought that it was impossible to fire people out here.

Friday night was fun! Going out I realize why the classy genuine silk ties I bought in a smart shop in Shanghai were so cheap – they are missing about six inches of material! I have tied it for the sixth time I now have it at normal length, with half an inch at the back. Have decided that I could make a good friend of the head of the Bank, except that he doesn't speak English, which takes the edge off it slightly, but the translator is suddenly getting very professional, but realize that it is also a serious career and social uplift for her mixing in this level of company. My translator is visibly growing in confidence in front of my eyes. She has gone from good local girl learning English to the centre of activity in the Jiaxing business community big time. She's a good girl from an honest traditional family and handling it well. I have decided to accept the invitation to Shanghai for the banking meeting. I am told that these tickets are quite precious.

The banquet was quite sociable. Mercifully there were no TV cameras. I have noticed that when you have a private room for dinner, someone always seem to turn up out of the blue, usually a drunk, who turns out to be invariably

41

quite important one at that, rolls into the room after dinner to introduce himself with a glass in his hand. On this occasion the drunk turned out to be the head of the local Tobacco Monopoly, more ganbei. Oh what a coincidence and I consequently I have been invited to another banquet with him sometime soon. This is part of Chinese culture and basically you do business with your mates! I appear for now, to be everyone's pal. Anyway, the upshot is that the senior management team of the bank are inviting me away for several future weekends for me to have interesting looks at Chinese culture and so that they can practice their English. We have a deal, another red wine toast. My poor translator is worrying when this may be. It dawns on me that as I am so sociable tonight and speaking so much, that she has no time to eat all the fantastic food, she is working hard at her job. I was informed that I was drinking the best and most expensive red wine in China (?).

I keep trying to convince these guys that they need to build a golf course in Jiaxing, at which stage they point me in the direction of Shanghai. I say that if they want real investment money here, they need the Japanese; therefore they need a golf course to attract them. They are listening seriously. That said, I was told that a golf course in Jiaxing city was not a part of the city's urban plan, although there was one an hour's drive away in the counties.

On the way home I drop into my 'local' where the band plays as it is Friday night. I am soon on stage receiving a cigarette lighter as part of my prize for buying a raffle ticket that I didn't buy. I find out why there were no TV cameras at the TV Broadcasting centre – The entire broadcasting team were all here in this bar! I am introduced to the producer of Jiaxing local TV who is there with there with another guy I am suddenly a friend of the Sport's reporter from Jiaxing Radio, who is there with the Editor in charge, and apparently, they are all turning up at work on Monday to see me! They have my business cards, the details of which will I am sure now be all over Jiaxing. So much for my quiet beer in a corner.

I am also learning to keep a wide birth of a certain type of local lady who shouts out in the street 'Hello, you teach me English'. Call me sceptical, but I suggest that learning English is the last thing on their minds, even if I am large! I am getting quite professional at the dismissive, polite, and smiling 'no thank you' and keep on moving!

Finally got the safe changed for one that works, but the poor guys really weren't happy about bringing up another one and taking the old one away.

Sunday, my pal phones up and suggests that we go to the local open fresh food market. On the way I notice the frog sellers on the streets with bags of live frogs for sale. Some were in the process of being gutted and skinned for eating – yuck! The open food market is something else. The vegetables look good – lots of them and lots of choice. The poultry section has such a wide variety of chickens, duck, quail, pigeon, and their chicks; in many colours and patterns, all of which would make an impressive specialist collectors farm at home, all alive at this stage. The difference here is that they are for sale to eat, and animal rights don't enter the equation. I am told that you just chose one; they will de-feather it, gut it and wrap it. I decline to choose one but observe the process when another purchaser arrives. My hunger dies away somewhat. Oh yes, they also have white rabbits in the poultry section. The pork section is mercifully pre-killed, although the collection of skin, tongues, pigs' tails, hearts, liver, kidneys, and other bits are not attractive – although the chops do look good. The beef section looks okay, but are they what I think they are? I think so; I have this shrinking feeling in my groin. Vegetarianism suddenly seems attractive. Abattoir would be a better description.

The fish and shellfish section are fascinating. Nice looking fish, crayfish, catfish, prawns, big black fish etc, but the eels and freshwater snakes don't look good. Look even worse when they are having their spines and skins removed. Decide that I will skip lunch!

Monday I am off to Lanzhou. No translator on this occasion, as my Sales manager says he can translate. This probably means one of five things:

This is a cost control exercise – it would be very expensive to bring the translator.

He wants to control the conversation!

We are going to drink lots of alcohol (The translator doesn't really drink!)

The living conditions there really are as bad as being suggested!

There is a security risk, which has been hinted at a few times, with the word 'Muslim' being translated.

I choose not to speculate and will see what happens, potential to be a farce. Lanzhou is in the province of Gansu, very central/north of China and near to Inner Mongolia. I'm informed that conditions are very basic. We are flying via Xi'an. Strangely, I am looking forward to this experience.

Heard today that another plane has come down, this time in Taiwan. Worrying!

Some observations this week:

> *Folk often turn up at meetings with a clear tubular vessel that to me resembles one of those old medical museum sample/specimen bottles with a removed bodily piece marinating in alcohol inside. In these cases, it is just Chinese tea leaves inside. If the tea is made hot enough, then the tea leaves sink. If not, you get a mouthful of what tastes like seaweed. Refreshing though when you don't have mouthful of leaves – I suspect, as I've not yet managed this feat. Tend to participate in meetings looking like I've been eating spinach!*

> *I've noticed that women also find the need to clear their throats loudly, usually followed by a good old-fashioned gob. This is most disconcerting and usually happens when you least expect it, perhaps it's just the effect that I have on them!*

> *That my deputy, has a standard phrase that goes "It's okay, it's no problem", which I am quickly learning usually means exactly the opposite. My discomfort levels in this situation are rising.*

> *Rules are rules! There are Government rules for everything in China. Seems to work though, driven by the fact that the penalties are high, monetary penalties! Something else that we could learn at home in the West.*

> *Teeth quality is variable! Young people seem to have good teeth. In contrast the older businessmen often seem to have bad teeth and don't seem too worried about it. An example is the president of my local bank, who is probably forty-five to fifty years old, smart suits, smart haircut, trim physique, professional presentation in every sense,*

but one – his teeth are chipped, brown and black! Maybe too much banqueting and Chinese firewater 'ganbei' have removed all the enamel from his teeth, combined with smoking. Perhaps a toothbrush for Christmas may be a nice touch. Dental hygiene hasn't always been a priority it seems.

There are some interesting TV channels and programmes. One invariably seems to be running continuous tapes of how to use the 'Windows' on your personal computer. There are benefits to the set up here. What better way to educate 1.3bn people quickly in the use of new technology?

School children ALL wear tracksuits to school as school uniform. Looks very practical, very smart, and very sensible. Perhaps one idea we should think about at home. They must be purchased by the parents, but the rates are subsidized. Wearing is compulsory.

People are starting to believe that I am rich! Made the mistake on answering a question over dinner the other night about my family's hobbies. Said riding, yes that's horse riding. When pressed I confessed that we had our own horses and that we kept it in a field next to the house. In fact an ex-racehorse. Somehow, I think that this bit lost something in translation. They now seem to think that I race horses at home and that I am loaded. They go even starrier eyed when I accidentally mentioned that I once went to Buckingham Palace and met the Queen. Less impressed though when they found out that I hadn't met Princess Diana!

Contrary to popular belief, the Chinese do not actually eat that much rice at banquets. This is merely incidental filler at the end of a meal just to fill you up, if indeed you need it at all. Only had rice a few times when dining out, and then fried rice. It is though, a staple in day-to-day life at home especially at lunch and dinner.

Meetings take forever. Not only does everything have to be translated both ways, but also everybody wants to 'make a speech'/diatribe which goes on forever, and you are not allowed to interrupt, or it is perceived *as being rude. Then they start again with another speech, after the first one has finished. By the time they have finished I have forgotten all my questions and certainly missed the moment to maximize impact and to make my points. Darn this; things are going to have to change. I need a questions right clause in proceedings.*

I am getting to like the warmer climate.

I notice that Taiwan is getting much closer to China, which is encouraging, or at least that is what the English language China Daily says. Then it is pointed out to me that what I am hearing is the Chinese English News and their interpretation of events. I was starting to believe the propaganda! There remains a significant distance between the two, although given China's move towards capitalism, it is only a matter of time I'm told.

For years, until the mid-late 1990's the only western music allowed here was from the 1950's and early 1960's – a sort of time warp. The only modification to this was the introduction of Richard Claydaman and the Carpenters! This all changed with the Internet, although in CD shops the selection of western music is still often limited in variety selection at this time.

w/c 27ᵗʰ May 2002 - Monday morning at work I was afraid to stand still unless I got painted or polished. The general work rates are accelerating as we find things for people to do, and the place is a comparative revelation. Our cleaner now cleans around me in situ whilst I am sat at my desk, just to make a point. I am informed that I have made a very popular start, whatever that precisely means.

Thursday was the day of the good housekeeping competition at work. Place not too bad, but long list of things still to do. Wandered down to get a haircut. I had got my secretary to write down "good trim, not too short and especially not too short at the back". Heck, something got lost in the translation! I now have long hair on top and virtually nothing at the back. Feeling suicidal and wondering where I can hide for the next few weeks. Perhaps I should get a sun hat? Going to look silly at work though. Perhaps my secretary was getting her own back? I don't think I said anything wrong to the hairdresser – I can't say anything? This is China; I will never know what happened!

Friday is my fellow Brit's last day at work, so we must celebrate. Another banquet at another 'special' restaurant for twenty of us! Why do I do it? A real session, toasts all around, several of them, speeches, presentation and then downstairs to watch France vs. Senegal from the world cup. I spent the rest of the evening beating everyone at 'dice', which is not difficult as they are so drunk it's a wonder, they can see the dice at all!

Observations:

> *Little boys think nothing of openly weeing in the middle of the pavement. I have noticed this on four occasions now; no discretion and their parents don't appear to discourage it either.*

> *As a part of its environmental development programme, China publishes the daily pollution levels by city in its national newspapers. There has been huge investment in clean up systems, assisted by Norwegian consultants – these guys are serious.*

> *The President, Jiang Zemin, has just announced that China is to increase the speed of reforms to increase trade and integrate it further with the rest of the World – it will happen!*

> *Airport bus drivers are as bad as the road drivers, absolutely no respect for incoming aircraft priority!*

> *Big cars which are chauffeur driven, and always black, just pull out into main roads without looking, knowing full well that no one can afford to hit them! I close my eyes every time!*

> *In Lanzhou my deputy and the sales guy wore the same shirt for the 3 days we were together! Good job I have no sense of smell.*

> *I couldn't help raising a smile when eating at the airport with my two colleagues. They were both at first glance wearing nice 'Lacoste' shirts*

(the alligators). However on this occasion the alligators were facing each other! Now I am no expert on brands, but I'm sure that the original alligators were all looking in the same direction!

I have not come across any double-glazing yet anywhere. Let's just say there's a market opportunity and a need.

Ladies tights out here look as if they were made by pre-world War 2 machines, which in fact they probably have been. They are thick and a strange colour brown, not glamorous in any way, rekindling ideas about 'Nora Batty'! The 'pop' socks in the same material look utterly ridiculous.

I notice that plastic packaging specifications are usually poorly specified. The general rule of thumb is that when you need some strong plastic packaging, it isn't. Contrary to this, when you need something accessible, you have no chance of getting in! Quality and the need for consistent fit for purpose specifications I note.

w/c 2ⁿᵈ June 2002 - Had a brief walk around the evening outdoor market tonight and came across my first rat. I am not sure who moved faster, but it was a close call, probably thought that I would eat him, as everything else out here seems to get eaten. Yuk!

Got up early on Sunday to go to the Airport to pick up our principal owner who is arriving from the UK. I know that I have mentioned the roads before, but things don't get any better. Coming along the Motorway in the fast lane at seventy miles per hour plus and finding a road-sweeper truck going only five miles per hour without any warning is a bit exciting, as indeed are trying to avoid the farmhands who periodically wander across these roads, apparently oblivious to the traffic. I noticed that when someone breaks down, they sort of pull over to the right and then pull out one of the many newly planted trees and shove it out of the left back window to warn people off – Chinese equivalent of the European red triangle! Our company owner eventually arrived, and first stop was the counterfeit DVD shop would you believe.

There are times in life when I genuinely believe that I am a lucky boy!

Today, notwithstanding some quirky moments, was one of those days when I was most fortunate. Firstly, my boss and I meet the Chairman of the joint venture partner for an interesting meeting – Can't go into details, but this job could turn out to be something bigger than I expected. Now my boss moves in some high circles in a constant round of networking. We got invited out to lunch with the local Mayor, who runs the show in the Jiaxing City and his team of cronies; the powerbase. Good banquet lunch and afterwards we were given 'gifts', but I understand that this is the norm in China. Firstly, I received a gift-wrapped green tea package of Hangzhou's most famous Chinese tea. Next, they gave me two gift wrap books of ancient Chinese something – all Chinese manuscripts and pictures – very nice, even if I can't read a word. A nice touch was that it came in a Jiaxing Municipal People's Government carrier bag! Having met the city's 'leaders' who are on seemingly on the scrounge for invites to the UK for visas, it was a dash to Shanghai for an important meeting with potential financiers. On entering Shanghai, the weather is wonderful, and the buildings are spectacular with some weird minds obviously applied to the design of some of them, and I wonder if they are built with a better quality to the rest of China?

More importantly tonight was the chance to have dinner with the president of the Shanghai Tobacco Monopoly Administration, otherwise known as 'God' and a highly esteemed professor, who is apparently world renowned in the academic world and among other things a mate of our principal when he is not in China or UK, he lives in the USA. This is seriously high-powered stuff (outside of Property, the Tobacco Monopoly is the biggest business in Shanghai), and I was strictly informed to say absolutely nothing unless spoken to, don't even think about work and don't take my jacket off (The Professor was genuinely serious about high level etiquette)! We ate in a private penthouse room of a 'twelve star something star' Hotel that is coincidentally owned by the Shanghai Tobacco Monopoly Administration. Fabulous food, except that the conversation wasn't flowing, and as instructed, I had to say absolutely nothing and smile. I could have helped the evening go with the bang it needed and we could all have had fun, but no Jeremy was a statue. Now you know this is not my natural style. They took their jackets off within minutes, whilst I baked and sweated my way through the meal. The dinner ended positively though. We received an invite to go to the Shanghai cigarette factory on Thursday to meet one of our ex top customers! More gifts – two bottles of seriously up market Chinese wine, which was manufactured just for the hotel, with two very nice drinking vessel sets and an extremely impressive ornament of Chinese golden horses that is very heavy and meant to be extremely lucky. This is typical Chinese, quite nice except for the fact that the three horses have what looks like old six penny bits in their mouths, which to my mind detracted somewhat, but never mind – too much gold leaf, but hang on, they are very heavy! The son of God was an incredibly pleasant and well-spoken young man who is off to Edinburgh in August to study at university.

To cap it all we are staying in the old, world famous and very traditional Shanghai Peace Hotel on the Bund. Wow, old tradition and style, and everyone who has been anyone has stayed here – Bill Clinton, George Bush Senior, Henry Kissinger, Juan Antonio Samaranch, Lionel Jospin, President Mubarak, and various other heads of States. Fabulous views down the Huangpu River and of the famous Pearl Oriental tower on the opposite bank. Really impressed!

Couldn't resist a quick nightcap on the roof garden bar, what views of the Bund below and over to the newly developing Pudong area, and another in the jazz bar where the old guys playing from a bygone era reminded me of a few nights in Ronnie Scott's, London.

Wednesday, my boss is going sightseeing at a local 'old town' called Suzhou, which is actually a few hours away.

What a day! All hell let loose! Our biggest customer announces that it is turning up for dinner at four hours' notice, but they are not apparently senior people I'm told, and then turn out to be very senior people indeed! And they want to drink lots of beer and do Karaoke afterwards!

This was the busiest day I have had by far and the mill is short of many fundamental process supplies that I discover hadn't been ordered over recent months. One supplier turned up out of the blue (a good old Lancastrian lad). Everybody suddenly needs to talk to me urgently. My translator is absent with our principal, sightseeing in Suzhou and suddenly no one else seems to make any sense when trying to speak English. I haven't quite forgiven her for bringing me in a treat from her mother this morning, a particular delicacy – cooked frog meat - whole skinned frogs! I'm sure they are having me on here and it took to the early afternoon for me to realize that it was these that were stinking to office block out. Tried one, horrible, but took them home out of guilt, where they are still resident in my fridge! We then had to dash around and get some 'gifts' for our visitors. In the event, the banquet went well and as the senior guy, I managed to get out of the karaoke. A somber moment during the evening was when the head customer asked me if I had a child? When I said that I had three, a boy and two girls, he instinctively replied, "You have everything"; he was right, I am a very lucky man. He then sadly reflected on the fact that in China they are only allowed one child per family – there was genuine sadness and regret, I felt for him! Place went quite for a while, if we had had more to drink, we would have been crying, so we 'toasted' and set the place off again.

The customer visit Thursday morning went well, then back to Shanghai and the Peace Hotel again, before heading off to the Shanghai Cigarette Factory again to be welcomed by the President. I have discovered that he runs a reported $5Bn company – Biggest Cigarette producer in China, several hotels, Vineyard and 6,000 shops among other things, and comparatively a young man running it. For dinner back to the revolving restaurant in Jiaxing, but somehow, I got it wrong. I will never know whether it was due to a badly translated menu or the waiter writing down the wrong things, or me pointing to the wrong things, but I managed to order a large bowl of extremely hot green spicy chilies, a bowl with a whole large fish head in it, which was 99.9 per cent bone, together with bean curd and lots of very hot red chilies. At least the two spring rolls were good.

Friday and England are now world-beaters versus Argentina at football! I like football and life is good after that match! No fingernails left and was toasted at the end by everyone in the place! This bar with the large screen has been very quiet on the two occasions that I have gone in previously for football. Not tonight, they were swinging off the rafters and all seem like Beckham fans. I had to keep telling people that, no; he is not a friend of mine. The guys all want to introduce me their 'friends', which is a little wearing. Place went mad, I am happy, now for some sleep. Went to have a head massage on the way home but didn't – just practiced my Chinese. I have taken to having an occasional late-night walk along the canal roads to relax before bed. This is therapeutic, and I feel so safe.

Saturday I am off to my deputy's brand-new apartment for a house-warming lunch, so I must go shopping for a gift – this is a Chinese thing. I look for the gaudiest thing I can, but cannot bring myself to do it, even though I know that he will probably appreciate it more. I settle for three simple Chinese vases (The white with blue ones), and I also take the Johnnie Walker Malt Whisky.

I have concluded that the Chinese race is alcoholic! Lunch started at eleven o'clock, and I met a whole gang from work, his family, his wife's family (both father in laws turned up wearing white vests, which I thought was slightly different) and some new friends whilst drinking a shed load of Chinese white wine and toasting four large tables in the smart restaurant. Then back to the new apartment to watch some football, then oh yes, by the way, I am invited to dinner with his special best friends. This was unexpected, but also a great honour my translator informs me. She is fed up though – she wants to go home and has drunk too much milk! The apartment was nice, some similarities to mine, but a newer and slightly larger version in a nicely designed building, with a TV the size of a mini cinema screen in the front room. Everyone spends the afternoon playing an unintelligible Chinese game, Mahjong, which is in fact gambling. Some sleep, some are in comas, I watch the football and drink real water. Dinner started at five o'clock and was fun; I am really starting to get into the inner sanctums of Chinese society I feel. They are good people, but they drink too much.

I slept for ten hours solid – I cannot recall when that last happened. I get up on Sunday morning and make a major decision – I binned the frogs.

Observations:

> *I am starting to learn a few more words in Chinese, not the useful stuff, but various parts of the body, table and chairs, cups, clothes and a few other odds and sods.*

> *My hairdresser, the one who speaks English (a little), was explaining to me the evils of Western men, who take everything and think that money buys everything, no respect for anything and very 'material' – Mao has done a good job. My secretary confirmed these are the writings of Mao. Now I am powerful and evil apparently!*

> *Everyone sleeps at lunchtimes in their offices, which is quite disarming. I am not sure that they are ever fully re-awake after lunch given the pace of some of them. Mornings for*

most of them seem to be sobering up from the previous night's activities.

As a rule, folk simply disregard all 'No Smoking' signs. This will remain in force until somebody introduces Capital Punishment for this offence.

Some more dodgy translations:

More reverse 'N's on statutory signs.

Vehciles, meant to be Vehicles This Way, was at Shanghai Airport.

Zhang Xin Flypass, I think this was meant to be 'flyover', often also referred to as Overpass.

Publick Access, yes that is meant to be public, not pubic!

Multi-function Hall and Dinging Rooms.

But they will get there eventually. It is estimated that there are more people capable of speaking English in China now than in the USA, scary but apparently true.

There are an estimated 540 million bicycles in China, most of them quite old. This is a good way to keep the nation fit and healthy I have decided, but I'm not getting one! Too dangerous and too hot and sweaty.

There are no rubbish skips in China yet. Rubbish is just dumped in heaps on the ground and eventually gets picked up by men who put it in an open lorry. There is a market opportunity here for someone!

I have found another reason why people avoid big black cars – they are usually containing a government official of some type, who can be ruthless and unforgiving. I feel powerful suddenly, to compliment my evil materialism!

There are several street markets around the centre of Jiaxing; I have largely ignored these. Probably good deals to be done and from what I have seen have a nice atmosphere.

The sheer scale of China is quite intimidating.

Taiwanese Tourists all manage to look like American Chinese – very westernized in their clothing and demeanor. Usually very affluent looking!

Moving around China is now free; there are no closed cities anymore. I am advised that this is very different from ten years ago!

No one wears shoes in Chinese homes! You take your shoes off at the front door and put on slippers. I look ridiculous in size eight fluffy white or pink slippers with my size eleven feet inside!

The entire Chinese world works based on a network of 'friends' – being a friend is essential to do business – to become a friend you must firstly be introduced and then drink a lot! And....... maybe more.

Shanghai is as about as capitalist city as you can get! Stock Exchanges, very modern buildings, tourists, Pizza chains, big hotels, you name it!

I have now completed my first month in China. I have had a fascinating time, saw new things, and exposed to a new culture. I have enjoyed every minute.

w/c 9th June 2002 - Monday I meet our company insurers and they invite me out for a banquet dinner tonight. Right now it is pissing down (crude I know, but the most apt description in the circumstances), thundering, as black as an 'eclipse'. It is awful and I am just awaiting the plague of locusts to come over! 'Cats and dogs' would not do justice to what is going on outside currently, monsoon rains – and I must go out for dinner in it! The fact that I have a driver awaiting in scant consolation as I will be drowned by the time that I reach the car and I know what will happen – everyone will turn up dry and immaculate – rain, what rain? Even though some have probably cycled there!

Dinner goes extremely well! The stern looking insurance general manager suddenly brightens and becomes my best friend and has invited me to tour China! He is irrationally persistent, but we shall see, I suspect that he is very drunk! I was asked to recite my Chinese vocabulary to everyone at dinner, which is now up to forty words and climbing. They were very attentive and apparently very impressed; I am pleased with myself – although don't ask me to spell them. I had to laugh as by the time I had counted to five they had all joined in, by the time I got to seven they were ahead of me and then they lead me all the way to twenty. The whole table was well gone, there were some serious businessmen here counting to twenty in their own language like three-year-old's!

My deputy has set me up to go karaoke singing afterwards, I have no option as all my new friends that I made at the weekend at his housewarming will be there! Bless him! I go and enjoy it about as much as I always enjoy Karaoke.

Observations:

> *Haida is the biggest electric white goods business in China. It is huge. The unfortunate bit is that its logo is two little boys cuddling each other dressed only in skimpy trunks and they stick the logo on everything they sell. After several efforts I have managed to remove them from everything in the house. Bit dodgy to my mind and an unfortunate choice of logo – Child Protection groups would have something to say about this.*

> *The frontage of the building across the street from my apartment is typical 1950's Soviet train station architecture; they must have shared drawings. The worrying thing I suspect was that this building was probably only built ten years ago!*

> *A few miss-translations from the 'Coffee' Restaurant Menu*

> *Bam and egg fried rice (Ham)*

> *Steamed spate rids of pork (Spareribs)*

American t-lone steak (T-bone)

Black Peppei Lillet Steak (I'm saying nothing!)

Tiggling platter Chichen (I suspect sizzling chicken)

Braising pig intestine & intesti (They are trying hard to sell this to me)

Clombia Coffee (Columbia)

Sweet torn soup (corn)

France luckly lries pork steak (God alone knows)

France gooselivr (anyone can make a small mistake)

Lotus flavoured frogs with rice (I suspect they have this right!)

Facts:

Since 1998, everybody learns English at school from the start.

English learning goes from grade one to grade nine. To get into further education Colleges you must be able to speak English to at least grade eight (4,500-word vocabulary and speak it with fluency). Apparently, the standard of English spoken in the Hong Kong 'experiment' was not good enough!

There are eleven million people in Beijing and eleven million bikes officially registered with the government there!

Two billion tonnes of silt flows into the Yellow River and Yangtze River every year – the result is that there is a ten-year plan from 2001 to reforest eleven and a half million hectares of land – 'a lot'! six and a half million hectares will have seeds sown by dropping them from helicopters; sowing trees manually will create the balance.

There has been a 23 per cent increase in car sales in China this year to date.

There were an extra 11.22 million mobile phone users in the first two months of 2002! That is about equivalent from memory to a fifth of the UK population.

It gets light early here (04.30 hours) and people get up early. Dinner is at 17.30 hours and people traditionally go to bed early, although that is changing as the country Westernizes. There is also a twenty-four-hour element!

Chinese seem to have a dream in life that anything is possible. They have this in common with the Americans I muse!

Apparently in Chinese structures there are not 'load-bearing' walls. Having witnessed a new wall being built at work recently, I can only be grateful for small mercies!

A disproportionately high number of the population appears to have mobile phones. These are never switched off and ring at the most inconvenient moments. No matter, there is no discretion; the trick then is to shout into the phone as loudly as possible irrespective of your surroundings or circumstances. If you have a loud an irritatingly different ring tone, then all the better!

Even the Chinese burst into hysterical laughter when I occasionally refer to tap water as drinking water – don't touch the stuff!

I still can't get used to people belching unashamedly in meetings!

w/c 14.6.02 - Friday I reflected what a great meeting I had had with the chairman of the joint venture the prior day, leaving me in a good mood.

Today I contrived to buy an excellent dinner service and two, two feet tall typically Chinese vases (White China with blue on) for a total of £89. The vases together cost £21. The bone China dinner service was £68. I am happy, especially since the shop dispatched a 'man' to help me carry them all home. Place is starting to feel more like a home already.

Saturday I was off to Shanghai. On arrival at the Peace Hotel we were informed that unfortunately although we had booked a superior room, they had overbooked and they were all full...........................However, they were upgrading me to a Suite with no extra charge......oh, okay then! Brilliant, outwards facing, looking over the river on the Executive sixth floor, large bedroom, large lounge, and huge bathtub with Jacuzzi fittings etc, or the special large power shower as an option with stool in it. The nice touch was the TV in the bathroom!

At this stage I got a phone call to say that my biggest customer was turning up tonight (Saturday night) to have a meeting and dinner with me in Jiaxing (at three hours' notice!) – This is typically Chinese – tough, I am in Shanghai. My translator volunteers to go and make my apologies with a team from the mill – they will understand. I am fed up with this development, although I have made the right decision.……I am not used to this style of short-term organization.

I went straight out and up the Pearl Oriental Tower across the river via a special under the river flamboyant tunnel train. Then off to the famous 'Friendship' store which under previous regimes was reserved for senior communist officials and overseas residents only. Great stuff, but very high prices and visited at some stage by every head of states wives' from around the globe. This was followed by a beer on the Peace hotel rooftop area overlooking the river, old Shanghai 'Bund' area and the Sassoon family's old private Penthouse - a special moment; breathtaking!

Then there was the little matter of the world cup football. I walked up to the People's Park via the Nanjing Road pedestrian shopping centre and then took a cab to O'Malley's Irish Pub in the French Concession district, which turned out to be in a beautiful leafy suburb by the American Consulate in the middle of Consulate District. O'Malley's was busy and full of Brits and other expatriates, so it was off to a very good TGI Friday's restaurant where they had plenty of TV's and we watched the Football drinking good wine/beer and with good food….and well 3-0! Afterwards it was back to the 'Bund' for a late evening stroll along the brilliantly lit up riverside. The views closely rival those of Hong Kong, if not better, and the heat is tolerable, and everyone is out creating a fantastic atmosphere.

Next day was a leisurely start before getting picked up at 11.30 to be taken for lunch at The Hilton to meet the Bank leadership team. I joined fellow important customers of the Bank for a meeting. I am now officially a Senior Consultant to the President of the bank – I have a certificate! I also received a very pleasant framed original painting by a 'special' Chinese artist ('everybody in China knows this artist') – very nice, although a bit different. Everything was photographed and videoed all day along with their other foreign investors – three Japanese, two Koreans, one German, and a few Taiwanese. Yes, I am their biggest foreign customer, and they like me – sat next to the President at dinner and will be next to the President at the Orchestra, not the Opera that had been previously translated to me, private Black Limousine home. We all then got together for a large banquet dinner, where the President had a 'one child moment', before going off to the brand-new Shanghai Theater and a night with the Shanghai Symphony Orchestra. This was special, a beautiful new glass and steel structure, wonderfully lit and a great orchestra including six westerners – fantastic! The only slight edge off the day was that they allocated a lovely woman to be my translator. She had arrived expecting to show partners around Shanghai, when somebody dropped it upon her that she was to be my translator for the afternoon – no problem, she spoke brilliant English, even if she hadn't translated in a forum with thirty high powered people before, whilst being photographed and videoed. She got nervous and by the time I came to speak, she had lost it. Importantly though, most of the foreigners spoke English, so they could understand my unusually calmed and rational points – we got away with it! I was fine and in good form, she died of embarrassment, as did the bank official who allocated her to me! What a fabulous weekend!

There is an expression 'The best laid plans of mice and men' – I am learning in China that things often happen extremely well, obviously well planned by someone, but you don't get advanced warning. On Tuesday I arrive at work with a distinct plan of attack. This plan was destroyed within seconds of arrival when I received a very impressive invitation to attend a prestigious 'stone laying' opening for our joint venture partner's latest investment. 'That's nice, when is it' – 'In one hour's time!' Oh heck. I have managed to come out without a tie or jacket, so the driver was promptly dispatched back to the apartment to pick up a tie. I am not sure that is even a 'good hair' day.

At 09.30 we convened at the 'White House' the joint venture partner's HQ, where we were introduced to several local and provincial dignitaries, including the new Secretary of the local 'Party'. Then we were given sprays for our buttonholes and then into a people carrier to the nearby site. Then it hit me! We were welcomed at the building site by red carpet and company Brass Band. I was thrust to the front to stand on stage just behind the general manager and chairman of our joint venture and alongside the new Party Secretary behind the microphones. In boiling sunshine we were faced by about 1,000 employees in lines and ranks, some carrying umbrellas, some wearing coolie hats (The ones with the safety helmets on top of the coolie hats were a spectacle!). There were large helium balloons and slogans hanging from ropes, about twenty camera men and at least six video/TV camera men walking around – and I was in everything being stood right behind the microphones. Boy was it hot, but for once I wasn't too bad, which was more than can be said for the two new German guys who have arrived in town! One was wearing a brown-coloured shirt, which rapidly became a very wet dark chocolate shirt, whilst the other guy's light suit jacket started showing sweat on the outside! The speeches went on for a long time, the band played, then doves were released, balloons were released and then those darned firecrackers went off again – too close, too loud and for far too long! The bright red backdrop to the stage in the middle of a building site, the red carpeted stage, and the flowers all around were impressive! Sometimes they do things well! The foundation digging was starting as we left to the applause of the cast.

Then I even got to see their new machine, which is a competitive threat to ours! To cap it all I got a gift – a very nice Valentino Italian-Chinese JV 'Golf Shirt' – that looks far too small to fit me! Then back to work at 11.30 hours, spot on time for lunch – I had got nothing done this morning! My translator is again happy as she is photographed on stage and TV with all these important people.

Wednesday, I go for a head massage. At the hairdressers to night they were muttering about me and two of the girls were looking at me in a typically direct and Chinese way. The only one who speaks any English at all tried to communicate what they were saying. I thought they were saying that my son is very handsome and couldn't work it out (True, but how would they know?). Then I got it – they were saying that 'I must have been very handsome when I was a young man'! I was quite pleased with this and smiled until she went on and I realized that what they were saying was that 'I am now passed it'! Well there you go! These girls must be twentyish....... sod them, they will get old too one day! That is if they don't offend too many Westerners along the way. I was also please when the same young 'English speaker' kept telling me 'You are sweet'! What a lovely girl she is. However, after a while I worked out that she meant was 'You are sweating'! Not one of my more successful sixty minutes!

Thursday my job for the day is to re-audit the factory housekeeping. It is raining and extremely humid anyway, but even more so in the depths of the paper mill! I am dripping everywhere from places I do not wish to mention. By 09.15 hours I 'come up for air' to my office, looking as I have been for a swim in my clothes. At this stage I am approached my translator who is looking curiously concerned. She announces that our joint venture partner has invited me to have photographs taken with their chairman and the TV cameras will also be there. 'Oh that's kind, when?' 'Right Now!' 'You are joking right?' 'No'! Bloody hell they have done it again. I have a short sleeved light blue shirt on, an old tie, no jacket, sweaty armpits/everything – at least my shirt is a consistent colour and my hair is laminated to my head – the timing could not conceivably be any worse! The air was blue momentarily as I reflect on the fact that they have done it again – last minute notice – I will have to explain that this is not the way that I operate. This is where large air conditioners come into their own. Having dried myself off a little we head over to the 'White House' again, to be greeted by the joint venture partners 'board of directors' looking immaculate in suits. I have never seen this mob look so smart! They come to welcome me smiling, only to stand back in surprise when my translator, not instructed to do so, tells them upfront that I am seriously upset at the circumstances – well she is Chinese, but I could have done without her making this comment at this precise time. Back upstairs and there is my German friend, immaculate as usual, although he also claimed not to have had any warning this time! We then sat there in typically Chinese fashion talking and smiling at each other for a series of different cameramen and TV cameras. Apparently, these are for promotion brochures and the TV crew is from Guangdong for an investment TV advertisement. Brilliant! Pictures of a sweaty Englishman are going to be beamed to literally millions of people – what an advertisement!

I return to work for the production manager to tell me that his friend saw me on TV the other day at the 'bank'. I have also I suspect been on local TV at the supermarket, at the opening ceremony, in Holiday bar, walking down the street among others since my arrival, although I haven't seen any of the footage. The chairman has promised me a clip of today's events and has even asked me to go fishing over the next few weekends.

Observations:

> *When Chinese give speeches, they are invariably read from a script verbatim. I note that at the end that the last sentence or two of any script is shouted in an abrupt, clipped, and excitable manner in a sort of climax! Then applause is then spontaneous and brief.*

> *I must be careful how I put this, but I notice (from market stalls, shops and washing lines) that the majority of 'knickers' are very unfashionable and very large, but there are a few signs that this is starting to change.*

> *In a similar vein, bras seem not only to be highly padded, but also seem to resemble coconut shells, presumably catering for the vanity of a petite population trying to emulate Western film stars.*

> *The Shanghai Pearl Oriental TV Tower is special, although I am becoming a little blasé about these after The Twins Towers in New York, The Eiffel Tower in Paris, the TMP Tower in Sydney, The Sears Tower in Chicago, The Sinclair Tower in Boston, The Bank of China buildings in Hong Kong and the Tower in Kuala Lumpur – got to be done though! Another one off the list! I understand that the TV tower in Moscow is higher, as is the one in Toronto. The Post Office Tower in London resembles a toy by comparison!*

> *Our joint venture partners facilities are very impressive, a quick tour exhibited many brand-new factory investments, an impressive HQ ('The White House'), with lawns at the front and pond with Chinese style summer house at the back, A conference centre/cinema/convention hall that is straight out of the communist era, its own hospital, and so on.*

w/c 21.6.02 - Well it had to happen sometime – today my carry out lunch was of such a nature that I couldn't bring it to my lips. This was the first time since I have arrived. The meat was sliced and full of holes – I would not serve this to my worst enemy's dog! And then I had a thought......

Saturday morning and I set off on a one and a half hours' drive to the old city of Suzhou at the heart of the country's silk textile industries. This is a bigger city than Jiaxing and situated up the Grand Canal on a beautiful large lake. Firstly though I bought a couple of very expensive Chinese lamps for the apartment – pottery, blue, one about four feet tall, both with golden duck on, and I got a large plate to match – sounds gaudy and maybe it is, but I am furnishing an apartment in China, not a house in Devon. Intend to bring them home eventually all the same.

The Bamboo Grove Hotel, Suzhou, is a lovely five-star hotel. The bar area was novel, based somewhat loosely on a dinosaur/Jurassic background with jungle noises repeatedly being played in the background. The bar waitresses in 'Fred Flint Stone' outfits were something else. I am on the executive sixth Floor with our own tea area and separate breakfast area, with a rooftop view overlooking the small lake outside which is beautifully lit by night and like all water around here, well stocked with very large ornamental fish.

I went straight out to a local 'old garden', which was walled and quiet, despite the presence of Americans doing their best to destroy the tranquility. Usual stuff, at the top of their voices 'Hey Mary Lou, come and see this, honey!' stuff. Nice wooden rooms and artifacts, typical small hills resembling larva flows, with man-made, small pagodas, ornate wooden screens, photos of old Chinese types, water, exotic plants et al. I feel guilty about the impression of the Americans here, but it's just the fact of life; the way it is, loud and overconfident to the rest of us.

Then it was on the back of a tricycle taxi to the nine stories pagoda at the other end of the city centre. Very run down, but an ancient wonder – albeit looking out over a skyline of 1960's style factories polluting the environment. Nice gardens attached though. All courting couples, newlyweds!

Next a little walk to the biggest and best gardens – beautiful, a touch of mystique and very different. Lakes, plants, walls, mini pagodas, and summer houses. I was dropped off at a nice back street after a detour off the normal routes; some wonderful wooden stuff – bought two twelve-inch-tall rose wood

Chinese Lions that are very heavy! Well I like them! Suzhou is like a type of Venice with the old canals network and high-pitched bridges.

Then out to a local shopping street. Ended up buying two very nice paintings in interesting silvery thick frames for ¥700 for the pair (£60.00). These are traditional Suzhou silk woven paintings that are a speciality. Later saw similar ones in the hotel for ¥2,600 …. each!

At the Hotel, and dinner in the Chinese restaurant accompanied by three-piece young 'old' Chinese style musicians in appropriate regalia. Good meal. Considered a 'foot massage' afterwards in the hotel, until I heard a loud American male voice saying '……….and will she come to my room as well? How much?' Where do they produce these guys from? They must have lectures in rudeness, arrogance, indiscretion, and lack of diplomacy, but it explains why my former American employers had rules like they did! He was most put out when he was politely told that 'this wasn't that sort of place'. Whatever, I felt the need to be away from there!

Sunday traveling back to Jiaxing I note that the Grand Canal is the busiest inland functional waterway I have ever seen. It has direction boards and distance signs just like the roads; I note that the steering of boats is no better than the drivers on the road. Talking of which, on the way back having just overtaken a vehicle we were faced with a large dumper truck speeding towards us in the fast lane on our side of the dual carriageway! Such events are becoming the 'norm' and I am staggered at how calm I remain, despite being inches from death! Philosophically at least out here the drivers are looking for such things!

Monday more customers turn up later and meeting with my chairman first thing. Had to go out for dinner right after work with customers. Good dinner with the head of Honghan cigarette factory who insisted on having a photograph with me personally to go with his photos of 'many important Chinese people (Like Zemin Jiang, the President)'!

Observations:

> *The cleaner at work wipes off everything with a slightly damp rag, not a duster! This generally results in everything being dirtier after she has 'cleaned it' that before she started. Liquid smear marks are on everything – shame because she is trying so hard.*

Renaldo's silly haircut is modeled on Chinese traditional boys' haircuts pre four years old. I have since noticed this, but now wish I hadn't taken teased about his haircut over dinner one night! This was pointed out to me in a hushed silence.

Also over dinner last week it was suggested to me that Chinese food was very good for the mind, but not the body. I responded that with a population of 1.3bn people that it was probably good for other things too! My translator chose not to translate this, went a funny colour!

This country is coming. If the Western Press isn't reporting it, then they are naïve. The investment pouring into China is beyond comprehension and exceeding anything happening anywhere else in the World. Everything is being built new and on a vast and massive scale, benchmarked against the best in the world. Beware; this will be beyond anything the USA has to offer in the not-too-distant future.

More miss-translations:

> *'Main Office' – 'Please no Coming' (Uh huh! I suspect this is meant to be 'no entry')*

> *'Sweetwater Pearls'; should be freshwater pearls; another example of literal translations.*

> *'.Very pleeossantly food restaurant'.*

> *On the beachfront at Gulangyu: 'No Tossing' (I suspect something to do with litter!)*

From my hotel blurb in Longyan:

> *'Lodging Rdgualtions'*

> *'.......Uphold public oder'*

'.......*Racketing Gambling, porstititions, lecherous acts distributing re-actionary or pronographic articles'.*

'....... *radioactive materials are strictly forbidden' (Oh this is reassuring, but indicative of the prescriptive nature of Chinese rules).*

'....... *violations of any of the above will get criticized, warned, fine detained...in accordance with the 'Security Control Punishing Regulations' and the 'Hotelism Security Control Regulations'.*

All lorries and trucks out here seem to be painted blue! The same colour blue of course.

w/c 30ʰ June 2002 - Sunday was a time to relax. My nerves are still recovering from the previous night when we happened across a car reversing at high speed in the outside lane of the motorway from Shanghai. This was a close one and even seemed to unsettle my driver for a short while!

Tuesday, I'm off to Kunshan, an industrial city three hours away between Shanghai and Suzhou, to see a major supplier. Upon entering the city a banner proclaims 'Nation's cleanest city'; as my London friends might say, they're having a laugh, aren't they? Anyway, it improves somewhat, and the visit was a good one getting on extremely well with the expats Scot who is their Sales director. We quickly become big buddies and have plans to tour Shanghai. He tells me that he is tired having just had a three-and-a-half-week sales trip. I sympathize and then it dawns on me to casually ask 'Oh where'? 'Korea' he replies! 'Flipping heck, he was there for the world cup'! He only got to see ten games. Passed a large black limousine on the way back called the Nissan 'Cedric', which struck me as odd, but Nissan must consider Cedric an up-market name.

Thursday I am casually informed by my production manager that a typhoon will hit us tonight before he wandered off leaving me pondering what the implications of this may be or what precautions I should take? I am suddenly aware that all the cyclists are wearing rains capes and going faster that the norm; I am also intrigued by how far the newly planted trees outside of my office window, bordering the canal, can bend before either snapping or being uprooted. The road outside is starting to resemble the adjacent canal and some prat has left the windows wide open at the end of the corridor where we now have our own private swimming pool! Otherwise everyone seems quite calm ......well, you understand. It's very windy, but I wouldn't call it a typhoon .... yet.

Friday, I am hoping that the 'typhoon's' effect will have passed on by the weekend. I may have slept through it, but it was not much more than a strong wind with some rain at the end of the day – few trees uprooted, external pot plants blown over, high level cranes stopped operating (although they left the poor workers to keep going on the roofs), but I could not detect too much more.

I am becoming aware that some people do not do a lot of work. In the general office today I noticed that the 'statistics' lady was reading a newspaper at 10.15 hours in the morning. When I discretely asked my assistant why she was doing this, I was informed that it was because she was the statistician and she had finished her work for the day......... "Oh, okay, that's okay then!?!?" There are few others in this category – things are going to have to change! I've also discovered that our ISO registration that we got last year is a bit of a botch by any standards – a hell of a lot of work to do here.

Observations:

> *Taxi drivers all have displayed photographs of themselves that I swear have been taken wearing the same red tie and white shirt! Every taxi driver's photo, without fail is in a red tie and white shirt. The trick is to bear no resemblance to the guy driving the car.*

> *There is very little long-term booking of plane flights in China. This is partly the short-term nature of their day-to-day thought processes, partly that due to the huge infrastructure investments including in the airways, there is always excess capacity. This is changing as the economy develops and planning is going to become a challenge.*

> *Business in China is traditionally done through 'friends' who are basically drinking pals. This is starting to change in the big cities where*

professional standards are being introduced quickly, but I conclude that these friends main objective is to kill each other through liver cirrhosis. The better your friend the more aggressively you try and kill him. 'Moutai' (Chinese 'white wine' spirits) is about 55 per cent alcohol content. Business in China in many ways is impressive, but this feature is not one of the more impressive elements.

I know I keep harping on about the pace of change and investment here, but let me reflect on the global situation relative to what I am seeing in China, a strictly personal observation as at this moment in time:

> *The UK is a basket case from a manufacturing position, which it now constituting a lower percentage of GDP and the strong Pound damaging what is left for the long term, but who cares anyway as we can buy it cheap from abroad. People are conservative (a strength) and largely comfortable (which restricts ambition and stunts growth), I just hope that the economy can continue to develop on a tank full of fresh air! How long can the service sector, supermarkets and fast-food outlets keep the economy going? If the Pound weakens, inflation will be rampant as everything is imported and prices will shoot up with limited domestic alternatives as they have been destroyed. Long live the financial sector. Just the facts as I understand it.*

> *Europe is largely comfortable, bureaucratic, with over competition and a problem of uncontrolled immigration that it has not yet faced up to. It is also now a single State whether we chose to like it or not and that will bring growing pains and deflection of focus.*

> *The USA is in recession but has a vast wealth. It strangely lacks competition at times despite the PR and the quality of many of its products are inferior to their European comparisons. They have many under invested factories and have an entirely false and overpriced economy that helps most people live very well, although long may they keep it going! It works for them! Impressive though.*

South America is fundamentally corrupt I am told, poorly managed, and inadequately financed. It is run on the principles with which it was founded – by the ex-convicts of Spanish and Portuguese prisons who took advantage of all the locals. Obviously progressed but has its challenges of large populations and control. And drugs!

Russia is large, but has corruption, too many drunks, endemic inefficiency, and no money to modernize, although oil and gas is rapidly changing that! Rebuild job and will get strong again.

Australia and New Zealand live well, fabulous natural resources, but are not big enough in population terms.

Conversely Indonesia is big enough in population terms, but management problems, historical divisions and corruption pervade.

The Middle East has fabulous wealth, although unevenly distributed and with massive political problems and various religious influences that are self-evident.

Africa. It is currently Aids ridden in parts, indeed several medical related and nutritional challenges, corrupt, impoverished, at times arrogant, some of it at war, no money, tribal influences with diverging interests politically, lack of stability generally and few will to do anything about it, albeit some signs of change and China is waiting the help.

India has a huge population, the natural global advantage of English language and connections, is developing immensely through education, providing outsourcing for English language services, cultivating its diaspora around the world and its educated middle classes in technology and medicine. Modern migrations possibly a generation ahead of the Chinese. A lot of smart people, but not the ability to coordinate its development in the same way that China can despite strong networks!

China has wealth, resources, commitment, investment, and a large country. It also has an internal degree of control that every other country in the World is envious of and a dominant race of people who are proud and want to succeed - quickly! It has now also obtained everyone else's technology – just sit back and watch! Are your clothes, sportswear, plastics goods, furniture, household goods, tools etc made in China – If they aren't yet they will be soon! There is a pleasant absence of lawyers now; that is changing!

I am staggered by the amount of trading going on in stocks and shares in China. So many people seem to be making money on share deals – ordinary people. Daily people at work tell me about how much profit they have made.

Quotes:

The pilot on arrival at Shanghai – 'I look forward to having you all individually, one by one, during your next flight with Xiamen Air Lines' (Friendly fellow, it's amazing how far airlines will go to attract customers!). I edited the Chinese accent bits e.g. 'I look florlard....' (Forward), individllilly, etc.

A 'Classic' discovered in our old company literature:

Qrality goes beyond expectations'; which about sums it up!

I had come to China with an open mind and had a truly fascinating and enlightening first month which I embraced, despite the frustrations with a positive outlook. This was not going to be my normal sort of job, nor a lifestyle that I was accustomed to.

Part 2

The Way Things Were

Chapter 4

China's Drinking culture

Before going to China, I had done some basic research on the do's and do nots of the culture, but nothing that I had seen or heard prepared me for the alcohol drinking culture that prevailed there. This culture not only came as an immense surprise, but I was to discover that it pervaded all society from senior regional government figures to everyday life.

One of my first experiences was walking into the Diamond Hotel in central Jiaxing at five thirty for dinner welcomed by the sight of a man who was carried by two colleagues supported on either side, coming out shouting and throwing up all over the reception doorway and wall. Staggered by this I questioned my Chinese colleague who just laughed and said, 'Its normal, he's happy, they are happy'! I laughed assuming he was joking but I was the learn that he was speaking the truth as such events were to be all too common and considered entirely 'acceptable.' In comparison, I came from a country where I was brought up 'to know one's limits and hold one's drink'!

I often found myself pondering why people drank so much to extreme and often to oblivion, noting the alcohol consumption habits of the West in comparison where there is obvious over consumption for many, but it is obviously essential in China where friendship, relationships and showing it, was all part of the lifestyle. It was once said to me that *'you could see the true person when drunk.'* I had a feeling that it also had a relationship to the recent times of countrywide poverty, food scarcity and lack of other entertainment, combined with a communist system in place that led to a life scarce of activity that was repetitive and boring. There was nothing else when welcoming folk, except for quite cheap alcohol, and that getting seriously drunk was a distraction in life. In the north there was also the cold factor, a way to warm the system. No one ever denied this personal theory of mine.

There were other motives, sometimes drinking to distract the guest from the events and key issues of business, an attempt to keep them off balance, a clear tactic by some that I became aware of.

Drinking whether with friends or on business was relationship making, confirmation of 'friends' and building trust. For the most the drinking was set around dinners and lunches with very few bars around especially during my early days, although these were later to increase significantly to accommodate the demands of the emerging middle classes.

Early on as a part of my excellent welcome to the company that I was working with and with the city government officials, I was exposed to this culture full on and by definition, most of my banquet dinners and the occasional lunch were business related. I learnt very quickly that it was appropriate that business must be completed ahead of the dinners and that the dinners themselves purely cemented relationships.

These events usually started off ritualistically and slowly and developed their own directions thereafter.

Where I lived and worked red wine was usually the dinner drink of preference, another surprise, reflecting the gradually developing middle class tastes and the fact that at circa 13 per alcohol contents, it was a safer drink than the local white spirits. I was told that twenty years before that joint ventures had been establish with French experts to grow vines in China and develop the manufacture of red wine that has since developed into a thriving industry, both legitimate and counterfeit.

Alternatives to red wine were the locally produced yellow wine (Huang jiu) and the far stronger white spirits known as bai jiu.

I should explain the beverage options:

Chinese White Wine (Baijiu), a clear spirit.

Mainly distilled from sorghum although sometimes from rice, barley, and wheat.

There are many distinct brands across China although the two main ones are Moutai, made in Guizhou province and Wuliangye from Sichuan province. Some are extremely expensive and often packaged in clear bottles or white bottles which tends to make them look like firelighter spirit for which I am sure it would work. Often outer packed in luxury branded boxes.

This is a serious drink – varying between 28-65 per cent in alcohol strength, although most that I saw was in the range 35-55 per cent.

It is drunk neat and does not have the taste of for instance a fine Russian or Polish vodka. Mixers such as cola or lemonade were never options! A no-no, with one exception in my experience.

Drank traditionally in small shot type glasses at banquets, some very small. When drank from larger wine glasses or even bowls, things get extremely dangerous.

Red Wine (Hong jiu)

Red wine as we know it in the West, same bottles, and all. The majority made in China, increasingly imported and of course the counterfeited wines made in China but sporting e.g., high quality French wine labels and the likes. Circa 12-13 per cent alcohol content.

Drank from medium sized normal wine glasses for the most, but in the event of challenges large measures developed.

Yellow wine (Huang jiu)

A traditional Chinese drink made in the Zhejiang and Fujian coastal regions albeit available around China. This tends to be circa 15 per cent alcohol content and overly sweet, but the taste can be easily acquired and often used and semi formal dinner banquets, especially as often much cheaper than red wine and bai jiu. Our company accountants preferred us selecting this for company dinners. The most famous brand being Shaoxing yellow wine.

Western white wine was starting to emerge increasingly, but outside of large cities was rarely chilled. Referred to in translations as grape white wine. *My worst experience was getting drunk in Xiamen on a warm and sickly tasting white wine.*

Beer (Pi jiu)

China beer is weak at circa 2 per cent alcohol content and bottled, traditionally un-chilled. There are a few stronger brands, but the strong beers are imported, such as the extraordinarily strong Belgian beers and of course German beers with micro-breweries established in places like Shanghai. Beer tended to be used for informal meals, lunches and rarely for formal occasions. I note that the prime Chinese brand, Qingdao (brand name Tsingtao), originated from German breweries established in that city when they controlled it in times past. Budweiser was another strong brand, as was Harbin.

I do not know why Chinese beers are so weak but assume that it is a government population health and alcohol control mandated strategy.

With evolution, as bars become more westernized, then draft beers are becoming more available to the masses.

Banquet dinners were often pure stupidity, fun, new friendships made, and existing ones cemented through a haze of alcohol, although the aftermath and consequences not always so great. Attentive waitresses keep glasses topped up, aware of their bonus earning potential relative to sales.

The drinking etiquettes attached to banquets varied around China, although the basis is similar. The host sits that the head of a round banquet table facing the entrance with the most important guest sat immediately to his or her right and the next guest of importance to his or her left.

Thereafter around the table it tends to go by rank of importance away from the host, either side although in the north of China the host's *'number two'* (designated drinker), sits immediately opposite in the anointed drinker's chair.

The dinner starts slowly with a gentle and polite drink to start the meal before any food is touched. This is often accompanied by a few words and pleasantries from the host and a toast offered to the honoured guests and the table, the table first and then the honoured guest. In areas of northern China, the hosts have three consecutive opening toasts and then hands over to the designated drinker to offer the next three toasts. Thereafter things tend to free up and get happier. Around the country such etiquette would vary and sometimes one had the impression that rules were being made up spontaneously!

One never drinks alone! Drinking at formal occasions is always *one-to-one*, that is, if someone toasts you, you toast them back with the same amount of alcohol. The ritual known as ganbei, drink up, it is a question of 'face.' Sometimes this is a sip, often a bigger sip. Things tend to start deteriorating when one shows one's friendship through the competition of drinking half a glass to each other. Things then get plain silly when folk start toasting full glasses to each other!

The problem with drinking one-to-one shot style is that one does not really get a chance to savour the taste of the drink being consumed during a through-back and swallow. That does not stop expensive wines being used for the events as a show of face and friendship, but we rarely were to have fine wine appreciation discussions over dinner, except for the price!

It is also polite to toast everyone around the table during the meal, which is great, but consider the one-to-one drinking and the pure statistics involved of the number of people around the table. I think the largest banquet table that I attended had twenty-four seats although this was not of course the norm. Tables of ten to twelve people are common, but frequently there were more.

At times I was aware of the hosts taking advantage of their guests, in part to protect themselves as many officials were doing this routinely, even twice daily. Waiters were discretely serving the hosts out of one bottle on a tray and guests out of another, the guest ones being neat or higher alcohol content, and the hosts being diluted in some way. Typical dilutions included red wine with coke, an obvious spot when the red wine starts frothing; watered down baijiu; or serving e.g., 32 per cent baijiu to hosts and 55 per cent baijiu to guests! I have witnessed all these tricks and more on my travels.

Some of the dinners were brutal including out and out drinkers, *ringers*, invited there to do damage and as a foreigner I was often a clear target, a free hit. Often though the danger came from a pleasant younger woman, sat directly opposite strategically, who had sat through the meal not drinking, but come near the end, when one had had enough to drink, they stood up, walked around the table, and toasted me with a large drink, always difficult to refuse because of their 'face,' warm and smiling approach with everyone watching. I learned to become wearier of these secret weapons than the big drinkers at times. Women did not normally drink so much at these macho occasions but travelling around China I discovered that there were certainly some exceptions to that rule.

At larger company or friends and family celebrations, the women, except for my translator, were often condemned to a separate private dining room or rooms where they drink tea and chat amongst themselves whilst the men play.

At times, the host managed to get the restaurant owner involved, male or female, to come and drink a toast to the guest out of respect and to welcome at a vulnerable time. Likewise, they may also insist that one of the poor serving waitresses who were in no position to refuse, to get involved with a similar such toast.

When drinking baijiu with shot sized toasting glasses, one had a chance of monitoring consumption but drinking from larger wine glasses it was easier and dangerous to lose track of consumption quickly.

If one is the lone guest, by definition, one is likely to be in trouble. Do the statistics – at a table of twenty folk, exclude me, exclude my translator, which leaves eighteen. Drinking one round, one to one with everyone, that would be one drink for the others and eighteen for me! Dangerous statistics.

At large meals in open restaurants or a series of private rooms, one often had to go around and toast each table as a courtesy, especially if hosting. This though encouraged the return drinking toasts and certain folk felt compelled to come back repeatedly and pay respect to the top table and the host.

I took to focussing on the tactics and strategy for dinners such as taking colleagues along to share the burden and level the playing field, having a say in specifying the alcohol of choice for the dinner if given the choice, trying to go to smaller more discrete gatherings and dinners, talking up other guests so that they become the larger targets and so on. This approach became particularly important to survival and good sense.

I usually took a moment to warn foreign visitors as to rituals and what was about or likely to happen, urging caution with their Chinese colleagues and hosts. Too often this advice was not heeded in the moment, or events took over due to an over-confidence in their own drinking capability and the occasion. Invariably they were not prepared for the sheer volumes, speed, or strength of the tonic they were drinking with some spectacular 'failures.'

Once at an informal dinner of friends in the rural countryside, we drank white wine with red bull. Simple – put a large bowl in the middle of the table – pour in a couple of bottles of baijiu, add a few tins of red bull and the carnage starts. This was compounded by the diners having this concoction ladled into clean food bowls to drink out of. One has no idea how much one is drinking on every ganbei. Additionally, in addition to a serious hangover, one could not sleep because the body was also full of red bull!

In Xinjiang in western China, I once had a lunch in a yurt up a mountain, sat on the floor with a long wooden rectangular table. Ten people, only three large glasses that everyone shared as was the local custom. The host poured the three glasses with baijiu, he selected two people to drink with, draining the entire glass. One of the drinkers then nominated another two to drink with them and so on. Within a short while our sales guy was asleep flat out under the side of the yurt, totally wiped out! I left hoping the alcohol content was strong enough to kill any transmissible diseases acquired from the shared drinking glasses. On that occasion I did not drink.

I understand that the very senior central government officials drank more modestly. Of course, this was important for decision making clarity, but also, I suggest for health reasons, the legacy of decades of drinking their way up through the system and I found that many reverted to type given the opportunity and discreteness of the situation. That was the way that it was.

I recall a period of vast expansion when new office blocks were being built everywhere and on at least one occasion I viewed senior officials' new offices that came not only with private bathrooms, but with private double bedrooms for *resting* after lunches or dinners. I became aware that this was something of a norm but resisted any suggestion that I have a bedroom attached to my new office for the obvious connotations of what folk may think, and of course a lack of necessity!

Indeed, poor health was often the only real excuse that folk had to get out of drinking, and this was understood, especially as China developed and health awareness and facilities improved. The mention of liver cirrhosis was a free pass.

Looking back at this in my early days, objectively, a sizeable proportion of the country's senior officials were either drunk at lunch, drunk at dinner, or sleeping it off afterwards. This obviously had huge negative implications for work productivity, decision making, bad moods and individuals health, never mind their private family lives. Then of course the door was more open to corruptive influences. Most senior officials had reliable deputies around to help.

The sure sign that some had drunk enough was the face turning red, partly a cultural feature, partly health issues I suggest. At banquet dinners one expected to see many red faces.

On a couple of occasions, I had the misfortune to meet new senior officials immediately after they had enjoyed a liquid lunch elsewhere. Being sober myself, their lack of sobriety was obvious by their erratic behaviour, red faced, and they were extremely quick to temper, their irrationality was quite troubling. In one case extreme nationalistic tendencies showing, which I was rarely exposed to directly, as he was trying to do a deal to protect a friend through bullying tactics.

A couple of years before the end of my time living in China, President Xi Jin Ping in recognition of the dangers of prolonged binge drinking on health and decision making, introduced a number of measures for Party members (government officials in China included not just central and local government officials, but banks, insurance companies and state manufacturing companies). In addition to stopping smoking at meal tables, he discouraged heavy drinking at dinner and banned Party officials from going to KTV afterwards. This was one of several sensible corrective decisions made relative to the way the country was developing on the back of its success and increasing wealth, showing people that there are other ways to do business and enjoy life. Even so, many enjoyed an opportunity to quietly bypass these rules on occasions, choosing more select and discrete locations of meals, often at out-of-town venues, and using a guest such as me as an excuse. Old habits were to die hard!

After dinners, officials had drivers around to whisk them away, although there was a brief period when private cars were just starting out, that some chose to drive themselves home. This was quickly stamped out though through diligent police checks for drink driving as the problem became apparent, and Party rules implemented that came with stiff penalties.

After dinners, if one did not need to sleep, there were the options of continuing the *friendship* and bonding at KTV that I will cover elsewhere, or heading to a local bar street. These streets in the city were typically set up by the government where many bars can compete together in a typically Asian style competitive situation, which I first recall seeing in Japan with its electronic shops located side by side and opposite in the same streets. Dare I say that having most bars in the same area also assisted control of the environment. The drinking often continued in increasingly westernized styled bars, moving away from the seedier small bars that preceded them.

KTV of course was a chance to keep drinking, behind closed doors, which had its benefits at many levels and restricted potential events that can be the result of alcohol, like open fights, and if there are fights, it was contained to a discrete private room and was more manageable. Of course, this was a potential breeding ground for corruptive deals and commitments, as well as all the ingredients for extra marital relationships.

Whatever the option, there is the chance for continued drinking and all that may go with that with no official closing times. Dangerous.

Most of the private dining rooms had their own private toilets, but where there we communal toilets, it was not unusual to hear men throwing up or appearing from the loos minus shirt and dressed only in a vest as they had soiled their shirts. The sure sign of a fun time!

As time passed, I quickly learned to try and avoid dinner invitations unless necessary from health, family, and business viewpoints. It was a question of survival in the jungle.

All this of course is vastly different from the expatriate communities, hotels and bars of Shanghai which increasingly were set up to cater with western tastes with sports bars, draft beers, pool tables with an Asian twist. These modern bars were not the norm across the country during my time there, but the fashion was starting to spread, especially with increased numbers of foreigners working there, but also the increasing affluence of the burgeoning middle classes who has travelled internationally or more pertinently, studied overseas at school or university, and acquired a taste for the culture.

Increasingly there were demands for expensive overseas wines and spirits as tastes became more informed and wealth permitted, whiskies and red wines were popular, local counterfeit and original, expensive red wines from France, spirits, fanciful beers, and international shot drinks all adding to the available pot.

Interestingly, I was to discover from big city expatriate contacts that most of them had rarely experienced the Chinese style banquet drinking sessions, the intensity, the alcohol type, and the consequences! Most expatriates in the larger cities happily consume substantial amounts of alcohol in the western bars there, but protected from the reality that was much of China.

I have long held the view that half the world is inebriated at any given time given experiences in bars, airports, on planes, on holiday, at sporting events, business conventions, BBQ's, friends and so on. In this context it is fair to say that China has done its best to play a leadership role!

A typical wedding table greeting – alcohol, in this case yellow wine,
red wine and baijiu, and the ever present cigarettes. All topped
up with consumption and beer available for those in need.

Chapter 5

Food and meals

A major surprise to me from the start was how seriously China took its food, as, if not more, seriously than the French! Ordering meals was usually a profoundly serious and considered moment in life, often consulting the owner or waiters on freshness or culinary aspects, new dishes and more, a process certainly rarely rushed.

Being brought up in the UK where traditionally there were a limited selection of dishes, albeit that has changed in variety over recent few decades, I was amazed at the range of ways to cook food and the huge amount of regional variability that influenced things, from the spices used in food in Sichuan to the bread-based foods of western China. There seemed to be a thousand ways to cook a chicken and food was an intrinsic part of everyday society and culture. Each dish had a regional variation, and each region of course has its own specialities!

Prior to living in China I had always enjoyed Chinese food in UK restaurants but was quickly to learn that most food in China was not like that at all and that these restaurants were derivatives of Hong Kong-Guangdong style Cantonese cooking that had been sweetened and modified to suit Britain's tastes. I had also travelled a bit and previously enjoyed exposures to Chinese food in other parts of Asia such as Malaysia, Singapore, and Hong Kong, including such pleasant surprises as getting a bowl of live prawns ('drunken prawns') to cook for myself in the boiling water, in front of me, at the table, not untypical.

I had long mastered the use of chop sticks, a necessity in China, although my grip was not a traditional one, long the source of amusement to other guests at the start of meals and I usually got low marks for style, but ate.

Nothing though quite prepared me for Chinese food, although positively I can eat most things and did! Some of those things became easier to consume related to the amount of alcohol that went with them at mealtimes and trust me that was a definite prerequisite on occasions.

As I travelled, primarily on business, I was privileged to have been well looked after, welcomed as an honoured guest, and treated to local specialities, although at times I am sure there was an element of *testing out the foreigner*, both with alcohol and food selections.

It is fair to say that I ate in a complete spectrum of restaurants and homes during my time in China, from the spectacular and ornate gold leafed Romanesque palaces with their excellent services, through to the small rural roadside eateries with basic and frankly very dirty amenities. Let us just call them shocking!

China, it seems eats everything and anything, I assume partly culture, partly out of historic necessity given the famines and sheer size of population to feed.

These days with the westernization influences there are fast food outlets like KFC, which is extremely popular given China's preference for chicken, but also McDonalds. China also has its own variation on fast food outlets, although these rarely appealed to me. Steakhouses are starting to develop selling imported beef to the more affluent and are not cheap.

Chinese restaurants catered for all incomes from the small 'garage space shops' on ground floors surrounding apartment blocks, to the roadside barbeque stalls where cheap cuts of meat were cooked, with the government's hygiene officials increasingly chasing them away in their genuine drive to improve food quality, through to high class restaurants who seek to differentiate themselves with modern style dishes.

The preference is for large restaurants, and although they often had a communal dining halls, it was the private banqueting rooms with personalized waiter and waiter service that were in demand. These are expensive but impressive rooms with exceptionally large circular tables (I have sat at tables with twenty-two to twenty-four places around the perimeter), indeed all rooms with circular tables and *lazy Susan* glass turntables in the middle of it so that dishes can be shared around the table. The decoration was often fabulously ornate but strangely there was often a flat screen TV on a wall in the room showing news which may stay on with sound turned on throughout the meal and can be distracting. These though are places to develop guanxi and get things done.

Chinese tea is served pre-dinner at the table whilst ordering food and drink, and waiting for the meal and alcohol to arrive. Alcohol is not consumed before the food arrives and certainly there are not pre-dinner drinks as in the West. Evening mealtimes tend to start earlier generally in much of China at five-thirty to six o'clock and completed by about eight o'clock, although there are regional variations on this.

Formal places are laid out around the table and a cloth napkin is placed on the table with a bowl on top of it and extends into one's lap. This is fine but not if standing up to toast another guest with the habit of grabbing one's napkin as one does so, forgetting for an instance that the napkin is under your eating bowl, at which stage the bowl tips over the table, everyone laughs assuming the foreigner is drunk, and an attentive waitress quickly cleans up and changes the napkin, embarrassing.

So, what did I eat? About everything that was put in front of me, and rarely did this disagree with my systems, although I was quite ill on three occasions with food poisoning, each time due to eating contaminated street food on the way home (cheap recycled cooking oil, often extracted from drains became a scandal). This I assume because so much food is wok cooked and *terrible things* burnt off at the extremely hot temperatures, a different situation to say India. I ate all these things not just out of a natural curiosity and for the experience, but in the name of guanxi, to make relationships and promote friendship. I played the game!

Pork and Chicken were the most popular staple meats in Han China. Lamb or mutton is more associated with the west of the country where there are large Muslim populations and with the grasslands of inner Mongolia to the north. Beef in China was surprisingly in less supply although that was changing with increased imports of higher quality beef following the popularity of more western foods. Traditionally Chinese beef was not of high quality and softened by all sorts of tenderizing agents. Other poultry was always available, including ducks, quail, pigeon, as well as rabbit.

So, I will list the types of food that I can remember eating at differing times, these often being different to the general day to day normal foods that I had in my home city, albeit these often-included offal of several types:

Dog, yes, I did it. On a few occasions that I know about. This was a particular speciality of Guangxi Province where we had some loyal customers, and they prepared the speciality dog stews just for me. It was not terrible, but not great either in truth. Been there and done it! Please do not shout – it was the norm in certain areas, their culture and not for me to judge, right or wrong.

Fried wasps, fried bees, grasshoppers, and locusts as it was translated to me. Crunchy but simple to digest.

Scorpions. Indeed, three at one lunch sitting in inland Shandong, as my two UK colleagues passed on the pleasure, and it fell to me to please our hosts and keep our end up. The hosts pointed out that these were poisonous but not when cooked, although occasionally people did die from eating them, which was not overly re-assuring.

The entire soft shell of a rare soft-shelled turtle. Not great but the hosts watched carefully to ensure that I consumed it all. A protected species I was told afterwards, an honour!

Ants, fried, served in a bowl with spoon, quite a regular offer around China.

Chargrilled and entirely blackened baby chicks in Guangxi province, with their tongues still sticking out in surprise and shock from the initial experience of incineration. The bones were soft and eaten whole. The hosts always insisted that I ate more than one.

Shark's fin, the soup being considered an absolute delicacy in China and was quite common at one stage in premier quality restaurants. There was a lot of adverse global publicity surrounding this in the first decade of this century. I recall as lunch meal for UK visitors from Nottingham University to Nottingham Ningbo University and sitting opposite a lovely chap, a lecturer, who had been cautious about what he ate but really was enjoying the soup. He casually asked me what it was, and I told him that it was shark's fin soup, at which stage he violently spat out the soup all over the table in disgust and disappeared to the loo to freshen up. I have also eaten shark's stomach lining and other bits.

Chickens' feet, geese, and ducks' feet. I still do not get it, never acquired the taste of it but remains a popular snack in Chinese culture. I struggled chewing over a few of these things out of courtesy. No meat just bones and sinews. Arduous work with low return!

Sheep's eyes, sheep's brain, sheep's cheek, sheep's testicles, sheep's feet, sheep's heart, sheep's feet, indeed every part of a sheep. Eaten over two days in a restaurant and then a yurt in Xinjiang Province, western China. I know........!

I have drunk baijiu with a large, marinated deer's penis in it. I should clarify that I did not eat this and was reluctantly enticed into drinking it! The local theory was that it was "good for men"!

Grubs, fried. Yep.

Snake. I had tried fried snake in Zhejiang province which was okay. However, whilst visiting Fujian province I was treated to a speciality snake meal, a local speciality and, we ate every part of the snake. Even the green snake's venom was mixed with a strong baijiu white wine that somehow neutralized the poison and was consumed. Snake's skin fried, fried snake, boiled snake meat, snakes head were all consumed!

Ducks' tongues, which come with the jawbone are another popular snack. I recall one colleague, who was very weary of Chinese food tucking into these at a banquet as they were tasty and only one of the few things that he felt comfortable to eat. I recall asking him how they were, and he was enthusiastically positive. I then recall his reaction when I asked him if he thought he was eating chicken wish bones - at which point cottoning on to the realization of a potential problem he dropped the tongue and said, "what is it"? When I told him, he was sick, and I am sure he never forgave me for not telling him earlier of indeed at a prior meal. This was to be a breach of trust between us thereafter.

Smelly tofu – it simply stinks, horrendously so by design, but is delicious if one manages to get it to one's lips. One of so many ways to cook tofu with each province having regional variances, but this is a classic dish in Zhejiang province. The same colleague who ate the ducks' tongues at the same meal again virtually vomited having this smell on the table and he certainly was not going to have this near his sensitive stomach, and he willingly drank three full glasses of red wine as a penalty for his request to have it removed.

Tofu is another dish that have different styled specialities in each province and mixed with many things, sometimes spicy – soaked in blood is a typical favourite.

Fisheyes – considered a delicacy and important for improving one's sight apparently! My translators often chose to tuck in to improve their vision, the positive being that it also protected me from having to do so.

Fish reproductive glad. There you go, again a delicacy and too often offered to the honoured guest, which I often was. This pushed my limits of food tolerance and although not retching, I had to quickly wash it down with something. A horrible slimy texture.

Bull's testicles, indeed, other testicles, sheep and I think pigs, but will never know! And do not care to!

Pigs' anus – I know! That is what the translation said on the menu.

Dim Sum in Hong Kong, and Guangzhou – wonderful! A terrific way to eat snacking and varied small portions of a variety of dim sum. A clear favourite of mine.

Offal-Intestines-Lungs is quite standard cooked in various formats and included in many standard dishes. Usually from pigs and often mixed with various fresh vegetables.

Pigs' trotters – something that I did not recall seeing much in the UK since my grandfather's generation back in rural Cornwall.

Frogs, bull frogs and toads, some poisonous I was informed. Some protected as well. Never a great fan of these. Lots of small bones.

Chicken often appears in a stew, *the entire chicken*, feet, pope's nose and all, neck, and head which someone around the table will always gladly have a go at. The most annoying thing to me about chicken was that it was often just literally chopped up, legs and all the bones which means picking up pieces with chopsticks and trying to negotiate not swallowing bone chippings and fragments, sinews and so on. I used to die for a simple piece of meaty chicken breast but no such chance, unless I went to KFC. The inclusion of the head, neck and feet were often more of a surprise to foreign guests and to many terminated their interest in eating this dish.

Fried tendons – chewy – not sure from what animal, but not something that I would look for again. Truly horrible and as close to inedible as feasible. Strangely popular to some.

Sea cucumbers/Korean Sea Slugs – which I first had in Qingdao on the coast of Shandong province, a seafood town but popular all over especially in classy seafood restaurants. Specialities, but to me horribly chewy and impossible to bite and chew. Strange texture in one's mouth. Near the top of my list of least favourites but have eaten on many occasions.

Hairy crabs – popular on a seasonal basis especially in Zhejiang and around coastal areas. Small crabs that are a lot of arduous work for small returns in crabmeat. No utensils provided so one must use teeth to crack the shell which sometimes is not a clever idea, otherwise pulling apart with fingers and sucking meat out of the leg shells. All of course whilst removing the glands under the top of the shell that are poisonous and not to be eaten! Messy and demanding work for low return.

Around other southern coastal provinces I did get to eat larger, meatier crab with appropriate eating utensils, but in my experiences this was a rarity.

Horse's penis really, yes apparently I was told although after translation there were suddenly some 'shushes' and things went quiet; it would have been nice to have known before. Certainly, other horsemeat and donkey meat and sausages appeared along the way.

Whole ball joints from animal legs, along with knuckles, not great! Something to suck on and to try and extract bone marrow at times. Again messy and sometimes noisy.

Eels – chewy, greasy, and slippery.

Pigs' ears – chewy and as per the name on the tin (Sow's ear)!

Camel meat – in the west where there are more deserts areas.

Uncooked raw lamb marinated in garlic.

Beach worms, yes, plain, and simple.

Fish – usually fish appeared cooked and arrived whole on a plate in the middle of the dining table. Usually, this fish up until about half an hour previously, was swimming around in a fish tank in the food ordering area of the restaurant and had been especially selected by the host. Some of these Asian fish are beautiful, or incredibly ugly, and strangely different to fish we have in the West, but the thought remains fresh in your mind when pouring over the bones of what are usually delicious fish. Traditionally I had an ongoing concern about the water quality of the inland freshwater fish had been bred in and the effect upon the fish but learned to burry that thought, but I know from first-hand experience that some of these breeding ponds were none too clean.

Animal tails, that I assumed to be bull, although I have seen dishes of pig's tails as well, curled up, fried on the table!

Abalone, like shark's fin, a delicacy and an expensive one! Marine gastropod molluscs; "Ear shells" to some, a seafood. Pleasant enough!

Sticky rice, wrapped in a banana skin with a piece of pork in it was a local delicacy. Zhongzi.

Of course, there are the standard foods that we enjoy around the world such as Beijing crispy Duck with pancakes, also a premium and overpriced meal in China, often with lots of skin and not much meat. The slight variance being is that the removed bones are often fried as an option and put on the table in a separate bowl to chew through as well.

I should say that I never knowingly ate rat, which does not mean that I did not. I do recall my first translator telling me that a doctor had once prescribed her to eat rat for medical reasons. I was not re-assured by translations that struggled to differentiate mice and rats.

An increasing fashionable style of restaurant food, especially in winter, was the hot pot meals, stainless steel pots with water in the middle of the table that is heated and allowed one to cook one's own food. These pots of hot water were divided, one half for water and simple spices and one half for spicier tastes. Now this was good – a selection of meats, pork slices and vegetables. I once saw brains being added and indeed tried, but this was not the norm. That bit was not great!

Barbeque foods were also becoming extremely popular, especially as meat quality improved and in part a development of the Korean style barbeques that had long been popular in the north. Cheap meat barbeques became popular on the streets for a while, cooked on skewers, but meat quality to put it mildly was often dodgy.

I once had the pleasure when eating seafood of drinking baijiu white spirit that was marinated in a bottle with seahorses.

Drunken prawns were not uncommon, a bowl of live prawns delivered to your table to cook yourself in boiling water.

Potatoes were often either sliced or shredded and usually a little hard and undercooked in my view; popular dishes though in a rice-based society.

Chinese vegetables are plentiful, fresh, and excellent. There are a wide range of Chinese vegetables, examples including:

Lotus roots

Bamboo shoots and bamboo

White radish

Soybean sprouts

Chinese cabbage

Bok Choi

Tree fungus – quite popular in several parts of China.

Seaweed is a standard, boiled or stir fried.

Mushrooms

And many, many, more, one being a particularly long type cucumber, many times the length of our western ones, with the joke being that it was exceptionally good for men; the follow up joke at the table being that it was even better for women. My translators always had trouble with translating that one.

Given such dishes one was not surprised that various foreign visitors to our company who claimed to be vegetarian when arriving in China for their first banquet. I recall one senior company manager from the UK, a lady, who asked me as the meal was being ordered to ensure that there was vegetarian food, to which I enquired "I did not know that you were vegetarian, how long have you been?" to which she replied, "since I got off the plane at Shanghai four hours ago"!

Vegetarianism is, or at least was not common. Vegetables traditionally in China are great and abundant, stir fried, never eaten as salads, which is something that has developed more recently through western influences and with water quality improvements. A problem is that vegetable courses are often cooked blended with meat or fish juices and chopped meat pieces for example, so trying to get a straight vegetable dish is sometimes challenging. On more than one occasion I had to work hard on translators and the kitchen's chefs for them to get it – vegetarian food has no meat, fish and that includes the juices!

I recall a company board member from the UK, a modest and affable gentleman who was vegetarian and asked for vegetarian food when ordering the meal. After several attempts to order vegetable dishes and indeed rice without any meat or fish in them there was a lot of frustration from the host, the well-travelled translator who could not understand the requirement, nor for that matter the waiter. Total disbelief at the request. Having eventually resolved this with curried white rice and two vegetable dishes, or so we thought, the host asked the director what alcohol that he wanted to drink? To which the director replied that he did not drink, at which stage the exasperated translator gave up translating and just barked at him 'What's wrong with you'? As perhaps to be expected the first vegetable dish on the table included chopped meat pieces!

There were other many various shelled seafoods and crustations that are popular but challenging work, including large prawns coming with shells on that are difficult to remove and messy to do so in formal situations with fingers. I have seen one gent, and one lady who popped a whole large prawn into their mouths and proceed to separate the shell from the meat with their teeth and tongues alone; no simple task and took some time until they spat out the shell still pretty much in its entirety having swallowed the prawn. Yes, my mind did work.

Many of the above dishes are specialities served in good restaurants. Daily dishes can be mundane and varied, usually economical with rice or noodles.

Breakfast varies by region, but typically includes as examples:

Chinese dumplings, either pork or vegetable in dough casings of just vegetable. Fried or in soup. Fried is delicious and a regular choice of breakfast for me – there is no cereal in China traditionally, no decent Western bread outside of the big international community cities such as Shanghai.

Chinese pancakes fried with potatoes and various greenery and some meat included delicious.

Rice soup – rice in a bowl of water, translated as rice porridge, added to with such as left-over foods or pickles or the likes. A staple, but not for me.

Fried eggs or hard-boiled ones

Long sticks of fried Chinese bread, Youtiao – delicious.

Many roadside breakfast specialities included combinations of the above, such as fried bread wrapped in pancakes and so on.

Often washed down with some soya milk. Cow's milk has been traditionally limited in its availability.

Lunches and snacks typically include:

When not eating in a restaurant, noodles, soup noodles or fried. Both can be delicious but fried is best! There were many distinct types of noodles available.

Dumplings again.

Rice based dishes, half boiled white rice half a meat and vegetables.

Dim Sum – a southern speciality and simply wonderful.

Across China there are so many regional varieties, most of Han China in the north, east, central, and south have rice and noodles-based meals, whilst the western provinces tend to be bread based and some delicious breads there are too, with lamb and mutton the predominant meats there. Central Chinese foods of Sichuan, Chong Qing and Hunan provinces are often very spicy.

During the mid-autumn festival September annually depending upon the lunar calendar, moon cakes are in high demand, a huge commercial opportunity. Generally looking like small pork pies, sometimes with ornate decoration of the pastry and containing egg yolks and the likes, but are strangely sweet. Many variations and traditional gifts to be consumed during the festival.

Western style cake shops have become extremely popular during the last decade, specializing in birthdays and weddings, customizing designs often being the norm. Less sweet than western cakes, without the heavy icing, but lots of cream.

Overall diets have improved significantly as wealth increases with decent food supply, wider choice, more availability given the urbanization programmes and supported by government initiatives to improve food quality and hygiene. There was though always concerned rumours about the degree and legality of hormone contents of pork and chicken, as well as ongoing concerns about the effects of illegal but effective pesticides used on the crops. Coming though from living generations where there was starvation, limited choice, and quality concerns there has been distinct progress.

That said with increased wealth and fast-food outlets multiplying there has been a notable increase in obesity. When I arrived in China I seldom saw overweight children, but this noticeably changed over time, compounded by a lack of exercise in schools and the move away from bike riding to powered travel options.

Knives and forks are rarely used although are being introduced for western dining courses as steak dishes increase in popularity. Chop sticks remain the main utensil for eating.

This all of course ignores the likes of Shanghai which has every type of global food now and culturally developed citizens in modern China.

Fresh food markets

These fresh food markets, of the type that is allegedly the source of the coronavirus 19 virus outbreak, were typical when I arrived in Jiaxing, the prime source of food supply and I think there were four main markets around the centre of Jiaxing city. The Chinese like fresh food and distrusted frozen foods partly because the food was perceived as being not fresh and partly there were genuine health issues eating frozen food in those days as food was often frozen, unfrozen, and refrozen etc in the supply chain as links in the chain tried to save money by turning off the freezing systems at night and in transportation. The most evidential example being ice creams one bought that we often deformed beyond recognition having obviously melted and refrozen.

The fresh food markets were to become a part of my tourist tour of Jiaxing for family and visitors, a real curiosity of the type largely unseen in the West. Fascinating.

Within a few years supermarkets, often foreign joint ventures, started to develop and reduced demand on many of the fresh food markets which were gradually scaled down and many closed, thereby improving the hygiene and safety of the food supply chain.

Food, whilst so important a part of China life, did not feature in many TV programmes. I recall reading in the Chinese English language press that China deliberately banned TV food programmes which are so popular in the UK and elsewhere in the West, for fear of making the population fat!

China has a wonderful variety of cuisine and the quality of this food through the supply chain is improving continuously, as indeed is the food hygiene standards and regulation in its supply chain and preparation.

Food in China is a serious business!

An example of a modern palatial restaurant in the city of Jiaxing.

A typical superior quality banquet large dining table in a
private room. This one laid up for eighteen people

Chapter 6

China's Leisure and Relaxation Industry

I remember early during my employment in China, towards the end of a well-oiled banquet dinner, that the head of our Chinese joint venture partner company stood up, welcomed me formally in front of several banquet tables of colleagues, invited his team to look after me and make my time there comfortable. He then stated what I was to hear many times over the coming years, translated in the slightly quaint old English expression that *'he is very handsome.'* Then *'we must find him a wife here in China'* (as translated), *'it is important that he is happy here in China,'* which was quite surprize to me at the time in its openness and would have been a considerably more shocking to my family if they had heard it. He was not joking it seemed despite the laughs. I also remember somewhere in the translation, mention of 'little sister' (xiao Jie), two words that I would hear repeatedly all over China.

It became clear early on in my stay that the needs of Chinese men in society shall we say, were well catered for!

Strangely and quite out of character, on an early trip to China by my then wife, who never normally talked about such things, stunned me again by casually observing that *'you could have anyone that you want out here'!* This view being the result of walking around the city of Suzhou and observing the attention that I received and the female reactions. Instincts.

In 2003 a new British colleague came to work with me in Jiaxing, separated but not yet divorced, he was seeking a girlfriend. Enlightened and trusted friends and advisors informed me, un-solicited, that there is no way a nice middle-class educated Chinese girl from a rich family would get involved with him or any other foreigner as he was still married. Their families would not let them date him. This was followed by the assertion that once he was divorced then they would be pleased to make appropriate introductions. It was not about playing around, he would have to make a serious commitment to a permanent relationship quickly, which is the way things worked apparently. This was not actually what he wanted at that stage and was not therefore too encouraging. I was curious about the perceived need to '*make introductions,*' '*find a wife for him*' and what that entailed.

It was said repeatedly that 'if he wants to play then it is better to pay,' transactional and no commitments as it was put to me, none of the problems associated with '*love.*' When questioned, it was pointed out to me that this is normal in China, there is always money or some benefit involved; this was simply the way it was, which I interpreted as prostitution, but I was told certainly not!

Now then, '*prostitution is illegal in China.*' I know this only because it frequently appeared in the poor English translations of many hotel rules and regulations one found in the bedroom folders as I travelled around inland China. This was the sort of bureaucratic rule that one came to expect in Chinese hotels along with the likes of '*it is illegal to bring nuclear materials into your room*' and '*Don't steal the TV or you will be charged for it.*' Indeed, the regulations often included a price list of the contents of the room and the rooms were always physically checked for damage or theft ahead of check out payments, paid in cash, which slowed departures down.

Out of casual curiosity I found myself drawn to seek greater clarification on the matter of prostitution and therefore Googled the word, before Google was blocked in China, and good old Wikipedia immediately presented me with the following definition '*prostitution is the business or practice of providing sexual services to another person in return for payment*', which is pretty much as I had understood it to be.

Suddenly, I was struggling to reconcile this clear statement of the laws of China and the reality of what I was becoming to understand about the situation in the society that I lived in. Of course there may be an element of interpretation and indeed cultural translation to be considered, as for instance there is a price for everything in China, the old anecdote of 'there is no such thing as a free meal' taken to a more extreme point of view perhaps. Incidentally, the ever-useful Wikipedia also confirmed that prostitution is illegal in China. The hotels were right!

Still, I continued to struggle with this all. For instance, *basically every hotel in China was a brothel*; again perhaps a sweeping statement that no doubt again requires more clarification. I should say that nearly every hotel that I had stayed in openly offered services that would come under the definition of prostitution, a range of hotels from five star to lower quality hotels in towns and cities across China, but the services available were something that was obviously the expected market norm for the male population. I had no reason to suspect that these facilities were solely confined to the hotels that I stayed, indeed comments from friends and colleagues had confirmed the fact that such services were widely provided. The evidence for this were manyfold including the hotel spa's that were seriously marketed including in-room massage services, repeated 'sales' phone calls direct to the room, regular knocking on doors, messages pushed under doors, 'display rooms' of waiting young ladies in rooms off the reception areas, even questions from the doormen. I recall on my very first trip to China, day one, jet lagged, walking around the floor below reception of a nice smart westernized hotel in Jiaxing and finding a clear glass fronted room full of young ladies sat in uniform rows of chairs, maybe thirty of them, all dressed in white sports shirts and shorts, all looking at me with beaming smiles and I was to learn later, were all available awaiting a call, awaiting to be 'picked'. Quite surprising and indeed shocking. It is also fair to say that levels of discretion varied depending upon hotel quality and location.

The few hotels where such arrangements were not available were either in the stricter controlled Beijing area at times of purges, had a name like 'International Friendship' hotel, which were strictly regulated, or ones which have had an 'incident' of some kind. This could vary based on hearsay, from some drunk seriously abusing a lady, something that could not be kept under the radar, or the 'right people had not been paid'. When I questioned this statement with a knowledgeable Chinese friend, with a leading question that was 'do you mean the police or the mafia?', the response was a wicked laugh and the proclamation that 'what is the difference? They are one and the same'! The facilities were available, but apparently the hotel and the girls must pay a cut to this mysterious body of folk who seem to unofficially run much of China! The presence of either fit or fat strong men with cropped haircuts, wearing t-shirts and gold chains around their necks were often giveaways.

Anyway, hotel house rules were obviously misleading, prostitution was widely and freely practiced in China, in its hotels and elsewhere. In the hotels it was just a question of asking for a massage, one may get the question 'massage or xiao Jie', one can get a genuine massage in one's room, but the main availability is the *xiao Jie*, who will probably be a very hardworking and diligent lady who will work all day or all night in accommodating fashion to earn her income.

In some hotels folk could go to hotel reception annexes and select a lady to take or be sent to the room, some young, but I have to say that there was never the suggestion of any girls under-aged. In some hotels the girls were encouraged to be more proactive, knocking on one's door or phoning one's room. I have been in hotels in Shanghai where I have received phone calls, in up market managed apartments, at 05.00 hours in the morning with my wife lying next to me asking if I needed company, in English. At other times I have been awoken at 03.00 hours and again by the same lady at 04.00 hours and 05.00 hours just checking whether I needed a massage; active marketing. Unfortunately, such calls, which happened all too often, did not do much for marital trust. Phone calls in the middle of the night in hotels in China was a very common and recurring theme, which didn't help sleep patterns either.

After one long business trip, I eventually arrived in a small hotel in Luohe in Henan Province, only to have lady knocking on my door, two minutes after I checked into my room, asking if I needed a massage at one o'clock in the afternoon. It was immediately obvious to me that she wasn't dressed too much like a masseur adorned in a skimpy mini dress and heavily made up.

It doesn't take long to work out the sheer numbers involved in providing these services across China. The scale was immense, and I am sure these young ladies all go home to their families at the Lunar Chinese New Year bearing money and gifts and informing the families that they work in make-up shops, factories, offices, or hairdressers. It was a question of economic circumstance and the market demand sadly.

Now there is a subject, hairdressers. Of course there were genuine and proper hairdressers, many high end, then there were 'hairdressers', small shops, often along side streets, with girls sat in chairs looking out of the window, a couple of barbers chairs and a mirror, sink and some hair treatments, but not smart. The girls looked out encouragingly and invitingly. To enter one would find that the ladies in the 'hairdressers shop' could offer a wide variety of basic services, except perhaps to cut your hair. Indeed if audited I bet that they would struggle to find a pair of scissors between them all. I also suspected that one could probably catch every disease known to man as well if one tried, indeed without trying too hard. I say this is deference and with respect to the real hairdressing shops, the difference is tangible. These shops were sometimes on busy streets open and obvious to the local community but staffed by ladies from out of town.

The list of such female company outlets went on and on, not hidden, albeit not so open in nature when compared to the overtly public showings in for Thailand or the Philippines.

Showering centres were very popular. These started I believe as functional places for the populace to get washed, say once a week, for folk who didn't have showering-bathing facilities at home who needed to clean up in a basic way. I witnessed private apartments where the tiny shower rooms in the bathroom had become storage rooms and not functional. Again these were places that one could clean up but also go and relax and even sleep over at, popular with travelers as a cheap overnight option to a hotel. Over time these commercialized and developed as high-quality showering centres that offered a far greater range of amenities, a place one can go to for a shower, possibly a single sex communal bathing pool, be body scrubbed all over by young men around the poolside with something akin to Swarfega with grit in it, showered again and then issued with nonwoven shorts, a gown, and shown upstairs to a private room, where one was presented with a very impressive menu of different massage types that one could have, in Chinese of course. I recall in Shandong, one drunk, friendly, and fluent English-speaking official that I had just had dinner with, entering my room as I arrived for a basic back massage (everyone at dinner had gone on to the massage centre), and offering to translate the menu. 'Do you want a back massage, head massage or a sex massage with oil'? All said very matter-of-factly and oh yes, the ever-present Johnson's baby oil, although it was probably a counterfeit oil, one of the main supplementary tool of these ladies who undertake this work I gather. I should also clarify that there are many places that offered pure massage services with none of the frills; genuinely therapeutic and relaxing. I was to learn that many local governments around had their own private showering centres for their officials and guests, generally discreet and private behind gated entrances and with high walls.

The rumours of the types of body massages available were let's say intriguing, but let's leave it at everything being on the table. Some western colleagues joked about remembering their favourite number on the menu's just like food options on Chinese take-away lists.

I recall an experience very early on in my time in China that I heard about from a trusted friend. *'However, the world being what it was, after a very good dinner and having imbibed copious quantities of red wine, the host took his guest for a foot massage, which somehow developed and the guest was shown to a backroom, which had a double bed in it, and to where two young ladies were shown in to greet him. Now it was said that he apparently slept exceedingly well and was gently awoken sometime later and shown outside to the reception area, where his host was waiting to pick up the itemized bill. Yes, itemized bill! He encouraged the guest to sit and rest why he took care of things, but after a while he approached the guest quietly and discretely but looking slightly concerned, 'did you have two girls?' to which he replied 'yes, you sent two in', to which the startled host replied, 'but you were only meant to pick one'. It seemed that these 'benefits' are not necessarily cheap, and the host would have to explain this entertainment bill to his boss!'*

I was to discover that the itemized bills could be embarrassing, with one translator arguing with the checkout reception of a luxury showering centre that there was obviously a mistake on the bill as the overseas company boss did not have that service, 'he would never have had that', whilst the embarrassed chap in question sat quietly in a chair nearby waiting for her to simply settle the bill and get out of there. Then the penny dropped with the translator and then there was silence!

KTV (karaoke in private rooms)

Then of course on China there is KTV, a national pass-time for primarily the male race and where so much 'guanxi' was developed, making friends, whilst cementing business deals behind the closed doors of private rooms. The KTV industry, karaoke to most of us, was simply huge. At one end this was a pleasant chance for a few friends, male and female, to go out and sing, but the industry has taken a whole different turn. Huge KTV palaces appeared all over the country, lots, and lots of rooms, often palatially decorated, with huge and comfortable sofas where there were full KTV sets organized for the business community to come and drink and be merry. Of course, to do this one should be accompanied by a young lady to drink with, for which the host will pay, sometimes selected on a graded scale depending upon the beauty or shall we say, the social flexibility of the ladies.

Upon arrival at these glamourous KTV buildings one was greeted by lines upon lines of young ladies wearing elegant long dresses, all shouting 'welcome, welcome', in a unified chorus to you as one entered the reception. This was impressive. Later line ups of these girls appeared in the usually large and extremely comfortable private KTV rooms, a chance to select someone who you thought would be a good match for the evening during the karaoke. Regulars often had their favourites on speed dial on their phone and called upon arrival which could cause issues of conflicts of commitments at times. She would then join encourage one to spend your money, drinking, smoking, being happy, sing and at the end pay to her a big tip for sitting with you, closely to you if wished. If things had gone well, then for a fee and by negotiation, the girl may go home with someone, but for this there were a raft of serious costs – the KTV place, the girls themselves, the agent, the *protection* and so on. Taking girls home afterwards was certainly not the norm for KTV participants but was certainly a viable option for some if circumstances suited. I was to learn that some senior officials were at the KTV rooms nearly every night, entertaining clients.

Then there is the singing part, something that doesn't come naturally always to us foreigners, who tend to be reserved, but encouraged by alcohol and the privacy of the rooms, folk generally loosened up and joined in. The western song menus improved significantly over time. My singing party piece progressing from Frank Sinatra's *'My Way'* in my early days to Robbie William's *'Angels'* later in my time, with several epic failures in between. It should be said that there were many embarrassing moments relative to singing performances. I never learnt to sing a song in the Chinese language.

A senior banker from Hong Kong once told me that a serious and creditable business analyst there once studied the industry in China and estimated that KTV comprised 12.5 per cent of the Gross Domestic Product. I was shocked by the scale of this. He justified it though when considering the properties and buildings involved; the decoration and fittings of these, not just a bit of paint, but special lighting, pictures, glasses, ornate sofas and so on; then there is the KTV sound systems and large flat TV sets; of course there were the girls, often hundreds of them at one venue and the waitresses who serve, the salaries, charges and tips; the girls dresses which were often something else; the make-up the girls wear; the huge alcohol bills; expensive Chinese teas; tobacco – often best quality and most expensive brands of cigarettes; the revenues charged per song added up very quickly and then there were the gifts involved. On the black-market side there were estimates for the 'protection money', the cash for employees who work there and female income. Mindboggling!

I was never sure quite how all the labour processes worked, but there must have been very organized supply chain systems in place across the country to attract out of town young ladies to these roles. Often, although certainly not always, there were tiny tattoos on the woman's hand somewhere, often between the thumb and forefinger, sometimes in the inner wrist. This was explained to me by colleagues that it tied them to local migrant gangs………..the word 'mafia' kept coming to mind.

More recently from the 2010's I heard that for some guests of a certain preference that young men also were available to accompany them at KTV. This was told to me in hushed tones but showed the development of China becoming more open about such things as homosexuality was never mentioned or recognized openly in my first decade or so there.

In recent years President Xi Jin Ping has slowed all of this down by vigorously restricting Party members from going to such places as things were getting out of hand and as a part of a major corruption clampdown, and as other more acceptable sources of economic income became available. He was obviously mindful of the facts that so many young women in the country were involved directly in the leisure and relaxation industry. I think that is the most diplomatic way to phrase it. About this time a video of a senior local government official appeared on the internet in a hotel room with a young lady – a huge scandal given that these were traditionally private areas, but a clear message to all Party members to moderate their behaviour. Then another such video appeared just to reinforce the situation. I guess it worked as a deterrent!

I struggled with all of this though. I understood as reported in national statistics in China, that there were forty million less women than men in the country. I.e. if all the men and women were married off, there would be forty million blokes without a missus who could legally be their married wife. This is where I got confused, because so many of the available women are tied up in the sex industry or associated relaxation processes, who I assume will one day settle down into married bliss, many provinces away from where they practiced their profession. I do suppose though that at a practical level that it works the other way round as it spreads the women around to take care of the needs of the male population.

Massages

In my early days my main source of relaxation, in amongst the boredom of being home alone every night with no foreign friends around, indeed no friends, was to wander down to the ground floor of my apartment block to a small genuine hairdressing shop for a head massage, which at that time was cheap and entirely innocent. This was highly relaxing in a reclining barber's chair having one's scalp, neck and back massaged. All very therapeutic as I adjusted to life in China and although I spoke absolutely no Chinese at that time, a colleague's wife had explained what to do and as the only foreigner around the ladies in the shop already tipped off. This basic head massage migrated as China innovated to also have an ear clean with cotton wool buds that was an interesting experience, although I was always terrified of someone pushing a bud in too far and doing damage, but generally it was all very relaxing and for a while I had the cleanest ears in China.

China is always trying to innovate and differentiate to get a competitive edge, seeking continual improvement to get more money. For a while, and this will still be an option, the fad was for body massages with delicate ladies walking up and down one's back, using their feet to manipulate the muscles expertly, or not as the case may be. Then later there were the small fishes added to the foot massage soaking tub, the idea being that they eat all off the loose skin of one's feet whilst creating an interesting sensation at the same time; a real novelty. This trend lasted a while but came to an abrupt halt suddenly and reputedly due to a link between these fish massages and the spread of hepatitis!

The traditional and ever-popular foot massages, appropriate for all, were very relaxing and beneficial. The basic routine was that one selected the ingredients to go into a large tub of water, the foot massage lady trying of course to sell the most expensive cleansing treatment and massage therapy from a menu, then soaking one's feet for half an hour in very hot water to cleanse, soften the skin and relax the muscles. Remarkably I was never burnt despite the scolding hot water added at times. This all whilst sitting in a reclining chair and usually watching a movie on TV and drinking Chinese tea whilst snacking on fruit. Then the massage lady, one by one took the feet out, dried them, added a massage cream or oil, and massaged your feet and legs below the knee, working every pressure point. Some, using skills learnt of old Chinese pressure point know how, could diagnose problems with health in other parts of the body. Then perhaps a slapping around the thighs and a neck, and back massage to end things. Along the way it was typical for a fellow to come to expertly trim one's toenails, not using scissors but a razor-sharp fine chisel to cut toenails, including cutting down the sides – ideal for getting rid of ingrowing toes nails. These same nail cutters would clean off any layers of hard skin callouses that had developed as well as lose and flaking skin, and or cut out any foot contaminants such as verrucae. Despite the sharpness of the chisel I cannot recall ever being cut, just as well given that the same tools were being used on multiple clients daily in a country where various hepatitis disease was prevalent, but they were routinely dipped in a sterilizing solution.

Increasingly male foot masseurs started to appear to provide for the demand from female clientele.

These developed throughout China as high class, highly acceptable foot massage venues, popular with the middle classes and far more acceptable for business relaxation and families, albeit not cheap as costs exploded. These often proved popular with foreigners, many of whom I was to note had neglected their feet. Indeed I took my mother and family there on occasions. Afterwards one could stay there and relax/sleep for a while before leaving and paying an itemized bill.

The reported variations in massage options were eye watering and best left to the imagination – assuming one has a vivid imagination.

Some expatriate contacts boasted of the experiences of the 'oral' relaxation shops in Shanghai, often in rooms set just off main roadways in the old French Concession, such as the affectionately named such as 'birdcage 1' and 'birdcage 2'. These places contained a welcoming area, serving canned beer and small cozy wooden un-soundproofed booths, where a man could disappear to with a lady who would provide a certain relief; he still sipping his beer and she continually sipping a tea like drink that was assumed to be a bromide containing sterilization refreshment for obvious reasons.

In many of the massage parlours, the young ladies wore sportswear, such as golf type shirts and tracksuit bottoms. For a while these became associated sadly with the profession and for years the middle-class ladies would not be seen wearing these in public for fear of association. This being prior to the more recent booms in gyms.

Bars

The traditional bars, often small and seedy before the westernization of many, developed continually but were usually staffed by young ladies and with that goes all the temptations of a combination of sexes and alcohol that can occur anywhere is the world. What differed through was the dice game 'shidze'. Quite simple, a waitress and guest play one to one and both roll the 5 dice under an upturned plastic cup, then each try to guess what combinations were under the cup such as two sixes or five sixes and so on. When the cup is lifted the closest guess wins and the loser must ganbei, drink a full glass (usually sensibly small glasses) of typically beer. This encourages lots of drinking, the waitress gets paid commission on each bottle of beer or wine consumed and everyone gets happy, or at least usually. At some stage later in the evening this often all results in someone falling over. The game could be played anywhere with any type of alcohol. Not good for one's health, terrible for the barmaids health!

Tea Dancing Halls

Another experience in my early days was a tea dancing hall, which a foreign colleague took me to. This was an interesting experience, although these halls tended to disappear as other options became more popular. It involved a large dance floor, sitting down in booths of two seats opposite two seats with a table in between, drinking tea served by waitresses and young ladies around who would join and dance with you – ballroom dancing, which was so popular in post revolution China. The music would play for fifteen minutes, and everyone would dance, the music would stop, and folk would sit down and drink some tea with the dance partner who the guest would buy tea for. Presumably she would be on commission. Then a couple of minutes after the tea arrived, the lights would all be turned out, totally pitch black for ten minutes, which made for a different type of social contact shall we say – all very different but an early exposure to China's social activities! A small tip was paid. I chose not to go back.

Throughout I remained very weary of these activities at many levels. I was married with a family, I was concerned about the inherent safety, I was concerned about local community perceptions of me for going to bars (which were laughed off as me being a daft foreigner for the most) in a city where I was a lone westerner for a long while, in a responsible position and how it would affect my credibility. I was terrified about the consequences of disease in China, not just the sheer unknown numbers of HIV/Aids (which were not reported for many years, publicly ignored, before belated major campaigns launched), but the more routine hepatitis, whether it be strains, A, B C or whatever, which many speculated could even be caught by sharing meal dishes with chopsticks or even dirty glasses despite being well vaccinated.

The fact was though that prostitution, as per definition, was alive and well and thriving in China, a reflection of economic circumstances, demand, the need for financial betterment as well as the influence of historical culture. All illegally it seems. China is changing though, with rules and restrictions introduced that addresses much of this landscape.

Chapter 7

Doing Business

Prior to living in China, I had worked entirely for publicly listed companies with responsibilities to the business, shareholders, the board of directors, customers, suppliers, communities, and employees alike. The businesses were managed professionally and ethically, complying with prevailing laws and with prudence, driving initiatives, looking for angles and advantages, yes, but with no thought of operating in any other way. I took those responsibilities very seriously and focused upon delivering the best returns for the business and took the view that if the business did well then everybody, including me, would see the benefits of that success in whatever way those benefits presented themselves, but always legally.

Businesses were developed through good external relationships, developing great well trained and experienced employees, optimized production efficiency, excellent product development, consistent product quality and compliance with requisite health, safety, and environmental regulations. Whilst of course delivering competitive products that were fit for purpose, on time and satisfying customer requirements.

From and early stage I became aware that in China things were different, vastly different! Of course, guanxi, the relationship networks, were an essential cornerstone at every level and I was to focus heavily upon this, having initially evaluated the situation that the company that I was responsible for was in, and looking forward for additional new investments. The relationship and the base understandings were there – guanxi was essential!

What it took me a little longer to become fully aware of, was that in all the discussions and business developments, it became apparent that our Chinese contacts were always asking themselves *'what is in it for me? What can I personally get out of this? Along with my cronies.'* Of course, there were clear targets that had to be delivered in line with policies and the laws, as well as the business plan objectives, but increasingly in the new China the emphasis was on getting rich, piling it up, and hence the focus upon ways to get money out of the business at many levels.

One Chinese colleague once privately explained to me that China culturally had a different approach to westerners, with a *'let's just do it. A can-do attitude,'* unlike so often in the West where opportunities were evaluated more extensively, especially in financial respects. It was explained that Chinese entrepreneurial businesspeople often made commitments, without a detailed support plan and then worked out how to deal with it afterwards. In my early days, the banks were operating often on brief plans for what may or may not have been clever ideas and lending based upon their assessment of this but also of course the relationships that prevailed with the leaders of the companies making investments. Sometimes I suspect that these banking investments would have been made under pressure from government officials, either with personal gains to be had through commissions, the lure of lucrative foreign investment or an urgent need to meet government targets for their fiscal year, so that officials could get their annual bonuses paid. These were the days prior to the introduction of professional banking ratios regarding lending practices. Hence there were high flows of lending support from the banks on all sorts of expansive investments, but they were also making far too many bad loans, stacking up bad debts to be dealt with over the coming decades.

In this environment my view was that foreign investors and businesses were seen as a cash till to provide this wealth through their initial investments and to garner the banks to support on the back of credible foreign investments. Then of course it would be good if the business was successful and made great ongoing profits, but that was not a necessity in many cases and anyway the banks would often provide fresh working capital loans.

Funds came in and these were picked over and divided up as required to provide personal security, employee security, keep *'all supporting parties happy'* and trying to keep enough money in the business for it to trade, before going back to the banks for more. One company leader once explained to me that he needed a large *'personally controlled slush fund,' no records kept,* which he solely controlled and would make the necessary payments anonymously *to make things happen*, whether it be for customers, government officials or whoever, but he would not be specific. When challenged he incredulously explained that *this is how things are done in China* and that everyone did this! I cannot help assuming the fund had the potential for personal gain.

Land for investments was provided on designated new sites by local governments at beneficial rates, often free in development zones, with attached development timelines and conditions, to which there may be some flexibility within terms. Buildings, much larger than required were built at the front of these sites, a costly over investment but an ambitious statement of future expansion plans to everyone taking notice and a clear demonstration of 'face' with the investment. These usually contained huge offices within as statements of importance. All large and shiny on the outside, often behind large fences, which were gated, and landscaped, these will often have laid empty or underutilized for years. These buildings were like mini versions of the opulent new government buildings that were built in every city around the country and in every case the rumours were that the local government significantly overspent the budget allocated.

Many businesses failed, which left opportunities for new investors to pick up assets cheaply and develop the business plan ideas with new cash injections, innovative ideas, and resources. Many businesses of course were extraordinarily successful and grew quickly, others just failed and disappeared. This though was happening at an incredible rate, all over China, with massive swathes of land being allocated to new factories and buildings as part of *China's plan to be the factory for the world*. Areas so large that it is incomprehensible to most western countries and the developments happening at such a rate that was simply mindboggling. Mistakes were made, rules were bent, legislative compliance ignored, but these areas, under government pressure were developed. Undeveloped land was eventually reclaimed by government and plan B's implemented with land being reallocated to another business bringing more investment. This was a centrally coordinated strategy by the Chinese government to ensure expansion and modernization programmes as the factory of the world and the West happily played ball, shifting their manufacturing to China, thereby abdicating a degree of control of their supply chains, and exporting their environmental responsibilities, thereby handing power to China. As the saying goes *'If you've got them by the balls their hearts and minds with follow'* and China duly warmed its hands.

I witnessed this with direct involvement in several provinces, all similar with a local spin. My home city of Jiaxing, and its surrounding districts, benefiting from location close to the coastal ports and with a fabulously effective overseas investment team, expanded hugely. Inland cities and towns, despite having land in abundance, developed more slowly due to their relative isolation, but increased rapidly following the major infrastructure investment programmes connecting the land with wide roads, trains, and planes.

There was one joint venture deal whereby all employees were to get an apartment with deposit paid in a newly built apartment block as a part of the deal with low mortgage costs, built very near to the centre of the city, right opposite the government buildings. Land where property was to rise in value extremely quickly, the rate of which reminded me of property rises in the UK in the 1980s, but in China they seemed to keep rising and rising. It was said that it is very typical for there to be spare apartments included in such projects, given free of charge, to government and other officials in the planning and financial approval processes. This is how so many assets quickly accumulated within certain individual's personal wealth, ownership often in the names of children or other close family members to spread the wealth and distract regulatory attention.

The view was that many deals were competed in the KTV parlours around the country.

China initially, as well as developing export markets, developed a thirst for making products that were previously imported, thereby eliminating import duty tax, reducing costs through competition, shortening delivery lead times, and reducing costs using cheaper local labour and avoiding global transportation costs. This provided a better control of its own destiny, and generated huge profits. Importantly in China, jobs were created and more mouths fed. In this respect it was remarkably successful. Banks lent money in abundance and in many cases there was over investment in excessive market capacity, made as provinces competed to grab market share, but objectives were achieved, and it was a case of the survival of the fittest.

Employee quality and education was enhanced with the advent of many new private companies. State controlled companies floated parts of businesses on stock exchanges to raise funds and started to modernize although this took longer. Non-state-controlled companies evolved rapidly, free of the traditional state-owned mentality and its burdens, harder working, with tougher disciplines and incentives. All round employee security improved through legislated social funds, including pensions, that companies and employees contributed to. Training and education improved, and qualified, more worldly graduates entered industries as opportunities expanded, a reverse if you like of what was happening in the UK and much of the western world. Younger people had more opportunity at young age suddenly and all the drive and ambition that comes with youthfulness. It reminded me of South Africa where under apartheid often young whites were often given a lot of managerial responsibility at a youthful age. Different situation in China, but younger, educated folks were given responsibility free of traditional thinking that constrained older generations, but always with wise heads, mentoring, not too far away. Increasingly, bright young minds who had studied at universities overseas were incentivized to come back to China with the lure of a bright future.

Employee incentives improved rewarding successes with bonuses, often undeclared (cash), in addition to the traditional '*13ᵗʰ month*' bonus at Spring Festival time. The adage that no one could be fired changed as the state system was diluted, with fines for inferior performance more common and demotions permissible. The rewards and fines system in China worked given everyone's focus upon the importance of money.

The increasing overseas interaction through joint ventures, trade, working abroad, visits, trade shows and more, enabled China to improve its knowledge and access the requisite technologies of products and industries, increasing its skills capability and setting baselines to take things to the next level through its own innovation or refinement.

Environmental and regulatory requirements improved continuously, but often playing catch up.

In amongst all this there were always suspicions and concerns as to various practices and ethics.

I also always had in the back of my mind though a meeting at a Muslim run factory in Malaysia in the 1990's. Upon entering we were asked to take off our shoes and escorted into the owners office. Our salesguy at the time commented as we walked through the factory that it was very apparent that all the workers were Muslim with no Chinese there despite the local town being a mixed community. The owners response was to grin and then said, *'I would never employ a Chinese person, as they work for you for a few months and then take all of the knowledge, set up a factory next door to you and then directly compete with you.'* He said it, not me and an interesting thought and perspective which stayed with me.

In a slightly similar vein I quote from my diary as an example of the business circumstances for foreign investors that were to prove telling:

w/c 28th August 2010 - China's lust for money seems to continue all fronts and I notice its effects all around in everyday life now.

My working life in China is just so frustrating and it is interesting to read articles and quotes by many western CEO's now:

'Few company chiefs speak out against China for fear of hurting their prospects, but their numbers have been swelling recently. Peter Loescher from Siemens and Jürgen Hambrecht from Germany's chemical group BASF told premier Wen Jiabao last month that the playing field in China is increasingly tilted against foreigners.'

'Jeff Immelt, the head of GE, vented his frustrations in Rome, complaining that the company's efforts to gain a foothold in China were failing to pay off. 'It's getting harder for foreign companies to do business there. I am not sure that in the end they want any of us to win, or to be successful,' he said.'

'Steve Balmer from Microsoft said early this year that China's software piracy was a constant thorn in the side. 'China is a less interesting market to us than India or Indonesia,' he said.'

'The American and European chambers of commerce in Beijing have issued reports about subtle barriers, dubbed the 'Great Wall of China'. They are particularly concerned by China's central bank's actions to hold down the yuan.'

'The European chamber said the investment climate in China was on a

'declining trend', as moves to open the economy and lift curbs on foreign capital had reached stagnation. It said Beijing's 'Indigenous Innovation Policy, uses procurement incentives to help Chinese firms at the expense of foreigners in fields such as software and clean-tech.'

'The US chamber said its survey found that 38% of its members felt 'unwelcome in the Chinese market', up from 23% in 2008. China is also becoming a more expensive place to operate, with rigid labour contracts that make it hard to fire workers and a rising tax burden.'

I have noticed the less welcoming climate of late in China, indeed for me over the last few years really, but China now has what it needs. – It has the technology, it has the developing skills, it has the infrastructure, it has the internal markets, it has the cars, it has the houses – it is on its way like a developing child and doesn't really need the West anymore, except for its markets that is. It has done things in a hurry to great effect. It now thinks that it is very clever and to some extent it is, but there are still a lot of very average qualified people around, some in very senior positions of power; I wonder what the future brings?

Of course, there were penalties for being caught for some of the illicit happenings that went on, but those caught seemed to be on a selective basis at times. I recall meeting a senior contact in Taipei, Taiwan, who over dinner enquired how did I find doing business in China? He then clarified that he has many Taiwanese friends and industry contacts working in China but then stated with a wry grin that most of them were in prison there as China penalized them for breaking rules in business. Following up that Chinese nationals then took over the businesses that had been set up with Taiwanese money. I did not hear of many Chinese contacts going to jail despite some obvious infringements, perhaps the odd one as an example.

Employment laws in many ways did not differ so much from international counterparts as they evolved. However, I often heard that whilst foreign investment companies were willing and indeed had to comply with employee payments in addition to salaries, for pensions, medical funds, apartment purchase funds and so on, that many Chinese companies, particularly smaller and medium sized ones, did not make these payments either through hardship or not just wanting to. This did not assist the competitiveness of course of the foreign companies versus their Chinese counterparts.

Somehow Chinese companies for so long managed to avoid paying tax, or at least to the level one may have expected. One of my first duties upon arrival as the new general manager of a joint venture, was to be awarded a smart plaque for being one of the leading companies paying the highest amount of tax per size of company in the province, the narrative being that if one paid a lot of tax, one had enjoyed high profits! Many of my contacts visibly laughed at this, as Chinese companies would never have 'been caught' paying that much tax; why show the profits? In later years, our company received awards for paying the most overall tax per employee (employee social security funds) for a certain factory size and so on, under the guise that we were an efficient business, whilst we were just complying with legal tax requirements; the obvious implications being that other companies in the area were not!

During my time, irrespective of genuine and normal business issues that occur with running, investing, and developing enterprises across several different provinces I was to suffer all sorts of frustrations that tilted the equation against foreign investors, examples of which included:

Land is allocated to businesses by the government, on a timed agreement, not given on a permanent basis. It is also valued according to its designation (such as industrial, commercial, or residential housing) at very differing rates at times, an issue of course when it comes to realizing the value. It was obviously important to recognize simple contractual tricks like ensuring that 'right of land use' ownership was legally transferred to the joint venture at the time of contract and not remaining in the name of joint venture partners who previously held ownership, as conveniently there were transfer problems due to government approval and no one thought to tell the foreign investor, nor did the senior Chinese working for the JV. Potentially highly valuable land in the middle of cities could be suddenly found to be designated as industrial use at basic nominal usage valuation, resulting in low compensation for any forced factory relocation, especially with foreign company involvement. In reality of course, such land was immensely valuable commercially and one could only speculate who would get the benefits between nominal compensation and the actual commercial sales value, or indeed how the profits cake would be carved up? One thing for sure, there would be considerable barriers to foreign investor seeing full potential value as the system of joint venture partners and local government conspires against them, sometimes blatantly, sometimes subtly. The response to questions was so often a simple 'It's difficult,' as eyes averted their gaze elsewhere.

Competing with joint venture partners. It is simple, set up a minority joint venture with an overseas company, the foreign company provides investment, technology, and knowhow, the Chinese partner the land, some plant, employees, services and logistics and the company makes large profits. Then the Chinese joint venture partner sets up its own wholly owned production line, the investment courtesy of banks loaning money against those initial joint venture high profits, a larger, more efficient and state of the art manufacturing process. The most profitable joint venture business sales are then transferred to the new production lime, maximizing its profits as a great investment, the returns for which the Chinese shareholder gets one hundred per cent, not say 40 per cent as they did prior as the minor joint venture partner. In such circumstances it does not matter to the Chinese investor if the initial joint venture struggles and partners fall out. A question of *contractual interpretation* of course with local government support.

Joint venture partners can come in diverse types and legitimacy, the warning is to ensure that an honourable and respected partner is selected before entering an agreement, but also the location and local environment from a government viewpoint. Sometimes rural environments are less regulated and dare I say less honourable, and it is never a clever idea doing a joint venture whereby the landowner is in prison for corruption and land bought via proxy or that the JV partner had previously had multiple bankruptcies!

If investing in a wholly owned foreign invested company, do so without of any historical joint venture legacy of conflicting issues, land ownership, service supplies, local legislative compliance, and sales arrangements. A 'clean' new site, independent, with no legacy issues or commitments of contention is necessary.

Land is owned by the government and allocated to businesses for use, often 20-50 years dependent upon laws and agreements. Often though, especially in rural areas, locals can still have access to land. Factories in cities can be easily secured, security fences and gates, staffed to ward off intruders. Land in the countryside though can be different, one example being that the locals used to fish the lake in hillside land, wandering where they liked and doing what they wanted, it was their right! They ended up taking all the fish and draining the lake amongst other activities and then threatened group violence towards shareholders when confronted about it, with local government ignoring it all. The countryside folk have rights and an attitude to match! Usually not educated and not always friendly.

Contracts are key in any business and there can be contractual disagreements anywhere, within countries and between countries. I was aware in my early days that a lot of people said that the written contracts between parties was not the important thing, but what was important was the understanding and goodwill between the parties and that if this were okay then solutions could always be found without resorting to the law. That was how things were and if the original people party to the contracts remained in place then there was often a certain debt of respect and 'face' in terms of commitment to honouring agreements, to some extent at least. However, things can change over time. When original parties move on either due to retirements or business ownership changes, this bond is suddenly not there, and a wariness can develop.

Likewise, over time the power of the law changed emphasis from simplistically being a seal authorizing stamp on a piece of paper verifying things, towards a more sophisticated and literal translation of the contractual and investment agreements in place that had to be registered with the government bureaus as a true record and official copy. Obviously, there are merits to this process. Over this time the sophistication of lawyers changed, albeit slowly, as did the business approach of the newer managers and directors that were emerging. Under new joint venture ownerships, or with changing moods or circumstances, contracts were pulled out and scrutinized in detail, with foreign investment joint ventures contracts usually being in both Chinese and English, but with the Chinese copy taking legal precedence if there were any doubt in agreement. At this stage there are a few things to consider, including whether the translation of the agreement and its points were accurate and were there differences in meaning.

Early foreign investment contracts were set for international arbitration in e.g. Switzerland, a traditional venue, but increasing as positions strengthened these arbitration venues were set in Beijing, as the investments were in China. Oh yes, and if there is a dispute between the two versions of the contracts, then the Chinese contract took legal precedence! Oh boy, especially when one starts getting into historic detail and finding out that the actual translations do not reflect that same version of events between contracts. If the contracts were indeed accurately translated, there is the cultural issue of interpretation and I was to discover that local governments always have the 'same interpretation' as the Chinese joint venture partners, who had obviously prepped with government officials with credible and logical explanations. Suddenly, disputes were not just between parties, but one is fighting the system, especially as local officials were friends of the Chinese partners! Read between the lines. Even friends of mine, genuinely trying to find solutions, used to conclude that *'it's complicated'*! It became apparent how certain contracts were written so cleverly as to set up for misunderstandings.

If purchasing local services from community or partners, always ensure that there are extremely specific agreements in place regarding quantities, quality, and their specifications, and vitally timescales, whether it be water, effluent, electricity, steam or other. Processes can suddenly develop problems out of its immediate control if the quality or quantity of these service supplies fail in any way. For a long while cities around China suffered growth pains, including routine power outages due to lack of available supply capacity, having all sorts of consequences including late sales deliveries and the higher costs of process inefficiencies. In other cases variable supplies directly affected processes, their quality and efficiency and one had to ask at times, was this ignorance, a lack of control or simply malicious? There were strong views by some as to the answer.

On occasions the government just unilaterally decided to shut down factories for a variety of reasons for periods of time, whether it be visits by important visitors, compliance with central power allocation, environmental compliance targets for the year, extraordinary events such as the Beijing Olympics, or other. Obviously, such outages were a time-consuming nightmare and protracted negotiations with officials trying to meet customer delivery targets whilst playing ball with government mandates.

I was to learn over time that it was quite normal, most prevalently with private companies, for wives, girlfriends, or other relatives to be on the payroll, despite not working for the company. Apartments were bought, cars provided, educations funded and much more, paid for by the company to suit the owners personal needs and preferences in life. Sometimes it was friends, sometimes it was an employment 'ghost account' to enable a friend to get a bank mortgage or loan, a stamp on a piece of paper providing the evidence.

All agreements, as per international conventions have rules documented relating to the activities of the board of directors, their voting rights and regulation. I was to discover that in China, in many cases, this did not work. If the Chinese joint venture partner, even as a minority shareholder, did not want to do something or agree with proposals, then directors would not recognize the basic premises by which board of directors operate, ignoring votes, voting rights, protocol and board requirements upon the chairman and legal representative, who for convenience, was usually a Chinese citizen. Difficult, especially when their boss is driving it and he has influential mates in local government. Frustrating as the company's articles of association were usually virtually identical to those of western companies, but just ignored and with little hope of legal redress.

At Chinese New Year, officially for a couple of weeks, one can write off a month, with basic functions such as China Customs at ports closing early or opening late as folks went for holidays or returning to their homelands, thus can create chaos in planning, supplying international customers and receiving vital raw materials. Often there would be a solution, at a price, but very time consuming and distracting!

There is always a huge and symbolic fanfare new businesses and for opening ceremonies including all key parties, media coverage and usually lots of firecrackers and fireworks. There is no escaping the ceremonial side of this all, which is extremely high profile, visible and a celebration of commitment. Very necessary culturally.

Lots of red tape bureaucracy especially in the early days that was 'jobsworth' stuff, which was all time consuming and wasteful, although with computerization, and increasingly *joined up* systems this was improving.

On a personal basis I was to discover that despite the introduction of foreigner pension schemes several years ago, that the system does not work if one does not stay resident for a prolonged time. For years I had been contributing to the pension scheme paying my own contributions based upon the size of my salary, which was obviously much higher than average factory employee wages, and the company contributions, as per the employment law, were much more significant than my own contributions, so it seemed 'all good.' Upon leaving China I requested to draw my pension and was told that I was indeed entitled to a refund of my personal Chinese pension investment. However, it materialised that the rules, given the company circumstances at that time and my last designated responsibility, were explained to me as:

As I had not been paying into the pension scheme for fifteen years, I could not draw my annual pension entitlements. I suspect that the majority of foreigners would not stay that long.

That I would get a refund of my personal contributions only.

But that the company contributions to my pension scheme on my behalf would be kept by the tax man (all that money, contributed by a foreign company, simply kept by the state).

My personal refund would be based upon the number of years multiplied by the average wage for the factory, way below my salary, a small lump sum.

Effectively my pension disappeared to the State, having worked and paid taxes for fifteen years and been in the newly introduced pensions scheme for foreigners for about seven years. China kept my pension!

Anyway, there was no Chinese pension payable for my time working there and something of a warning to foreigners.

These examples of 'frustrations' and influences, apart from direct business impact, took up huge amount of time management, all consuming, like wading through treacle. Bureaucracy, meetings, shareholder involvements, legal considerations were all significant, but more so the hidden implications of being distracted from focusing upon the running the business under normal operating conditions.

When partners come to breaking points, various other complicating factors can kick in such as the Chinese snub, where it is literally difficult to find someone to talk to, in order to find resolution and one finds oneself scrambling, looking for 'friends' to try and broker a solution. I got tired of hearing that *'it is complicated'* as a standard response. I have seen situations, and heard of others, whereby senior overseas investment appointments, senior managers, were locked out of their own factories by the minority shareholder Chinese party, with the support of the local government who were cronies of the joint venture partner leaders. Likewise, they just grabbed assets, took them, and set up their own security militias to protect them. The local law courts, also apparently in on the plot, these coups, did not act, nor did the police!

There will be those in China who would argue that the foreigners caused problems and at times there may be some validity in those comments as business cultures mix the way things are done, however, the basis of stances taken by foreign partners were usually taken due to total mistrust of Chinese partners and their support team of local government officials and banks. A consistent approach across differing provinces with similar agendas, something that muddied the waters when more honest partners were involved. It was also evident that over time that complete lack of trust worked both ways at times given actions taken. The dreaded tit for tat spiral just wasted time and worsened situations.

As one chairperson of a foreign investment company put it, *'we are at an impasse while the Chinese try to work out what and how much they can steal'*!

Many Chinese friends just shrugged it off as *'it is just business'*! But not as we know it............ Playing to a different set of rules and often on a different playing field!

I refer to my diary notes as a few examples as how I was feeling at various times and the challenges, business-personal and business that were experienced.

w/c 4ᵗʰ June 2005 - This being China, life is full of red tape and bureaucracy, and I am still amazed at the inefficiency of service from government bodies on so many issues, seemingly action still only really depending upon whether you have a 'friend' there rather than receiving a service because one needs that. Anyway, I have now been issued with a host of updated employment certificates from various bodies all inconsistent in length of time of validity. I have my Foreign Residency Permit now valid until 6.1.2007, whilst my Foreign Experts Certificate is valid until 6.4.2010 and my Alien Employment Permit to 27.5.2006, leaving me wondering what the differences are? I note that my Z Visa is valid until 6.1.2007. That said, with all the work issues, I am not sure that I will want to. That's not a serious comment, although my frustration at the blatant lying and tinkering by the partners is increasing. Not for me to say that they are corrupt, manipulative, devious, cunning, conniving, untrustworthy, overly proud, nationalistic, arrogant; but some may say that and indeed have. There is an attitude problem from the past originating, but no red guards at my door yet! Believe me, today I am ready for them.......and there had better be lots of them!*

w/c 26th August 2006 – Today was significant in the calendar of my life as I formally resigned letter, offering six months' notice which would take me through to the end of February 2007. Our CEO was very understanding of my reasoning that I had spent enough time resident in China and that after the completion of my contract I would have been in China effectively five years. I now must wait and see what I do next, and in amongst my busy life I really need to turn my mind to this topic. Not an insignificant moment in life so full of experiences.

In the event my parent company persuaded me to stay longer and then life was to change.

w/c 7th November 2009 - Settling into the airport, I start to get my mind around the requirements of this very important visit to St. Petersburg, Russia, only for my mind to be blown by a call from the new British general manager at our Shandong company. In typical British understatement, he introduced that 'we have a little problem here' as I heard an American colleague yelling away in the background on the phone to his secretary 'Are you okay'?

There has been something of a coup at our company there and the minority shareholders, led by the JV Chinese leader, have decided to 'dismiss the two foreign executives;' something that is not inside of the law, nor the articles of association for the business. More seriously they have taken away their transport, stolen their bags with lap top computers, passports, and possessions in and kidnapped their two secretaries, also removing their mobiles to restrict communications. Upon arrival at work, the foreign colleagues had been barred and physically removed from site and their translators who were kept separate to them also having their mobile phones removed. Therefore the two-majority appointed foreign executives had found themselves shaken, shocked and stood in the local police station, without anything, unable to talk with no translators, no transport, no passports, but did have their mobiles back and phoned me. The situation is awful and the timing for me just as bad!

Whether to go to Shandong instead? I also have some time for a considered decision and that depends upon what action we can muster and physical wellbeing. I got onto my Chinese deputy and a series of calls. He in turn called the police station whereby the police faithfully promised that that the foreigners would be safe and that they were secure the 'release' of the secretaries. The local Development Zone President was mortified and went straight to the factory and police station to secure the situation.

The irony of all of this is that following some strange legal actions last week, I had informed both my colleagues to notify the local Party secretary, mayors and police chief, and any other Bureau relevant, something that in their wisdom that they decided was not necessary, but in hindsight was mightily foolish and might have avoided the current situation.

My deputy informs me that all parties are safe, and that the local government is having a meeting this afternoon. I confirm this by phone who are all shaken, but okay. On this basis I make the 50:50 call to go to Russia as planned, as losing this customer would be a disaster with even greater consequences. This issue will run and run though and has extremely serious ramifications. What a start to the week and against a backdrop whereby our business in Shandong is strengthening, the Brit GM is getting some control of the company and an imminent new investment is likely; this is not what is needed, but has been coming for a long while. My deputy is going up there later today and is better placed than me to sort things out from a Chinese official position and communications.

The crisis has worsened as the Chinese have also stolen the 'company stamp,' the ability to authorize payments and documents, and the city government is in on the 'coup,' or at least unable or unwilling because of the connections, to *do anything about it all. This is unbelievable, the effective 'theft of a business' in front of our eyes. I will have to get involved despite our parent company's reticence and steady approach that has contributed to us getting in this mess. All the activity, including alleged theft, breaking business laws, assault, and intimidation, both to our guys and their secretaries, but also their families have been threatened apparently. This is not the act of modern China, although many Chinese may like to do this to foreigners, but the act of bandits in the bandit country of rural Shandong Province.*

This could take the business under with all sorts of legal issues. Our lawyers are highly active in the courts and administration issues.

w/c 14th November 2009 - Tuesday I was up early and on my way to Shandong, not really knowing what to expect. The Chinese joint venture partner did at least have the good grace to organize a car to pick us up and I took along a neutral translator. It is colder up there, but dry although still evidence of a significant snow fall on the ground.

Wednesday was a dire day, though I did manage another meeting with the JV partner today and his henchman, sorry Labour Union representative, but no progress was made, although they agreed to come back again tomorrow. In the meantime, as instructed, we issued board resolutions firing the Chinese chairman, the finance manager, deputy general manager and the office administration manager; all to no effect though as they are not enforceable without correct signed original legal documents from the British based CEO and the backing of the local government with whom they are all mates. 'Rules are rules,' Chinese relationships drive you mad some time!

A meeting with the main bank confirmed that they were continuing to co-operate with the coup takeover. Attempts to approach the ruling provincial government officials were not responded to, or at least not as one would want.

Thursday I had another meeting with the joint venture partner with absolutely no result, a brick wall and I am not sure whether these people are stupid, bone headed or both. They certainly are not clever, but they do have their interpretation of events and there are genuine issues with both shareholder parties.

Later we went to the police station to make a statement on the situation, repeating what my foreign colleagues had done weeks prior. I have never been in trouble with the police and am not now, but it was strange giving a statement lasting three hours and well into the evening and then having to witness it by signing with my fingerprints in red ink!

Friday morning I was at my band-standing best – I went into the bank and blasted them accusing them of being an accomplice in a massive fraud. Then it was into see the director of the Development Zone (EDZ) and I let him have it too, a show of strength. This is what was needed, although it should be said that great progress has been made since my arrival, though certainly not resolved by any stretch of the imagination.

We are witnessing old style powerplay, countryside communism and at a time of significant rise in nationalism as well, which is disconcerting with wide ranging consequences.

w/c 28th November 2009 – Thursday I, our CEO and my deputy met the minority shareholder leader, he being the representative of some sixty-six rebellious minority shareholders. The meeting though was delayed, awaiting the main joint venture representative who was allegedly in hospital getting post heart attack treatment before meeting much later in the day for a constructive meeting.

I am fed up though – this situation is serious and no obvious solution in place. The government have stood back and done nothing despite re-assurances and the company has been 'stolen' by the minority shareholders who have refused the two onsite expatriates, the interim GM and technical director, denying their translators access and are acting illegally. It is also deflection away from our other interests here in China.

Friday the partner delayed the eagerly awaited board meeting. Then our CEO sacked the Chinese leader! This dismissal was an impulsive call, angered by his noncompromising reaction to reasonable requests and whilst technically is the right thing to do, is bound to inflame the situation more having taken some face away from the partner, stoking up his mob of minority shareholders. There is now total loss of trust between shareholders, although this was the case before.

In amongst this the business though continues to run and I discover from a local bureau that due to local incompetence (or, much worse), that I was never actually registered as a director with authorities, despite having been assured at board meetings that I had been, recorded in board minutes as such, translated as such and Chinese documents provided and signed by me! This legally gets me out of all sorts of potential liabilities, although I have been acting as a director for three years. We had a EDZ dinner meeting at their own restaurant with a couple of low-key junior guys, the key guy dealing with our case has disappeared to Egypt for two weeks, and his deputies were powerless. For all the EDZ's re-assurances they have done absolutely nothing over the last four weeks to progress a dispute resolution and one must wonder how far the local networks extend in this seemingly corrupt environment.

This afternoon we achieved a breakthrough of sorts as the EDZ finally applied some pressure and compromises were made that enable our expat managers and their translators to go back into work tomorrow morning. Not totally happy, but great progress and then dinner with an ex-mayor, and relaxed. It was good to see him, and released the pressure on all of us to relaxed, except for our American colleague who is struggling with life as this completely unreal situation understandably takes its toll.

Monday we were at the factory gates early. Things seemed back to normal, but not really. There is nothing normal about anything going on up here! There seemed an uneasy peace – a bit like Israel and Palestine really, but our team are at least back along with a set of conditions for the minority shareholders. It is agreed though that there is a total breakdown in trust between investors and that somehow and quickly, there must be a separation of the ways.

w/c 5ᵗʰ December 2009 - Here I am stuck in Shandong for the weekend. There appears to be no 'rule of law' in this part and no will by the police or government to get involved. So here we are consoling our two expats and their translators who effectively do not have jobs or any payments of salaries or expenses currently. They are beyond frustrated and are now angry at the UK shareholder who in truth are unable to influence this mess quickly.

Much of the morning was drafting necessary documents, frustrated at the lack of availability of people over the weekend. We wanted to meet the legally named twenty-five minority shareholders to talk sense directly, but their leader says that he will not let us meet them. Then at short notice we get an indirect message via a secretary that some shareholders will meet at the factory. It was arranged for police to go and monitor this situation and for the EDZ to supervise it as they had promised and to provide translators who were neutral.

The shareholder meeting was a total nightmare, the worst that I have ever attended anywhere. On the way we discovered that the EDZ will not be there, nor will the police, and that the EDZ had refused to provide facilities at their offices. The driver said that it would be a difficult meeting and upon arrival there was no translator which immediately threw my trusted deputy straight into the fray as a stand in; although he speaks great English, he is not a translator.

To add to the situation there were all sixty-six minority shareholders (un-officially unregistered) in the room looking at three of us and this was an angry mob. Angry at their leader's dismissal, angry at the foreign shareholders, angry at the expats, angry that none of the foreign investors family were present, angry at ongoing business issues and angry for the lack of return on their investment. Our CEO effectively decided that he was leaving after they started to heckle him and instructing me to say absolutely nothing. My style has always been to take these things head on diplomatically and just as I was about to try and rescue the dire situation, my deputy jumped in and saved the day with a diplomatic speech, but not before our CEO had phoned our expats to call the police here as we were being prevented from leaving the meeting room and getting abuse. I and my deputy just sat there, aware that leaving would provoke a serious and aggressive response and was amazed at how flustered the situation became and ended up saying nothing to the attendance that was useful and that frustrated them more. This was a total and utter cock up and damaged credibility more. We came out furious, frustrated, disappointed. I am reminded 'This is China'! With a baying mob.

We departed; crest fallen after a useless meeting. Our CEO was naturally intimidated by the crowd and did not understand Chinese cultural reactions. I did not feel physically threatened. Later he said that I misread the mood, but he does not understand China despite coming here so often and this was not a normal situation for anyone.

As we left the police turned up, too late and ambling across the road pulling their uniforms and hats on, in no hurry. We retired to the hotel to be met by the EDZ and a guy from the foreign investment department; as I explained that this was company theft, no one was doing anything and that this would kill all future foreign investment; finally he got the message and vowed to go away and do something. There was though a total loss of credibility with the minority shareholders in a part of China where perhaps they see anger as strength and saying nothing as weakness!

We were to discover that a not dissimilar situation had occurred with another international paper company who had entered a joint venture with a local manufacturer and had the company taken over and western employees locked out, also in Shandong province and not too far away. That obviously became the playbook for the minority shareholders. Not sure what the end point was at that company, but it remained unresolved a few years later I understood.

w/c 12th December 2009 - All is quiet now and a telephone call from our chairman last night suggested that he is against coming across to China and does not want our CEO along with him in case they 'get kidnapped together'! China is spooking people at present as I believe this to be an overreaction!

Friday, and Interestingly as a complete aside one of our visitors in Jiaxing was from Zebo, in Shandong. Unsolicited he stated that the city where we had the joint venture was a 'terrible place' speaking very seriously. I asked him what he meant, and he said that it was 'terrible in every way and was amazed that we had a factory there'! This follows the comments from an UK educated friend who is from a nearby coastal part and once said 'That is bandit country and be careful, you will get cheated there,' again an unsolicited comment. We got the message!

Obviously, some of these examples are extreme, but indicative of how the system worked in certain parts whatever the causes. Many examples were not dissimilar but less obvious and less overtly confrontational. The Shandong situation was eventually resolved, but the pathway was an unusual one.

I had some exceptionally good, trusted, well connected contacts, who genuinely sympathized as best they could in different situations, but the constant reply was either "*it's complicated*" or "*it's just business.*" But not as I knew it.............

There are of course ethical and successful business folk in China as well and I appreciated that in business partners, but frankly there were just far too many examples where things just were not right about this playing field.

A stone laying ceremony to commence building
the foundations at a new site in Anhui

Chapter 8

Government

The Chinese government and its communism is well documented elsewhere, so I have no intention to compete with that level of detailed analysis, although as ever there is often a level of unbalanced reporting of the situation or the context and certain obviously historical events are used as caveats to any successes.

China is widely criticized in the western world, particularly by the USA, a natural competitive situation of the two biggest economies in the world operating under different legislative rules of engagement, and different sets of rules beyond that. Many times, I have talked to American contacts and colleagues, some who had not previously been to China, but had well entrenched ideas about what China stands for and how it operates, never mind the shocking idea that I chose to live there, "a terrible place" apparently. A clash for world leadership, economically and militarily. I have had conversations with folk in England, usually casual ones, who are overly critical of China and how terrible a place it is and the standards that they apply to its people, its animals, its minorities and so on. I even have had teachers suggesting that the Chinese are not really that good musically, which differs significantly to what I have witnessed first-hand. At times I struggle to calibrate what I hear with the reality of the situation, views driven by emotion and biases, and I am often left wondering if western societies have had a good look in their own society's back yards of late; they are not always so attractive, ethical, stable, or secure.

Hence, I conclude that much of the West does not really know what is going on in China and how it is developing.

The irony being that the free and capitalist western world, and the rest of it for that matter, was happy to subcontract its manufacturing to China, either giving China free runs at markets or outsourcing the manufacturing processes of products consumed in the West at significantly reduced costs. Quality of these products for a long time suffered and many times through perception. The goods were often as specified, but often the initial specifications were to change be changed by the manufacturer to reduce the costs and went unnoticed until there was an inevitable problem – a management process control issue. Often these products were cheap and cheerful by design for western consumption and fell apart, not a Chinese issue as much as a specifying issue to make a quick profit.

China got rich on this, operating as the factory of the world it exploited world market opportunities through trade, all the time using this as the basis to increase the rapidly growing wealth of the middle classes demanding all that goes with that, thereby also developing a Chinese domestic market that would be sustainable should export markets be interrupted. Simply, a huge part of China's wealth came from capitalist mantra of the western world, who sacrificed jobs in the process of closing factories in their own countries, but just as impactful was the fact that governments effectively exported their environmental issues and their impact by closing domestic factories that polluted their own environments, some old and inefficient, some not so. Decisions making it easier for the western countries to celebrate the achievement of their own environmental standards and targets. The implementation of 'Net Zero' global targets should be interesting for China.

This was a free trade situation, implemented through the World Trade Organization policies since China entered the WTO at the end of 2001, but with a separate set of rules predominating within China, its 'system' somehow enabling its own interpretation of requirements.

China's government is all powerful and all-embracing with strictly implemented 'big picture' strategic aims. If China sets a policy, then it goes and achieved it. Government is strong at every level, centrally, provincially, in its cities and towns, although its degree of control traditionally diminishes in the countryside. The central policies are delegated for enforcement, monitored by the *Party* mirroring, and monitoring the local mayor's power. It can act and control the populace in a way that Western leaders must be jealous of. Party training is strong and routine, important when managing and communicating to large numbers of people and strictly implementing policies.

Whatever the viewpoint and objections, some from within, the system within China seems to have worked for China with its uniquely large population. I say this personally, not as a politically orientated Socialist or a Communist, but as a traditional Conservative from rural England.

Much is made of the lack of opposition political *Parties,* and this is a fact officially but note that behind the scenes within the Party there are differing factions with quite different viewpoints and interests; a real power struggle at times, vying for leadership with their own agendas and policies throughout Presidential terms awaiting change, but something that is rarely observed in public.

Its underlying principle is that of *social stability*, the avoidance of conflict and armed struggles, seeking negotiated settlements. There are no publicly owned guns permitted in China, something that is rigorously enforced. Knives are everywhere for the kitchen, but rarely used in conflict despite a few tragic high-profile attacks by some less than stable individuals; something that can happen in any society, but in China these cannot happen with guns!

The government is indeed all powerful, but I do not recognize many of the restrictions reported emotionally in the Western Press. Of course, there is the serious Xinjiang situation and others, but every country has social issues of one type or another and China is unapologetically dealing with it in its own practical way through its long game policies. The western world is changing culturally through mass migration and universal inclusivity, ongoing wars linger in various parts of the globe, whilst sections of society in the USA are uncomfortably far from content with life and lifestyles, a recent example being the Black Lives Matter movement as obvious illustrations of this.

Every modern society needs rules, control, and discipline to avoid anarchy and the breakdown of society. China with its infrastructure is incredibly well placed to enforce the rule of law. Given it is not too distant history of regional warlords, civil war, attacks by Japan, and the communist revolution, it is very aware of the need to have control given its huge population. Social insurrection is a no-no! The police force is extensive, so is the military and wider policing roles. The Party is prime and when we talk about government it is totally intertwined with all walks of live – central government, but also state industries, banks, insurance companies, technology companies and so on, albeit with increasing entrepreneurial companies emerging usually with greater independence. It is all embracing; that is the system.

In my first few years in China, it was not untypical for main roads to be shut down at every junction, manned by police as a fleet of the small state coaches carrying very important people passed through, although over time this practice waned in its use. Indeed, though I personally experienced and saw the benefits of this in Beijing in 2005. This was a visual sign of power, something that as a youth I related to the 'official only car lanes' in the USSR and other communist states.

Main roads and entire cities can be closed at an instant through toll booths and perimeter police stations at all main arteries to cities. All aimed at social stability and control. China's Coronavirus lockdown, once started, was effective and all embracing, unlike the western attempts and failures at lockdowns which were tragically comedic in comparison, a situation driven by people's freedoms or political demands for freedom rights. In China some of these 'unwise' freedoms are not tolerated.

Once in Shanghai I went to the main 'bar street' to enjoy western beer and a Saturday night football match, only to find that the entire street had been simply closed and moved elsewhere. The bar street was later to be moved again by police. Another time in Shanghai I took visitors to a bar that was dead. Inquiring I discovered that there was a major international conference in the city that was hosted by China and that the government had shut down, or folk warned away from, all dubious places, including bars for a month!

The elephant in the political room currently is the human rights issues most specifically with the Uyghurs of Xinjiang, which garners so much time on CNN and is so politically emotive to the Western world. I do not know enough about it frankly to comment but would observe that the world has a race issue between Muslim extremist factions and their own cultures. When 911 occurred China, interestingly along with Russia, showed solidarity with the USA, recognizing that it has its own self-designated 'Muslim problem'. Accordingly, China is trying to deal with its 'problem' in a managed way to find a long-term solution through re-education processes whatever that means, again the aim being social stability. Inevitably there are casualties and wrongs in the process, but China acts to protect its Han culture and avoid acts of terrorism.

When I first went to China I was aware of the unrests in the western province of Xinjiang, a few years later, China used these unrests as the excuse for shutting down Facebook, Google and Twitter in China through its 'Great internet Fire Wall', in part a cynical action to promote its own competing software and social media industries, which have become immensely successful, but also seemingly to prevent the Muslim minorities using Facebook and similar platforms to communicate their coordinated terrorist activities off the Chinese grid so to say. I was aware from my Han Chinese employees and colleagues that they were afraid for their own personal security when they visited Xinjiang, reflecting the obvious unrest and attacks upon Han Chinese there and the stories behind the spread through Chinese whispers.

In the West we have seen the response to out-of-control Muslim based societies around the world – The invasion of Iraq, the invasion of Afghanistan, the attack in Libya, Syria, the ongoing Iranian conflict, the situation in Israel with the Palestinians and so on. There have been no easy solutions, certain no 'one size fits all solution.' There have been wars, terrorist attacks, countless killed, the emergence of ISIS, huge migrations, huge military costs to the Western countries, the loss of western soldiers' lives and on and on.

China, aware that it also has other significant minority populations in other provinces, including Tibet, is very aware of these issues and the potential for huge insurrection across the country. It carefully controls individuals 'hukou's,' where a person can legally have his or her registered home and live, controlling the minority populations in Han Chinese cities and their activities. At one stage in 2002-2003, the whispers on the streets was that Bin Laden had crossed over into China and was being sheltered there.

At one stage during a political celebration of the longevity of the Chinese political Party, I happened to have a senior police officer in my office on another matter. During our friendly small talk, he said that his department's biggest issue over the coming week's was monitoring the Muslim community and travellers as Jiaxing was the birthplace of Communism and that the famous 'Red Boat,' Communist Party Museum and government buildings were considered potential targets for Muslim terrorist attacks. This brought home to me first-hand the concerns that the government had and their proactive approach to such a potential issue from 2,500 miles away that had not previously occurred to me.

When I went to China, I found the systems so bureaucratic, laughably so, only mirrored by my frustrating experiences getting visas to Russia.

However, returning to the UK I now find that the UK has caught up with the bureaucracy that I encountered there. The bureaucracy was there for good reason – to avoid system abuse, corruption and to maintain control. The UK lost control of its immigration system over recent decades and now out of necessity is striving to regain control by imposing onerous visa application demands; all for good reason though. Likewise with its benefits systems that are reputably abused. Modern societies must have adequate controls to adjust to global progressions.

ID cards are an emotive subject in the West, although I never understood why, given that if you were a law-abiding citizen then you had nothing to be afraid of, whilst if you were a bad guy then certainly you would not want to be identified. In China it seemed to work exceedingly well – your name and number that accounted for you in everything you did where needed, from ordering train or plane tickets, booking into hotels, opening bank accounts, buying cars or houses and so on, never an issue. In the Western world, so long afraid of big brother, we now actually have big brother through the extensive IT online networks that prevail, so why not ID cards? So much simpler than carrying around one's passport as ID. I was issued with a green card, a permanent residency, should I have wanted and at that time in made sense, this was on the same lines as the Chinese ID card. As an overseas resident I could be clearly identified, which made sense to me and no infringement of my freedom.

Modern China was shaped through the Communist Revolution under Mao Ze Dong, *Chairman Mao*. Millions died and the culture changed. Positive comments from observers within China centre on the fact that Mao did two important things 'He unified the country breaking down the regional factionalism that prevailed and cleared out the opposition Kuomintang.' The result set up the baseline for what was to follow decades later. The narrative being that China could not have achieved what it has today without first levelling the playing fields and associated controls in place.

Conversely there are those, often in minority dominated provinces, who saw Mao as a monster destroying everything and creating mistrust, whilst living very comfortably himself. Just as telling as one senior executive who once told me that he hated Mao, as 'he destroyed my education, as universities were closed or restricted. It ruined my life and the lives of my generation.'

History cannot be changed although there are always those who wish to rewrite it. My only surprise during my time in China was that as the country opened increasingly and moved lifestyles and trade towards western style situations, that Mao was not quietly removed as the poster boy of the Communist Party. More people, more confident within the new China and more with access to biographies of Mao, were more openly critical of him. I was sure at one stage that it would go that way, but President Xi Jin Ping, having established himself, slowed down certain progressions that were changing China's culture and the presence of Mao remains.

It seems true that many of the 'Princelings,' the offspring and future generations of the revolutionary leadership teams, have become fabulously wealthy and powerful, exploiting the opportunities that went with their power and influence as Chinese opened and was allowed to get rich. The irony being that reputedly that Mao's family is not wealthy nor influential. This wealth is often well hidden and built or converted into legitimate investments, and in many cases the offspring educated abroad under aliases, setting the trend for the rest of the more junior officials' families the developing middle classes to emulate.

The Chinese government can act in a way that no other can act. Its modernization programmes as an example have happened at such pace with the building and infrastructure projects that have been able to happen and to be implemented without barriers regarding land ownership. This is in stark contrast to the other great populous country, India, where I understand that private ownership and legal rights, just as in the UK, slows processes down as the laws of ownership and free market economies need to be worked through. In China, the land is simply taken and buildings, whether it be factories or housing, people and businesses relocated, albeit with appropriate compensation.

China also had the ability to simply close factories for any reason. Often, relocating old state-owned factories out from inner city areas to new purpose-built sites outside of the city or indeed elsewhere, often inland, and often very lucrative to many even after compensation given the huge jump in land values over the last two decades. In other instances, in competitive supply industries where obvious successful companies were taking market leadership and the stragglers struggling to make a profit, not complying with modern managements standards and processes and or polluting the environment, the government has been known to just step in and shut down those companies permanently, whole swathes of an industry sector, thereby creating instant competitiveness after the cull. An incentive to invest, modernize and compete within the countries risk and rewards policies.

There has often been high profile reporting globally of the poor Chinese who were dragged kicking and screaming from their ancestral homes by a ruthless government so that they can develop the land. The highly visible focus of this was the Hutongs in Beijing in the years running up to the Beijing Olympics, where swaths of blocks of traditional housing were removed to make way for modern development. What I would observe is that these pictures were usually of the last ones remaining who have held out, but also that their removal would have been long negotiated in terms of compensation and relocation. I am aware of many examples whereby countryside folk were relocated off their small holdings to urban city areas and given a new apartment, sometimes more than one. Many of the inner-city one-story hutongs lacked basic adequate sanitation and infrastructure, were not very quaint and rat infested, without heating or air conditioning. In China *'new'* predominates in a culture that believes that *'old'* is no good and new is great. In buildings terms, old relates to many unattractive buildings built in the 1970's and 1980's. Sometimes there is little sense of permanence in the culture, although conversely there is considerable emphasis on ancient tradition.

I was aware though that through first-hand experiences that government at all levels listened with a view to improving their own situations, big and small. Small examples included queuing arrangements at banks to become orderly, fair, more efficient, and confidential. Likewise, personal medical confidentiality in hospitals, the application of western management techniques and incredible use of technology.

A big example was related to an old town development that I had a direct involvement in. Jiaxing was a traditional canal city set on a network of canals off the Grand Canal in the flatlands of the vast Yangtze River delta area. As a part of its development in the early 2000s it was bulldozing its old town communities in the city set along the canals, ramshackle and poor looking traditional housing disappearing, and the bulldozers rampaged along. I knew of this because every morning I was up early and out walking on my circular routes along the canals for an hour every morning, a chance in private time peace and solitude to observe the ongoing processes. I was shortly after at a dinner with the city's mayor and his senior deputy mayor. I took the opportunity to enquire what the plans were for these areas and was told major modern redevelopments. Thereafter I talked diplomatically as a 'friend' and resident to point out that in many great cities around the world, there had not been widespread demolition of traditional old towns, but within city developments, old towns had been rejuvenated attractively and become popular with both local populations and tourists alike, reflecting part of their cultural heritages. I used as examples Cape Town's Victoria and Albert redeveloped waterfront out of South Africa's oldest harbour that was drawing substantial numbers of tourists. Likewise, the Rocks area in Sydney, New York, London and more. I agreed that there was obviously a need for new buildings, but highlighted that Jiaxing had a unique situation, the home of Communism at South Lake, beautiful canals, and a rich Zhejiang Old Town heritage, thus asking the question whether it would make more sense to redevelop the canals near my apartment as a traditional old town. In reply I was told that the area already had a specialist old town, Wuzhen some 40 minutes' drive away, but I countered that this new development would be an integral part of the city centre area, readily accessible and a part of daily life. I was aware that the table had gone noticeably quiet and that I had the undivided attention of all present, but especially the powerful decision makers. I was the quickly asked to another dinner with the deputy mayor and asked to write an official letter to them outlining recommendations and suggestions for Jiaxing by the local government to consider, based upon my experiences elsewhere. This I duly did, but coincidence or not the bulldozing stopped the next day I observed, and everything remained untouched for a considerable period as it lay, a pile of rubble, many evacuated old houses and everyone withdrew, no progress. Over the next few years this area was to be redeveloped into an extensive old town, with tourist shops, art galleries, souvenir shops, restaurants, and its own bar street all in very traditional style. This I consider no coincidence and reflects a time when the leaders of Jiaxing were incredibly open minded to ideas that would improve their city and that this played no small part in the city's recognition of my friendship. The point being – China listens and learns! I respected this approach!

The laws and policies of the country are developing all the time in increasingly complex situations. For so long the laws were implemented purely relationship-based situations. I was to find out that in truth the 'law' was 'a stamp on a piece of paper;' the question is how to get that important piece of paper stamped by someone in power to do so? So often it was the results of relationships, 'face' and interpretation in a particular way that was justifiable in the mind of the person stamping his or her approval.

China's policies are clear and well communicated through is management procedures. There is the official policy. Then there are the variations of policies applied either through ignorance of officials, or lacking understanding, experiences, or education. Lastly there are the rogue interpretations by official with corruptive self-interest or under pressure from cronies. China continues to work to eradicate anomalies.

The year 2021 China celebrated its 100th anniversary of the birth of the Chinese Communist Party, it is publicizing its achievements and states its future objectives and aspirations. The successes are obvious, while critics point to Xinjiang, coronavirus origins and atrocities of history such as Tiananmen Square incident some thirty-two years ago. Whatever the points made, China has improved the lot of its citizens dramatically with a positive future to look to.

I include a few selected diaries extracts relative to China's government supervision of the country to illustrate examples ongoing activities at that time relative to government approaches and some of the issues it was contending with:

w/c 13th September 2003 –

> *Air China claims that it will be the World's largest airline by 2010. I wouldn't bet against it!*

> *Last Wednesday was 'Teachers Day' in China, which takes place annually to recognize the importance of the teaching profession in the Country's development. Although the teacher is very highly respected in China due to long historic reasons, I cannot help thinking that Britain could benefit from such similar recognition.*

Suicide rates are disproportionately high in China running officially at least twice the rate of western countries, brought about primarily by the radical rates of changes to the society and the implications for individuals. Suicide counts as the highest cause of death by far in the 15–34-year-old age group.

The travel industry is being freed up and the first majority owned joint venture has been signed with a foreign country – a German Company, who owns 75 per cent!

'Care for Girls Day' has also just been launched in China's poor western provinces in areas where girls are 'just not considered as important as men'. Big issue and will take place in another eleven provinces next year.

There are lots of new rural middle class housing estates being advertised suddenly. Individual houses resembling my memory of 1960's modern architecture – box shaped, flat roofs, lots of glass etc.

The Government is starting to make a few noises about concerns over a potential SARS comeback as the autumn approaches. Many people are having flu jabs this year at far higher rates than before.

America is actively lobbying for China to float its Yuan currency, as at its current valuation it is favourable to China in terms of trade competitiveness. They are right, but I can't help feeling that they are trying to distract thoughts away from the problems of their own society problems.

w/c 27ᵗʰ September 2003 -

I discovered over dinner another element to Chinese population control regulations. Apparently during the Cultural Revolution and until recently, it was illegal for a man to get married or have children until he was twenty-two years old (twenty-three in Chinese years). If he did there would be a very heavy fine as a penalty.

The Chinese government, concerned that the changing weather may bring SARS back into play, has resumed its daily public information releases, although no cases or suspected cases have been reported.

A copper sculpture of a pig's head' that was an ornament in the Old Summer Palace in Beijing has been returned to China after 143 years. It was lost when British and French troops looted the palace in 1860. This is a part of China's policy to reclaim its antique treasures and this head is a part of twelve animals in a set. In 2000, the ox, monkey and tiger heads were bought back for US$4.2m at auctions in Hong Kong. Big project, but Britain and the US have not signed an agreement to cooperate upon the return of these artifacts.

China is annoyed that a US report has listed China as a major drug producer and trafficker. In my part of China, drugs are not an obvious issue and many of our party last week were shocked in Hong Kong when the tour guide pointed out drug addicts on the side of the road.

w/c 11th October 2003 -

Over four hundred of the World's top five hundred companies have operations in China, thirty of which are the Asian headquarters.

Tourism in China – over the Golden Week National holidays on first to the seventh October, ninety million Chinese travelled within China. Foreign tourism numbers are increasing again but have not yet recovered from the pre-SARS levels.

Lord Howe is making a big speech out here at present and is receiving a considerable amount of interview coverage. He is an affable elder statesman with credibility – especially after he was there when Britain gave Hong Kong back to China!

China has publicly spent US$ 2.2 billion on its staffed space programme.

China has introduced 'anti-monopoly' legislation for its information technology sector.

Shanghai now has piped natural gas from a 1,454-kilometre pipeline from western China's Shaanxi Province.

w/c 4th October 2003 -

Golf is starting to get a higher and higher profile here:

There are 195 Golf courses currently operational.

The first was built in 1984.

The biggest is called 'Mission Hills' and is set in Guangdong Province, adjacent to Hong Kong. This is the Chinese home of the David Leadbetter Academy.

The main foreign input from golf pros is from Australia.

There are 30,000 golf club members at present.

There are about 200,000 playing non-members at present.

There are currently 1,500 golf courses under construction, which is not under planning, which is as it says. No mention of how many are being planned.

As a part of the encouragement to the masses to continually drive forward their education, Beijing has announced that it is now seeking to recruit PhD's for the best Civil Service jobs over the next ten years.

Watch the applications for PhD courses shoot up, as these Government roles are prime jobs.

w/c 24th October 2003 - The day starts early as my driver picks me up and we head out to the Shimao hotel to collect our CEO. He was told at his check-in yesterday, to be checked out of his prebooked hotel room and the hotel by 09.30 hours today due to the imposition of 'Marshall Law' (The temporary imposition of direct military control and suspension of civil law) from that time for the next twenty-four hours, as the hotel will be taken over by the Government for purposes unknown. This is the first time that I have come across such actions and am curious as to why but guess that I may never know; Chinese behind closed doors stuff. That said, we picked him up to be informed that overnight the Government had changed the day of Marshall Law until Monday; hey hoe, we will have to find him another hotel so that he doesn't have to keep repacking. He was commenting that he trusted that this 5-star hotel was being compensated for its loss of business. We later discovered that the hotel had to be vacated to accommodate the Former President of China, Jiang Zemin, and his entourage, who is still God as he remains as the Chairman of the Country's Military Committee and leads Beijing's wise old heads gang. I guess that makes it okay, what a marketing coup for the hotel and apparently, he is staying in Jiaxing to make a speech at the official birthplace of Chinese Communism at South Lake during this week's festivities.

w/c 5th March 2005 - Over the last few days the Party at the Chinese People's Political Consultative Conference (CPPCC) have been having their annual gathering in Beijing where they proclaim the policies and way forward for the coming year and thereafter. This event that goes on for a couple of weeks or so is universally reported on all channels and in all media publications. Serious stuff and this year to date include:

> *An anti-secession law to put pressure on Taiwan to integrate into the motherland and not to progress a path of independence. This is taken very seriously, but positive President Hu is urging peaceful*

reunification, whilst the USA and Japan have been advised to stay out of this matter.

The bolstering of the military forces by increasing huge funding to modernize, although the 12.6 per cent rise this year is described as modest, US$ 30 billion seems significant to most and its timing giving the implied threat to Taiwan is also alarming to some.

The resignation of the seventy-eight-year-old Zhang Zemin as Chairman of the State Central Military Commission and handing over to President Hu Jin Tao, thereby completing the transfer of power.

New sexual harassment laws to protect women are to be introduced into China for the first time this year.

Senior party leaders from all over China are being encouraged to 'share their opinions' with their colleagues and leaders and all State Council Departments are being encouraged to listen to them. This truly is significant where until recently sharing your opinion would have got one into deep water, maybe worse and everyone officially listens only to the proclamations of the leaders! These ideas include:

> *Increased suggestions related to economic and social development.*

> *Make contributions to building harmonious socialist society.*

> *Bring the role of non-Communist Party members and people without party affiliations in the CPPCC into play.*

> *Work harder!*

The 2005 economic growth targets have been lowered to 8 per cent, 1.5 per cent lower than 2004.

w/c 10th March 2007 – Over the last week or so the Chinese Government has been holding their National People's Congress in Beijing, held at a time where after five years there are many government changes; there is a lot going on, but general news includes:

Prime focus is upon 'social harmony' and stability.

Two hundred million people have come out of poverty over the last twenty years in China. There are still 150 million families in poor rural areas who are living under difficulties.

Development is still 'un-balanced.'

China is going to build thirty-seven new airports and expand significantly thirty-one more around north-west China over the next four years including Tibet's Lhasa.

GDP grew by +10.7 per cent last year (2006).

China is failing to achieve its own pollution targets, attributed to high growth, but it will take more radical precautions in future. (The environment is extremely high on the agenda and being talked about openly and with resolve. China is really starting to get it, or at least the leadership is, so it will improve).

China is going to harmonise tax between Chinese and foreign owned companies (This will adversely affect our interests – potential tax grab from foreign business investments, but let us wait and see specifics).

Sex education for Chinese migrant workers – there are > 120 million of these, 30 per cent of which are women. It was recognized that this is estimated and could be much higher. (For the record that is over twice the population of the UK on the move and with more to come).

A 17.8 per cent increase in National Defence spending was approved.

It was also announced that Terrorist camps in Xinjiang with connections with Al-Qaida and trained by the Taliban have been raided. They are called the 'East Turkistan Liberation Movement.' (This subject is of increasing concern to China)

w/c 30th May 2009 - I see that it is the twentieth anniversary of the Tiananmen Square incident, something that China obviously wants to put behind it and try and forget about. China has never openly admitted to casualties that night with the tanks it seems, but most independent estimates say that 3,000 people died that night on the streets of Beijing in 1989. Amazingly the 'tank man' the guy who stood in the way of the tanks, has never been identified and the identity never released or discovered even by the most ardent protestors. A bad moment in history, but a defining moment on the way forward. China isn't reporting this and is restricting movement around the Square to avoid any protests. However, it is not interfering with a massive protest of 150,000 people being planned in Hong Kong.

w/c 4th July 2009 - The last week interestingly has demonstrated clearly how China can act, shutting down the internet in blanket form in Xinjiang, although it must be said that it has had the desired effect as there have been no updates over the last few days that have been meaningful regarding the riots and unrest. Then there was the arrest of four senior Rio Tinto executives, one of whom is Australian, for supposedly stealing State Secrets, the catch all term for stopping things that it wants. This action, supposedly relating to some bribes, was not clever as it has spooked the overseas community here. And then there is the fact that Facebook and other such websites have still not been switched back on in the country. Yep, China is flexing its muscles and demonstrating its controls again.

w/c 11th July 2009 - Elsewhere in China I was intrigued to note that one hundred Africans had held a protest in Guangdong after one African died jumping out of a window trying to avoid a police passport check. Bottom line – there are illegal Africans in China, clampdown in process! I suspect this situation will be dealt with clinically.

w/c 22nd August 2009 - Elsewhere in the press it is reported that over 300 million people that are now living in the Chinese countryside, the equivalent to the entire population of the USA, will move into cities over the coming fifteen years. China is proud of the progress to date noting that no slums have been seen developing around any city, unlike similar mass migration situations in India, South Africa, Mexico, Brazil and so many cities around the world.

w/c 26th September 2009 - I am very aware of the impending celebrations of the 60th anniversary of Communist rule in China; this is obviously a big thing here in China and it must be said that last ten years have been magnificent for this country whatever way one dresses things up. The progress has been phenomenal, and China and its people should be proud, with the young people under thirty-five years of age having no direct memory of the Cultural Revolution that killed three million people and the bad aspects of the regime in the early days such as the Great Leap Forward that resulted in an estimated forty million deaths, many through famine. The young China has never experienced things so good, and it determined to have it even better in future. During this time, whatever the critics and rationale, China has been transformed from a chaotic, barbaric, and poverty-stricken place, survived Japanese invasion, and survived civil war. In the wake of these achievements the scale of Mao's wrongs are for now at least ignored, a history of the Party's leadership that reportedly left over seventy million dead along the way as it enforced its theories and its associated practicalities. China's success has been though the way that it has broken away from the central control of the government in a measured step by step approach which has resulted in vast fortunes for some and more personal freedom for most that at any time in the preceding sixty years of Communist rule here. 1978 is the key event in all of this, not 1949, when Deng Xiao Ping introduced the 'Opening Up' process that allowed what we have today to occur. I am sure that we will hear more about all of this over the coming days and weeks in another bout of extreme Chinese Nationalism at a time when the country needs a bit of a lift. This to me remains a worry and what will be the backlash on others who are not Chinese if things go wrong at some stage with this modern capitalist society that is shunning many Marxists values? China has a history of pillorying, whilst admiring the foreigners!

Interestingly the celebrations planned in Beijing look huge and look to at least match the Olympics celebrations of last year and no doubt will be matched by the Shanghai Expo next year, not only to keep China in a position of prominence, but out of the inherent competition internally between the city leaderships of Beijing and Shanghai. The security around Beijing is immense it would seem, with China fearing a terrorist attack from Xinjiang terrorists in Tiananmen Square at the time of the Communist Party's sixty years celebrations.

Jiaxing is descending into a sea of red as the National Holidays and anniversary approaches. There are red banners and red Chinese flags are everywhere as Nationalistic fervour takes over. There oddly seems a lot of excitement about the military parade about to take place in Beijing, where China is expected to demonstrate its military might. I understand that the small Chinese flags attached to every taxi and many private cars have been issued by the government free of charge. In the news China seems to be flexing its muscles all over the globe, from the successful G20 forum to huge oil trades in Nigeria and increased trade all over Africa; the pace of progress is immense.

Thereafter it was a day of the TV and the National Day October 1ˢᵗ celebrations from Beijing that dominated everything. This is a huge event and is punctuated by shots of famous cities, scenery, and landmarks from all over China as well as the fifty-six minorities who make up the balance of China. This is China's Day, and they are going to make the most of it and the Nation seems to be truly captivated. The official ceremony kicked off at 10.00 hours and whilst not my cup of tea as they say, it was mightily impressive with a formidable array of military hardware on view and Tiananmen Square full of folk perfectly choreographed. For obvious reasons, China is fabulous at organizing lots of people and this was demonstrated again, the minutest detail covered.

Somehow, they managed to organize the weather, apparently using eighteen planes to spray anti rain formulations to disperse the clouds over Beijing and it worked, blue skies and sun, where much of the rest of China had rain and low cloud; the scientists succeeded again. After the military and the fly pasts, came the floats and marchers.

w/c 3rd October 2009 - This afternoon our purchasing manager's eight-year-old son came into work on behalf of his school as it is "Flag Angel Day" whereby he presented me with a small Chinese flag and we discussed the success of the Party in China and life in general, all whilst my translator was translating, and his father was videoing and taking snapshots which he informs me will be put on his classroom wall at school.

w/c 21st November 2009 - In another TV article, on BBC World, I note that China has a 100 per cent monopoly on the mining of 'special metals', used in all sorts of devices, electronics, computers and perhaps most importantly in the west's armaments developments! Scary for the future.

w/c 26th December 2009 - I read that China has unveiled its latest achievement, although I struggle to catch up with them all – the world's fastest train. It can take folk between Guangzhou and Wuhan, some 1,069 miles, in just three hours, averaging 350 km/hour, with a maximum speed of 384 km/hr. This average speed compares with France's top speed train of 277 km/hr and Japan's at 243 km/hr. What next for China? Well, the Expo next year in Shanghai will be impressive and I note that the high-speed train connection with Hangzhou from Shanghai is coming along at pace alongside of the motorway with the concrete pillars and platforms all but finished.

I see that between 2004-2008 that the number of private companies in China grew by 81.4 per cent to 3.6m, whilst State Owned companies fell by 20 per cent to 143,000. I also note that China has budgeted investments of US$ 104.8 billion for agriculture, farmers, and rural areas – hence the amazing developments going on that I have just witnessed in terms of infra structure in the Chongqing countryside. It is worth observing that China spent more than US$ 133 billion in public spending so far in 2009. The Chinese economy continues to boom, with retail and housing sales continuing to climb. One rarely sees Mao Ze Dong style uniforms around these days.

w/c 9th January 2010 - Then I see that Google is threatening to shut down its Chinese operations due to increased censorship. I note that Facebook, Twitter, You Tube, and the likes remain shut down in China anyway. You Tube is owned by Google and there are ramblings from the US Government again about human rights in China and restricted freedom of speech. Microsoft though have committed to staying in China, as I guess has Cisco Systems that provide most of the operating systems for China's networks.

w/c 30th January 2010 - With at least some time on my hands I look at some 2009 data announced during these boom times:

> *In 2009 there were fifty-one million 'outbound tourists' from China, a record and up 7 per cent upon the prior year.*

> *There were 480,000 'foreign experts' registered in China in 2009.*

> *Mortgage lending was up 48 per cent in China in 2009.*

> > *The government though is taking all sorts of measures to slow down increasing house prices including much higher mortgage loan rates and transfer property taxes.*

> > *New housing prices rose 7.8 per cent year upon year with second-hand houses rising 6.8 per cent year on year as of December 2009.*

> *CPI (Inflation) rose 10.9 per cent in December 2009 after nine months of decline. Overall, for 2009, inflation was down 0.7 per cent upon 2008.*

> *Car sales in China rose to 13.6 million cars in 2009, up 46.6 per cent from 2008 and a massive increase from the 4.39 million sold in 2003, my first full year here.*

> > *The city of Beijing now has four million registered vehicles.*

There are 65,000 kilometres of motorways in China, the second only to the USA, with another 4,719 kilometres added in 2009 and work on another 16,000 started in the same year. The target of 100,000 kilometres of motorways by 2010 is likely to be achieved long before that date.

China created 11.02 million new jobs in 2009 in urban areas. The plan is to create fourteen million more jobs in 2010.

Foreign direct investments in China in 2009 was US$ 90.03 billion despite the global recession, just 2 per cent down from 2008. The main target was manufacturing industry.

Exports of mechanical and electrical goods, which comprise half of the country's exports, rose by 10 per cent in 2009.

However, overall foreign trade, in and out, fell by 16 per cent.

Ominously China's overseas investment last year was US$ 42 billion!

w/c 20th March 2010 - The news here is troubling, dominated by the trials of the Rio Tinto Executives for bribery (receiving them) and Google's position in China, reflecting the current anti-foreigner sentiments.

w/c 20th February 2016 - On the plane I read an English Language Chinese Newspaper, something I rarely read anymore, but the point that last year Chinese domestic consumption increased to its highest level ever at 66.7 per cent of the Chinese GDP was notable, meaning that China is less and less dependent upon overseas exports than it once was and this I have always predicted, but I also note that the exports remain important and that is largely driven by the rest of the world's demand, which is turn brings money into China that helps pay for the domestic GDP consumption. The other key point that I noted was the apparent Chinese ban on new outrageous building designs in favour of something more conventional and cost effective, thus ending the modern designs of large buildings all over China, but which are especially prevalent in Shanghai in places. This has been interpreted by some as censorship and control, but seems to make sense given some of the results witnessed that would seem impractical and inefficient!

In closing this chapter, I would offer that if China were a stock exchange listed company, then investors would be immensely proud of the returns that it has made over recent decades! Not all is right, it is long term work in progress, but progress it does.

Chapter 9

Cheating and corruption

I originally entitled this chapter *'How to get screwed in China,'* fully aware that the title was ambiguous and that was deliberate. However, I reflected and decided to call it what it is. Cheating and corruption as defined is endemic in China as people frenzy for money, for their children, a better life, long term security, not to be left behind the rest and indeed to try and better others, and to show it! Money drove everything, no matter how much. This cannot be denied.

I was aware of it sort of early on in my stay, but it never directly affected me in as much that I was never offered or given a bribe and never asked for one, but these things were endemic around me. It took a while for the penny to drop in my understanding how much it purveyed society, although it would be wrong to tar the entire nation with this claim, but it seemed to be the way things worked.

Again, I start by highlighting the initiatives by President Xi Jin Ping to curtail or at least reduce this corruption with some high-profile actions taken against a Party Politburo member being caught out and separately Beijing sending a troop of central government investigators into Chong Qing province having removed the mayor and others for graft and corruption. These where clear signals of intent, albeit to those who may have been out of favour and showed their gains too publicly. The fact is that the top Party officials are incredibly rich, and, or their family wealth now legitimized having acquired it on the way to the top over time. Indeed, when a clean-up of government and the Party were announced, they were given a prolonged period to clean their act up appropriately to enable them to pass an audit.

Rightly or wrong, though, I concluded that everyone was at it in some way. That is the way the system works, traditionally all cash, but that is changing with tighter banking and technology tools such as the equivalent of PayPal.

That said, I personally never found or heard any issues of this nature with the local Jiaxing government, hardworking professional politicians and managers seeking to develop the city of Jiaxing, seeking direct investment, or trying to support investors for joint venture partners by solving issues as best they could, but there were always difficult and conflicting issues. Certainly, I did not see overt corruption that I became aware of elsewhere in China but at times there certainly were conflicting agendas and interpretations between factions that were to challenge our businesses on many fronts.

I outline random examples that I know about and heard about over times:

> It was suggested to me indirectly and in all seriousness, not by any mayor or anyone close to him, that the best way for me to curry favour with someone senior was to either support his child during their time studying in the overseas in some way, the amount of support not specified but substantial was implied, or offer his wife or family member a job in our company, paying her a monthly sum..............but don't expect her to do any work or indeed turnup! This is how things work to guarantee support, I was informed. I declined on both counts!

> More normal was the request to give folks sons and daughters a job in the UK based parent company. This was a routine request to help their visas and prolong their stays, assisting their education and CV's and leading to marriage and living abroad. There were occasions when to ensure cooperation that our parent company agreed to the occasional job request but for limited periods of time only and where there was a genuine fit or need. Many more requests were gently turned down.

> There was the strong rumour through Chinese whispers that a very wealthy businessman's wife in Hangzhou 'lost $1 million' to the wife of a senior provincial Party official playing in a mah-jong game, a Chinese gambling game that was banned under the Cultural Revolution as Mao clamped down on gambling, but this

ancient Chinese traditional game was allowed to creep back in with great popularity. The obvious implication was that this was legitimizing payment from the businessman in return for favours or commissions. Of course, I had no proof of this, but this was openly talked about at all levels of society including government officials and seemed to have credence.

I was asked to give people jobs requested by 'friends' to ensure cooperation, but also to help their debt of friendships to the family members to whom these individuals were related. I did this once on a limited period as it was very clearly explained to me that I had to do this in a joint venture. Whilst agreeing on that occasion I made it clear that there would be no repeat, so go away and this was respected. I cannot honestly say that other managers in the company did not have some influence on appointments unbeknown to me. "This is the Chinese way," I was told.

Driving tests – it has been widely reported that company car drivers to officials have been known to take the driving test for that official or family members in their places and passing their license successfully, the examiner somehow missing the fact that the person taking the test was not the person registered to do so, but ably comforted in life by a wad of cash I gathered. Commonplace apparently when more individuals started buying cars from the early 2000's, but again increasingly clamped down on by government over recent years.

Driving instructors take lessons with usually a carload of learners together, normally say four people crammed into the car and each taking turns to drive. I gather that after a few driving test fails by the team it is common for these four individuals to group together and donate a lump sum of money to examiners who then pass them, thereby enhancing the wealth of the examiner and saving face in the career of the driving instructor. It is of course quite possible that the examiner in some cases is not going to pass folk anyway until they have paid!

Guanxi – developing friendship through a social network, which is how China works, building trust and making friends through dinners, gifts, favours and ....I suggest there is no limit to how far this could go dependent upon circumstances. It certainly works in getting things done.

House and apartment sales are often discounted under negotiation, sometimes significantly, the trade-off being that a significant amount of the discount be paid privately to the individual estate agent selling the apartment, shared if you like, unbeknown to the house builder or house selling company.

It was discovered that a company driver, an honoured position in the company as they drive senior managers and officials and often do a lot more, was using the company car fuel card to buy fuel as approved but was abusing this by using it to secretly fill up many others people's cars or cans of fuel at the company's expense. Let us just say the situation was very abused, over a prolonged period, and was known about by the financial department, but they did not flag it because they accepted that "this is what happens" and my known reaction. Eventually it was all too much, reported to me and he was dismissed with the condition that he paid back his agreed illicit gains (I am sure understated) so that the theft was not reported to the police. Afterwards, a senior deputy to me, a respected sensible fellow, explained that 'all the drivers in the state companies, joint ventures and other companies' did this, the implication being that the other driver did it too, an unsaid perk of the job, '*but he took too much, too obvious*'! Oh boy!

At work we made tea bag paper at the local factory. Strong lightweight papers that were absorbent and strong, ideal as basic wipes, for disposal. Indeed, in the UK such internally rejected materials were sold off as 'seconds' to local garages to wipe spilt fuel. These papers came like large toilet rolls. We discovered that some employees where smuggling these out as a pastime and supplying many of the local small restaurants in the area at a cost for table papers to clean up food and splashes. Ideal use, but not right and a cost to the company.

Wastepaper sales from the process at work were subject to an implied power struggle between members of the sales team wanting to do this job. We were later to find out that whilst trusted, the certain sales persons were getting significant kickbacks from the paper recyclers who bought the scrap paper from the company that was unfit for purpose quality wise. Again, disciplinary action was taken against very apologetic employees although frowning at why the foreigner cared about this all – it was company money, a state-owned legacy belief.

At work we had two translator/secretaries who shared responsibilities in booking things. I was to discover that they both used separate travel agencies to book tickets for plane or train travels and hotels. When I suggested that we standardize the travel agent that we used there was hell to play, initially quiet resistance hoping that I would go away and forget, but later increasingly defensive and aggressive. Then the beans got spilt – they were both getting significant commissions for their respective travel agents that garnered all sorts of suspicions. Anyway, we did standardize the travel agents and eventually one of the translator left the company a little later, the one who was overtly benefitting.

A production manager came into my office one day, bemoaning the terrible quality of nylon type ropes used in the production process, which were falling off the machine after short life spans and causing considerable machine downtime. Now these ropes were imported from the UK and renowned for their excellent quality internationally, but he swore that they were terrible, and we needed to change supplier immediately. It turns out that he was personally cutting the ropes partially, causing them to fall off the machine and by changing to another supplier ropes he would get a commission personally from this supplier. Anyway, we did not change, and he left the company shortly afterwards, very shortly, but an example again of how personal gain came into conflict with the company's objectives and indeed individual's own direct responsibilities.

On another occasion another production manager was being sponsored to take a master's degree privately in Shanghai the condition tied to employment tenure for a number of years. As time went on, he was not making much progress with his degree and further investigation showed that the finance department had been paying him the money personally, albeit upon submission of invoices from the university. Unfortunately, he was using this money to partly fund his new apartment and its decoration. Again, we agreed that he repay this money over a short timescale to avoid reporting to the police and he was to voluntarily leave the company not too long afterwards. I often wondered what the police may have done if we had reported this fraud and other similar ones them given the commonality of it all?

At one of the company's joint ventures up in Shandong province, where there was a western general manager, I was walking around the site on a visit and noticed a nice, new four wheeled drive car. I was informed that it was the purchasing managers car. Now I knew their salary and even though the company was assisting buying their apartments for them, there is no way she could have bought that on her legitimate company income alone. I heard later that she got a rollicking from the joint venture's Chinese chairman for driving her car to work on the day that I visited! Heavens knows what was going on in that factory in an area that a western university educated friend from the affluent coastal areas of that province, referred to as '*bandit country*'! Let us just say that the team up there lived well relative to the performance of the business itself.

Shortly after I went to China in 2002, we had a major quality problem with raw materials supplied and I demanded an immediate meeting with the supply company on site with a very well-spoken Chinese English speaker who I had come to know, at ten o'clock on a given day. I was therefore incredibly surprised to see the supplier representatives sneaking into a senior manager's office at nine o'clock, something I caught out of the corner of my eye and was not told about beforehand. They then all arrived in my office as agreed telling me that all issues had been resolved, but when I listened, they certainly had not been resolved and the correct questions not asked. I was told that we could use up the substandard quality chemicals in lower quality grades without penalty, which I refused in front of some very grey and glum faces. I was to find out later that the issues that had been resolved were the private 'commission' payments to some at work, given the potential of these materials for rejection, not whether they were fit for purpose or not.

A westernized Chinese social friend of mine who once lived in the USA, decided to open a bar and at short notice I was invited to a dinner that he was hosting, I had to attend to add to his credibility, where we dined with police, fire brigade and other officials related to security and the issuing for licenses necessary for running a bar. A merry time was had by all as guanxi was developed and they all agreed that his bar could open on time as planned and that all licenses were approved. My only benefit was a free dinner. At the end, after debate among the group, my friend asked me to leave the private dining room and leave them alone which was strange but as I left, I saw him carelessly taking out some thick 'red envelopes' (gift envelopes containing cash) and start to hand them around the table to the attendees. I was later to understand that this also included 'protection money' for his bar, something that I had only previously been exposed to by watching New York police-gangster movies! The bar owner later confirmed that 'everyone had to do this, or else there will be trouble.'

Company tax evasion or avoidance, whatever the interpretations of the difference, was rife in the early days I understand. Tax was monitored at many levels and meticulously by government statistics. One of my first duties was to collect a plaque for our 51 per cent foreign controlled joint venture as the previous year, prior to my arrival, the company had paid one of the highest tax rates in Zhejiang province. I.e., the company had made a lot of profit, so it paid a lot of tax and there was official recognition of this fact. When the dust settled I was informed by an external friend in authority that the local community was laughing at us – 'Why were we paying so much tax? That would never happen to a Chinese company!'

Many years later in a much larger Jiaxing I received another award for the government of one of its two main districts, this time for our one hundred per cent foreign owned company, for the most tax (all taxes including pension contributions and insurances etc as well as employment tax) paid per employee ratio. Again, I felt foolish – our company was abiding by the employment laws of China and paying tax strictly in line with that and this was being officially recognized – let us just say that others were not!

Gifts were and are a major part of Chinese society, a sure sign of friendship and appreciation and certainly for most of my tenure in China these were legally not declarable for tax reasons. I was the recipient of many small gifts especially in my early days, less so later. I did not in any way let these influence my judgment or decision making and certainly did not consider them a bribe or direct influencer upon circumstances, as accepting them as a cultural norm. My parent company also accepted this was the situation. Gifts came from Banks, Insurance companies, government officials, customers, suppliers, agents and so on. None of them materially significant in value, but happy memories to me of moments in life and folk's kindness.

Examples included pictures, ash trays, sculptures of the various 'Year of the ....' artifacts, tea pots, vases, commemorative coins and stamps, teas, and so on.

For a while I lived near a teacher. On occasions each year I think from memory just ahead of the school year starting and certainly just before the Chinese New Year, a succession of cars and boxes would arrive. At other times he was to unload all sorts of gift packages from the back of his car, once with a noticeably large wad of cash stuffed in the back of his trouser pocket – I can only assume from appreciative parents seeking favour for their children, especially as I understood continually that such practices were normal. This was only my assumption though.

After a trip to Guangxi province in in circa 2004, just prior to the Chinese New Year, we were heading back to the airport at Guilin in the back of a mini-bus and were in a hurry as we had left late from a rural town. At the first village a police officer, two, stopped the vehicle and demanded on the spot payments for a brake light that did not work. The driver even tried wielding me out of the car as part of the negotiation to avoid a fine and delay, but they were not phased; they wanted money. After a prolonged debate we went to the police station and the driver duly paid the 'fine' in cash. Technically correct, but this was viewed by traveling colleagues as pure corruption, and I witnessed it face to face. At the very next village the same thing happened, exactly, and another fine was paid on the spot. This clearly was not right; indeed, it was very wrong, but the police had the power!

I do not have first-hand evidence but understand that when housing developments are approved the house building company must grease the palms of various government officials, bank officials, insurance officials and various associated officials for approval to take place. This could include the provision of free apartments given in family members names of those officials.

I had it on good authority from a European supplier that a brand-new machine for a factory was delivered to China from Europe by an engineering company. This was a large piece of plant and required numerous containers for all the parts and frames. The first item out of the first container delivered was a top of the range Mercedes car for the company owner, free of charge and no punitive import duty paid.

Private 'commissions' paid to company officials by suppliers, especially from within China are legend.

I was delighted that overall, our one hundred per cent foreign owned business was 95 per cent export sales, and our major suppliers were renowned international suppliers and imported, thereby at one stroke avoiding any significant such issues mentioned with any sales to China handled by an independent agent or joint venture partner. Our products had a specific customs export code allocated to it for duty free, or low duty, to be paid at the ports for these exported goods. This was tried and tested for our product and proven to be correct. However, periodically, usually just ahead if the annual Chinese New Year festivals, a customs officer at Shanghai port would question this code allocation, quite seriously, impounding the container being exported and thereby delaying shipment to the customer. The customs officer would randomly state that it should be allocated under another paper grade code and therefore liable to much higher duty payable, so this was serious, because if implemented ongoing this would wipe out profit margin on the business's products. This after consternation, worry, explaining delays to customers, was usually resolved by a nominated shipping agent representing the company ensuring that the Customs agent clearly understood the product code allocated and when the officer had understood something clearly at last, the container was released, and everything returned to normal. I will never know how much money the freight forwarder had to pay the customs officer to ensure that he had clarity of mind and I am sure that this would be denied by all parties if asked.

Red envelopes, a cash gift in a red envelope is an integral part of Chinese society. Prevalent for children at Chinese New Year, weddings, birthdays and so on throughout. A gift of cash that makes things untraceable. This is usually a simple gift of cash, but can be so much more!

Once when with on holiday in Xian there were two incidents that left me extremely upset to say the least.

One was at the Terracotta Army site where figurines were being sold outside by pedlars and by this time, I knew about negotiation so having been shown a box of five warrior figurines, inspected it, I negotiated and agreed a price. Having given them the money I immediately became suspicious when the cash went straight behind his back to a passing assistant who disappeared into the crowd immediately. I was then not given the gift box with five figurines but handed one only! At first, I thought this obvious conn was a joke and suddenly the seller lost any command of the English language, but it was a fraud. All hell let loose, I lost my temper in front of a massive crowd creating immediate attention and it took all my strength to prevent my rugby playing son from planting a punch on this guy. In the end we got the box I believe, but the brazenness of it all.

The next day we were buying plane tickets, in cash as was the norm, in the hotel's approved official tourist agents office in the reception area. There were three mature ladies present in the office. They typed the amount of money to be paid into a calculator as was the way to show me and I carefully counted out the money, twice, and gave the cashier the notes. She then in turn carefully counted the notes, twice, as was convention sorted out the notes, put them in her cash draw and bundled it with other cash notes and then turned to me and told me that I had not paid her enough money and that owed another ¥500, approximately £50 at that time; are you kidding? I knew exactly what I had paid her and now she was telling me that I had underpaid and the problem I realized was that there was no way of proving it as she had already mixed the cash and two ladies behind her were nodding in agreement with her, partners in crime in this obvious fraud. I called my secretary and deputy on the phone, and they talked to the travel agent cashier and then they told me that I had underpaid, and if I had not, they confirmed that there was no way to prove it. So pay the extra and get the plane tickets.

Life is about learning experiences indeed.

An overseas visitor from Europe came to see us in Jiaxing and after a few days he asked to go to Shanghai for a day alone over the weekend. I caught him up a day later for a lunch and visit to some tourist spots. When I met him, he was ashen faced and explained to me a story that was tenuous as best on the lead in, but the end outcome was scary. Apparently, walking down a busy Shanghai Street he was approached by a young lady who was begging for some money for tea, which is the odd bit, and would he like some tea as well. It seems that out of the kindness of his heart he followed her down a narrow alley off a major street and into a room whereby he was accosted by a gang of tough looking men who said he was disrespecting the girl and demanded money or else they would beat him up and made him get his credit card out and use it in a portable transaction machine, twice, each time for €1,000, after which they let him go. Feeling stupid, he was now wondering how he was going to explain the loss of €2,000 upon his return to Europe. I never did entirely believe the first part of the tale.

I am very aware of somebody giving me an exceptionally fine bottle of top-notch baijiu. This was extremely kind and very much appreciated, but he did not buy it himself. A worker in a state-run company, he knew the purchasing accountant who owed him a favour, so he cleared the debt by getting him to buy the bottle with company money, such resourcefulness.

A lot is said about *quality* in China. Part of the quality consistency process is to gain ISO 9001 Quality accreditation and certificate that says a company has adequate quality systems in place and adheres to them consistently. I was surprised at some companies that I saw around China that were ISO accredited or at least to the Chinese state equivalent version. Systems seemed scant and superficial, but companies kept being accredited. We started up a new company from scratch and the Quality certificate along with the Environmental systems and health and safety were all essential parts of the company's development, indeed we needed to be at far higher standards to satisfy international expectations. Having prepared well I was staggered ahead of the first audit when senior managers started suggesting that we needed an amount of money on top of the official audit fee, 'to make sure that there aren't any problems'! The auditors expected a bribe to ensure a company was accredited, at which stage I stopped the process and had a deep and meaningful internal discussion along the lines that we are an international company, we do the right things, pass accreditation based upon merit and so on. Under no circumstances were we getting into separate payments et al, a dinner for visitors, but nothing more. Members of the team had to go away and explain this to the audit firms. It explained though why so many other companies had ISO certificates – they were bought basically.

In one area of the north of China, although nothing specific local officials had to be paid to get anything done. That was how it was reported by the local Chinese management team at least and occasional verified by the overseas nationals there.

I regularly heard that officials often appointed family members to key roles – loyalty, trust, wealth, and power. Also though that others paid for their jobs, bribes of lots of money paid to officials through a fixer, often a trusted family member, who would coordinate the appointment process. Lucrative and again simply explained as *'this is normal.'*

Quite quickly I was to become aware of corruptive activities via the Chinese and English language media and my diary extracts reflected this awareness - *w/c 15ᵗʰ March 2003:*

- *The Courts here are getting tougher on crime. Supreme court cases are up 46 per cent over the last 5 years and local courts up 22 per cent, with smuggling, tax evasion and inferior quality goods cases up 68 per cent. 90,000 people have been sentenced and US$1.67 billion of assets recovered.*

- *Similarly the fight against corruption cases have been stepped up, with 207,000 cases heard over the last five years and 12,800 against officials above County or Divisional level. A deputy governor of Jiangxi province and Vice Chairman of the National Standing Committee have been executed for possessing property 'from unidentified sources', whilst the former vice Minister of Public Security (Re: police + more) has a two-year suspended death Sentence for accepting bribes and dereliction of duty. The government is now concentrating on mafia-style crimes that are apparently endemic.*

w/c 25ᵗʰ January 2003:

The National Audit Office in China has announced a crackdown on the assets of the big State firms. The reason, last year twelve state firms lost US$871m worth of state property through malpractice. 32 per cent of the state firms falsified profits and overall malpractice involving US$ 24.7 bn were discovered.

China is clamping down on the imports of African animal products, like ivory. It has just seized US$242,000 worth (mainly ivory products, but also crocodile skins), but is on the trail of a lot more.

w/c 22ⁿᵈ February 2003:

President Hu Jintao has called for a cleanup of corruption. Since 1998 there have been over 200,000 criminal cases involving government *officials, including 5,500 major cases of serious bribery or misuse of public funds of more than US$120,000 in each instance. Twenty-five officials at ministerial level have been sued.*

There is a clampdown on book piracy, with 10.24 million 'pirated' books seized between August and October 2002.

Six people convicted of trafficking and selling drugs in Guangzhou have had all their personal property and assets seized and have been sentenced to death – immediately; case solved, won't do it again! Swift justice, no problem.

w/c 22ⁿᵈ *March 2003 - The government here is also clamping down on fake food products. Last year the Government confiscated 55,000 tonnes of fake food (presumably illegal branding), worth US$ 38 million. They claim to have 100,000 government officials on the case, and apparently there were 114 fatalities in 104 serious food poisoning cases that resulted in 5,900 people being poisoned in the first ten months of 2002. This is though, 56 per cent down upon 2001.*

w/c 3ʳᵈ *May 2003 - The Government is cracking down on all sorts of things at present, including my little DVD shop:*

Twenty-eight folk have been arrested for illegal pyramid selling in Guangdong.

170,000 wildlife police have blitzed illegal trafficking, killing, selling, or buying protected wildlife. During April 10-19, over 838,500 endangered animals were confiscated, 45,000 of which were supposedly under 'first class' State protection. 1,423 suspects have been arrested.

Fake computer printer ink cartridges for Epson, HP and Canon printers have been seized, worth US$9.7m. Lot of cartridges!

w/c 4ᵗʰ *November 2008 – Today I discovered that an ex-buyer, one of our main customers and someone who was doing very well, was just sentenced to ten years in prison for corruption, taking over ¥1 million in bribes (£75,000 at the exchange rate) whilst dealing in tobacco leaf. I suspect that this was only the tip of the iceberg, no wonder he could afford to send his daughter to the UK to be educated. I cannot help feeling though that he was 'unlucky' as from what I hear everyone seems to be at it in China – he must have upset the wrong person somewhere along the way. Worryingly, he was a big friend of my then deputy, although no evidence of wrongdoing.*

w/c 17ʰ October 2009 - Captivating China at present is the massive corruption purges going on in Chong Qing, whereby huge mafia gangs have seemingly developed massive wealth and corrupted all aspects of government and life there. Beijing has cracked down upon this in a massive way, sending a signal to the activities being mirrored all around China and I am sure that there will be significant implications. With China's increasing wealth, there has been the rise of the Chinese gangs that were once stamped out by the Communist's regime. These gangs in turn have become a direct threat to the very government that runs this country. This story will run and run. Also in the news are stories about bribery and corruption and again back in Chong Qing, it is reported that one leader took £10m in bribes in recent years; now that is a lot of money wherever one lives. The stories of butchery and barbaric behaviour that are coming out is extraordinary including attacks on passengers on a plane with guns and machete attacks which the police ignored and were never reported in the media!

Thursday and in the national media there is ongoing reporting of the huge mafia and corruption scandal that had engulfed the city of Chong Qing. There have been nearly 5,000 arrests, many senior folk including the deputy police chief and so on. This attack coordinated in advance in secret by the Beijing government was I am sure the high-profile action, sending it a future political heavy weight as governor, but it was therefore no surprise when in Jiaxing today I hear that the Chief of Planning and Construction for the government has been arrested for bribery and corruption along with forty-six others; turns out to be in Pinghu, one of Jiaxing's satellite towns. This will run, but one must believe that everyone is at it and that he has been caught because he has upset someone higher up the chain or just been too open about it, reportedly taking ¥2.8m in bribes, £280,000, but you just know that it was a lot more than that!

And on and on it goes, probably so many more examples that I have forgotten or do not merit to be mentioned here, but indicative of the society. Work was complicated by all of this, indeed I got to know quickly in unexplained situations that were a problem, when my translator used the phrase *"it's complicated,"* that money was involved somewhere, either that or a powerful family friend or relation was leveraging power to a situation.

Chapter 10

Security and the Police

It is inevitable that with a population of 1.4 billion people that there will be breaches of the laws, security, and random incidents as well as issues that happen when there are economic disparities and a huge migrant populace.

I say it as I found it, I found China to be incredibly safe! That is not to say there are not bad people or bad situations around, or unsafe for some, but unsurprisingly given the size of the police force, domestic security was generally very good, especially given the immense population. Crime though was all around, with gangland type conflicts talked about certainly not as overtly evident as it is in many western countries, but controlled in many proactive ways and civil stability maintained.

The whole ethos of how China is run is to avoid conflict ensuring social stability by finding agreeable solutions through negotiation, often vigorous, partly cultural style, partly the history of China with its factional warlords, the civil war and more recently of course the Communist Revolution.

Maybe because I was a foreigner I had a special pass as such, touching foreigners aggressively being considered generally taboo with severe penalties, but I tested out the streets of Jiaxing and other cities around China at both ends of the day, often in the dark, either walking home happy from a late night of social activity, business or my exercise routine of long early morning walks often in darkened quiet streets and through semi-rural parks and along canals; I never, ever felt seriously threatened at these times. No thoughts of racial attacks. No thoughts of knife attacks. No thoughts of shootings. No thoughts of muggings. No nothing, just a safe environment. This is the converse of many cities in the western world, or indeed Russia, where I would not be out walking early or walking home late under any circumstances. In 2012 I was cautioned not to go to an NBA game in Atlanta, USA on a free evening in the city as it was in a *dangerous* area and there were unsavoury folk around. In the Mid-West of America in the 1990's in a rural environment I was told not to go outside of the hotel jogging as my safety could not be guaranteed. In the Philippines, Makati, Manilla indeed, there were bomb attacks on hotels, one time enduring a 'lock-in,' and often we were told not to walk outside of certain blocks, the safe blocks openly protected by machine gun bearing soldiers. In South Africa, well, one just did not venture out of the hotels unless escorted by someone who knew what they were doing. In the western world there has been an increase of homeless roaming the streets, some often apparently under the influence of substances and frankly intimidating. And so, the story goes on around the cities of the world. In China I experienced none of this!

The security environment was quite the opposite frankly to what I had experienced in for example the USA, where gun and knife crime are rife as are muggings, robberies, domestic physical attacks, drug fuelled rages, no-go areas in certain parts. In China there are no privately owned guns; it is against the law, and this is rigorously enforced. The only guns that I have seen have been under Marshall law situations, such as Presidential or senior political visits, armed police in certain situations, passing military folk and armed bank collection trucks who tote what I would recognize as sub machine guns as a deterrent.

Knives are a part of the Chinese culture, especially those heavy large blade chopping knives that are used in domestic life, but folk would not think to use them in an inappropriate way. In 2003 I did hear in my earlier days during a rare visit to the chattering expatriate community in Shanghai, allegedly leaked by consulate officials, that there had been a massacre of a German family with a machete in Nanjing, by a Chinese guy who just went mad, slaying the German, his wife and two children. I will never know if this was the truth or not, but the expatriate community in Shanghai certainly believed it at that time; this was never reported in any newspaper at least the ones that I saw, with all parties content to keep it quiet.

Later there were several random attacks on schoolkids around China at schools which garnered high national profile with kids and teachers being injured or killed by mad knife wielding attackers. The government response was to quickly put two armed guards at the entrance to *every* school in the country, often retired police, or the likes, as a deterrent that appeared to work and certainly gave some assurance to parents.

I have seen some physical altercations, the result of too much alcohol with often a girl involved but nothing that was too aggressive or damaging.

Drugs it seems were around, but I never personally came across them bar noting some white powder dust on the sink surface of a high-class bar a couple of times. Not I suspect the heavy stuff though, whatever that may be. That all said, drugs were available and there was once a double murder of two fighting drug dealers that I became aware of in our city.

I was never sure about attacks on women though, but there were obviously issues and I suspect not isolated ones. There always seemed to be an underlying concern. I am aware, either due to preventative training or events, that my translators and female colleagues often noted the taxi driver's taxi number when getting into it alone and messenging it by phone or sending a photo to their families or friends either to dissuade any thoughts of the driver or just in case something were to happen. Attacks obviously happened and at times there was shall we say awareness and fear of men. Stories abounded of girls being abducted for trafficking by gangs, whilst other rumours related to strange guys taking children, never to return; hence parents watched their children closely.

Taxis always had steel bars across the middle of the car segregating movement between the back and front seats, then increasingly a strong Perspex dividing partition between the driver and the front seat passenger. These were there for good reasons and out of necessity.

Proactive prevention also seemed to be the approach taken to home security, building security into its systems, fuelled by various paranoia that went with a talking community. Apartment windows for so long were built with bars on the windows, strangely irrespective of which floor the apartment was on or its practical accessibility. These accessories became more useful as shelves to hang drying clothes and meats on than preventing access by intruders.

Apartment doors were often double doored affairs, two doors, the inner door being wooden and decorative in nature whilst the outer door being steel door with at least two key locks, more resembling safe doors and in no way were decorative. Over time many of these multiple key locks were to be replaced in part by the finger-print door lock or similar technologies.

In the cities people lived in gated type communities, primarily several high-level apartment blocks with one or two secure main entrances staffed by security guards and security perimeter fencing with security cameras and touch sensitive trip wire alarms on top, controlling people flows in and out and dissuading any approaches by casual intruders. It was these gated communities that enabled China to so rigorously control its masses during their covid 19 lockdowns.

More recently, with the advent of technology, apartment burglar alarming and close circuit TV camera systems boomed for the middle classes to protect their homes. Again, this seemed to be very re-assuring and folk always referred to the fact that the issue was with poorer migrant workers from other provinces.

In the countryside communities, the communities tended to know their neighbours and look after their own; I always got the impression that anyone causing trouble would be 'dealt with' off the record.

I became aware of the presence of plain clothed police officers around directly on three separate occasions. The first one was when I was in a quiet bar on a main street, one that was isolated from other bars and the main street shops around were shut. Late one night someone in a drunken state threw a bottle of beer onto the floor, as he did this the bar owner immediately made a short phone call. Within a minute, there was a plain clothed police officer in the bar investigating, tattooed, looking fit and cool in tee shirt, but also showing his police credentials and a very sober and sensible figure he proved in defusing the situation professionally, having materialized out of nowhere. It got me thinking about plain clothes police, but also the bar security arrangements that prevail.

The second incident that I was very aware of was in a nightclub bar, not the type that I would normally go to. I had just enjoyed a lovely dinner with a local government fellow who used to be a police officer. He was plainly happy to see me and had become quite a good friend, however over dinner he explained that he does not normally drink too much as he likes the 'fight' whilst doing so. That was the translation, I did not catch on quickly, but I interpreted this statement as meaning the challenge of 1:1 drinking challenges with others at dinner, sometimes referred to as fighting. Afterwards he insisted on taking me to this bar with a male assistant of his in tow and a female translator who was not my normal translator and was bemused by it all; and excited to be going to a nightclub. Anyway, a busy place it was too and upon entry we crossed to the bar, not a packed bar, on the edge of the dance area. At this stage it was just he and I drinking, together with my translator, and having received our drinks he immediately picked up his beer bottle and threw it straight past the bar man into the optics behind him and into all the expensive spirits bottles on shelves behind the bar. No warning. Immediate pandemonium! His assistant, ever deferential to seniority dived right in the protect his boss, not overtly restraining him, but blocking his path anywhere. I suddenly realized what he meant by his comment that he liked *fighting* after a drink. He was a drunk aggressive, not to me, but there were obvious demons from somewhere. Then suddenly, out of nowhere in this busy bar, he was surrounded by thirteen plain clothed police officers (I counted), not one of them saying anything, no one grabbling him, but totally surrounding him, arms down by their sides, thereby controlling his movements and one step at a time walking him outside the building where his assistant drove him away. I was left to work out quite what had happened but remembered that as a police officer prior to his government role, he had been the boss of these plain clothed police, hence no one restrained or arrested him. I am sure this incident will somehow have been swept under the carpet amongst friends being not major in the scope of things, but the following morning I received a personal phone call from him in his very broken English as a sad, genuine, and truly regretful apology. He must have said sorry twenty times. But the key awareness take away for me was the presence of all those policemen amongst the party revellers, their cover at least for that night, well and truly blown!

The third occasion which seemed altogether more sinister took place on a business trip to Beijing with colleagues. We were in central Beijing in need of a taxi home from dinner, with many foreign tourists around. This though in pre-'Didi' (Chinese Uber equivalent) call a taxi days, was proving a challenge, but eventually we managed to hail a cab at roadside just as we would do in Shanghai or Jiaxing and gratefully got in. Immediately as the taxi tried to pull away, four plain clothed police officers descended upon the taxi, ignoring us, ignoring my presence as a foreigner, one grabbing the driver ID Number and photo displayed in the front of the car, ripping it out. Two others simultaneously got hold of the driver and without warning or explanation physically dragged him out of the car onto the pavement, whilst a fourth watched the perimeter. No real explanations, some shouting, and he was just taken away by the police leaving us stunned and startled on the curb side. The taxi driver was not allowed to be hailed to stop in this area and could only pick up from taxi ranks and the laws were being enforced, with force by guys who could only be described by me as thugs acting thuggishly! These officers did not come across as nice guys, were not customer service friendly, no smiles or courtesy explanation, just functional and physically aggressive in doing their job and this was a truly massive over reaction to a minor taxi driving offence. A new experience for me and this was Beijing where things were done differently, but I was surprised by the show of aggression in a tourist area in the early evening. I will never know if there was something more to this episode.

As an aside it is worth noting that one of the benefits, a significant one, of private KTV rooms was that any alcohol fuelled aggression was naturally contained within and dealt with quietly and out of sight of prying eyes. There were moments when I witnessed minor outbreaks and I was to become aware that there was always a secret back entrance to these places, unseen by the public for removing troublesome folk and indeed to enable folk who should not be there to enter.

Another incident that I had with the police was when an employee who I was insisting on disciplining for a serious offence, dismissing him, decided to issue me personally with a death threat straight to my face, in my office, translated through a stunned and breathless secretary. Having talked to my translator and deputy, they said it was not abnormal as it was not normal to dismiss someone in the old state system, who he had worked for previously before joining our company, and such a response was a face-saving threat. I was not convinced and called the police, who went on to explain the same thing, that this was a normal thing to say in China, but he had no intent on following through! Heck, I wanted this on the record and action taken. They undertook to talk to him, which they did, and promised to put plain-clothed police watch on my apartment for a week. Interestingly I found out later he was quietly given a job in our joint venture state owned company that he previously worked for within a couple of weeks. The benefits of 'relationships.'

There was a strange involvement with the police during the Chinese New Year 2005 that in part was a clear example of relationships. My British colleague's wife and daughter had arrived for their first visit to China, I refer to my diary:

w/c 5ᵗʰ February 2005 - Thursday and the weather theme remains the same, wet, grey, and miserable. I work from home again before hosting a large and important dinner to celebrate the festivities at the prestigious Sun City restaurant for twenty folk – the chairman of our joint venture partner, his son in law, my Scottish colleague, the president and deputy president from an Insurance company and the head of the Jiaxing police department, along with their families, for whom was the first time that we have met an as it turns out was a truly memorable one; maybe for the wrong reasons!

This dinner went well, set in the largest and best room in the place on the top floor. As may have been anticipated the meal had a liquid nature to it, driven by the fact that there were so many people there and the fact that the head of police could drink and wanted to, despite the disapproving looks of his wife. Strangely it wasn't driven by my friend who it seems had already had a lunchtime session, and it showed both in his consumption and his translation ability, which I would best describe as a drifting translation. Anyway, it went well, with my colleague's wife and daughter enjoying the experience and the occasion thoroughly and we all went away happy; me congratulating the police official on how secure Jiaxing is and that there is never any trouble! 'The place is safe'!

I was still happy after paying the bill and catching up my colleague and his family for a last nightcap at a bar. Unfortunately, when getting out of the taxi I somehow caught my feet and fell over myself and out of the car – headfirst. The upshot of this was that I now have some serious grazing on my forehead, resembling the blood birth marks on a former Soviet leader, a heavily bruised hip and elbow......and I know what everyone will think and know that I will get no sympathy! Looking back, the incident must have been a little like the scene in which Dudley Moore fell out of his car in Arthur when the butler opened the door! At least this brought a smile to my face.

And that was one of the better bits of the night. Next my Scottish colleague just disappeared, as he is apt to do after a few drinks, unannounced, back to his rented apartment, which is someway from the city centre and taking with him the only copy of the address written in Chinese for taxi drivers and leaving his wife and daughter. Unfortunately they, inspired and in holiday mood, did not want to go home and I found myself baby-sitting them until a group of American teachers turned up and we drifted around the town in celebratory mood. Then disaster struck, someone stole my colleague's wife's handbag, which is bad enough, except that her husband had insisted that she always carry their daughter's and her passport, as well as just about every other valuable she had brought. Panic and chaos in the bar, where it had been picked up from a barstool! This necessitated the police being called, a trip to a small local police station (including my first ride in a Chinese police car) to cope with all the red tape associated and thankfully along with a young American, who spoke enough Chinese to get us by! There was relatively scant interest from the police interviewer at this festive time initially, until it dawned on me to produce the business card of the head of police for the city explaining that we had just enjoyed dinner with him and his family. That did the job and gained instant reaction, he suddenly shouting for colleagues to join him, and the report was made. Wonderful, we were unable to rouse my Scottish friend by phone, his wife was unsure how to get home and I wasn't wholly sure either, but we eventually grabbed a taxi and pointed the way there, getting to his apartment at about three o'clock and finding my colleague awaking and reality setting into them the implications of losing their passports, confirmed after calling the British Consulate's emergency numbers:

> *They would not be able to go to Shanghai tomorrow for a three-day holiday, as they need their passports to register into hotels.*

> *They would not be able to go home on Monday as planned as they have no passports or exit visas and would not get the latter until next Thursday at the earliest due to all Government departments being shut for the Chinese New Year until then, and then there are no guarantees.*

> *They had lost about US$ 1,000 in cash.*

> *Their two plane tickets were non-refundable or transferable.*

There were two credit cards in there.

Their expensive digital camera with all their Hong Kong and Jiaxing holiday snaps were in it and my colleague hadn't downloaded them yet.

A whole host of other things, including the fact that they may not have renewed their travel insurance policy.

And so on ......the mood got soberer and soberer, and the married couple started sniping at each other. I spent a few hours asleep on their couch before we started chasing everyone in site for help; this is where the value of my close Chinese friend from dinner comes in handy and he responded immediately and positively, mobilizing forces all over the place. He had the delegated unofficial power and authority to do such things.

Red tape is a problem, and the day was spent chasing police reports, walking the streets looking for abandoned handbags, getting all sorts of folk on the case and a lot of frustration as my colleague and his family could not go to Shanghai, which was planned as the high point of his family's holiday. Along the way it materialized that he had not registered his wife and daughter with the local police in Jiaxing, as is the requirement for foreign visitors staying anywhere for over twenty-four hours, and not staying in a hotel, unless they have a Z visa. Whoops! So now they are declared illegal aliens and the police will not give them copies of the reports required by the British Consulate to help them get new passports et al. We all agreed that there was as much chance of getting this stuff back as finding a needle in a haystack.

Now I have no time at all for criminals, especially thieves, but I suddenly feel a little sorry for the poor person who stole the handbag, not knowing that tonight we had dined the top police official in the greater Jiaxing area, a fact they may have noted when opening the handbag and finding his business card inside. This is suddenly a matter of 'face' for the police chief, his professional credibility at stake in the face of the top western guests in his city being first time friends. Someone had now seriously embarrassed him on his patch. I hate to think what went on behind the scenes, but I did pick up from my friend that there was a considerable amount of activity and that the police chief, had taken personal charge of this case. I have to say that I had visions of bamboo shoots under the fingernail jobs going on everywhere around the city (my imagination only), especially as it was also spoiling his Chinese New Year family time.

On Friday afternoon I was at my deputy's home with other work friends with my Scottish colleague, miserable and down on his luck at home in his apartment, when we got a phone call – The handbag had been retrieved with everything in it except for the Chinese cash! Bloody unbelievable. Again, I understand that the police had visited the bar owners' home among other places, I feel a little sorry for the thief, well maybe not, but this is a country where seemingly people are apprehended one day, they tend to be sentenced the next and then executed the day after {my exaggeration, but indicative of processes}, which is normally one day before the formal appeal procedures kick in!! Anyway, my colleague got away with his brood to Shanghai, albeit a little later than expected and his family departed as planned. I never did find out what happened, but the translated word 'mafia' was muttered.

One of the few major incidents that I became aware of was w/c 17th March 2007 – I received a call from a well-connected good friend this evening inviting me insistently for a quiet dinner. He informed me that the popular SOS bar, that I infrequently visited, was now closed as there was a double murder there this past weekend following a fight between two out of town drug dealers over a girl. Drugs was becoming a significant problem in Jiaxing of late. He was giving me a warning to make me aware and for me and other foreigners to remain careful and discrete. This though I believe to be a comparative rarity in Jiaxing.

The police were to modernize big time during the first decade of the century, with their equipment. In my early days, the typical mode of transport was aging motorbikes and sidecars that did not travel so fast but had a gentle impact flashing light and some ineffective siren. These to me were almost comical, a veritable keystone cops' picture if you like, with a motorbike and sidecar with a weak alarm rolling up, slowly. This was certainly to change radically with a brand-new fleet of impressive vehicles, cars, riot vans and motorbikes, replacing the old ones over a noticeably brief period.

I rarely witnessed mass demonstrations, although our joint venture partner, a state-controlled company, had a serious employee problem at one stage when wanting to introduce many changes to modernize. The gates were locked, and mass crowds appeared outside blocking the road, quite excitable at times. The police did not use force to clear them and there was animated ongoing discussions over many days at the gates and beyond before resolution. That all said, despite the disputes, the 'system' kept the factories running, somehow getting goods out and raw materials in via the unattended old canal access and dock, that the masses gathered outside had ignored. The senior management team though took the threats seriously enough to move their families out of their apartments in various large hotels around the counties as a precautionary measure, in some cases for a few weeks.

Where I did see any other demonstrations, they were anti-Japanese ones, Japan an emotive subject given the history of occupation and the atrocities that took place in Nanjing, something that stuck in the national psyche. Japan had become the default setting for international demonstrations and these demonstrations seem to be tolerated for certain lengths of times before breaking up amicably, indeed I suspected they were encouraged; a veritable rent-a-mob with TV cameras in tow to report feelings.

From the 2010's there were larger and extensive uses of CCTV cameras everywhere, as private security, building and factory security, employee monitoring in offices and factories, in the new malls and supermarkets, on motorways, at stations and so on. A huge investment to track the nation as required. I was aware enough to check my office periodically for hidden cameras!

The police and security departments in China are wider ranging in their overall powers and content than many in the West and included also the entry-exit immigration department, passports and visas within their ranks Simply, they do their job and the system works for China.

Chapter 11

Nationalistic Traits and Observations

China has a huge population that has evolved through many dynasties and wars and with the most recent of significance being the Communist Revolution. It has a proud, traditional culture that has developed in its own way demonstrating some genius at times as well as some less impressive moments. Isolated from the rest of the world for so long during the early years of the Communist leadership thereby fixing many traditional thoughts in what is now the older generation, but more recently opening and taking a proactive global leadership role. Accordingly, it has its own traits and view of the world. The Chinese government is communist with its central planning and controls, but in my experience many of its people, especially the younger generations, seem intrinsically capitalistic in their instincts and approaches to life, albeit 'within the system' and the influences of history.

I share selected observations of note:

> Apart from the sheer numbers of people, the first thing that I became aware of is the lack of personal space, and immodesty that went with it. Simplistically I just put this down to having to fight one's way through life, taking advantage of what space is available within its densely packed population. There is often just no physical gap between people at times. I witnessed this daily, whether it be the multitudes of bicycles and motor bikes coexisting somehow without even more accidents, whether it be crowds queuing too closely and getting physical, sitting next to people, whether it be work colleagues leaning over a computer screen – it is all too close.

China accordingly has learnt to successfully manage large numbers of people quite well at events and public places, impressively so, although some of it remains work in progress.

Money – everything is about money and the need to get rich. Money is important everywhere in the world, but coming from a more traditionally affluent society such as the UK with various safety nets in place (The National Health Service, various state benefits and state pensions), we are a little immune to the economic hardships of the real world around us at times. I put this money driven culture in China down to historic poverty, real economic circumstances of much of the nation and a lack of security such as an absence traditionally of pension schemes and money required for medical treatment, but *everything* seems to revolve around money. Every conversation somehow involves money as a default setting.

Traditionally China has been a cash society, although in recent times with modern technology and processes like Alipay, using their mobile phones, watches and of course credit cards, this is changing. It was not uncommon though to witness folks carrying around bags of cash to buy cars, apartments, or houses outright and pay entirely in cash. I witnessed this several times, one time surprisingly I was in an HSBC branch in central Shanghai whereby a middle-aged couple withdrew vast amounts of cash and filled several large grip bags stuffed with wads of cash. It was like witnessing bank robbers from a movie stashing their cash although not dropping any notes. Red envelopes remain in cash!

Ambition – hand in hand with money goes ambition. China is so ambitious at all levels and the opportunities are there in the new China. Ambition is far higher than in the West which for the most through circumstance has become comparatively decadent, 'fat and lazy.' Boundaries to doing things are truly tested and indeed not sure China even sees these boundaries at times, certainly there is lots of blurring around them at times. Anything seems possible!

Tied into money and ambition is the lust for a good education. China is competitive given the numbers of people and apart from guanxi life's progress measures start with school exam results and university placements. Parents and families have made huge personal sacrifices to strive and ensure that their children have a good education to support a good future, with an overseas university education being the goal. Their little Emperors and Empresses will do well academically and all that comes with it!

'Show' – The Chinese love to 'show' that they are doing well, whether it be adorning expensive handbags, watches, fashion brands, expensive cars, new houses, household decoration or increasingly their travel experiences. In the UK we used to refer to this as "nouveau riche." The evolution of their own social media such as Tik Tok has only served to exacerbate this demonstration of show. China now celebrates and follows the cult of celebrity, despite central government's apparent disapproval of this.

The *pace of change* is just incredible, far faster than what I see elsewhere in the western world. Infrastructure, buildings, apartments, shops, technology and so on; everything changes at an incredible rate. China was way behind the world at many levels, it started to catch up, it caught up and changed gear to an exponential rate of change, overtaking the West in many things that it does and is still sprinting! It has rebuilt and recreated itself and now has its eyes cast globally.

Competitiveness and Jealousy – I found China to be both incredibly competitive and jealous. In the West we have the phrase 'keeping up with the Jones's' but that interpretation is nothing compared to China's motivation which is at a different level. The grass is always greener elsewhere no matter how green one's own grass is, and China wants that grass, and whilst there the house as well. The competitiveness is most evident amongst the parents of children and the desire to do well, even with close friends being incredibly competitive, in a supportive sort of way.

'Face'

I must comment upon this. Despite my time in China remains something incredibly difficult to understand and explain.

This was clarified by the famous Chinese writer, Lin Yutang who wrote that '*face cannot be translated or defined*,' but added '*abstract and intangible, it is yet the most delicate standard by which Chinese social intercourse is regulated.*' The closest translations include 'pride, dignity or prestige' but these do not fully cover it.

I was aware of it, aware of some early mistakes and thereafter learnt to try and find diplomatic solutions that did not let anyone, friends, colleagues, customers, suppliers, other contacts, lose face.

A very American Chinese who lived in Hawaii tried to assist me late one night during a visit. He explained that a person's face was so strong that he can never backdown from a position that he has taken, explaining that someone could be in a meeting, knowing 100 per cent that he was wrong on something, but could never admit it and would argue until he was red in the face, knowing that he was wrong and lying, but could never backdown........unless there was a way out of it for him. I took this to heart, trying to recognize the signs and constantly trying to find diplomatic face-saving solutions that enable satisfactory agreement without backing someone into a corner that they could not get out of.

I recall my first management meeting in my first role in 2002, a new concept to the team. After initial introductions, I asked an open question about the business and what was their opinion, trying to make it easy for them to answer. Nothing, no response at all, not in Chinese, not in English. The silence was deafening. I asked again, and again, nothing. I said say something, anything; nothing! After what seemed like 10 minutes of these excruciatingly awkward silences, I ended up saying that we were staying here until somebody said something and that I was not trying to catch anyone out, I just wanted their honest opinions. I said that we would go around the table starting on my left, to the horror of the gent sat to my left. His answer was, 'well what do you think'? And that was the story pretty much as we went around the table. 'We are interested in what you think'? 'We will do what you tell us to do.' Eventually my deputy general manager jumped in with some brief points, followed by one other. Later that afternoon in the privacy of her office, one of the senior managers who spoke excellent English, explained that it was all about face. Everyone was terrified of saying something that I may disagree with, or indeed the deputy may, something from which they may not recover. We got over that hurdle with further explanation over the coming weeks after developing something of a mutual trust or at least understanding, but it was not easy.

At another management meeting we were discussing what was a total lack of discipline on one shift and why the shift manager was not dealing with it and not taking disciplinary action? There was a simple solution, and it was not being implemented, even worse I could not get a reaction from the management team and certainly not an adequate answer as to why we had this situation; more than a little frustrating. The same manager as before took me to one side later to explain again ' is all about face. The shift manager is related to some of his team and lives in the same area as the others, he just cannot discipline them because of face.' 'Also he is in the Party and so the management team must support him.' Even more disheartening was when I asked if this applied to the other shifts and, she replied 'yes'! Goodness! *Supervisors who cannot supervise.*

I recall a discussion with a senior bank official at a time when our company was starting up a new business. A shrewd and affable guy and someone who I considered a friend and had met on numerous occasions. I had met with him three times before on an important subject, with three different translators unusually, and each time he had agreed to provide a $3 million working capital loan in addition to the capital investment loan. This was much needed, in fact desperately needed but had not been provided on the time scale promised, which was essential to the major manufacturing process start up and frankly we did not have any immediate plan B's lined up because this had seemed like a slam dunk certainty because of his prior promises.

At this fourth meeting, he said not only was the money not available, but, and this was the astonishing bit, that he had never agreed to this and never said that he would provide this loan. He was adamant. I was incredulous and frankly under pressure and this challenged my patience, stunned by this. We got into it some more with me very clearly stating that he had said that he would, three times (I had my written personal meeting notes from each meeting in front of me), which was stepping outside of the bounds of diplomacy and, things were now only going in one direction, not a good one. Then we got into it, the bank deputy president and customer service director, also a friend, weighed in hard, '*it must have been the translator's fault*'! All three of them on three differing occasions? It became clear very quickly that they were protecting their boss, passing any blame away from him to the meeting translators even though all three of them had said the same thing, that he had agreed previously.

Although a mess, I realized thereafter that there was a 'face' situation here, he had changed his position but was unable to admit it. In hindsight he was caught by the changing governmental and banking policies that were being applied during this time span. Chinese banking had until that time primarily been heavily reliant upon good relationships with their clients, supplemented by some basic paperwork supporting it, albeit credible paperwork, readily handing out loans. China's banking industry though was professionalizing their banking policies and principles after years of bad loans and some spurious circumstances, introducing stricter credit limits and started using international professional banking ratios to evaluate loan applications. Relationships had a part, but quite correctly these new rules were being strictly applied and it was more than one's career's worth to break them. Under these new schemes, they had concluded that despite a great mutual relationship, that with heavy expenditure on other new ventures around the group in China, that they had loaned us enough, so no working capital loan! For us this was disastrous in terms of timing, but he had no way out given our previous close relationship and what he had previously promised. He was now denying it all, rather than the obvious thing to do, which would have been simply to explain that there had been a profound change in banking policies and as a result he could not forward us any more loans. 'Face'! This sadly was a major breach of trust between us, and face, and new rules, resulted unfortunately in a more distant relationship thereafter. Sad.

Confidentiality

This is quite a simple concept, there is not any confidentiality in China!

Chinese whispers just seem to prevail, with folk talking and talking, communicating perceptions, opinions, and facts, not always correct but the chattering continues, and facts seem to just get out. I was to learn that government and company 'policy' was often allowed to leak out in advance so that everyone could discuss, understand, and get used to the decision made ahead of announcement and implementation.

My first overt experience of this was when I decided by dismiss the factory production manager based upon a long-term review and careful assessment. He was not popular as he was from outside of both the Party system and the local community, so had struggled with the adversity of this and all the lack of cooperation and decision-making overridden by others that went with this. Sad as it was, I decided that he had to go, but had kept this close to my chest.

Late on in the day, just before closing I called the deputy general manager into my office and explained that the next morning at eight thirty, I was going to call the production manager into my office and dismiss him quietly and discretely, he spoke English so there was no need for a translator. I explained that this is highly confidential and that he should not say anything to anyone, and I would get my secretary to call him up to my office tomorrow when I arrive. He agreed and said that he did not want to be part of it, which was fine. I then called in the personal manager and went through the same process with him and re-enforced the need for confidentiality. I note that he and my deputy were both Party members and close, but he agreed and that was that.

The next morning I duly arrived at my office to find the production manager stood outside of my doorway waiting for me, apologizing for the failure of his performance. He knew about his impending dismissal at eight o'clock the night before as did everyone in the factory who were talking about it and the shift supervisor phoned him up at home to rub it in! Turns out that the joint venture partner senior managers knew all about it as well, as did the joint venture partner HR departments and the joint venture partner's Party leaders and his severance package all agreed and buttoned up before I met him! A learning moment in life!

Astonishing! As always it was explained away in this case by my deputy, as 'this is China' or 'this is how we do things in China'! That was to change, at least within our company.

This told me a lot about the system and the culture and how things worked and started to wonder what every else knew about anything.

Salaries and wages information were not confidential either. I was stunned to hear that in the company accounts of a company that the chairman's salary was listed at the same rate as a machine operator, which had obvious tax implications, but also patently was not true. Some though chose to believe it, and everybody knew about it and funds were obviously provided in a separate way

On another occasion a supplier, negotiating hard ball, walked into the offices quoting confidential employee social security information from records stored in government computer records; courtesy of a cousin who worked there in the government's social security department who obviously felt the need to share with his family connections.

I was to discover in my first month at work that everyone in the factory seemed to know my salary!

As for medical confidentiality…………..well.……

Blame Culture - I became aware early on that there was a strong blame culture in China and when someone got blamed watch out. Related to face I reckoned, 'it can't be my fault so let's blame someone else'! Another default setting. Huge issue at times.

'Friends'

In China you cannot get anything done without a friend. A fact and a phrase that I heard continually. This is true, hence the need for guanxi to develop relationship networks for assistance. If you have friends in the right places then you can get anything done and quickly, noting that the law, although evolving, was effectively having a piece of paper with an approval seal stamp on it. Having the person with the power to sign that paper as a friend is more than useful, or failing that, someone who can influence that person or at least get quick access to them.

How you develop that friend is another matter and the options have an obvious theme. If you do not have a friend, even with menial procedures, everything becomes harder work and took longer, bogged down in bureaucracy and sometimes with no result at all. It is the way the society works.

China's views are rapidly and continually changing in everything as public education and its opening up develops at pace.

I recall a conversation with a bank president who joked that in the past that all the rich people were fat, and indeed admired for that (noting that Chairman Mao's pictures were allegedly adjusted to make him look fatter and hence more prosperous), and that thanks to McDonalds and KFC and other fast-food chains it is becoming the poorer people who are fat, noting that the middle classes are becoming more aware of their health, eating and drinking less, going to gyms and getting slimmer.

Perception of other countries and views based upon ongoing feedback:

I long held the view that privately everyone in China wanted to be an American given the rights, freedoms, and lifestyle.

Failing that then Canadian, Australian, a New Zealander or European.

British education is held in high regard, but it is not understood why Western children do not study as hard as Chinese children, and why Western children have so much emphasis on sport, holidays, and general relaxation time.

Admired though for its NHS and other government benefits such as child benefit.

Undoubtedly due to education and lack of exposure issue, but traditionally China was cautious about Africans. This is extraordinary given what is happening now with the huge investments that China is making in Africa, buying commodities whilst providing fundamental infrastructure and wealth to many African countries, effectively colonizing much of Africa through trade in a way that no western country could ever do currently given the history of such activities. This view is changing, and the government is working hard on this historical perception, with more Africans gaining visas to work in China, many as English teachers.

Japan – China hates Japan. Lots of history and the invasions by the Japanese from Manchuria across the country. The pinnacle though in everyone's mind are the Nanjing massacres that were a terrible time in history. The rapes, cruel murders, enforced comfort girls and tortures are long in the memory. It is easy to get Chinese activated in anti-Japanese protests and there were various rent-a-mob type protests Japan over the years, when it suits, although Japan's huge investment is always very welcome.

India – a natural competitor in many ways given its presence in Asia and large populations. There is caution and suspicion, although like every other country there has been Indian investment in China.

I was once at a large trade dinner in a prestige Shanghai hotel, an industry do, and sat on a table with a professional and eloquent internationalized Singaporean Chinese man who had worked in Mumbai for two years before moving to Singapore. He told a traditional Chinese story unsolicited and in genuine seriousness about China's view of the Indian businessman. *"If you are walking along a path in the mountains and come to a fork in the road and are presented with two options. One path takes you down to where there is the deadliest most poisonous snake on the planet with no way around it and certain death if bitten. The other is towards an Indian businessman. Which path option should you take?* After a pause for effect but before an answer could be given, he followed up with *'Go on the path with the snake as the Indian businessman is far more dangerous, untrustworthy, and unpredictable!' Um!* He pointed out that this was profoundly serious and how Chinese think about India. I was to hear this story repeated over the years in various forms.

A separate type of example of perceptions was when an Indian/American colleague was coming to China to travel round for a week and try and open new markets together with a female customer service colleague. A few days before his arrival I was confronted by this genuinely concerned and distressed female sales manager about the visit, exclaiming that *'Indian men are rapists.'* Since discussing this visit privately, she had experienced regular input from her husband, in-laws and friends given all the high-profile reporting of such things occurring in India that had been highlighted in the Chinese media and social media. Obviously, this was not the case and was not to be an issue, but it took a lot of my time trying to settle things down ahead of his visit and understanding how to re-assure her family. I realized though that this perception was the reported narrative in China.

At work in one of our joint ventures were had a professional young Indian national working in a senior position. At a large gathering of Chinese customers at a celebratory dinner he, quite out of character, became incensed, raging, and we had a matter that we had to deal with the next morning away from the glare of our customers. He was adamant that a Chinese general manager had used racists comments against him and the fact that he was Indian. Next morning the anger had not subsided, and he was not accepting that he was an Indian national working in China taking what he considered were racist comments – took a lot of trying to resolve and then not entirely to his satisfaction. Later separate colleagues confirmed there was a degree of anti-Indian sentiment that prevailed in China.

Westerners (Europeans, Americans, Canadians, Australian, New Zealanders et al)

I would have to say that in balance I was treated well with courtesy and respect. Not always the case and even when being treated well there were often differing agendas and outcomes.

I do remember reading about social media reactions to the sexual activity of foreigners with Chinese women that was very emotional at the time and drew angry negativity on the internet.

I also recall walking down a street in Jiaxing with a female colleague once in 2002 or 2003, nothing between us, but at the end of the road she said, *'sometimes Chinese people are not very nice'.* When I enquired further, she would not tell me all the detail, but explained that they were calling her all sorts of names and suggesting that she was a bad woman to be seen walking with a foreigner.

There were times though when tensions and views came to the fore or at least I was made aware of them. Most memorable was in 2004 and I quote from my diary - *at an impromptu karaoke session afterwards with an insurance company leader and a dinner guest of his who turned out to be the head of the local electricity company. He was really drunk and quite obnoxious with it, making it clear that he didn't like westerners – out and out racism – a situation that came genuinely quite close to blows until somebody decided that it is time that he went to another room. This is the first time that I have witnessed this sort of direct racism and Chinese 'old style' cultural thinking, directly to my face and I didn't like it. It is just as well that I hadn't understood the things that he was saying at the time, as although I am not an aggressive person, I would probably have undoubtedly 'planted him' if I had. The translators decided not to translate, the silence really didn't help much. On the way back my translator suggested that he had probably never met a real westerner before and that the drink had brought out the worst in him. No one was impressed with him, especially the fact that he physically hurt one of the waitresses as well. Prat; drunk was not an excuse for this sort of behaviour, and this was by a 'senior guy'! The next day I had a friend on the phone on behalf of our host apologizing for his guest's behaviour which had also upset him considerably and informing me that he was planning to send me flowers as an apology! An hour later, our host phoned me himself, speaking in broken English; yes, he must be embarrassed, a Chinese 'face' issue. Rumour had it that the troublesome gent lost his job over these incidents, although I never bothered to verify.*

Not so much in Jiaxing, but many times around China, especially in northern China, I was aware of the local translators being put in exceedingly tricky situations relative to business matters, the idea being that she should work with them against me and fellow westerners with the calling card *'Remember that you are Chinese First'!* An obvious attempt to influence and intimidate translators who were working on behalf of our company and getting paid to do so.

At a wedding in Jiaxing, my driver was attending (not driving) and got drunk with his friends on baijiu. He had been a trusted colleague of mine throughout and never an apparent issue between us of significance. By chance, also in town and attending was a senior western colleague from the north of China and his female translator. My God, did things kick off with my driver apparently delivering a very vocal nationalistic tirade against her for associating with and working with the foreigners, leaving her hugely distressed. My colleague was stunned but not surprized as he was used to this sort of abuse in his northern province, but I was taken aback that this was my driver, my personal driver who loyally looked after my family when there, but I was never to find out what precipitated the outpouring of his emotions, apart from alcohol consumption, but I became increasingly guarded thereafter.

China has a huge respect for Germany, its engineering and technology, with German engineering and industrial equipment often involved in new investments. These contributions have assisted China is setting up its competitive manufacturing bases. And of course there are those famous German car brands regarded as 'the best.'

China has a 2,000-year-old loose tea drinking culture, green tea, and some yellow tea! Tea is to be appreciated and held in high regard in the psyche. Tea given as a gift was an honour and tea drinking tea shops and ceremonies dominated prior to the explosion of coffee shops.

This did not fit well with our company's plan to manufacture tea bag paper in China. The logic was that as China modernized it would want and would consume everything from the western world driven by the increasing middle classes, the volume of returning students who had lived abroad and the lust for all things western. And boy did they consume, that part of it was right. What did not change was the tea drinking culture, with the thought of drinking tea out of a tea bag being considered low class and disrespectful. Over time the demand grew steadily, especially in hotels, imported teas, black teas though and not the traditional Chinese teas, or used for weight loss tea drinking substances, but much of this was imported. This obvious experience enlightened me to the power of Chinese tradition.

Chinese quality

The Chinese people regard Chinese quality of goods made there as poor and are very highly suspicious of anything made in China! This view remains as the masses 'know something.'

Even if living or traveling overseas, Chinese always check labels in order not to buy anything 'made in China' and are extremely disappointed in themselves if they accidently do buy such products.

This belief remains despite the modernization and huge progress made in respect of quality of goods made in China. This I believe is the culmination of many influences over time:

The old inefficient underfunded state factories with lack of process and labour control and attitude resulting in inferior quality.

China's fascination with low costs, resulting in specifications being implemented, or even if a higher quality was specified originally, then someone somewhere in the company made the unofficial decision quietly to reduce the specification over time to reduce costs.

Outside of China often lower quality was specified by the foreign buyers for costs reasons and when goods performances rapidly deteriorated then reputations developed. I.e. there is a specifying and a short termism issue at times, not a manufacturing one.

None of this helped my cause many years later, when despite having a world class invested process, western standard manufacturing processes and controls, a well-trained workforce, using international leading raw materials, selling tea bag paper internationally, a food use paper globally, which we did successfully, but the perception was always that goods made in China 'must be cheap' even if made with international commodities at same market costs. A challenge that we met through selling to over fifty countries, there was the occasional lapse in quality that could only be put down to 'cultural influences.'

China lusts for foreign brands and goods, the more expensive the better. This is partly because of quality perception, but also due to the huge amount of counterfeit goods being made in China which they look down upon. Then of course there is the prestige of owning overseas goods.

Ownership of foreign goods demonstrated show, face, prestige, quality, and wealth.

Overseas trips usually are accompanied by a burdensome shopping list for friends and family who have given them the money to buy overseas goods from them, whether it be prestige high class goods, western medication or more standard, baby milk powder, after the scandalous outcry relative to the health of babies using domestic baby milk. Anything made overseas is viewed as being better than Chinese goods, usually with historical good reason.

Goods often made by foreign companies in China, even like BMW, were traditionally looked down upon compared to the foreign imported equivalent, for no reason other than the fact that it was made in China.

Chinese, particularly the women, have a very deep fascination of mixed blood children, particularly a western-Chinese baby. The 'Hunxue.' These children always get lots of attention everywhere they go and in many respects, they are put on a pedestal.

China is a proud and ancient culture and increasingly nationalistic as it gains in confidence from its successes and strength. I witnessed this national pride first-hand at the Beijing Olympics, followed by the Shanghai Expo and on many occasions since. At times there is something of a cultural superiority. This confidence continues to grow, a natural feature of its increasing successes and achievements.

Despite the inclusions about great food and restaurants, most Chinese when not entertaining are frugal with what they spend on food and for the most eat cheaply, aware of the need to protect their income for other things in life, such as old age provisions. This is changing with the advent of the wealthier middle classes, but remains a factor.

'*Chinese snubs*' as we know it are very real. I have been on both sides of friendship and the Chinese snub is a very real 'cancel culture' tool. Difficult to find a way back from at times. Irrespective of any face issues, it is darned frustrating and challenging in getting things done!

I had understood that China did not have religion when I went there. That was not right. Buddhism was everywhere pretty much, and the temples rebuilt and expanding - a place to visit on tourist visits and at Chinese New Year, burning scented josh stocks to pray for everything from family to luck and wealth. Christianity is around and in evidence in large cities, but not prevalent. In the West of the country there is a strong Muslim faith and culture, which does not sit well with the Han majority at times. Muslim populations living in many cities is restricted I gather.

China can be critical of itself and privately folk often are, but as a foreigner do not even think about it, one cannot say the same things. National face. Although they can be couched in diplomatic, constructive ways to assist the cause of needed. It is quite possible that some of the contents of this book will not be appreciated.

In day-to-day life the Chinese are very direct, saying things straight out, which can be slightly disarming. Typical among the older and less educated generations. At times there is a definite directness when meeting people, a most disarming example when I first arrived being women telling me directly how handsome I was, which initially I was not sure quite how to take at all. A cultural greeting, not an open invitation.

In factories, health and safety and good housekeeping let us say needed lots of work and instruction as it was not in the DNA traditionally. Procedures and controls are improving fast, but many will have seen the video's circulating on the internet of Chinese safety failures.

I saw lots of bad road traffic accidents on my travels including fatalities. I could never understand why people all seemed to gather around the scene watching and apparently 'smiling,' which I always struggled to get my mind around, but was a constant. A friend explained it as a discomfort reaction, like an awful embarrassment despite the tragedy and hence the smile; odd!

The Chinese can be incredibly strong willed and resourceful in getting what they want. Flexible and prepared to try anything to get what they want. Resourceful, resilient, and determined.

A diary extract - *w/c 2nd May 2009 - I reflect upon life of the Chinese. I heard earlier this week, that the ex-boss of a company contact in Guangdong, ran off four years ago to Australia having sucked US$ 24m out of the business and business associates and simply 'disappeared' with a new identity and fresh passport all pre organized for him and his family who were already there and settled. You hear these stories so many times and thus the government restricts the travel of partners together a lot of the time. There is no doubt though, with a population of over 1.3 billion people and greater travel freedom that more people from China will settle all around the world. Many of the children of middle classes who go abroad to study marry and have families abroad, many escape and emigrate increasingly to Australia, New Zealand, and Canada, but indeed everywhere. This undoubtedly, given the sheer numbers around will have a profound affect upon the demographics of the world over the coming one hundred years as races mix, new communities are formed with differing priorities and cultural practices and so on.*

Chapter 12

My Friendship Award in Beijing, Media, and Others

The Chinese Friendship Gold Medal Award

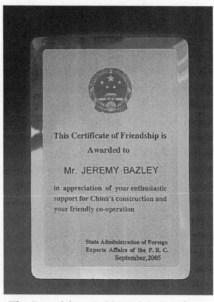

The National Friendship
Gold Medal

The Friendship Gold Medal Certificate

The week commencing 24th September 2005 was a special week in my personal memory and a somewhat heady one. For this I largely refer to my diary notes.

w/c 3rd September 2005 – I was back in the UK and just before I left for a business meeting, I noticed from my mobile phone that overnight I have missed several calls from a good friend who was very senior Foreign Affairs in the Jiaxing government. Having finally taken yet another call, she was very excited and officially informed me that all my friends in government are very excited as I am to be awarded the 'Chinese National Gold Friendship Medal' for 'outstanding contribution to China by a foreigner'! Seems from what she said that this was a top award that can be awarded in China to a foreign national, that I am the only person in the whole of Zhejiang Province to receive this award this year and that the medal will be awarded personally in Beijing by Premier Wen Jia Bao, who coincidentally I was just watching on the News with Prime Minister Tony Blair on his trip to China. I will see how this pans out but I have been invited to Beijing for four days by the State at the end of this month to receive the award. My first thought when the phone call ended was 'did I need to make a speech'? Quietly I am quite excited by this award.

Gradually a little more information emerges about these awards. The awards first started in 1950 by the then Premier Zhu Enlai, Chairman Mao's popular deputy, but unsurprisingly disappeared during the times of the violent sociopolitical purges of the Cultural Revolution (1966 to 1976) and its fall out. These Friendship Awards were then re-established in 1991 and in total there had been about 800 awards made to date in total, with generally about fifty awards made each year, although exceptionally there had been a total of eighty-four made last year including to Nobel Prize winners, ten Brits including the Chairman of BP China and the Chairman of the China Chamber of Commerce. Officially the Friendship Award is awarded by the State Administration of Foreign Expert Affairs 'for outstanding contributions made by foreign experts to the development of Chinese society, economy, technology, science and education'. 'The highest award that China is able to bestow on a foreigner'. It seems that at this time there were 250,000 foreign experts registered in China in 2004, therefore this award represented one in 5,000. It has been suggested that this foreign expert registration has climbed sharply to 400,000 in 2005, but I guess I will have to wait to find out more. Anyway, the awards ceremony and Grand Reception will be held at the Great Hall of the People, Tiananmen Square, Beijing; a rather notable address if there ever was one.

Jesus, this is bigger than I had thought it was! I retreat from the internet and pour myself a small drink after my long day's travels, partly in celebration, partly to help me sleep at this late hour of one o'clock in the morning. I scramble through the drinks cabinet to find a decent malt whisky to sip, eventually downing a Glenkinchie ten-year-old. I reflect that I have been in China three and a half years and have achieved more recognition there than I had managed in my entire prior life in the UK, with these awards reported in the National English-speaking newspaper, the China Daily, on the internet and on National and regional TV channels. Certainly this is not something that I envisaged in my life years ago. Where are people in my life to celebrate these things when I need them? Usually I am stuck in my apartment in China all alone, now I am stuck in my own living room at my home in the UK; all alone!

This is exciting for me, but also exciting for the government of Jiaxing who will be represented and recognized at these national proceedings.

w/c 17ʰ September 2005 – This Saturday night I went alone to the big annual Mid-Autumn Day celebration for foreigners living and working in the greater Jiaxing area, held outside at the top of South Lake, hosted by the city's mayor. I was double booked as I had been asked by our UK principal to go the city of Ningbo to the new University of Nottingham campus there and to meet with John Prescott and his delegation who is there again representing the British government in a follow up to Blair's visit a couple of weeks ago. This was to be high profile, but I declined given the importance of this mid-autumn function and the need to honour the city's kindness.

This is the night of the year in Jiaxing when awards are made and there is entertainment by local musicians and dance troupes as well as caveats from foreigners who are resident in the wider Jiaxing area in celebration of the festival when it is traditional in China for families and friends to get together and to eat 'moon cakes', reminding me that this is the fourth time I have experienced this festival. To my knowledge this is the third such event of its nature held for foreigners, certainly the third that I have been to and seem to recall the comparatively modest first event. It's getting bigger and bigger in stature with every year, with the whole of the Jiaxing government's senior team turning out as politicians anywhere in the world does, especially here in China when an opportune photo call with foreigners. The entire event was as usual being filmed by a battery of TV cameras and press photographers, as well as the home video brigade from various departments of power.

I was seated on the top banquet table in the position of honour next to the mayor, with the visiting mayor of Jiaxing's sister city in Bunbury, Western Australia, sat on the other side of the mayor with his wife. Many awards were made, but this turned out to be a big night for me as they formally announced my National Award and called me onto the stage in front of about 600-700 folk to receive a huge bunch of flowers from the Party Secretary of Jiaxing, officially the top guy in the pecking order of government, a fellow that I had met before, but never had a private dinner with. Great evening and I had a few TV and newspaper interviews to deal with, as well as many old friends traipsing up to the top table to congratulate me during proceedings, reminding me of just how many friends of influence and power that I had here in Jiaxing. In an area that now includes 3.7 million people, walking through the streets home this evening was like walking through a small village, with knowing and smiling faces at every turn. Heady stuff!

Somewhere along the way, probably gleaned from their foreign trips, some government folks seem to have decided that it is appropriate to hug good friends. This is a trend that a good friend started some time ago and he keeps it up. I am not overly comfortable with these male hugs but was entirely appreciative of the hug if not somewhat awkward hug in front of all and sundry at the top table by the good lady from foreign affairs who organized much of this. The hug style and technique seems to be to approach me, throw their head to one side, tuck it under my arm somehow, noting my comparative height, and bear hug me, which is exactly what the deputy mayor repeated when he arrived; now that was embarrassing and left me guessing that he had also had a good dinner before arriving at the event.

Monday just before leave home I am flicking through the channels on my TV and see a slot in the local news from Saturday night's event – a speech from the Party Secretary, my fluent Chinese speaking German friend reciting his rendition of 1,000-year-old Chinese poem in Chinese, then I heard my name "Bay Ze Lei" and there I was, on stage receiving my flowers, smiling, and looking a lot more relaxed and comfortable than I remembered under the bright lights. Then I was being interviewed at the top table, then I was together with the mayor receiving my gift bag of mooncakes and then a wide shot of the table, where the mayor looked tiny sat next to me.

Wednesday morning started with an interview and photo session with the city's newspaper, the Nanhu Evening News, all related to the circumstances of my award. A photocall outside in the baking heat with them encouraging me to move my hands in all sorts of gestures, was followed by a two-hour interview. Apparently, a few other senior folks in the city are being interviewed about me and the article will be front page!

w/c 24ᵗʰ September 2005 -Saturday morning was not a rest day as I am up early and off to Shanghai at the Invitation of the ICBC Bank and their fourth Special Consultants Conference, of which I have been to three, missing last year's as it clashed with my trip to Canada.

This event had simultaneous translation in into English, with similar translations going on for the Japanese who as usual seem to comprise the bulk to the attendees. This year's event was held in the Oriental Riverside Hotel which is a part of the International Convention Centre in Pu Dong, right on the riverbank and with magnificent views over the Bund. I had once planned to stay here, but it never happened and so this is my first visit and was quite impressed. This place has been the venue for many important international events including the IPEC summit a few years ago with George Bush, Chancellor Kohl, Vladimir Putin, Tony Blair etc all attending – thus the excellent and world class conference facilities available.

After a buffet lunch we got down to business and this year the format was different with several guests from various other bodies making speeches, thereby providing some variety. With thirty-six 'special consultants' present, visitors, and bank folk the attendees totaled around seventy or eighty. This was followed by a dinner on the seventh-floor restaurant looking directly out over to the Bund and dinner was great; all very social with some old friends and new ones along the way, some of which will be important contacts such as Jiaxing Customs and Quarantine senior officials. My German friend got totally wasted, pushing things far too far, but it was great because he got targeted and I was very happily relatively ignored and the fact that the bank people are nice and sensible. The gift today was a special local painting that are very popular at present and the first that I have been given, my only decision now is where to put it.

Sunday was also the day that the Jiaxing's Nanhu Evening News Weekly Edition was published and there I was on the front page in full colour, with me looking particularly fat and glad that I had donned a long-sleeved shirt and red striped tie to cover my recently expanded middle a little, although failed to mask my three chins! Awful photo, and why did they use one from that angle? And what was I doing with my hands, well-being expressive I guess as the photographer had asked me to be – distinctly out of the Prince Charles mode, although there the similarity ends. The photo is the main item on the first page along with what appears to be a short article about me below, which seems very short for the two-hour interview that I had, but I realize that Chinese characters take up a lot less space that the English language, although there may be other things about me in the paper, although none are particularly recognizable. So the upshot is that the paper is very similar to say the Mid Devon Gazette or Express and Echo in terms of page size and I guess that the area dedicated to my photo, the article that I recognize and headline takes up about a third of the front page; actually I suspect that the article below is also about me, although from the Chinese characters I don't recognize all of my name written, but suspect that my name is written under my nickname "Lao Bay" meaning 'Old Bei' but in a very respectful way that is very Chinese. Everyone has nicknames in China, and I have verified several times that this is okay. In fact I eventually deduce that the bottom article is also about me so basically, I consume about two thirds of the front cover. The newspaper lady at the stall on the corner near my apartment, who I can honestly say I have never noticed, knew all about it and excitedly summoned me over and showed me the paper, selling me three copies in the process.

Monday and these though are interesting times, and I was interrupted by a procession of employees wandering into my office to show me the newspaper and find lots of smiling faces walking around the factory. I never quite know how people at work react to these awards, sometimes on the one hand pleased to be associated with, but on the other hand I have come to learn that many folks can be less than generous in these situations and then start to moan about their own lot and what's in it for them.

Tuesday morning I set off for Shanghai's Hong Qiao Airport convinced that I have packed for every eventuality. I am told that I will be greeted at the airport and taken by government bus to the International Foreign Experts Hotel, which is a four-star amenity on the fourth outer ring road in Beijing and directly north of the city centre.

Things in my life never seem to happen in halves and before departure to the airport; my secretary asks me if I can go into the factory for some more publicity photographs. It seems that the Company is now seriously being considered for a major award as one of the top investors in Zhejiang province and supported by the Chinese shareholders. Suddenly I feel a little uncomfortable as I know from previous experiences in life just how quickly these things can turn on one; however, let's make the most of it whilst I can!

Hong Qiao Airport is better these days following the upgrade of one of its entrances. However, the loos in the old end are still a dump. After a delayed flight and what seemed like an endless wait to get through Beijing's large airport, I was taken by special taxi, just beating the ring road traffic rush hour to the Beijing Foreign Expert Hotel, which in truth was fine and extremely functional with its apartment's style, but slightly disappointing and very Chinese. I was greeted by a welcoming committee seated at the entrance behind banners and a long table who were to deal with everything and enlighten us, which they did in part, but no name list of award winners, although I did finally get an itinerary. It was at this stage I met Garth from New Zealand who is setting up a business in Guangxi, Guilin to be precise and has been here almost permanently for over two years although has been visiting a lot longer, nearly twenty years, but has had a heavy presence here for the last five or so years. I hooked up with him for the evening discussing life over a buffet meal and an in-house foot massage which demonstrated that this is a very starchy State-run hotel with folk in very starchy which coats. I also met a Professor from Denmark and a French investment guy, Michel, who was a seventy-year-old talker but obviously a successful one who has been employed by the Shandong government to promote external investment in Yantai and in all has been in China for twenty years.

My fifteenth-floor room was a suite-apartment with two TV's, including satellite CNN and BBC as well as kitchen, washing machine, bathroom, broadband, balcony and so on. Just a little drab and unloved that's all and the service there with it generally, which is a shame, but maybe this is the difference between old State-run style Beijing and modern flamboyant Shanghai.

Discussing matters with Garth, I discover that he was a University Professor who has moved into the commercial world; he doesn't mention family, but seems to have discovered a plant in Guangxi, the only place in the world where it can be found that is 400 times sweeter than sugar, but has none of the downsides of sugar, including no calorific value. Accordingly he has bought out the rights, set up a company and is going to produce and market it worldwide with seemingly all the big boys interested to help him make his millions. He was awarded the Provincial Gold Medal by Guangxi last year for his efforts. Whilst awaiting Garth's arrival at dinner I tried to check out the 'list of award winners' from the Chinese hosts. A quick glance concludes that I am the fourth youngest, there being one forty-six years old, one thirty-nine, and one thirty-two-year-old University lecturer whilst conversely there is one eighty-six-year-old and one seventy-seven-year-old! Most though seemed to be in their mid-fifties and early sixty's. The large majority of the fifty award winners, of which only forty-six will be present, will have their wives with them. I talked to Garth about this who had received the same wall of silence, but had challenged as his girlfriend wasn't allowed, but he had wanted his sister, but no, no translators, nothing other than spouse with security reasons being cited. I note that the number of award winners this year are back to fifty after an extraordinarily high eighty-four last year – policy change I am told; they want to keep this a prestigious award! I like that bit. Others seem to include a Ukrainian and a Danish Professor and his wife who lives in Copenhagen and a few Japanese and maybe Korean. I am sure that I will find out more as the week develops, but it must be said that there are a few distinguished looking folks of different nationalities wondering around the place.

Tomorrow, we have a morning's presentation about the Beijing 2008 Olympics, tomorrow afternoon a visit to the Forbidden Place Museum followed by dinner and a visit to the Forbidden City Concert Hall for a Peking Opera. Thursday there is a meeting amongst the Economic and Technological Experts of which I am one before departing to the Great Hall of the people East Hall for the actual Friendship Award ceremony, followed by a reception dinner for the award winners back at the hotel. Friday, we have a look around the Beijing Planning Exhibition Hall before going to the He Bei Hall of the Great Hall of the People to be received by Premier (Prime Minister) Wen Jia Bao for a photo session, followed by a National Day Banquet in the Banqueting Hall of the Great Hall of the People – I just hope that my cold doesn't develop. This could be quite a week if I can stay well enough, with all the talk about bird flu they might not let me attend of I come down sick! It may be small talk among the guests but there is also chat about Hu Jin Tao, the President, being around at some stage; I am more skeptical.

Wednesday, I awake to a miserable grey fogginess that reminds me of a St. Dennis, Cornwall from my childhood, the difference being that my room is overlooking two of those very bland Beijing apartment blocks which are peaking out of the fog towards me and the motionless Beijing traffic filling the fourth ring road below.

Thinking about this event I conclude that it was probably ten years ago I have a similar experience, or rather equivalent type of visit in the UK when I went to Buckingham Palace in London to meet the HM the Queen and HRH the Duke of Edinburgh. The difference being that on that occasion we were collecting a Queens Award for Technological Innovation, whilst this is a more personal award, albeit due to the nature of my job.

This morning's meeting was led by Wang Wei, Party Secretary for Beijing and an Executive Vice President of the fifteen Man Beijing Olympic Organizing Committee who gave a quite excellent presentation about the preparations for the Beijing Olympics. This included such facts as:

> *There will be thirty-seven venues and sixty-three training venues. Of the thirty-seven venues, thirty-one will be in Beijing and six outside: the equestrian in Hong Kong, the sailing in Qingdao and soccer pre-qualifying in four other places including Shanghai.*

> *All construction will be completed by the end of 2007 and there will be forty 'test' events at these venues by the end of 2007.*

> *The cost of staging the event is estimated at circa US$ 2.4 billion.*

> *NBC will contribute US$ 1.4 billion.*

> *There will be twenty-eight sports and > 300 events.*

> *The biggest concern: 'The high expectation both inside and outside of China'!*

I met a few more people this morning by way of introduction, Gilbert, a Belgian who has lived in China for donkey's years and now lives in Beijing where he is advising upon the Olympic Games preparations and strategy. Bob, or more formally Dr. Robert, and wife, an Aussie Professor who is an agricultural specialist working on grassland development and re-habitat of the deserts. The very formal Dr. S. Solomon from Lucknow, India, and his elegant and traditionally attired wife, who is from the Indian Institute for Sugarcane Research and only the second Indian ever to be presented with this award. Then there was a third-generation Japanese American, and his Los Angeles based wife, who are an environmentalist and a teacher up in Ningxia Province, one of the most polluted areas in China, they inform us. After the meeting Garth and I chatted for another hour getting to know each other better and we get on well. Then there was Henry and his wife, Germans from Kunming also involved in Environmental Protection, but whose overseas home is now in the Canary Isles. I note that almost all the other award winners appear to have a lot of letters after their names, with numerous Professors and PhDs spotted and a host of MSc's and the likes.

By afternoon the fog, re smog has not lifted, nor much improvement in the road congestion as we head out to the Palace Museum at the Forbidden City. This is all becoming a little unreal as our five coach convey set off lead by a police car with flashing lights a few hundred yards ahead and a stretch black Mercedes 600 lead car with massive horn and flashing lights; upshot – at every junction, and this is central Beijing, congestion and all, the traffic was stopped to let our motorcade through and twenty minutes later we entered the back entrance to the forbidden city, straight up to the main gates watched by bemused westerners and local sightseers wondering who these VIPs were – yes little old us; everyone in the party was impressed. The Forbidden City was, well the Forbidden City, same one that I have seen twice before, but scrubbed up a little more in places with more being cleaned and repainted ahead of the Olympics and was no less impressive than before, especially as we had electro chip earphones and commentary tracking every step and cutting in with the correct commentary in the right place.

Most impressive though for each of our parties of eleven or twelve, was the four white shirted Imperial Guard bodyguards allocated to each party, one on each corner, looking outwards for anyone who may want to do anything bad to us; now this really did impress us! Along the way I got to chat to a few more new people, namely Haydn and his wife, originally from Adelaide, but resident for the last three years in Wuhan, trying to stop the Han and Yangtze Rivers flooding the place; big project this. Then there was a more elderly Dr. Ramis from Toronto Canada, a volunteer expert who has been assisting the government in China for twenty years on several fronts all over the place, but more latterly up in Inner Mongolia. Also contacted a Japanese expert, Hayashi, but not a clue what he was up to as there was no translation. Another was an American oil man, Michael, and his wife, of a similar age to me and with three children of a similar age, who started life in Texas, but have lived in London for three years, Aberdeen and Calgary for several years before coming to Beijing four years ago to oversee his company's offshore oil drilling operations; bit uptight this gent though – corporate American; end of story! One thing is becoming clear to everyone though – 'This is our fifteen minutes of fame' or at least it feels that way to us. Our convoy made it back to the hotel in only ten minutes, the drivers keen to impress! Sadly the sun never really made it out today!

So after yet another buffet dinner in the hotel it was off in convey again to the Forbidden City Concert Hall for the National Day performance of Peking Opera and the Peking Opera Orchestra. Feeling distinctly rough with my cough and cold I was in no mood for 'strangled cat music' as we have come to describe the whine of Peking Opera singers. That said, this was brilliant, set in a wonderful theatre in Zhongshan Park with a truly wonderful orchestra, accompanied by a Chinese specialist instruments player and singing by Peking Opera singers. Not good for the ears, but this was something else!

Tonight I got chatting to Dr. Olaf from Eindhoven in the Netherlands who input in glass technology has contributed to the company that he was assisting down in Hainan Island for the last seven years to become the world's largest producer of glass; yet another scientist I note, leaving me wondering if I am the only one who isn't? Sadly, the convoy's moved slower tonight, unable to escape the congested Beijing traffic systems.

Thursday I am up early for a meeting with one of the deputy directors of the Foreign Experts Bureau who explained that:

> *Of the registered foreign experts working in China, 28 per cent are Japanese, 15 per cent Korean, 12 per cent American, 6 per cent German, 4 per cent French and then 'the rest' that comprise 34 per cent.*

> *These awards are categorized into International Trade and economic cooperation, senior management and technical, Education and Academic contribution.*

The Friendship Ward is the highest Award that the State can bestow upon a foreigner.

There are fifty awards this year and they hope to limit it to this in future, which given the increasing number of foreign nationals working here, means that this year was the most competitive ever.

China is seeking excellence as the world's largest underdeveloped country, with challenges in its land and water, e.g. 22 per cent of the world's water, but 7 per cent of the world's land area and much of that mountains or flood basins!

There are sixty million handicapped people in China, thirty million very poor 'farmers', half the population still working the land in the countryside with 200 million surplus labour – this presents real governmental issues!

Resources per capita are only 25 per cent of the world average, with 400 of the 600 cities in China suffering a shortage of water, with 110 of these having severe shortages of water. There are similar issues with electricity and so on.

China is seeking sustainable development and needs foreign expertise in which to do this, hence our presence!

We all then had to give short presentations for which none of us were prepared, confirming our views that whilst schedules were well organized, the pre-visit information and subsequent was not good. I had a chance to talk to Jim, a chairman of a large American semiconductor who had flown in overnight, a German forester called Klaus, more research doctors and so on. Positive moment except that the translator seemed to have more trouble understanding my Devonian accent than expected but also French or German English which was a little embarrassing.

After lunch we set off for our presentation ceremony at the East Hall of the Great Hall of the People where we are being presented with our medals by Wu Yi, a lady, and Deputy Premier of China. When talking to Chinese she seems very popular and commands a lot of affection from the people. On the *way there Garth takes a call from the New Zealand Ambassador in Beijing who congratulates him upon his award and invites him to attend a party at the Embassy later tonight. It turns out that many of the others have had similar direct, personal, and unsolicited contact from their respective Embassies or Consulates, particularly Australian, Canadian, German, and French, but oh no, not me, I am British, leaving me wondering a little more about the British policy on China – no wonder we are losing out in trade competition to the Germans, French and the Antipodes! Entering the Great Hall there was this air of exhilaration about entering such a famous building created in the Communist era on the edge of Tiananmen Square. Perhaps a little as expected it was large and a little stark inside although there were some marvelous large wooden carved screens around the place and in the Hall, itself was the large standard red banner proclaiming that this was the awards ceremony for the Foreign Experts, as there always is for such events is China and there are lots of ceremonies in this formal country. Before the ceremony Garth and I decide to visit the gents in a large marble loo overlooking Tiananmen Square and conclude humorously that we are standing in the footsteps where Mao himself had stood many times!*

We are invited to sit in our numbered order at three rows of tables facing the dignitaries with wives (most other wives had been flown in business class by the government for the events) and government facilitators at the back and sides. We were allowed cameras into this event, but there is a battery of photographers and TV cameras. As I am number fifty on the list, I suddenly realize that I will be presented with my award last, which is unusual for me as I am never last for anything and with a surname beginning with 'Ba' at school and elsewhere in life I was often first up or very close to it; this was a strange feeling it itself. Next to me, forty-ninth, appeared the other Brit, young Daniel who came to Hunan Province nearly eleven years ago after graduating and has stayed, teaching English to senior people at the Agricultural University in Changsha and developing a side career as a serious environmentalist the combination of which is why he is here and the youngest ever recipient of the award.

Each row received their awards from different dignitaries, so I was not actually presented with my medal by Wu Yi, but the senior deputy chairman of the People's Political Consultative Conference in China, Bai Li Zhen. In the queue waiting to go up I was trying to work out with my compatriot what

217

order the presenter was presenting the medals in, i.e. what was the routine such as bow, handshake, pose for photo etc. Sadly there was no routine, and I teased my colleague about Rowan Atkinson's Mr. Bean sketch where he met the Queen, bowed at the wrong moment, and laid out the Queen with a head butt! We momentarily had hysterics, but he regained composure enough to get it right, as did I, a handshake, bow for the medal to be fitted, turn, and pose for the camera together with my certificate which is a solid wood book with a metallic certificate attached inside, and another fine and warm handshake as I was the last. Even the Chinese guy attending the line said to me 'They have saved the best for last!'

A photo taken by a fellow attendee of my presentation from distance

The official presentation photo taken at the same instant by Bai Li Zhen, Deputy Chairman of Chinese People's Political Consultative Conference (NPPCC).

Afterwards the elation amongst everyone was incredible with spouses basking in their husband's glory and a chance a milestone in many people's careers and marriages. The high continued all the way back to the hotel especially as the motor convoy seemed to have more zest and sped through the dead traffic. Upon arrival back at the hotel I ended up talking to my father with pure emotion overtaking me for the first time that I can ever remember out of happiness; this is unbelievable. Here I am, grew up in Devon watching the annual May Day Communist Party Marches and tanks going up and down outside of The Great Hall on TV and thirty-five odd years later I am not only inside it but being bestowed the highest honour that the Country, the second biggest economy in the world and the most dynamic, can offer to a foreigner. This suddenly is just all too much for me to cope with, but I felt alone. Poignant moment.

I suddenly start to wonder about anyone knowing about this award and how they would perceive me, for instance I muse that in the USA some folk would probably consider me a dirty Communist sympathizer, assisting another superpower to compete and taking jobs away from the North American populace. Maybe the same in Europe, but the fact is I don't care; let them think what they want. Throughout the day I have met with more of the award winners from Canada, a University Professor from the University of California, another Environmentalist, a German Radio Broadcaster who has helped develop and popularize Beijing Radio over the last eleven years, an elderly lady from Thailand who has had close cultural links with China as well as an even older Swedish Lady, Stephen a senior environmental engineer from Vancouver Island in Canada.

Then it was downstairs in the hotel for a celebration dinner with the Minister responsible for Foreign Experts. In his speech he pointed out that the gold medals are pure gold and worth about US$8,000 each, joking that they had raised the National gold reserves to provide these. We were also presented with other gifts including a wonderful wooden carving of a cockerel, this being the Year of the Chicken. Everyone is just overwhelmed by the degree of attention and support that we are getting and are in party mood, albeit mutedly so. I got to bed late, still shaking my head in disbelief at what has happened these last few days and with more to come tomorrow. Outside of marriage and the births of the kids, this was quite possibly the biggest day of my life; it is a simple as that!

Friday morning and finally the sun is trying to get through although quickly disappeared and we set off for the Beijing Planning Exhibition Hall that is eighteen months old and a copy or at least styled along the Shanghai version. This though was more impressive with 3-D films and a fantastic view of where the city originated, has been, is and where it is going over the next few years up until the Olympics and thereafter. Again, this is simply unbelievable! The ambition in this country will seemingly stop at nothing and the technical skills and foresight amazing. Some of the building designs for the Olympics and CCTV are incredible and will be there for the world to see soon.

We also note that there is a large article about us on the front page of the China Daily although only two of us are mentioned and only one photographed. I learn that the award winners are from twenty-one different countries and that there were thirty-five economic and technology awards and fifteen for culture and education. There have been 850 such awards since 1991. The internet is also starting to clock up articles, although no name lists are given as a matter of Chinese policy which is intriguing to us all. Article is also front page in the Shanghai Daily and there are a few regional articles it seems. The exposure is significant given the vast population of the country and the fact that they read newspapers religiously.

This afternoon was part two of the event, being privately received as a group by Wen Jia Bao, Premier, at the He Bei Hall of the Great Hall of the People for photographs (this time there were no private cameras allowed) then hosted by him along with many others at a State Banquet. Wow! In the photos we all lined up, interestingly, together with spouses on a stand, with senior folk at the front and tiered up thereafter, me ending up in a central position three rows up and a couple places away from Wen. Then Wen Jia Bao, gave us a ten-minute-long speech and sat with us along with other senior Party officials for two official class of 2005 official photographs.

温家宝总理会见2005年度"友谊奖"获奖外国专家合影
2005年9月30日于人民大会堂 大会摄影

The group photo taken with Premier Wen Jia Bao. I am pictured
third row, ninth from right of photo. I recall that I was originally
stood in the second row, two places closer to Wen Jia Bao, just over
his shoulder, but somehow got moved back and out one place by the
photographer's assistances in getting the photographic balance right.

That completed we were ushered through the large and grand red carpeted corridors and stairways into the Banqueting Hall which was enormous and apparently contained 1,600 guests for a National Day dinner, which in the event was somewhat brief, but a wonderful experience. This dinner was also attended by Hu Jin Tao, President, the entire Politburo and all the Ambassadors, Senior Party folk, Military Generals and so on. We were joined on our table by Jean, a delightful diplomat who was the Representative for Haiti in China, which as Haiti has its Chinese Embassy in Taiwan, meant that he is not flavour of the month at these events and thus could not sit with the other Ambassadors and senior diplomats on the table adjoining ours. Still, he was great company, and I couldn't help but mischievously asking about the main industry in Haiti and the state of its tourist industry.

Concluding the week, we headed back to the hotel for several goodbyes, collecting a couple of official photos and tidying up the arrangements for departure, the end of an unbelievable week! I go to bed knackered and with something of an empty feeling and realization that the real-world beckons again. The official 'team' photo, taken by the Xinhua State news agency is good.

October the 1st; this is National Day in China, celebrating the 56th Anniversary of the Communist Revolution and the New China since 1949. This sparks a five-or six-days holiday for many, which often means 'travel' and getting together with families.

It was a fantastic week but also a strange week, but I must put that all behind me now and move on to the next challenge and back to business.

I reflect on a conversation with the Haitian Diplomat last night who noted that generally in that community it is said that the ideal combination for a diplomat is 'An American Salary, an Italian or Japanese wife, and a Chinese cook/servant'. He had an Italian wife, but not the rest we were informed. Nice guy who spoke French, Spanish, Italian fluently, and English although he claimed not, and spoke functional Chinese. These guys seem to have a great lifestyle in the diplomatic core – nice locations, free rent and board, great pensions and mix with power.

Beijing Airport's domestic terminal is a little crowded, perhaps not surprising as it is the National Day Holiday, but acceptable and the terminal is more modern and seems to have more flair and efficiency than Shanghai's which I find a little surprising. The incredible thing is though that they are building better and much bigger terminals adjacent apparently to replace these and which will be opened in 2007 ahead of the Olympics. I saw the model for this new terminal in the Planning Exhibition Hall yesterday and was designed by Sir Norman Foster, the British architect of international acclaim and who has contributed so excellently to global architecture generally. I am informed that he is a past Friendship Award winner, and I start to ponder who else maybe in this category but guess that I will never find out as winner's lists are not published. I am still amazed at the style of buildings being built up here, but this won't really be effective until Beijing rids itself of its air pollution and severe traffic problems, both of which the government are addressing with vigour building new public express transport systems and doing all sorts of things environmentally.

Sunday I can find no mention of me anywhere in the publicity in China with only a select few getting interviewed and a handful of Xinhua news agency photos released mainly related to Beijing related types. I am aware that articles related to the awards have appeared at least in English in the China Daily, Shanghai Daily and Shenzhen Daily and that there are several articles on the internet, which I found by typing in 'friendship foreign experts' into Google. Brief reports were also made on CCTV 1, CCTV 4, CCTV International and the Main Beijing news.

Back in Jiaxing a close government friend gave me a gift in recognition of my award, this time it was a piece glass which looked more like an ashtray, but could be a paper weight, from Liu Li Gong Fang from China's only artistic glass studio.

I recently wrote an article about China for Paper Technology, the UK Paper Industry Technical Association journal that was published in the October edition, titled "China – The New Land of Opportunity"! The result being that I have had a lot of email contacts from lost friends and suppliers who visit China or want to.

I gather that the Mid Devon Gazette have been on the phone, presumably someone has tipped them off regarding my award! Well there you go – a somewhat smaller circulation in the UK than in China.

This though, although, not the end, was the culmination of a succession of prior recognitions within the Chinese guanxi processes and my personal recognition by regional and provincial governments, heavily supported by Jiaxing.

Before this there had been several formal recognitions of my efforts and a few afterwards:

Foreign Expert Award

My first award was a standard recognition as a designated *Foreign Expert*. Many foreigners receive this, a small red book that informed me that I am formally a foreign expert, a recognition of technical collaboration.

In my case somehow, they have extended this to include a three-year residency visa, which would make my life a lot easier and was extremely kind. Again I defer to my diary notes on the occasion.

w/c 13ᵗʰ July 2002 - Tuesday, back to work and reality. I am still as weak as a kitten, sweaty and people are keeping a wide berth from me. My deputy GM produces a nice surprise casually during our multi topic conversation. 'I need your passport'. 'Why?' 'Because the Municipal Jiaxing Government Administration 'Party' is going to increase your Z Visa from one year to three years!' 'Why?' 'Because things here are now far better than they used to be and you are a really good manager, this is good for the future of Jiaxing' 'But I am still on trial?' 'No problem... you will be staying!' 'But what about board approval of my appointment?' 'They will approve it!' 'How do you know?' 'They just will'. 'But my passport expires in February 2004.' 'Give me the passport – It is no problem!' 'Okay, Well thank you'. I take this as an extremely positive Chinese compliment – they are quite a modest people at times (less so at other times), so statements like this are big ones! There is something afoot that I don't understand, and I bet my bosses back in the UK don't know about this, especially as they have the deciding vote, but I reckon that it can only be a good omen.... I hope? It also confirms my views that the rules and regulations out here are rigid and totally unbending under any circumstances whatsoever, until you can find a friend who can fix it for you. Sounds like I had better continue the Chinese lessons. It briefly crosses my mind that a three-year visa may be useful in getting other opportunities out here should I need them, but my mind quickly comes back to the task at hand; more than enough to keep me busy and interested.

w/c 8ᵗʰ August 2002 - Monday and it's back to work with all the associated issues to catch up on. I believe that I have some meeting to attend at some Government building. Later in the morning, as I am catching up, my secretary reminds me that I have a meeting at the Bureau of Public Security together with a few other foreigners. 'Do we know anything more about it?' I asked, 'No' the reply, which I am getting uncomfortably used to. Twenty minutes later a somewhat perturbed secretary reappears. 'This afternoon you have to make a ten-minute speech'. 'To whom?' I ask. 'Jeremy I am very nervous. To several hundred people, the mayor, Zhejiang provincial president, and many other important people from Zhejiang province and Jiaxing and I must translate!' 'And oh yes Jeremy, the television cameras will be there'. I asked again, 'Why is this happening?' 'You are being given an award?' 'For what?'. 'Three years residency certificate'. Okay, so we are back on that track......better get speech writing. I am right back into the swing of things – my deputy GM who I thought that I had arranged an urgent meeting with for this morning is AWOL again and nobody knows where he is; Our overseas mail seems to be going astray, we suspect being intercepted by our joint venture partners; No information is available about anything; and I won't have any time today to revise for my Chinese lesson as I had faithfully promised my teacher last night. But I wouldn't want it easy, would I? I am encouraged by the fact that if I had a week's holiday when I was working in the UK, I would return to a one-foot-tall pile of paperwork and a zillion e-mails; here I have one envelope, three pieces of paper and nine e-mails, four of which are personal – the pressure is devastating! Early days though.

On the way to the Bureau, my secretary casually informs me that I am one of twelve foreigners getting an award, the majority being Japanese or Taiwanese. Because 'so many important people' are there in the audience, the organizer is very nervous about what we (I) may say, and she has apparently been asked to 'control' my speech should I become controversial. However, she has a copy of the draft of my speech and is happy that there will be no problems.

Well that was different! The bureau of public security, or as I was corrected very precisely, the 'Public Security Bureau', turned out to be the bloody police station, albeit a very large up market one, newly built and comparatively palatial in nature. I also understand that the police out here have a much wider scope of responsibility than at home. About 200 people were present and there were about forty awards of varying degrees made, not the twelve that I had expected. I had also understood that all award winners were to make speeches; not true, only three of us, a local Chinese guy who was deputizing for his GM reading verbatim, a Taiwanese guy who was apparently witty but went on too long and me, who was second in proceedings. The other two guys spoke Chinese, so I was the only one with a translator. Now it's funny how things hit you at moments like this, but as I am walking towards the podium, I realize that my secretary is wearing a rather skimpy summer dress – white with pink flowers, lipstick that was close to matching the colour of the ten red national flags behind the podium and high heeled elegant shoes. All very fetching, a different side to her that I have not really seen before (literally!), and far better than the alternative jeans and orange plimsols. However, as we are going up, I realize that this dress is totally transparent, with her wearing blue and white striped knickers and I suspect that there is a possibility of a very skimpy bra — and this is all being filmed for local TV. I wonder what impression that this might give, but quickly return to the case in point — my speech, which was fine and finely translated by my suddenly Californian/ Italian style attired translator. Somehow my speech script managed to resemble a fish and chips wrapper by the time I came to read it, but I survived. Anyway, I am told that it will be on one of Jiaxing's three TV channels tonight. All in all an entertaining afternoon. This was a very formal occasion and typically Chinese — Eight Officials sat in a straight line with microphones facing the audience, big red banners proclaiming something deep and meaningful above them, beautiful bouquets of flowers in front of them, speeches conscientiously read out in monotone fashion and always one of the senior mob with sideburns and brill-creamed back hair, white and off red tie, therefore resembling a Chinese equivalent of a 1970's UK trade Union shop steward.

In 2003 I was awarded the Jiaxing friendship award

*w/c 12th July 2003 - Anyway, the day personally got better, when I am informed that I have won the "South Lake" Friendship Cup, having been entered by Minfeng into a competition with other foreigners who have 'contributed significantly' to the prosperity of Jiaxing. Surprisingly, there are a great many foreigners working and investing in Jiaxing, but most of them are either Japanese, Taiwanese, or Korean, and therefore for some reason they do not appear to carry the prestige and general attraction of westerners. I am honoured by this, but don't know when I get this award, what it is or when I will get it. I am especially humbled as I have only been here fifteen months and I am sure that there are poor fellows out there working far harder than I have and indeed been here much longer; maybe they don't have the same friends as I do. I also understand that I have been nominated for a Zhejiang Provincial 'West Lake' Award for friendship, but I will have to wait to find out about this. Hey ho, my predecessor received this award, but as a leaving reward after seven years. I am just pleased to have been considered for nomination..........
or perhaps they are telling me that it is time that I left! Just as I come to terms with this, my secretary runs in to tell me that this is a false alarm, someone has maybe said something that they shouldn't — the final decision has not yet been*

made and won't be until mid-August. That sounds ominous, someone has made a cock-up somewhere, oh dear, never mind.....................there is always next time! Strange feeling suddenly! Typical Chinese mistake though. As the counter news came through at five o'clock it suddenly seemed to have a major deflating effect, not upon me so much as the folk around, who had got quite excited about it all. As they tend to say out here 'no matter', but the gossip has started now – who is covering up what? Probably will never know. The one thing for sure apparently is that I have at least been nominated for both awards!

In 2003 I was awarded the Zhejiang provincial friendship medal.

w/c 13th September 2003 - Didn't get any better after a major machine breakdown but did improve somewhat when I am informed that I have been awarded the Zhejiang Provincial 'West Lake Friendship Medal' and Cup as a foreigner who has made the biggest contribution to the province in terms of impact. I am informed that this is superior to and more prestigious than Jiaxing's 'South Lake' medal. Makes sense though as the greater Jiaxing has a population of over four million, whilst I really don't know the population of Zhejiang Province, but conservatively it will be at least ten times that; truly conservative. The bad news is that I am due to be awarded it next week in the Provincial Capital city of Hangzhou on twenty-fifth, the day that I am going from Hong Kong to Macao for a day with customers, leaving me with a dilemma – maybe I won't be able to collect it personally. This is a nice touch on the back of my new promotion two days prior, but I could do without all the work problems at present. Maybe I can try for the 'South Lake' award next year.

w/c 27th September 2003 – Tuesday morning and the Jiaxing divisional chief of the foreign affairs office arrived at my office with only a little notice to belatedly award me my medal. I was told to expect to receive four people, one of which would be a reporter from the Nanhu Daily (South Lake Daily Newspaper). In the event at one stage I had fifteen people in my office as the officials were joined by the chairman of our JV partner and the chief executive of the partner Group, all sorts of aides, cameramen with both still and video photography and two journalists. All of this surprised me somewhat and took me a little aback; I am never good at times like this when the spotlight is specifically on me, but I coped, and the presentation of the medal went very well. It is strange that many of the awards I have received during my life have been on behalf of the Company or for winning team events, i.e. basketball. This award was for me personally but was not a comfortable feeling. I am becoming a little frustrated at the lack of facts and information about things in China, in this case my translator had informed me that I had 'won the cup' individually, which was put in traditional Chinese tones of compliments and exaggeration. In truth I was one of thirty-two foreigners to receive the Medal this year; the others being a cross section of Japanese, Taiwanese, Canadian, Americans and of course, Germans, who are dotted all around the province. As always in life, the facts give a more balanced perspective to events.

I reflect that this is the first medal that I have received since my basketball days, the last meaningful one of which was winning the northwest counties championships way back in about 1986 and 1989, I guess. But none of them were like the one that I had hanging around my neck today from a red, white, and blue striped ribbon. The short narrative that came inside the leather medal case stated 'Zhejiang Provincial People's Government issues the West Lake Friendship Award to honour the foreign experts who have made great contributions to the modern construction work of Zhejiang province. The medal contains 3.60 grams of gold with a purity of 99.95 per cent.' The Chinese narrative added that it was 24-carat gold, but I also suspect that the Chinese version may have added 'gold plated'!

The divisional chief added that this award is the highest honour that a province in China can award a foreigner and all the while we are being filmed, interviewed and I am also presented with a 'mock' cracked traditional Chinese tea set and a certificate, nicely bound in red silk. Then it's time for another interview and I am told that a feature on me together with photos will be appearing in the Nanhu Evening News on the eighth of October, the first normal day after the impending holidays, taking yet more photos and extremely curious about the family given the prominence of their photos in my office. There were lots and lots of questions about the gang as they sought to understand lifestyles in the west. Everyone went off happy, leaving me all a little stunned at events, but equally as happy. The only slight disappointment is that the medal case states that this is a 'Fiendship Award' rather than the hopefully intended "Friendship Award"!

During my first few years, as China continued to open and become a little more inclusive, I was invited as the first foreigner to attend the local National Congress meeting in Jiaxing, in a packed newly opened Opera house with all the senior government officials and Party members in attendance. This was considered a great honour and garnered considerable local media publicity at the time. Again, this was one of those privileged moments in life to participate in such a forum, although the poorly anointed government translator for the day quickly gave up and I was to spend much of the morning sat at the front of the balcony, trying to look attentive and smiling for periodic photos and TV shots, as well as glances form attending members.

w/c 15ᵗʰ October 2005 - Wednesday morning I get a call from a great friend at the Jiaxing government who has decided that tomorrow I must go to the Jiaxing TV Centre for an interview. I could honestly do without this but cannot put them off any longer. A lot of life seems media orientated at present as I gather that an article appeared regarding my award this week along with a photo in the local Mid Devon Gazette, and apparently next to an article about Josh Stone buying a house in Culmstock. I also now have two framed photos in my office, one of me receiving the award and one the larger group photograph with Wen Jia Bao, Premier of China. Locally, everyone informs me that I have become very famous, with lots of people knowing me; this fact worries me a little as I value my privacy but suspect that everyone always knows my movements. I also got to finally find out the full name of the gentleman who presented me with the award in Beijing, a certain Bai Li Zhen it seems, who is Deputy Chairman of the Chinese National Political Consultative Committee. As a result of various company press releases, I am also listed on several industry paper websites at present at present, raising my profile within the industry again for the first time in a few years, this being assisted by my article in paper technology about China, which has brought some mixed comments and responses.

Thursday and my day are consumed by the decision by the government foreign affairs department to arrange for me to go to the Jiaxing TV centre to do an interview for what they told me would be ten minutes. No chance.

Having picked up by my friend from the government who is translating for me we went off to the Jiaxing TV Station for what is my first formal interview in a TV studio in front of cameras. I have done several impromptu interviews in external locations and have made a few company videos over the years, but this is another first for me. I have been given six pre-ordained questions the previous day to think about and which my translator had translated for me, but the problem was that for some reason that there were nine questions and she had only translated six of them, including missing out the first two! Luckily this was picked up in the pre-interview 'interview' but didn't help relax me any as the first questions and answers are often the critical ones. Having got that sorted out we went into the studio, sat opposite the female interviewer with her translator sat behind her and my friend behind me. I look around noticing that there are three cameras trained on us, but also noticing the main news desk across the studio and another sports desk alongside it. Anyway the whole thing took about one and a half hours and will be cut and pasted extensively due to all the translation and for any mistakes and I am told will be cut to anywhere between a twenty-minute slot that will be televised next week, and they seemed reasonably pleased at the end of it all, although relieved may be a better sentiment as I am not sure that this interviewer had interviewed a foreigner before. It will be interesting to see the result and I was aware that I was using my hands a lot again.

w/c 29th October 2005 - Monday and today we are having videos being taken of the management team for our company promotional effort which takes up much of the morning and is an unwanted diversion; indeed it was far more than that. A government crew turned up in my office at half past eight saying that they wanted to video me, then proceeded to toast me with ark lights for half an hour before my video statement and then asked why I was so red? Useful afternoon and had another meeting tonight with the head of our joint venture partner; an emergency one, which was a shame as it clashed with the screening of the first half of my TV interview.

I did get home in time for my TV interview at eight thirty which lasted a fraction over ten minutes. One half of me is very disappointed in as much as the fact that I am now overweight and it shows, magnified by the TV cameras and against the slim and heavily made-up female interviewer who looks more attractive on TV than she did in the flesh. Conversely, at least with this set of questions (Why China, views on China, personal security, management style, safety, etc?), I feel that I answered them well and intelligently, avoiding a couple of pitfall questions with 'politician style' holding responses and then answering them in my way. Did look a little startled to start with, but I am actually very pleased with the interview, and they had edited it very well and my Scottish colleague phoned to say that it had come across very well, which pleased me so much that I joined him for a quick drink at Hei Mei Gui, where they inform me that they had all watched my interview in the bar together, obviously not knowing in advance that it was going to be on but catching it by accident. They had left my voice in place, presumably for any English-speaking listeners to hear direct and then added subtitles, unusual in a country where it is typical to talk over and turn down the foreign language, but it allowed my dulcet Devonian tones to come through and added I believe to the impact of the interview; just hope the translations are good! I am fed up with my fat neck and three chins, or no chin, whichever way you look at it. I just hope though tomorrow's questions are answered as well and come across well again. Um? Later my translator cheered me up by saying that I looked awful on the TV, not at all like she knows me in real life; just what I needed to hear!

What I hadn't planned for was that the local news and interview were re-screened at midnight and had given no thought to the fact that most of our local bars had TVs on the local TV Channel. One would never have assumed that they would be watching local news at 00.30 hours, but it seemed that most of them were, and I received phone call after phone call or text messages from a variety of destinations between 00.30 and 00.45 hours; brilliant – how to get back to sleep?

w/c 20ᵗʰ November 2005 - Today a newspaper article appeared about me in the Nanhu Evening news following my interview yesterday with a female news reporter who turned up in our offices demanding a session with me. The article, carried on page three together with a photo was apparently complimentary about me, but seemingly carried some stuff that I didn't say and started off 'He is a tall and handsome Englishman with excellent manners, he even opened the door for me and encouraged me to go first'. My Mum will be pleased! This of course brought a lot of attention at work and hilarity in the sales office where my translator brought me down to earth in front of everyone by saying albeit jokingly, 'but Jeremy we know that you are just old and fat'; it is a good job that I can laugh at myself, whilst my Brit colleague felt that it was sad that a man of my age had taken to placing articles advertising myself in the newspapers, whilst another wondered why I hadn't included my telephone contact number. Like I said, it was better to laugh!

By 2007-2008 my star had faded slightly due to ongoing conflicts with state represented joint venture partners, my weight had increased and there was a need to freshen the foreign profile of Jiaxing. I wasn't therefore chosen to run a section of the Olympic torch carrying in Jiaxing, an honour which went to another foreigner, a newly arrived Swiss gent. This was a slight disappointment but understood at many levels – the city needed a new foreign face and I suspect they would not regard it as good luck if a foreigner dropped dead of a heart attack whilst carrying the Olympic flame, nor attention drawn to one whose company was having some interesting challenges with its local JV! Interestingly though many folks talked to me about this.

15th November 2015 – Ten years after my previous Nanhu Evening News front page appearance, I was to appear again, this time parading with school children at what was considered Jiaxing's premier state school, in a pseudo-Olympics type event around an athletics track. My two daughters were at the school, and I offered an international presence to the event.

Chapter 13

Education

China has a lust for education that few foreigners can start to comprehend, a veritable fanaticism. In truth it is an 'Asian thing,' but in modern China, with all its ambition and developing wealth, education, and all that it includes, seems to be at the top of every middle-class family's priority list, with sacrifices made in many different ways. Never mind the expensive holidays, although that is changing, education and one's child comes first. This is especially pertinent given the effect of the 'one child policy' and whilst that is also changing its effects remain – the entire family focus, of two parents, four grandparents, goes into the upbringing of the single child and with that the focus, resources and pressure that goes with it! This policy has been well documented elsewhere, whereby that child is spoiled, but also pushed and pushed by *Tiger Mums*, often brought up by the grandparents, usually the father's parents, as both parents increasing work to provide more income for the family, or are migrants living elsewhere in the country.

The other practical point is that if the child is successful in life, then they will have high income and the funds to support grandparents in old age, noting the limited pension provisions for the elderly in China. This point in terms of mindset should not be under-estimated as a motivation, again a question of traditional economic circumstance and security.

I was also reminded from time to time of the history of it all and why China focuses on education – many of the parents, but more so the grandparents did not have any, certainly limited high school, or few university opportunities as Mao sent the educated classes off to the fields in the deeply rural provinces. I recall one senior manager in northern China going off on one when I mentioned Chairman Mao and I sat and listened through a translator to a monologue of criticism that stunned me, the first time that I heard overt criticism of Mao, although I was to hear more elsewhere during my time. Cutting through most of it, the main criticism was that all his generation had their education destroyed by Mao's policies, he was from a well to do family and they got moved to work away from their home in the countryside with poor education in the local schools and no chance of a university education as a result, noting that university entrance places were severely curtailed during these times. The comment that 'this lack of education destroyed the lives of a generation' sticks in my mind! Younger, educated Chinese understand that their parents 'don't know so much,' an expression that I regularly heard.

The other big take away that I had was how much respect Chinese society had for its teachers, indeed there was an annual Teachers Day when pupils took in gifts for the teachers in recognition of their gratitude and respect. This though was a big issue for me given the sometimes-indifferent levels of respect in western schooling systems for its educators, with a serious lack of discipline in some schools and classrooms with the teaching profession often mired by political learnings, a lack of educational ambition and awareness of the benefits in comparison. I saw this as an incredibly positive feature of society and started to wonder why more countries did not encourage this recognition and the benefits of discipline and respect in creating a better learning environment, but also carried forward in future life.

In educational issues the 'Tiger Mums' come into their own. Jealousies and competitiveness abound. This of course can happen everywhere, in the West we have the expressions 'keeping up with the Jones", but in China this is taken to the next level, supported by the associated Chinese whispers. I learned to never underestimate the power, resourcefulness, and drive of the Tiger Mum in her efforts to achieve the betterment of her child-children!

Towards the end of my time there my two daughters were in the primary school system, and it was a pressure cooker. Firstly, there is pressure to get into the recognised best schools with the best teachers. In a densely populated situation this is a challenge and a competitive one for limited places. In our cases the girls got into good schools largely as I was a senior foreigner in the city and was well contacted and known. If one does not have the benefits of these circumstances, then frankly greasing of palms takes place off the record, to teachers, head teachers and or educational department officials, higher, anything to secure a place for their sons and daughters. Money solves so many things in China in conjunction with guanxi. I heard stories of lots of money changing hands for a school entry place to be allocated to children at these schools, state schools, lots of money and at times some additional relaxation as well! Then of course there was the times when political pressure was applied, from genuine politicians who were friends of prospective parents.

Once in the school this process continues as parents continue to curry the favour of teachers for their children to give them adequate, indeed preferential attention and treatment and to get good marks. This was important at many levels as class sizes at a good primary school were typically 45-50 pupils, staffed by one senior teacher and a junior assistant teacher. Discipline was good!

The teaching system and exams in China are different and I do not intend to get into this too much. I do know that the many western teachers who came into Chinese schools were privately critical of the Chinese system, insisting that they just learned to reproduce information from memory, and they did not develop problem solving skills through learning to think out of the box for themselves. That, but I know that most Chinese kids were darned good at maths, albeit did not seem to know much about geography or their knowledge of history in China, knowledge as a westerner knows it, was dodgy reflecting their teachings. I do know, despite smug criticism, that many Chinese who go overseas for secondary education often excel at maths or sciences.

Outside of school there are extra lessons to be had and art (drawing), maths, English and Music, the latter being a traditional sign of middle-class success.

The discerning middle-class child, his or her parents often from the countryside, plays music as a sign of status and education. This of course is a cost to this all, but once engaged the practice efforts are long, hard, and demanding. Teachers often engaged through messaged nightly videos at home pushing, monitoring, and challenging every note played, in addition to their normal face to face lessons. This is a sign of status and the piano the ultimate musical tool.

I recall that when my eldest daughter was four years old that my wife came home and said that we needed to buy a piano for her to play on and learn at home, not a keyboard, not a second hand one, a brand-new piano! Accordingly, we became the proud owners on a new Kawai piano, incidentally, bought, delivered, and tuned on the same day, indeed within a few hours, with the delivery lorry and squad of lifters following us home from the music shop and the piano tuner turning up shortly afterwards! Another example of how things work in China. Quick, customer orientated response and service.

That evening I was enjoying a banquet dinner with colleagues and Chinese suppliers, and I told this story, joking at my own situation simulating the ridiculousness of it all. No one else laughed, just the silence of a prolonged awkward pause and I realized that I was onto something. Then my ever-diplomatic Chinese deputy said, 'that's right, I bought a new piano for my daughter when she was four years old'! Thereafter three or four others including our purchasing manager, declared that they did the same. As usual in these situations, I was educated with the phrase that 'this is normal in China' leaving me to humbly laugh off my embarrassment at my lack of prior awareness. It was also nice to know that my wife was not out of step on this issue as I had briefly suspected. Not a cheap option though!

Something else that surprised me was that increasingly young children celebrated 'graduation ceremonies' from their primary schools, adorned and photographed in mortarboards and black gowns, scroll in hand and often wearing bow ties and collar, simulation just like a university graduation. This is all a part of new China and the motivation and incentivization to try harder to succeed.

The English language was necessary for children and is taught at most schools. For most university entrance places a command to a given level of the English language is mandated and I have to say that this policy has been impressive by China as it seeks to develop trade and development throughout the world, noting that the most widely spoken languages globally are English, Mandarin Chinese and Spanish. That said, many kids spend many years learning English and still do not have the confidence or knowledge to speak it well, especially outside of the big cities. Others are mightily impressive, growing up in China without the benefits of travel, but learning English fluently, unfortunately many with an American accent given the learning tapes available. Thus developed an entire industry of private English learning at evening and weekend schools that grew to meet demand, both formal groups and personal 1:1 learning. Hence the demand to recruit armies of foreign English-speaking teachers, often TEFEL trained, to help the children to learn 'real English' and to get a wider cultural experience!

Homework is all a part of the pressure cooker environment and a challenge for the parents to ensure the child gets it all right and completes everything so not to 'lose face.' My girls also played the piano, and I can remember them practicing many an evening, more the rule than exception, to eleven o'clock at night – these were primary school children! The joke in China was 'That's a great school, the parents get lots of homework there'! In part these were pressures applied by the schools to parents to ensure that the schools achieved the grade results necessary to maintain their position in response to government targets and the pressures associated with that.

As I write though I understand that the government has introduced measures to cancel the additional support schooling industry, or certainly to moderate it, as they seek to reduce pressure on children and open different avenues in the best interest of their children's welfare.

All these efforts are to try and ensure their children have a great future, with education viewed as being the key to success in a competitive world.

Sports are not as prevalent in the good schools as compared for instance British independent schools, especially not much team sport. This I am sure will continue to change as football develops and the ever-popular basketball game prevails - the American NBA being the focus of China's sporting ambition. I noted from an early age that certain children of a certain build, for instance gymnastics were streamed within the system and kids pushed to develop prowess young. Often when a child elects a sport, outside of school, they are drilled and drilled through shot/stroke repetition without the ball to get the basics right from the start – Personally witnessed this approach with table tennis, tennis, badminton but also swimming with extensive practice before the kids enter the water.

Joint venture schools with overseas names and education techniques were introduced, lots of Canadian school I noted and a few British Schools such as Dulwich College invested in Shanghai, in part to support the increasing expatriate community, but also the wealthier Chinese who often see these schools as a stepping-stone to further education abroad.

Indeed, this investment was also at university level with Nottingham University opening a campus at Ningbo with the high profile opening by the UK's Labour Deputy Leader, John Prescott, a ceremony that I was privileged to attend. On that note, I had never met John Prescott before, and only imagined the news headlines of a brash inarticulate dour political slugger, on one occasion physically going after someone who threw a rotten tomato at him. Based upon what I saw that day I could not have been more wrong – he was supremely articulate, immaculately turned out in an expensive well-cut suit and his humour and kindness shone through. It reminded me of my days back in the UK visiting the Houses of Parliament on several occasions and coming away with the view that once politicians started talking one could never stop them, whether they were right, wrong, knew what they were talking about or not, they talked. Despite media coverage, these are clever folk and extraordinarily articulate plying their trade.

In the UK look at our universities and independent schools, many with high numbers of Chinese students who are learning and westernizing with the promise of a higher paid job back home when they return home, along with the prestige of it all. They are incentivized to go back, one of the lure's being the chance to gain the precious residency status in Shanghai with a highly paid job, whilst overseas governments have correspondingly tightened their immigration policies. It is the same in many parts of the world – America, Canada, Australia, New Zealand and throughout Europe. For decades, the senior communist party leaders have been quietly sending their children overseas to be educated, thereby setting the trend with this oft expressed example.

The Chinese have ambitions and want the best universities, which is the pure ambition with every Chinese family knowing about Oxford or Cambridge, Harvard, or Stanford. Then they want the best schools to feed them to those universities. That is the dream.

Another motive though is for the children to go overseas and eventually stay overseas in employment and gain local passports – and then the family follow to move to a new life. The children get their residency in a hard-earned way and many parents are now wealthy enough to 'buy residency' visas through investment and house purchases. This is getting harder as international immigration rules tighten, but it is a well-worn and prove past.

I have long held the personal view that many Chinese 'want to be American' lured by the western openness, freedom, and the perceived affluent lifestyle of the rich there. Decadence and the power of celebrity gains increasing following, and attention as China strives to balance this.

Education comes in many forms and one of the policies in the first decade was to encourage state sponsored overseas travel, for enjoyment, for business learning, awareness and understanding, but also to understand knowledge, lifestyles, practices, and culture of the rest of the world. As wealth increased there are increasingly foreign family holidays, usually at much cheaper rates somehow than other international holidays costs. Again, with this an industry developed to coach folk in how to behave and not embarrass themselves abroad, a range of issues, from not clearing one's throat and spitting on the floor to how to use knives and forks, disciplined queuing, littering and so much more. The government planned this overseas travel programme as a part of its education, something that has now gained its own momentum.

The bottom line is that China's massive population is getting educated with increasing momentum supporting the increasing middle-class goals and direction. This knowledge raises the benefits for all parts of society and paves the way for China's future. Again, this policy has been immensely successful in developing global awareness and of course encouraging so many innovative ideas and practices gleaned from these experiences, to be applied back in China, driving new markets and the development of the economy.

In 2006 I had the pleasure of going to the opening ceremony for the University of Nottingham, Ningbo. I refer to my diary notes:

w/c 18ᵗʰ February 2006 – Monday morning and our principal arrives for this week's Nottingham University official Opening Ceremony at its Ningbo Campus as he is on the Board of Governors. He comes with various associated visitors and guests including 'John' who turns out to be John Prescott, deputy leader of the Labour Party and of course Deputy Prime Minister of the United Kingdom. Dinner this evening was in Jiaxing with the Party Secretary, officially higher than the mayor, who surprised me with how much he drank, especially in the presence of his well-educated daughter who had just returned from her degree course in Beijing and surprise, surprise, is looking to take a master's degree in the UK.

Thursday we were off to Ningbo, my first visit there, a progressive city in the south of Zhejiang and about three hours by car; on the way there I am reminded of how hilly west Zhejiang is compared to the Yangtze delta flatlands where I live in Jiaxing. This is a long trip from Shanghai currently, about 4 hours around the top of the estuary on motorways via Hangzhou, but by 2009 there will be the longest road bridge in the world connecting Shanghai and Ningbo, which will shorten the trip to an hour. Ningbo is a city of 5.6 million people and an ancient port in Eastern China as signified by the western cathedral in the city centre off the modern Zhangyi Square, in a very modern and progressive city, mirroring Shanghai in some respects and certainly its coastal location will have exposed it to considerable foreign exposure during its history.

We are staying at the Nan Yuan five-star hotel which is fine and after a banquet lunch in a private room we were dispatched by bus to the University of Nottingham, Ningbo, which is a recreation of the traditional British Trent Building back in Nottingham with newly landscaped surrounds. This was a Sino-British joint venture of considerable esteem, whereby the University of Nottingham has set up this university here, transferring many of its lecturers to the city and all of the lectures, mainly business-related degrees, are given in English, thereby creating a great chance to learn excellent English and its culture more cost effectively, but also for British students to have the experience of studying in China for a while should they want. Anyway, it is the first of its type in China and has a high profile with Tony Blair discussing it during his visit to China on its prime CCTV 1 channel.

This was quite an event, and our principal was in his element as a council member of the governors for many years and one of the few to invite a contingent of Chinese guests, including joint venture partners, bank presidents from Jiaxing and Hangzhou, Party Secretary, the local Tobacco company leader, and government officials responsible for inward investment. Apart from its resident lecturers, the university had flown out sixty of its senior staff along with local press, but the press corps were dominated by the national press traveling with John Prescott as well as a matching Chinese press contingent, making for a large event indeed with cameras and TV cameras everywhere.

I had a great chance to network including a Singaporean Pathologist who had studied in Aberdeen at the same time as me, another gent, Herb, who as a British African was also there in 1980-81, the Chief Executive of the Nottingham city Council, John from Hong Kong who knew a close Vice Chancellor friend of mine and various lecturers.

I also met Sir Colin Campbell, President and Vice Chancellor of the University and the famous Chinese professor Yang Fu Jia, who I once had a dinner with in Shanghai shortly after I arrived here, as well as a host of Brits. The guests of honour where Madame Chen Zi LI a State Councillor, former education Minister and now a Cabinet Member from Beijing. The deputy Minister of Education from Beijing, the Party Secretary from Zhejiang province, and of course the Right Honourable John Prescott, Deputy Prime Minister, and Secretary of State for the UK, who it must be said was a hell of a lot more impressive in real life than he appeared on TV and entertained everyone with a well-constructed and polished speech. I sat six rows behind him as one of the special VIPs along with our company principal and our contingent. After the ceremony there was a tree planting ceremony, then a traditional English tea in the Robin Hood Centre, or at least as close as one is going to get to an English tea set in China, accompanied by some excellent student musicians.

This project had been well supported all along with visitors prior to the opening ceremony including Sir Christopher Hum, UK Ambassador to China, the Lord Mayor of Nottingham, the President of the University Council, James McGreevey, the former Governor of New Jersey, the Deputy Governor of Zhejiang, and the British Council amongst others.

John Prescott's speech, which included some bits of humour that the large British contingent howled at in laughter, but which failed miserably in translation leaving the Chinese wondering what was so funny? A stark reminder of the need for extreme care and attention to translations. The main one was when Prescott said that he had met a group of Chinese students in Beijing, one of whom wanted to be President, another an Actor, with Prescott dryly adding that many people did not know the difference between the two (actors and politicians), at which moment the place fell apart. This was not translated properly and without humour – one does not criticize politicians in China even with a little alacrity – not in public anyway.

More ominously, Madame Chen's speech was good and humourous,

241

but added that there was now real competition between the University of Nottingham in the UK and the one in Ningbo, adding that the Chinese would win! She was not wrong, and the situation is quite worrying as China could indeed dominate everything around the globe; something of which I am increasingly aware!

The Chinese were also in a complaining mood, complaining about the excessive costs had to pay for education fees compared to English kids at English Universities; point made, bullseye! Afterwards I counter this discussion over tea saying that for each Chinese kid, there is a British kid displaced from higher education or the university of their choice and of course that education is indeed also a business – supply and demand! Sometimes here you just must state the facts and put the situation straight; that said the Chinese only ever seem to see it the Chinese way in situations like this!

Education and learning is one thing, but presentation and sociability is another. Chinese children are often quiet and deferential and often their social and inter-personal skills limited. A neighbour's son once approached me to interview him as a practice for his entry interviews to an excellent American University, taking place in Shanghai. I knew this lad, an extremely clever boy, consumed with learning and a hard-working diligent lad. When I asked him the preprepared questions he had given to me to ask him and then to check his responses, it was evident to me quickly that he 'knew everything.' He was brilliant, but he demonstrated no communication skills, no presentation skills, no interpersonal skills, mumbling his answers whilst talking to the floor, walls and ceilings, weak handshake, looking all serious and dour. After a few minutes of this I just stopped him, told him he knew his stuff, but we need to practice different things, he was stunned but being the bright respectful teenager he was he listened and learnt. So as per my coaching, he went out again and tried things differently. He knocked on the door assertively, looked me in the eyes when greeted, shook my hand firmly, smiled and remained engaged throughout the interview, talking directly to me, shoulders back and head up, more relaxed, and open. There you are, perfect. His interview to get into Carnegie Mellon University went well, followed by Stanford I believe, and he was to go on to have a successful career in the USA that befitted him. His interpersonal skills issues though were not isolated and one to be worked upon and with signs of changing as China opened up.

Education, education, education – China is and has been doing a fabulous job in educating its children, but the pressure!

Chapter 14

Buildings, Developments, and Infrastructure

I had been to Manhattan in New York, and I have enjoyed going up many other towers around the world, many prior to my time in China including in Auckland, Sydney, Toronto, Kuala Lumpur, Hong Kong and Singapore, as well as the Empire State Building and the Twin Towers in New York, even the 1960s old GPO Tower in London when younger, but nothing prepared me for the buildings and associated infrastructure that suddenly sprung up all over China.

My hometown of Jiaxing, a small, underdeveloped city, but still it had managed to build a twenty-five-story hotel with a revolving restaurant on top in the middle of the city, something that pre-dated my arrival by about eight years. Not overly stylish in many respects, but certainly impressive compared to its surrounds.

In Shanghai, some of the most magnificent buildings were to be built. The famous Pearl Oriental TV Tower (the one with the 'balls') in Pudong was a great starting place, 468 metres high and completed in 1994 as China set out to turn the swamps of Pudong over the river from the establishment buildings of the Bund, into the "Manhattan" of China and Asia. This was quickly followed by more tall buildings built adjacent in the Lujiazui part of Pudong, the Jin Mao Building, 420.5 metres tall with eighty-eight functional floors plus five more in the spire, completed in 1999 and was the tallest building in China. In 2008 the Shanghai World Financial Centre opened remarkably close by with 121 floors (the bottle opener to some given its shape on top) at 492 metres tall, with a hotel on the 93rd to 79th floors and an observation gallery at 474 metres high, making it the tallest in China and the second highest building in the world. Then in 2015 came the Shanghai Tower (The one with the 'twist'), again built very adjacent at 632 metres tall and with 128-stories.

Its observation deck is at 562 metres in height. This all made for a great tourist visit unless one does not like heights.

Around Shanghai, Pudong's skyline changed with the bank buildings that were built in and around the Lujiazui centre point and tall hotels sprung up. Each tall building in Shanghai seemed to develop its own identity with differing roof tops and increasingly elegant designs, appearing out of the ground which had formerly been low level housing blocks, such as in the old French Concession area. I can recall buying postcards of Shanghai only to find that they were out of date as the skyline had changed so much and so quickly.

The infrastructure to support all this developed, with a wonderful underground system, river tunnels, bridges, and overhead motorways, although the roads suffered the congestion of all big cities. Rail links to the Pudong international airport developed through the maglev (magnetic Levitation) high speed train. Airports were upgraded, new terminals built, and high-speed train lines and trains connected Shanghai to a considerable part of China.

China set itself targets to complete developments ahead of huge global events such as the Beijing Olympics in 2008 which saw the new airport opened there ahead of time and a redeveloped city including the uniquely designed China Central Television (CCTV) building at fifty-one-stories and 234 metres, in the same year. In Shanghai so much infrastructural development went into supporting the Shanghai Expo in 2010. Both prestigious international events fed were fabulously staged and China's confidence and pride as a nation, pseudo 'coming out' events if you like, demonstrating China's progress on a world stage.

Elsewhere in China the Ping An Finance Centre in Shenzhen, Guangdong was completed in 2017 at 599 metres high and 115-story, the second tallest building in China and the fourth tallest worldwide, again with an observation deck at 562 metres high also. This surpassed the Guangzhou Chow Tai Fook Finance Centre, also in Guangdong, which opened in 2016 at 530 metres high.

Beijing opened the China Zun building which was completed in 2018 at 528 metres high with 109 floors (plus eight more below ground).

Tallest buildings it seems is a competitive business, not only within China but with the others around the world.

And so it goes on! Many buildings had lights shows on the outside or changed colours routinely, every design boundary being tested, and I am sure not at low energy consumption costs. Impressive, yes, oh yes.

All over China, taller and taller building were built with international design and architectural inputs, high rise apartments shot up, increasingly stylish in design, albeit with regional influences, landscaped, fenced and with security controls in place. A country connected by great toll roads, high speed trains and airlines operating out of new purpose-built airports and with new fleets of airplanes. Within cities underground and overground train systems moved the people increasing to supplement the plentiful buses around. 'Didi' and Chinese equivalent of Uber taxis expanded quickly. Blink and something changed, indeed many cities became unrecognizable from their former selves, although key reference points such as lakes of historical areas remained, all scrubbed up and modernized for tourist consumption.

Industrial areas were designated or redesignated, far away from residential areas, parkland was developed for improved lifestyle use within its cities, new vast airconditioned shopping and food malls appeared, the fertile banks of lakes and waterways landscaped, and new housing developments came with landscaped gardens surrounds in many cases, sitting in blocks surrounded by landscaped roads.

Villas – separate individual houses, or semi-detached houses, were increasingly built to supply demand from the wealthy middle classes, often in overseas design such as Mediterranean, French, or similar, all within gated communities. The housing boom created so much wealth for individuals and prices continued to climb fast, providing huge and lowly taxed profits upon resale. Friends banded together to buy apartments as investments, often undecorated and unused for years, until the time was right to cash in. In Shanghai, as elsewhere, often at night many high-rise apartment blocks were only partially lit, confirming the lack of residency at that time.

A decade or so before China had built new city and provincial seats of government, new impressive buildings arose out of decaying sites. I am told all these always vastly exceeded their budgets and local 'face' drove design and implementation costs higher and cities and provinces competed to be the most impressive, controversially at times I gather. The same happened with hospitals, police departments, banks, insurance companies, schools, both government and private, entertainment venues, hotels, astounding restaurants and more. These buildings have since blended into the scenery, dwarfed by surrounding developments and seen and solid establishment.

Industry has truly modernized and competitive with innovative technology and new locations and factories. The tourist industry has demanded higher standards and the construction has followed to provide Museums that have shot up recognizing China's history. The entertainment industry demands increasingly to provide its wares to its increasingly wealthy clientele. Designs have become fabulous and impressive – all the time looking for the next 'Sydney Opera House' instant recognition and identity for their own buildings and cities.

Over the last twenty-five years China has rebuilt itself, with more to come as the middle classes grow. The countryside in many places remains comparatively poor, but apart from urbanization, the trickle-down effect is happening, access improves with investments and standards rise through education and informal benchmarking through Chinese whispers in this competitive environment.

This infrastructure has been essential in mobilizing China to achieve its goals.

Chapter 15

Environment

It is evident that China gets lots of criticism in the western media for its environmental performance and its impact upon the world eco systems.

Historically there was much justification for this as coal fired boilers for factories belched emissions into the atmosphere and effluent flowed virtually untreated into the waterways.

What I am aware of at first hand both through observation and being involved in businesses there, is that there have been huge, continued changes and improvements in the approach to the environment throughout my time there.

Conversely to the positive actions taken on environmental issues is the impact of the enormous growth in private car ownership and the middle-class sectors boom, the increased numbers of factories and in road freight to and from ports as China established itself as the factory of the world. These necessitated new roads and the inner cities clogged with traffic.

I was aware right from the start that there was a huge amount of tree planting going on everywhere, laughable compared to small voluntary plantings that I read about back home in the UK. Shanghai has long had tree lined roads, a legacy from the old French Concession that imitated Parisian life in so many ways. As cities developed all over China, they mimicked this lining inner city roads, creating new parklands and so on, but additionally all major new roads on the huge infrastructure spend seemed to be lined with trees of all sizes, often several rows deep. Central reservations on these roads were planned with evergreen box shrubs and more.

China, I note can physically move huge established trees successfully and replant them giving the impression that they have been there a long time, but also often saving the tree from other developments. Teams of men dig out the roots systems of large trees, keeping the key roots and binding them meticulously with rope after watering. These trees are then lifted by cranes onto flatbeds trucks and transported whole to inner city parkland areas where they are transplanted and maintained, hugely different from the old all concrete areas that prevailed under Mao's time I gather. There has been magnificent landscaping and provision of new parks in and around cities.

Huge forests have been planted and developed around China especially on Hainan Island for wood and wood pulp to reduce future requirements of imports. I hear plans and developments to plant the vast countryside as families move off the land and into towns and cities for lifestyle changes. Additionally tree planting as be applied in semi-arid desert lands to prevent erosion and to consolidate the soil thereby reducing dust clouds and increasing the usefulness of the land. Tree planting is only one part of the environmental system but is important, visible and China has been extremely proactive with this.

My belief and understanding is that the central government long planned to close-down and or modernize polluting factories that were clearly not compliant with legislation. As cities developed, factories were relocated out from city centre areas onto designated purpose-built areas and modern factories and processes designed to international specifications of environmental compliance. There was a lot of money involved in this as city centre land commanded high values for future housing and shopping centres, funding factory rebuilds with modern equipment and the processes needed to achieve that. Older and inefficient polluting factories in many cases disappeared at a stroke, often as the result of government led industry culls of non-performing companies.

Fundamentally China was a huge producer of coal that was comparatively cheap and available. The boilers it fed were often outdated and inefficient. Coals mines were often managed locally, unregulated and there were lots of fatalities, routinely reported in the media during the 2000's. Over time these mines were closed and modern, efficient, cleaner mines appearing.

A problem though all-around China was the local relationships between local government and factory leaders with an apparent reticence to close or deal with non-performing plants as local arrangements prevailed. Eventually laws were changed, enforced, and these compliance matters were dealt with directly by central government direct from Beijing, thus unfettered by local relationships, to positive effect. Online emissions monitoring was set up using modern technology and non-compliances rigorously followed up.

It is fair to say that these innovative approaches were needed. In northeast China in the early part of the century I was astounded by the heavy engineering factories up there which resembled dark satanic mills from a horror film. Old industries had moved on, some plants were closed. Chimneys belched smoke into the dust laden atmosphere, and everything appeared grey, simply awful. This was never going to be a quick fix.

In another part of northern China, I was taken to some old factories for sale in rural areas that needed investment and, they had no effluent treatment, discharging untreated effluent into open waterways. If the boiler chimneys had cleaning coal scrubbers on them, they were usually turned off as they cost money to run, if not by day certainly by night. As foreign investors in the country we always made every attempt to comply with legislation but were frustrated by having to compete at times with similar type factories in China who were financially unable or unwilling to comply but were still running and competing with lower costs bases. These were not level playing fields!

All over China during these times the abusers were obvious to me, black smoke filling skies and dirty waterways. That has changed for the most with factory closures, access to global technologies and a cultural mindset change, partly through education, partly legislative enforcement, and partly supportive funding.

Air quality has long been a challenge with senior friends warning me against running or walking in the mornings. China addressed this head on, firstly conducting air quality testing regimes in each city and publishing the results daily in prominent places in newspapers in a sort of league tale approach of offenders. Plans to counter were drawn up. Car sharing schemes were introduced in the big cities and cars number plates monitored with cars only being allowed into cities on alternate days to encourage sharing. This sadly did not always work as Chinese citizens resourcefully continued to find ways around things – in this case simply buying a second car, and often a bigger engine car given China's increased affluence and face, thus compounding the car emissions problem.

A big step-change came with the Beijing Olympics in 2008 that I was privileged to have a chance to see Finals under clear blue skies. Air quality over Beijing improved dramatically as many factories around the capital and surrounding provinces were simply shut down for a prolonged period ruthlessly. Unfortunately, after the Olympics some of these factories restarted and continued to re-offend, but an incredibly considerable progress was made.

Dust from erosion from the desserts of western China that so often blew across the country, has been addressed as the country seeks to avoid lost land from erosion and return to fertile grasslands. Agricultural efficiency to improve soil fertility and increase yields through crop rotation and alternative plantings is in place, increasing domestically produced food and reducing import demand for these basic crops. From the 2010's nationwide educational programmes for all were introduced to reduce food wastage that was creating unnecessary over production, to positive effect.

A great challenge to China was everyone's approach to rubbish and housekeeping. When I first went to China, I thought everywhere in the cities was so clean. It was not until I started my exercise programmes of walking miles of streets early every morning that I realized that there were massive amounts of rubbish dropped just everywhere and that every street seemed to have designated street cleaners sweeping and picking all this stuff up daily. Education was improving on such matters but huge migration of the less educated country folk coming to the cities was exacerbating this as they just discarded everything on the ground where they were or chucked it is a waterway. I was to witness the routine trawling of the waterways to clear discarded waste.

Coal demand for fuel was offset, being replaced by piped gases, newer and cleaner technologies. Nuclear power is in place. In Xinjiang in the west, I witnessed huge windfarms installed in arid deserts lands. Solar panels were in huge demand supplying the new housing project builds and constantly improving technology all over China.

At the time of the Three Gorges project, when the area was dammed, and the gorges flooded there was uproar globally and indeed it was sad to have lost those lovely gorges. The bigger picture though was that it controlled the mass flooding of the Yangtze Delta flatlands of Anhui province where every year lives were lost, farmers crops washed away, and houses destroyed at huge costs. The gorge dam though also provided for hydro-electric power to support the massively increased electricity demands, reduce coal consumption, provide fresh water to so any, as well as controlled irrigation.

These days city lakes have been cleaned up around the country and many ornamental lakes developed, landscaped surrounds and are magnificent features in the community, but much of this is recent mimicking the ancient lakes.

Waste, in the countryside and in cities was traditionally discarded into rivers, canals and ditches that were clogged and filthy, but there has long been an army of folk unofficially recycling the easily recyclable as there was a value in glass bottles, tin cans, cardboard and plastic bottles. It always seemed as if little old ladies scanned everywhere, often emptying public waste bins onto the pavement to retrieve and recycle such items for minimal return, and just leaving the waste on the ground. Of course, in recent years there has been considerable progress with huge recycling infrastructure in place for all main materials, but there remained scope for improvement at the time that I left those shores, with overseas imports of wastepaper and other materials banned, thereby reducing the global carbon footprint but more pertinently focusing the minds on recycling its own domestic waste efficiently. The waterways are now routinely cleaned for the most.

China has a lust for overseas prestige goods, but with increasingly high-quality manufacturing taking place in China to supply the demand of its domestic markets, the need for many of the imported products has reduced the imports and carbon footprints.

A major downside is the enormous number of cars, which have materialized over the last decade, hugely polluting despite cities attempts to control usages. What was very noticeable though during my last visit to China in early 2019 was the sharp increase in electric cars in the system, obviously set to increase further, together with visual evidence of adequate public charging points, pointing the way forward as the technology develops.

In and around cities they have been various transport systems introduced from underground systems to overland trains and trams to counter the increases in cars and to provide quick and efficient movement its people.

Environmental legacies will include the contaminated land of old factories that was often just built over with minimal adequate clearance as well as the burying of massive amounts of un-compostable waste from a huge population.

Importantly the younger generations are proving more educated and with more within urban boundaries, environmental awareness grows and is easier to control as new stricter policies are implemented, controlled and performances improved. The urbanization processes have enhanced the management control of the environmental situation.

Diary extracts from my early days as examples:

w/c 8th February 2003 - Beijing is set to be hit by ten sandstorms this spring according to meteorologists, due to poor vegetation cover and erosion in inland areas. This is a known issue and the sandstorm source control programme officially started in March 2000 with a planned investment of US 6.75 billion. The programme will take ten years and at the end 205,000 square kilometres of desert will have been revegetated. They don't do things in halves around here.

w/c 15th February 2003 –

Forestry revenues in Zhejiang Province have reached an output value of US$ 8.4 billion last year. The province has 60 per cent of its area covered by forest. I have obviously been looking in the wrong places and must get out more; are not any around Jiaxing. It planted over 46,000 new hectares during 2002.

China is now tackling forest diseases head on. Over recent years, bugs have devoured 170 million cubic metres of forest causing US$ 6 billion of economic losses each year. That is a problem! 8.7 million hectors will be infected in 2003 – amazing forecasting ability.

w/c 22nd March 2003 - Shanghai has just committed US$ 6.65 billion to environmental projects in 2003.

China made environmental improvement a high agenda issue.

Chapter 16

Counterfeiting

Intellectual property protection in China was a problem.

Counterfeiting was a huge issue for China, although less overt in my latter years than in the early 2000's. It must have been a lucrative industry, providing illegal market income for many. When I arrived, there was obviously a government tolerance of the blatant piracy of intellectual property over a range of goods that could be bought openly on the streets, in small shops or most high profile of all in Shanghai's counterfeit goods markets, the most notable at the time being the former Xiang Yang market, a 'temporary market', set on land awaiting approval for building development in the prestigious old French Concession area of the city. This market became firmly established as an absolute must for all foreigners travel itineraries to the city – an opportunity to buy many of the world's most famous branded goods cheaply. When one gets their mind around the unacceptable intellectual property ethics of it all, these were great fun to attend, and most foreign tourists had a visit to these markets and local expatriates shopped there routinely. I recall many senior expatriate executives there unashamedly sporting various purchases, often enjoying the sparring of the negotiation as much as actually buying these imitation goods that often were to make great gifts.

In the background was a steady pressure from the WTO, but to no real effect for a long while. It was a lucrative business, and many parties must have benefitted either directly or indirectly. Even after alleged clampdowns started and shops started legitimizing, shops always have a secret cache of goods somewhere in their shop, either above roof panels, hidden wall compartments or a *friend's* nearby storage premises that could be readily accessed for the discerning buyer.

After the Xiang Yang market was closed, the sellers spread around the city to other venues, one of the most obvious being the underground market below the Science and Technology Museum in Pudong. Restrictions were gradually tightened by authorities, but the secret compartments remained in more sophisticated guises.

I first became aware of counterfeit goods almost immediately upon arrival in Jiaxing through a local DVD/CD shop where I could buy the latest Hollywood movies on DVDs in English language, for the most a good copy with a few notable exceptions. Likewise western music CDs, although it was a while before a full range of up-to-date music became available but come it did. I knew that life was changing when the Guns N Roses CDs appeared, being hugely different from Karen Carpenter and the Eagles whose music prevailed for so long!

Wrist watches were a big item available in Shanghai and a sign of the growing sophistication of the counterfeiters. Like everything there were some good copies and not so good ones, with a recognized price differential between the two, but they usually always worked, with the main spoiling issues related ironically to the practical attention to detail related to for example wrist strap pins and the likes. I recall our CEO and a German executive both sporting the same exclusive diving watches in Shanghai, one the proud owner of an expensive original and other an owner of a cheaper, but decent copy. Careful examination confirmed that there was no visual difference, no obvious functional differences, the only difference we assumed being that one would work at two hundred metres below the water level and the other would not! And of course, a huge price differential! All the brands seem to be there – Rolex of course, but also Bvlgari, A. Lance & Sohne and a host of other high profile global brands.

Likewise, there high-profile branded bags and handbags were a popular staple, again the top global brands readily available. Some of these counterfeit bags were obviously copies, small visual examples being poor stitchwork or cheap internal lining material quality, or poor zip quality; others looked good enough to have come out of the backdoor of the same factory that the originals were made in!

Travel suitcases, grip bags and briefcases were all there, again all the leading brands and the trick for many upon arrival at the markets was to first buy one of these bags at a decent price and then promptly fill it with goods to take away, sometimes two bags!

I had always had a reasonable gold pen for business signatures and the likes, often a Parker pen. I had never had a Mont Blanc pen until I came across the counterfeit 'snow-capped' logo pens in Shanghai, wonderful looking pens. These, bought together with their presentation boxes made great gifts and were a regular purchase, much to the understandable chagrin of the Mont Blanc flagship store on a main street nearby.

Branded leather wallets were widely available, as were purses, grip bags, passport covers and cardholders, fancy heavy leather belts with large metal branded buckles, again coming in a range of quality levels that one soon got to know. Leather goods were always extremely popular.

The best silk ties were there, all labelled, the only downside being the occasional 'short ties' as the counterfeiter obviously had not picked its overseas market requirement for longer ties and had made to the shorter domestic sizes. A range of branded cuff links were great!

Branded clothes were around for a good while and excellent they were too with sports shirts, shorts, jeans, outdoor wear, and all but seemed to be one of the first category items to be snuffed out as authorities gradually clamped down. Sunglasses started to appear in large volumes reminding me of USA City experiences with these items, but I never got into those.

In a similar vein was the counterfeit golf market, from the clothing to the clubs themselves. Again, these appeared to come in two categories – incredibly good and a bit dodgy, but it was to become a huge market opportunity. The good sets, copies of all the leading brands, could not really be readily identified as different from the originals, indeed colleagues testified that golf club pros back home in the UK could not tell the difference, either visually or when using them to play. The not so good ones had the occasional issue, like a golf club head falling off at tee-off and cheap zips failing on impressive large pro golf bags but were still very playable with. I was once in Calgary airport awaiting my delayed luggage and got chatting to the Canadian pilots who revealed that on every trip to China, most pilots and their crew bought and brought back into Canada a full set of new golf clubs that they then sold on at considerable profit. I remember the phrase "same all over" to illustrate the scale of it all. I cannot exactly remember prices but seem to remember that a good set and bag costing just over £120 recalling in comparison that I once bought an impressive set of original Taylor Made clubs at the advantageous 40 per cent trade discount price of $3,700.

Early on I invited a visiting Scots colleague who knew Jiaxing well to my apartment and being a Scot I bought in a bottle of whisky. He did not initially comment but eventually declared that it was "fine but does not taste quite like the real thing"! This was my first insight into the counterfeit overseas spirits market and the ¥400 bottles that increasingly appeared in the bars to satisfy the needs of an increasingly aware and demanding public – so much of it copied.

I was to discover that the counterfeit red wine markets were huge with Chinese made red wines being bottled and exact copy exclusive French labels being applied; lucrative, selling for significant sums of money!

I recall a conversation in about 2004 with a very senior official European car producer in China, whose cars were everywhere there especially used for large taxi fleets. I had suggested that apart from new car sales there must have been a very lucrative spare parts business for them given the driving standards, routine accidents, bumps, gouges, and scratches on cars everywhere, pots holes in roads and dusty polluting environments. His response was depressing – there was a huge counterfeit car spare parts market in China, and this counterfeit supply chain had all the replacements spare parts market from bodywork, the engines, upholstery, and glass. And it seemed that despite every effort, at that time, they had been unable to do anything about it despite the laws that prevailed preventing such things.

Computer software copying was rife, endemic, with no licenses purchased, much of which over time became unusable as original suppliers found ways to make systems unworkable which provided challenges with backup systems and CD copies at times. Likewise components parts and consumables such as printer ink cartridges followed in the counterfeiting supply chains.

Cigarettes, a huge source of income for the state monopoly, were counterfeited, some reputably coming in from neighbouring countries.

Very prevalent when I arrived in the country, and very lucrative it was too, but the powers actively pursued this to shut down supply lines and bring revenues back in house.

I am guessing that much of this was tip of the iceberg stuff, but counterfeiting was rife and as a foreign investor, IP was there to be taken.

A diary extract related to news from the China Daily newspaper:

2004 - China has announced that it is making substantial progress with its 'piracy policing policy' in protecting intellectual property rights. Since the inception of a special department 182 illegal DVD and CD producers have been closed and that last year twelve million various illegal products were seized, and 2,542 copyright violators were fined US$ 338,000. Additionally, the were 34,000 cases of copyright infringement and 41,000 suspects arrested; remains a big issue for China though in terms of WTO credibility and its ability to act.

*2004 - I am not normally a shopper in these situations, but today participated, buying imitation and prestigious 'Mont Blanc' pens – eleven of them for a total of ¥100 (£6.67), a couple of branded leather wallets, a couple of branded polo shirts, one 'Polo' and one 'Boss' (¥40 each - £2.66), five long silk ties for ¥50 (£3.33 – that's total, not each) and a pair of canvas 'Columbia' brand knee length trekking shorts for ¥30 (£2). My overseas colleagues tried to clear the place and one even bought a fine fitted suit for ¥490 (£32.66). We all thoroughly enjoyed the negotiations and I discovered that I am now getting recognized by the street traders in certain markets and that I am now on the preferential deal list for taking my 'friends' there. I was also happy later to visit an up-market clothes shop and to see a tie like I had bought earlier.......
for ¥269, that is ¥259 (£17) more than I had paid!*

What I was to discover, was except for certain practical things like DVDs, spirits, wines and car parts as examples, the Chinese people did not want counterfeit branded goods and certainly frowned upon these as gifts, they wanted the real thing and had a negative attitude towards these fake goods, perceiving Chinese quality as being poor. The branded counterfeit market was primarily aimed at foreigners.

What I also noticed was the ingenuity and skills required for certain copies like watches for instance, the skills were there and now they had the technology and knowhow. I always considered how many skilled workers there must have been supplying this counterfeit industry and how these could be used in future legitimate industries.

For the original equipment manufacturers of these goods and brands it was all somewhat tragic and attempts to address it often futile. The World Trade Organization was on their side and pushing for control measures. Every now and again the government made very public statements that it was addressing the issues, but when there were open markets in Shanghai and elsewhere were publicly flouting the intellectual property rights, then one knew that it wasn't being taken seriously. Again though with time and as Chinese started to crack down on corruption and to legitimize its society, much of this industry was eventually sacrificed as it engaged the international community. Purpose served though, wealth created, product knowledge and skills acquired and developed, gradually legitimized.... move on.

Chapter 17

Driving, Cars, Bikes and Roads

This subject was one of the most overt signs of change and development in China.

When I arrived in China there were very few cars around and those were black in colour and always chauffeur driven by a professional driver who often seemed to double up as a confidant, friend and fixer looking after the needs of the official that he drove for. The driver would often be present during confidential phone calls and discussions with any guests in the car. The officials did not ever drive themselves, partly status, partly prohibited by alcohol consumption. The odd car was white in colour, but apart from taxis that was the extent of the colour schemes. I can recall that when I first moved into my apartment, I used to look out of the road below daily at seven-thirty and only my driver would be parked there waiting for me. Within a few months this was up to three cars and within a year or so the road was to be lined with cars, the expansion in car sales was that fast. The black cars were for government officials, including the senior management of the vast departments of state-owned industry, banks, insurance companies and so on. The driver was a trusted, respected, and well-paid position within a company or government department. I was privileged to have a car and driver and my first car was black, my second car a few years later being silver; a sign of the changing times. My driver was a kind and cheerful fellow, a great driver, and despite not speaking English we developed an understanding helped by my basic command of the Chinese language over time. He was to remain my driver throughout my time in Jiaxing, fifteen years, a loyal colleague, who got to know my family and foreign friends, someone who bought my breakfast, lunch and often came in at the start of private dinners and ordered food for friends and me before we developed independence. He drove safely and sensibly and was 'customer friendly,' something that not all drivers were I was to discover.

Traveling around China the driving standards of *professional* drivers was not always so compliant or safe. Indeed, the general standard of driving was simply awful. On a few occasions we found ourselves asking that they slowdown or take care, only to be smiled at and complacently assured that they were very safe drivers!

The roads though were dangerous, the killing fields, and controls were needed. A constructive comment of mine at a government dinner, that China was in danger of killing our children's generation on the roads, was not understandably over welcome but was acknowledged that there was a problem. The government continually strived to improve controls with traffic lights, crossings, speeding controls, fines, drink driving restrictions, elimination of 'false driving licenses,' barriers between bike lane and road, cameras, as well as on central reservations all contributed, supplemented by awareness campaigns, but it was a protracted process that is ongoing.

2005 – a diary note: *In between I find myself pondering some facts from an overseas article that confirmed my fears for road safety in China. China has 2 per cent of the world's car population and 15 per cent of the world's road accidents. The black market for illegal driving licenses is huge and the result is that 680 fatalities are being reported each day; I can believe this, and the situation is getting crazier and crazier each day. No one seems to be able to drive and certainly no one has any driving discipline! Each day I see more and more police at traffic light junctions, and more are wearing seat belts, but persistent offenders seem to be ignored by the law. It is quite simple – no one knows any better!*

By 2019 there were 398 million drivers in China, up from 137 million in 2009 – a 290 per cent increase over ten years. In 2015 China overtook the USA for the highest number of registered drivers, with the vehicle population increasing to 281 million in 2019, driven by the huge increase of private cars in circulation to 154 million. [Ref: Statista].

Taxis in my city, as many others, were green in colour, although purple appeared later, the colours provides a quick visual assessment of the city that the taxi was from and often or dated Volkswagen model or in some cases a French version, made at joint venture factories within China. Counterfeit spare parts market was an enormous industry denting the overseas investor profits.

Most prevalent on the roads when I arrived were push bikes, an awful lot of them, ridden by men and woman without modesty as I was to note during my first summer before shorts wearing became fashionable, with ladies cycling on bikes with short miniskirts in the extreme and saturating summer heat. Bike lanes were provided for on the new roads around the city, essential to try and keep separate from the lorries and cars.

Quite quickly these pushbikes were to upgrade to scooters and then electric bikes. The roads were often chaotic, and I used to liken the masses on bikes, scooters, electric bikes and eventually motorbikes as being like shoals of fish moving past each other in opposite directions. I was amazed at the comparative lack of accidents, although there were many and learnt that, as with walking across roads, to be decisive and just go, so that folk can see where you are going and plan their route for that. Any hesitation or quick change in route inevitably resulted in an accident in a country with one of the highest accident rates globally.

The electric bikes were branded by me as the killers of pedestrians, as you never heard them coming and they were coming at much higher speeds than pushbikes, often beyond the capability of the rider to come to a stop at short notice. I witnessed numerous crashes and near misses and locals became familiar with my Anglo-Saxon observations as a result. Traditionally many Chinese just seem to step out into the roads without consideration, almost deemed a right, which worries me more with the onset of the silent electric cars increasing.

Privately, in my early days, I was to see some very senior officials running around the city at weekends when not on official business, on their scooters, which I always found odd given their status within the community, but needs must.

Around China things varied a little. I recall an early visit to Longyan in Fujian province and discovering that real motorbikes were everywhere, of a type that I had not seen back in Jiaxing. This was known as 'motorbike city' as there was a motorbike factory in the city, its main industry, and motorbikes were the main source of transport. I watched incredulously at the number of people who could get on a bike, at one stage, my record, witnessing five people and a baby on a 125-cc motorbike.

I vowed early on never to attempt to drive in China, but many years later I changed my opinion. Firstly, China drives on the other side of the road to the UK, not an issue for me though as I had driven all over

Europe, USA, and Canada without issue. Then there were the chaotic road systems, which despite improved planning with great big wide roads, did not account for individual's driving tendencies, often migrants from inland China who were shall we say less disciplined in their approach. There was obviously also the issue with alcohol and driving.

There was also the fact that folk were worried about my security and wanted to control my movements suggesting strongly that I should not drive. Then there was the fact that there were no maps and few signs in English and in a pre-satellite navigation environmental this was limiting. I would have had to sit a driving test and at that time there were no written tests in English available and frankly the Chinese government did not want foreigners driving, another complexity. Control and restrict (an unwritten rule).

Then there was the vulnerability of drivers to the 'fake accidents' that were to become all too prevalent in due course, where folk would deliberately throw themselves in front of vehicles, experienced enough not to gets seriously injured but feigning a worse injury than a Spanish soccer player falling after a tackle, showing terrible pain and trauma following a minor tap! They would then just lie there in the middle of the road in front of the vehicle and just not move so that it could not drive away, with gathering masses of people looking to see what happened and the 'injured person' demanding money in cash from the driver, noting in the early days that these cars may not have been insured. These scammers, professional divers feigning accidents knew not to try this on with the professional government drivers who were weary of such folk, careful enough or alternatively were havening none of it. This was to become more prevalent with the increase in the less certain private middle-class drivers. I was warned from the start, when hinting that I may drive, that this would be my biggest challenge as I would be seen as a target and was dissuaded for many years about even considering this option. I did eventually take my driving test and get my Chinese driving license, getting ninety-nine out of one hundred on my computer theory test in English; I will go to my grave never knowing which question I answered incorrectly. I was to drive privately for a few years towards the end of my time there without issue, albeit with frustration.

Trucks were usually overloaded as a norm, vastly overloaded and often unsafe. This was to change within a few years when the government recognizing the dangers with increased freight imposed new truck loading rules – height, width and weight limits, in line with international health and safety standards, and rigidly enforced these rules, although initially all that it did was force the truck to move at night under the cover of darkness when they could continue to flout rules and of course allegedly make payments to escape fines. I became aware of it through business initially when our joint venture partner informed me that our company's freight costs per tonne had just doubled. Not believing this I investigated and found out that it was the truth. Loads of our products effectively halved in size with the associated significant increase in operating transport costs. These rules were implemented on the large toll roads and in developed China, but I was to notice that these were less rigidly applied in inland provinces away from watching eyes, where the flouting of the rules openly continued for some time – another example of China's low costs competitiveness.

Buses in an around cities were good, lots of routes to move the masses and regular, and cheap.

Small trucks and minibuses were much dodgier, often driving by out our town migrants from the countryside who did not recognize city driving rules. In the countryside it was more of a chaotic situation with drivers always assuming they had the right of way and rarely yielding to others.

During my introductory week in Jiaxing I was taken on a local bus and decided that it was not for me, small and overcrowded and I felt like I was in a goldfish bowl, a large foreigner wedged into a small seat. The city bus systems seemed to work well though at very economic rates, moving folk around the city and surrounds.

The newer intercity buses were impressive – modern buses with TV entertainment and loos on board, driven along fast toll roads. Professionally run.

Over time private ownership of cars and private driving was to become the fashionable thing to do by the middle classes. Driven by face and increasing wealth, people bought bigger and bigger vehicles to show off their wealth to their friends and neighbours, and boy were some of these impressive. This brought another raft of issues. Insurance was linked to new car purchases and driving licenses in a way that ensured that new cars were insured. There was not really a suitable leasing market for new cars and despite the prohibitive costs the car manufacturers wanted 100% payment up front. I have no doubt that this will have developed though.

That though did not account for the low-grade second-hand market, where second-hand cars were handed down to friends or family and ownership became less clear. Due to the relative newness of it all an appropriate second-hand car market did not really develop during my time there as people wanted 'new,' but it had to come through evolution as all those new cars aged.

Fuel was always comparatively cheap, unburdened by excessive taxes, this aiding competitiveness and affordability.

Driving tests were initially reputedly taken by drivers on behalf of senior company officials, in return for a certain payment. Medical conditions were ignored and in many cases test passes were falsified in return for a payment. Many driving licenses were 'paid for' and the standards of many was not acceptable.

My driving test as per my diary, noting that I only had to take a theory test, in English, as I already had a valid UK driving license:

w/c 27ᵗʰ August 2009 - Thursday and I still have not started learning my two hundred or so questions and answers from the 'Science Guide to Zhejiang Motor Vehicle Drivers' (which I note is also in French, Russian, German, Spanish, Arabic and what I am guessing is Korean and Japanese) for my written driving test tomorrow morning. This is also a Chinese type test, whereby it is multiple choice, and they tell you the precise question and answers beforehand; one just must learn them. The problem is that some of the translation is not good, and I am struggling to understand.

I later find myself laughing at the questions in the highway code examination examples – this could not be more divorced from reality. Laughable! The rules are generally very good and practical – the reality, as so often in China, is that no one takes any notice of the rules!

It has been years since I have taken a test of any sorts, I have a strange feeling, and I frankly don't want to be taking many more, but I was relaxed when I arrived at the Driving Test Centre at nine o'clock, as I was confident from my practice sessions yesterday. I had to wait for nearly an hour, for an overweight young Japanese guy to get off the computer, loaded with the English language questions on it. My driver and temporary secretary were in attendance waiting nearby and he indicated that he took the maximum forty-five minutes and got 91 per cent, thereby just passing the pass mark of 90 per cent. Most people seem to pass with about 91 per cent or 90 per cent, often after 'retaking'.

As I entered the room, from which my team viewed me through the window, I could tell that they had some concerns, but in the event, I took just fifteen minutes to answer the 100 questions and got 99 per cent pass, 99 out of 100 correct. The sad thing is that I will never know what question I got wrong? It maybe that I inadvertently skipped a question by entering twice; I will never know, but it is not important in life. I am though reminded back to examinations at Robert Gordon's and for my Management Diploma from Plymouth Polytechnic, whereby I worked based on not dropping any marks at all and hence I suppose the reason that I gained distinctions. Anyway I now have an official Chinese driving license, valid for six years until September 2015! Another milestone in life and something else knocked off the long list of things to do.

w/c 19ᵗʰ December 2009 - My newfound driving experiences are interesting to say the least. I confirm that most people should have no right to be driving; stopping at red lights seems arbitrarily optional; no one is ever in the correct lane for where they are going next and vehicles coming out from the right never stop and hurtle out like a missile. Still I was prepared for all of this and seem to be coping, although not for the unexpected potholes that appear even in brand new roads.

w/c 2ⁿᵈ January 2010 - China is developing a huge car problem, not only are car sales visibly increasing daily with the associated road chaos, but the driving standards are also hopeless, often lethally dangerous. Another issue though is that of car parking facilities and discipline, with people parking anywhere, just like they used to park their bikes and the results are absolute chaos, especially in residential areas, where the parking spaces costs money and no disciplined management is applied; this will raise my blood pressure, especially since there always seem to be cars parked in front of my garage doors preventing either entry or exit.

New housing areas had vast underground parking places that had to be purchased, but these often remained empty for this reason and above ground the parking was a mess.

Sadly, the older style bike tricycles were to die out as their use became restricted in the modern cities. These were cheap and effective, but less regulated and dangerous at times, but great fun at times, convenient, available, but less appropriate as the sizes of cities grew rapidly and folk lived further away from city centres. Also they were not too safe.

So, China changed, from a bike society to a car driving society and a big car driving society at that supplemented by huge volumes of freight transportation given their success as the world's factory. The consequence is that much of the positive environmental actions were directly offset by this explosion in traffic on the roads that choked cities and in not the most fuel-efficient vehicles, whether it be the new large engine variety or the old poorly maintained vehicles. China was though quick to recognize the benefits of electric car technology and is working hard to develop that industry. During a visit to China in early 2019 the rapid increase in electric cars on the roads was very apparent, the cars being very noticeable as they carrier special number plates.

Chapter 18

Hospitals, Medical Attention and SARS

China, surprisingly given its political system, does not have an equivalent of the UK's National Health Service with free treatment and subsidized drugs. Everything must be paid for.

Like everything else China has rebuilt its hospitals in recent years, modern buildings with modern facilities and improving services, it was not always that way. The cream of course being the inflated cost, medical insurance based, private hospitals in big cities like Shanghai that cater for the foreigners and the wealthy.

My first impressions of hospitals in Jiaxing were that they were filthy and there was more than a distinct lack of hygiene. Walls were filthy, doctors' offices and treatment rooms were poorly lit, paint flaking off, decaying, and crumbling. The walls, like the factories, were painted in a darkened blue colour from the ground up to about a metre in height to try and mask the dirt and grime on them, with 'white' walls above this; it did not work. The walls were simply filthy, brown stained not unalike a breeze blocked cow shed; horrible and didn't look like they had been cleaned anytime recently, noting again the absence of suitable cleaning degreasing fluids that were generally unavailable at that time.

The cause of the dirt and grime were the masses of people who entered the hospitals, many straight from the countryside or migrant workers, often in construction, the sheer numbers all pushing and vying for position in the hospital, all going in a differing direction with pieces of paper in their hands in an environment where there was a lack of obvious organization. Overcrowded, people brushing past each other, pushing, and shoving in the heat of humanity – an obvious environment for disease transmission to my non-medically trained eyes. That was what I walked into in Jiaxing 2002. Hangzhou, the provincial capital was ahead of Jiaxing in terms of general development, but at that time its hospitals still exhibited many of the same traits.

The doctors white lab coats, mandatory wear, seemed always worn through overuse and over washing, often with holes developing in threadbare patches, more often just dirty having not been washed, in some cases in a while, not assisting credibility. China's doctors, certainly at that time, did not appear to me to be held in such high regard by society as their western counterparts, a surprise, certainly not regarded as such a professional profession if you like. Comments from colleagues suggested that 'it was just a normal job' confirmed this. There also seemed to be lots of trained doctors, a point brought home to me when the government mobilized its military medical corps during the SARS crisis to staff toll booth check points and to provide additional checks.

I used to wonder what diseases that I may catch during my hospital visits, always accompanied by a translator who navigated me through the system. In some cases, I was to get accelerated access to a doctor by virtue of the fact that I was a foreigner, in other cases I waited like everyone else. As I was a foreigner, I always got lots of attention from the surrounding masses, many of whom would not have seen a real live foreigner up close before.

Personal medical confidentiality was non-existent, usually with many people present in the doctor's offices and surgeries at the same time, all hearing the conversations about other people's medical problems, often commenting on the diagnosis, and contributing to the conversation with doctors often talking to other patients about what was wrong with the patient he was examining at that time; unreal. In my case my translator had to fend off questions about my background and what was wrong with me? Others around listening to the doctor examine and question me along with the associated conversation, then looking openly over the doctor's shoulder to read his written notes or case notes. I was extremely glad that I did not contract anything of a personal or embarrassing nature! People talked and quickly everyone along the loosely defined queues lining the corridors knew what was wrong with me. Uncomfortable – a celeb by default at ones most private and intimate moments. A constant reminder of China's lack of modesty.

Our joint venture partner, traditionally being a large state-owned employer, had its own hospital. Functional and accessible it was, but the doctors consulting rooms were basic concrete construction, dirty paint flaking walls and contain aging wooden furniture that never looked like it had been cleaned and the doctor often smoking in the room. I could imagine that after a visit that within a short while that most of the 5,000 folk workforce would know that I had visited and what was wrong with me. A few times I was fortunate to be sent to the main private hospital 'house' which had private rooms for the treatment of the senior management team and in fairness that was much better; an early insight into the system differences.

The medication prescribed was modernizing, but untrusted by many, not aided by a high-profile public scandals whereby a leading drug company was prosecuted for supplying effectively placebos for treatment, tablets without medical ingredients in them, wholly unethically profiteering from the hopeful masses buying them. I cannot recall, but I recall drastic sentencing and a consequence for the drug company leaders involved as a deterrent to others!

The most common reason for hospital visits were for treatment for the common cold, of which there are lots and lots in China at certain times of the year. In the West I was used to popping a few tablets for congestion, throat, and headaches (such as paracetamol) and getting on with life as best I could. Not in China. Here people went to the hospital for a 'drip' treatment for the common cold, masses of people all lined up near each other affixed to a drip, some mobile, some fixed. An excellent breeding ground for bugs transmission I mused, but this was what folk did. A waste of an hour or two of either work time or personal time, but this was the norm and often repeated for several days in a row! Employees with colds seem to simply disappear with this genuine excuse for treatment.

Medication though was increasingly westernized with traces of traditional Chinese medical thinking involved. A translator once straight-faced examined that once a doctor prescribed the eating of 'rat,' yes, rat, to make her ailment better. I cannot recall what for as she lost me at rat.

Not all my local treatments were entirely comfortable, apart from the obvious modesty issues.

Another time I had to have a routine HIV test for western insurance purposes and decided to have it done in Jiaxing to save approximately five hours of traveling to and from Shanghai for the pleasure. Accordingly, as per system requirements I had to go to a non-descript facility, just off the main street, to go for an HIV test, something that had only really started gaining awareness in China, at least openly. The consequence was that I found myself attending the equivalent of the STD (Sexually transmitted disease) clinic in the city for testing, despite not having one! Uncomfortable does not come near describing my feelings. I recall entering and sitting there with all these men and my equally, if not more so, uncomfortable female translator, awaiting my blood removal for an HIV test. This was in the midst frankly of the great unwashed, and I could not think that Chinese senior management would be in such a place. All sorts of folk in dirty clothing, many obviously migrant construction workers, all looking at me and all talking, speculating! My abiding memory were the trays of multicoloured urine samples in test tubes lined up in racks on top of a table at the front that men coming out of the loo placed their samples in to for testing. Again, no modesty and there for all to see. I recall thinking that if some of these folks had been horses, they would have been put down. This openness of test tube urine sample storage in public though was commonplace in its hospitals testing areas I had come to know.

One time my then wife had to go for medical tests for her visa, involving a series of basic checks and tests. This included a standard eye test and when asked to read the letters ahead she did and did so well. Her eyesight was ticked off as excellent. The fact is though that no one had considered that she was wearing contact lenses, which she was, and which were not prevalent in China at that time, so technically she passed her eye test with flying colours, the reality is that without the lenses her eyesight was comparatively poor, but box ticked, let us move on.

The modern China uses its advantages in many ways and one of the most impressive is its immunization programme for children from birth, rigorously ensuring that children get the necessary immunizations as required through to adulthood, text messenging parents calling for their next jab to ensure protection to its masses. The system seemed to work very well. The child vaccination programme that developed was in my experience excellent.

The medical system is still open to corruptive influences. If an expectant mother wanted to deliver her baby by caesarean section, not for obvious medical reasons, then that is of course an option, it is a question of how much that the mother wanted to pay the doctor for the privilege, in cash of course. I hesitate to think what other medical treatment privileges could be gained in such ways.

I learned in time that apart from extremely basic ailments, to use my medical insurance and travel to Shanghai to the modern westernized facilities there, often staffed by Chinese American and European doctors and the likes working out of world class facilities and back-up in often joint venture hospitals. A stark contrast to the local hospitals.

Over time the old hospital facilities started to improve as the country benchmarked its standards against overseas equivalents. They often developed a separate wing for overseas visitors and VIPs, started to improve cleanliness and certainly queuing arrangements, privacy, and orderliness.

China was getting itself organized though, investing in new purpose-built hospitals and new facilities addressing all the historic limitations. New locations, large car parks, professional queuing systems, computerized systems, cleanly decorated with routine and adequate cleaning procedures, new equipment such as CT scanners and so on. Professionally attired, English speaking and younger doctors appeared. China flipped old for new quickly, mirroring the rest of its society.

I did find it strange at the start the practices in China of people going into hospital 'to find the best doctor,' a phrase I had not heard before. Folk put a lot of effort into finding the 'best doctor' for treatment and in Jiaxing I often heard 'he is the best doctor; he is from Shanghai'! I once asked a friend whether securing such an audition with these 'best doctors' involved cash, only to get the most startled look back and the simple response 'of course'! Long negotiations it seems.

Controls and confidentiality remained challenged at times. Once in 2016 I had to go to accident and emergency at one these new hospitals, and all seemed to be going well in the circumstances, except that to my surprise, my wife and two young children were admitted to the admissions treatment area to support me, where shortly after some folk in critical condition were brought in following a serious car crash, quickly followed by their families, wailing and screaming as their love ones passed away it front of them, everything which could be heard and partially seen by my young family. I will never be sure what effect that may have had on my children, but it was normal in China, even in these tragic circumstances. The lack of privacy and the right of family to be present is just accepted.

I include diary extracts relative to medication, treatments, and experiences:

w/c 8ᵗʰ February 2003 - From a China Daily News Health Supplement:

'In order to protect endangered animals and plants, Tongrentang is looking for substitutes for musk, rhinoceros horn, tiger bone and liquorice, which have long been used in the manufacture of traditional Chinese medicines'. Not to mention the snake's bile mentioned on my packet of cough mixture!

Tongrentang is a 330-year-old traditional Chinese medicine company. By 2005 it is estimating its sales will be US$603 million and that this will grow to US$ 1.2 billion as it is going to be a global drugs company. I just love all this ambition, and by the way, achievement as well!

The World Health Organisation fears that schizophrenia and depression will account for 17.4 per cent of all diseases in China by 2020. This is based upon the increasing pressures of modern life and the fact that an increasing number of Chinese between the ages of twenty to forty have been turning to psychologists for help and guidance in recent times.

China was addressing mental health awareness high profile in 2003.

w/c 10ᵗʰ May 2003 - The afternoon was enlightening as it was my first visit to the parent company's on-site hospital, which one could define as an interesting one. I had decided that it was appropriate to get proper medical treatment for my back problem, which although not too painful, is still preventing me from running. The hospital was bigger than I expected, more like a two-story farmyard than a hospital and probably built in the 1970's. I was ushered into what I thought was a waiting room but doubled as a back treatment room and doctors surgery. I was immediately lead to the front of the queue, where my secretary explained the story and there in front of everyone, I was asked to lie face down on one of four small beds in cramped and proximity of each other. I had forgotten from my entry visa medical test that Chinese hospitals are not private places and that interviews are conducted in the open where everyone can hear, leaving me wondering what I would do if I ever had any personal issues. Anyway I settled down on my stomach whilst my secretary described and translated my problem, assisted by my driver, and listened to with great interest by three doctors and ten other patients, all who appeared to be giving me a serious look over and debating my problem. The lead doctor soon found the spot on my lower spine, said a few words and then the treatment started (something about a disc), right there and then. First it was sensors from a machine attached to the area of my back for what I am told is electrotherapeutics – a twenty-minute massage of the area with electric current of some description. Then a doctor started a forty-five-minute massage of my back, inflicting more pain on my body than many could ever could have managed I muse to myself. This guy was firm at times and rough at times but gave me a real work over including sticking the end of his thumbs into me at the back of my knees and heals of my feet inflicting untold pain in the areas. Then I had the 'bottles' treatment, which apparently, as for obvious reasons I could not see, was three inverted spherical glasses with ignited alcohol in them, which were then 'sealed' to the skin of my back around the painful area. Traditional Chinese medicine stuff apparently and this process draws the skin and flesh into the glass spheres, leaving large circular welts on my skin. After twenty minutes of this and a trimming massage I was dismissed to return to work, bewildered and wondering what the bloody hell had just hit me. The hospital didn't seem that clean or sterile I noted.

w/c 21ˢᵗ May 2005 - Thursday morning I go to No. 2 Jiaxing Hospital for my routine medical as a part of my employment conditions in China. My predecessors used to have one annually, but a relaxation in the systems have meant that not only do I have to have one only every three years, but that I can now have it done in Jiaxing instead of Hangzhou, which is an hour and a half away. This 'convenience' is mixed with a slight nervousness about the lack of privacy and conditions here in Jiaxing, although I don't remember Hangzhou being that great. The hospital though turned out to be considerably better than expected, recently decorated and remarkably clean and well organized compared to my prior experiences, with the service element progressing significantly and privacy relatively good, although still a bit communal at times; maybe I am just getting used to the way things are out here. At first look everything seems to be fine, with a full investigation including eye tests, ear, nose and mouth checks, chest x-ray, ultrasound scan of liver, stomach, kidneys etc, listening to the heart, neck and investigation of glands, urine and blood tests and blood pressure. All conducted with high-speed efficiency, and I was out of there within the hour. I am left wondering about the slowness of the British National Health system in comparison, not knocking the NHS, but its speed at times.

w/c 10th March 2006 – Thursday after a dinner a bar stool fell on my foot bruising my toes slightly creating somewhat of a discomfort overnight.

Friday, I awoke and my toes or mainly the second toe on my right foot was a problem, distinctly black and blue and really hurting. Still I went into work to give the opening speech for a large employee sales training course before belatedly deciding to go to the hospital to have my increasing painful toe checked, although I was still tempted to just chuck some ice on it and even more so after I had arrived in administrative chaos amongst the masses at the Jiaxing No.2 Hospital.

First there was an eventual inspection, then an x-ray. Diagnosis via translation was that it was both broken and dislocated. Thereafter was one of the most painful few minutes of my life whilst the doctor replaced the dislocation without any thought of any local anesthetic. Then back for another x-ray and good, the dislocation has been sorted out and everything back in place as it should be. The 'fun' though was being wheeled around the hospital in a wheelchair, firstly by a young lady in a nurse's outfit who had no chance of pushing me either very far or straight and then by my ever-present driver who stepped into the rescue. I must say that neither seemed to demonstrate much awareness of the fact that my foot was incredibly painful and tended to steer it through the hordes of people in much the same way as a snow plough through snow, resulting in me having to take evasive action several times to avoid any further damage to my second pinky. The bad news is that the doctors think that I will dislocate it again easily if I walk on it and said that I must stay in the hospital for three weeks to rest it with my feet up; you had to be joking mate especially given my already overloaded work commitments. I eventually left after some negotiation with a small splint fitted, two crutches that were far too small for me and go straight home which was one hell of a chore in my suit and one bare foot along with my brand-new pair of undersized crutches. This is where I wished that I had an elevator to my fifth-floor apartment. By one o'clock I was very bored, frustrated and hurting and I ponder that I may take a trip to Shanghai to see an international doctor I conclude, but not today, possibly tomorrow, but will see how things go.

This trip to Jiaxing's No. 2 hospital had been disappointing, as the administration really wasn't good on this occasion, not helped by the fact that I had a new secretary who was unaware of the procedures and formalities there. Then I was in the old wing of the hospital, which was filthy, unhygienic, and poorly wired and exhibited all the bad factors of traditional Chinese hospitals, like lots of people standing around and being imposingly nosey. Then as I was waiting to leave, there was a young lady who wanted my secretary to give me her business card by way of introduction whilst smiling directly at me, which my secretary refused but then the lady tried my driver, but he also refused. All the time she was smiling at me directly in a way that would be best described as 'nudge, nudge, wink, wink'.

Eventually when my driver disappeared, the lady followed and caught up with me and shoved her card into my hand. My secretary read it and explained that she was promoting some medical products, but judging by the look on her face, her intentions had nothing to do with this, opportunistic, something entirely different.

SARS

I was to have lived through the SARS epidemic in China in 2003. This given the current covid 19 pandemic, can be viewed as something of a forerunner and practice run for China regarding wide scale infectious diseases. I include diary references from February-March-April-May 2003:

w/c 15th February 2003 - The 'pneumonia' outbreak in Guangzhou is officially 'under control'. 305 people have been diagnosed with it, six have died to date and there are a lot of critically ill people around. Accordingly vinegar sales have gone through the roof, on the back of the belief that it is a cure. Others say that smoking is good in the prevention of SARS!

w/c 29th March 2003 - In amongst a diet of Iraqi war TV coverage and hearing the fact that China has the 'SARS' epidemic under control. Most western countries have cancelled their business trips to China and holidays are being rescheduled, perhaps reflecting on the latest stats:

China	1190 cases;	46 dead
Hong Kong	780 cases;	16 dead
Singapore	95 cases;	4 dead
USA	72 cases;	0 dead
Canada	58 cases;	4 dead
Vietnam	54 cases;	4 dead

And a few others, totaling 2,223 cases worldwide to date and seventy-eight deaths as a result. Chinese and WHO are now quoting an 80 per cent recovery rate.

w/c 12th April 2003 - I ask our financial manager again if there are any government warnings about SARS or any guidelines from the travel agency who have arranged this trip by train for us – the response was simple, there is no guidance and Fujian Province (where we were going for a trip) is free out SARS; 'no big issue!' I buy this story even though there is suddenly a lot of coverage about SARS, although mainly self-congratulatory stuff that the spread is under control and no one should unduly worry, especially as it is confined only to certain areas.

Thursday, for the first time, I receive a circular letter, addressed to 'foreign experts', albeit in Chinese, suggesting that it has been hastily prepared, informing me of things that I should do to avoid catching SARS. This seems like odd timing to me and a little late, but I do note that over the last two days that the press and TV have been upping the ante regarding SARS.

w/c 19th April 2003 - I find myself setting off for the airport suddenly thinking about SARS. Yesterday, for the first time, the government in China has suddenly announced new and dramatic prevention measures, which suddenly seems over the top compared to the previously laid back and reassuring approach. This has the effect of un-easing me somewhat and raises in my mind the question, what do they know that I don't? All the way through this 'epidemic' as it now seems, the government has been understated and relaxed – It's a Hong Kong issue, cases are few, WHO very pleased with our approach and decisiveness and everything is under control. The situation has been contained. Now the temperature has risen.

I don't feel comfortable in myself and the 'SARS thing' continues to play on my mind, not helped by the fact that I have had a dry mouth for the last two weeks and have been convinced that I would be coming back to the UK with a cold. Last thing that I need now is to turn up to the airport, or indeed at home, sniffling! At the airport I am mindful of the men and woman doctors in white coats, stethoscopes, and all, wondering around and casting a watchful eye at all passengers boarding at airplane gates.

The airport is strangely very quiet and very hot, with far fewer westerners than I remember from prior visits. You can spot the Japanese visitors – they are all wearing facemasks. A few Chinese have elected to wear masks, virtually no westerners bothering to wear these things over nose and mouth. The Virgin flight is full, with about two thirds of the customers being young Chinese middle-class males and females presumably off to the UK to continue their studies. It crosses my mind that this is one heck of a potential vehicle for spreading SARS; straight into the universities, bars, and coffee shops. How the hell does one control this?

For my return trip to China I see on TV and in the Telegraph the reports of the rapid spread of SARS in China plays on my mind and makes me start to think about life even more.

It seems that so many people have colds, and I am worried about getting on a plane to China snivelling, as I have visions of being quarantined for a week upon my landing in China.

Every newsstand at Heathrow airport seems to carry magazines – Economist, Time, Newsweek – and newspapers all carrying the SARS epidemic on the front cover, which starts my mind thinking about the subject again. It has been evident from the occasional telephone call and emails over the last week or so that this is quite a concern in China. The first 'visible' evidence of this was when I went on board the Virgin flight to Shanghai– there was just no one there compared to normal levels of passengers and I overheard ground staff quietly muttering that there were only seventy odd people on this flight, out of a capacity of circa five hundred people. We are odd going there, only time will tell. Looking around most of the passengers were Chinese, but still a few westerners in transit.

26th April 2003 - I had put the SARS issue to the back of my mind, but as soon as the plane landed, I was suddenly aware that all the Virgin crew had donned masks as well as most of the Chinese passengers, although there had been no advice or warnings during check in at Heathrow or during the flight. The airport seemed comparatively empty; indeed this is an understatement, as there seemed to be no one else around apart from airport employees, creating an eerie and unrealistic atmosphere; surreal is the word that I am looking for. Prior to passport control we were all subjected to temperature tests by doctors and to have our health declaration forms stamped before we were allowed to progress. I was thankful that I had stopped sniffing by then. Baggage collection was a very somber affair before exiting to a very quiet reception area which is normally packed and a hive of activity – this time there is nothing, but for a very quiet looking my driver, who for once was not smiling; we didn't shake hands as per our traditional ritual. Every airport employee was wearing masks as were about 80 per cent of passengers, the only ones not being westerners, or more pertinently Brits; still with an aura of invincibility and stiff upper lip!

In the car parks, all attendants were kitted out with masks, as were toll booth employees, Police, Taxi drivers and so on. A phone call to my secretary confirms that everyone here is terrified and that there are two suspected cases in the Jiaxing wider region, one of whom is a student who recently returned from Beijing and has since been to church, coffee bars, on buses, trains and so on. Roadblocks have been set up at Motorway toll booths for passenger buses, everyone being checked for temperature, documentation etc, with coaches queuing back the motorway inside lanes. Sadly we witnessed the immediate aftermath of a terrible road accident, the driver of which sadly will not have to worry himself about SARS I suspect. My initial reaction is that the place is hysterical. If only the Chinese government, who I have had a lot of admiration for, had reacted properly in the first place, it may not have come to this; I am sure that they have got this wrong, with too much too late, and have no option now, but to overreact. They have come clean about their mistake, sacked some poor folk who had only been in their jobs a few weeks and are now doing their damndess to redress the situation. This situation must be calamitous to the economy here and heaven alone knows the longer-term consequences both in terms of human suffering and the economy. Feel sorry for the folks involved in the tourist industry here; there used to be one.

I get back to the apartment for some sleep and decided against going into work, where they don't really want me anyway, as I have been travelling. Travelers appear to be regarded as having pariah status at present and all our sales team has been grounded and those who were travelling when the decision was made had to stay at home for seven days upon return. After a few hours' sleep an expatriate friend from Shanghai phoned me to ask about

UK precautions for SARS, as he has just cancelled a holiday in Malaysia as he would have had to spend ten days in quarantine upon arrival – and he was only planning on going for eleven days! My deputy just phoned me to see that I was all right, which I was until he awoke me from a deep and wonderful sleep.

The world around here is now dominated by SARS – I am not allowed to go to bars, not allowed to go to restaurants, should not go shopping. This brings its challenges – no food in the apartment and can't go out; no fear as my secretary has arranged for food to be delivered to my apartment, although I am not totally sure of the wisdom of a waitress turning up at my apartment having been serving in a restaurant all day, but there you go. However, there are other issues – toothpaste, toilet rolls, and milk for my newly imported cereals, washing powder shortages, haircuts and so on. I get home to hear a press conference from the acting mayor of Beijing talking about cutting windpipes to help SARS patients' breathe and the necessity to handle stools properly, catches the attention. Whatever, Beijing has a problem; Beijing and indeed China, has a real fear problem now. Folk are simply terrified, and the fear factor is possibly worse than the reality.

Thursday is the start of the May Chinese Holidays, so all the staff are off work, but we are running the paper machines to maintain production requirements and satisfy sales demands. The other side is that I had to walk to and from work, which is the only option as taxi's are a no-go alternative in this SARS environment and the climate makes it a pleasant twenty minutes' walk.

Ten days ago there were 300 SARS cases reported in China. As of 29th April there are 3,106 cases reported. A ten-fold increase and an average daily increase rate of 270. As of 30th, there are 3,303 cases. By the 2nd it's up to 3,799.

- *139 people have died.*
- *1,395 SARS cases in Guangdong (South China around Hong Kong), 1,210 in Beijing (North China), 243 in Shanxi (North China) and 114 in Inner Mongolia (North China). Zhejiang (My Province) has 3 cases and Shanghai 2 cases. Fujian Province, where I went on my recent 'holiday', has 3 cases. I console myself that this is still a very small amount out of 1.3 billion people! In Shanghai there are 2 cases out of 17 million.*

- *Of the Chinese mainland cases, medical workers make up 610 of them, which may explain why there suddenly seems to be a shortage of doctors and nurses in SARS hotspots.*
- *India's Foreign Minister, is here claiming that the world's press is blowing SARS out of proportion, citing the fact that over 3,000 children are dying in Africa.*
- *There is a SARS education programme on TV right now, attempting to educate the public into taking precautions, also trying to alleviate the terror factor that has been created.*
- *It is claimed that people who are recovering from SARS in Guangdong are doing so as the result of a combination of traditional Chinese medicine and Western medicine.*

w/c 3ʳᵈ May 2003 - Tuesday, I notice walking to work that suddenly no one is wearing masks, save the bus drivers, but I do notice disinfectant everywhere in public places including apartment lifts. China TV is declaring that Hong Kong is now under control and that shoppers are now back to normal. There are, however, disinfectant wipes etc at every entrance to main stores and someone is permanently disinfecting lifts after each trip.

I receive a printed booklet entitled "The Brochure on SARS Prevention". This sparked a dialogue in the office, and it seems that despite apparent activity people are still really taking this seriously. The brochure tells me all about the symptoms and answers a whole load of questions and is quite informative and lists actions taken, including:

Suspension of theatres, cinemas, dancing halls (re bars and discos), karaoke parlors and 'underground' facilities (whatever the hell that means, but one can guess). Large public meetings and events are cancelled.

Schools are suspended if there are any suspected SARS cases.

Mandatory health declaration system at airports, train stations, bus terminals, docks, and travel agencies to detect any travelers with coughs or fever.

No doctors, Clinics etc can treat suspected cases, only designated hospitals.

There should be strict neighbourhood surveillance in suspected infected areas (i.e. people start spying on each other)

Step up disinfecting public places and intensify sanitary inspection and testing. Includes shopping centres, transport terminals, docks, public vehicles, schools markets, hotels, and restaurants.

Disease control areas arrange quarantines.

They are starting to get serious about it. With impeccable timing a friend phones me up whilst I am reading this is inform me that his prevention method is – drinking, smoking and women and that he has even found a safe bar that is open, although he is the only customer! That's my boy; I wish him well, but I'm sure that his life will be a short one!

/c 17ᵗʰ May 2003 - The number of SARS cases continues to drop quite dramatically in China. Seems like SARS has suddenly exploded in Taiwan.

w/c 24ᵗʰ May 2003 - Thursday I head off to Jiaxing No.1 hospital to get them to have a look at a wart on my left forearm, which is a little larger than it has been. Hospitals and I seem to go hand in hand at present for a variety of reasons. As we drove into the courtyard and had our temperatures taken, I saw a statue of a westerner in front of the main entrance, inscribed 'Norman Bethune'. Norman turns out to be very famous in China, and apparently, he was a Canadian who was a Communist Doctor and progressed through the Party hierarchy during the Cultural Revolution; one continues to live and learn. The hospital has been on this site, right next to the glorious old church ruins, for eighty years and was founded by the French, who had also built the adjoining church, monastery and planted all the trees along the roads. The main building was seventeen stories high, but not in great condition and the conditions cramped. I noted many patients being moved around in beds from ward-to-ward and from building to building outside, in many cases the family members pushing the beds around.

I arrived with my secretary at eight o'clock to be greeted by her friend, David, who I had met some months prior at the 'English Corner' meeting. He is a delightful fellow, and an eye doctor at the hospital, and was on his day off, but came into ensure that I got the best attention possible – this is how things work in China I am reminded – though friends. David was charming, organized a doctor to look at my arm and diagnose it, then arrange a minor operation to remove the wart, then the blood test, which is mandatory for all operations. All done with a minimum of fuss and quite efficiently and I was pleased to see that my blood was okay (was tested for a long list of things). The blood test cost me £2.00 and I was told to come back at 14.00 hours for my operation, which I understood to be a simple slicing off the offending wart. I has been seen by a very presentable doctor, who David informed me was from Shanghai and the 'best doctor' in the hospital; he was certainly very pleased to see me, as were all the other doctors in their rest room, which David had taken me into to meet this guy. The hospital, despite having a Chinese grubbiness about it; was professional and I had checked that all the needles were single use needles and the hygiene conditions seemed okay.

At two o'clock I duly turned up at the operating theatre to be greeted by the young surgeon and two others all in full surgical gear, which I thought a little OTT for a simple slicing off. Laid out on a bed under an operating light, they gave me a local anesthetic and told me to look away. Twenty minutes later, I heard the words 'beautiful' in reference to the last of the seven stitches that they had inserted into an incision that must have been an inch to an inch and a half long on my forearm; I will have to await the removal of the bandages to be more precise. Turns out that the wart was a benign growth, which was much bigger than I would have liked, about the size of my little fingernail, but nearly spherical. Heck, I wasn't expecting all of this and suspect that I will have quite a scar on my forearm in future, but at least the growth has gone. Thereafter, it is dressed, and I am told to go back on Monday to have it redressed and in two weeks to have the stitches removed. Then there's the antibiotics for three days and only thing left is to pay for the operation at £20.00. I left the hospital with my arm in a sling and very grateful for David's assistance on his day off, and frankly a little stunned at the speed and magnitude of events.

It's amazing how much attention a sling can get one and I am pleased that at work I get some sympathy, along with a degree of mirth and laughter at my predicament.

I don't like hospitals! Never have done and never will do. On TV hospitals are being described as the amplifier of SARS, which is brilliant as I have now been to three hospitals, six times over the last three weeks! This place was again very public, and my presence enhanced everyone's nosiness and interests. Queuing is a scrum, and I was delighted that David managed to find ways for me to jump all queues. Medical records are left on the side for all and sundry to read and problems discussed openly in front of all within hearing distance, many of whom shouldn't be, but have huddled around in general interest. No one seems unduly concerned at this. In the reception area, there were two large dispensing chemists, one labeled in Chinese and English 'Chinese traditional medicine' and the other 'Western Medicines'; I was interested to see that the queues at the western medicine counters were significantly longer! The computer network seemed very efficient, linking all departments and as I visited folk on the first, second, tenth, and sixth floors, I can confirm it works well, although I would still back Chinese word of mouth to spread information, and disinformation, faster. They are the World's biggest gossipers! The hospital was typically unclean, but with a specific ruthless efficiency in amongst all the chaos (!). My blood test results were completed in fifteen minutes, producing a long print off the findings; I am advised that I am normal with no problems.

Friday, I find that my arm is not as sore as I thought it was going to be and I feel in good form after a solid night's sleep. The news on SARS is all very positive. Cumulative cases are over 5,000 and sadly 327 have died, but 3,121 have recovered and about 1,500 are under treatment or being observed. As the day goes on my arm gets a little sorer despite the painkillers, mainly because I seem to have spent the whole day typing on my PC.

I got into work, without any dressings left on my arm only to be chastised by my secretary in the central office in front of everybody, who were equally as concerned at the sight of my stitches. My secretary went on and on 'It is obviously infected.' 'You must not take your dressing off' 'You have had an operation, not just a small cut' and so on. My driver is immediately summoned back, and I am dragged off to our JV partners hospital. Upshot – no problem, would healing well, a little redness around the stitching is normal, no infection. Oh and, nice stitching. My secretary is suddenly noticeably quiet, but unremorseful.

w/c 21ˢᵗ June 2003 - I also look at the scar on my forearm from my operation and remember my translator's comment on the plane last week, when in her typical cheerful style having been surveying the damage, she said, 'Jeremy, it is not so beautiful'. She is right and the cut was lateral across the forearm, not vertical.

Anyway, I lived through and survived both SARS and the older Chinese hospitals!

Chapter 19

China's Toilets

Right, let us get right into this, as going to the loo is one of the most basic and necessary functions of the human body and in China the situation has traditionally been darned basic in dealing with provisions for ridding the body of its fluids and wastes.

Over recent years China has made great strides forward in terms of its toilets, facilities and habits, but I recall reading a book about a Chinese American who referred to "China's stinking toilets" in the 1960's and 1970's and in all honesty, I can say that until the last decade or so that there was really not much progress as I was to learn very rapidly that this was no exaggeration.

I am British and accordingly probably by definition I have some hang-ups relating to toiletry habits, usage, and cleanliness. I never coped well with public toilets anywhere and especially the squat holes one used to see at service stations and lay-bys in France during my school summer holidays. These though were clean places in comparison and did not prepare me for the situations that I was to face in China as I travelled around its various provinces.

The first thing that I discovered that there was never any toilet paper in any of the toilets. There was paper everywhere else though given the country's bureaucracy and tissue paper stacked in the middle of every dinner table for eating purposes. Therefore, whenever anyone left the dinner table to go to the loo, they had to grab paper to take with them, on the presumption that they knew in advance how much toilet paper they would require. Put bluntly, everyone knew that who was going for what bodily function when they left the table by the amount of paper they took. One quickly learned to discretely carry around a packet of tissues in one's pocket! The reason that there was no toilet paper in the loos as

I understand, was that it would get nicked and taken home for usage in China's frugal society; I jest not!

And this brings me to the immodesty of the Chinese people in such situations, there is not any! Less common these days, but it was the norm for lady cleaners to be cleaning the loos and urinals in the men's toilets, whilst one was using them and inevitably as I was a foreigner, they would discretely sneak a peek as they mopped the floor around me!

Public toilets remain for the most the 'squat toilets,' a ceramic hole in the ground with a flushing mechanism of some sorts and this remains the preference of most folk as they see it as more hygienic than the contact western sit-down toilets. The Asian squat continues to prevail in public places including modern shopping centres, hospitals, restaurants, and schools that are not internationalized.

Often instead of paper, there was often simply a water flexi-pipe for washing oneself, which I have never totally got my mind around, especially as there is no paper or other for drying purposes.

If by chance one did have paper then as a rule one did not put it down the toilet after use as historically it would have blocked the pipe system, a 'no-no', but one had to deposit in a plastic wastepaper bin next to the loo, stinking with no lid, which is not always a pleasant experience I should say, either visually or odour wise and a party fest for the many flies and mosquitos.

There is an issue in China with men and urinals, particularly that for some reason, folk do not stand close enough to the urinals and pee all over the floor, splashing all over the place and leaving a pond on the floor. At international airports there are often educational signs as hints stating, 'Please stand closer to the urinal' and in Shanghai's Pudong airport in more than one occasion I have witnessed poor cleaners, mops in hand exasperatedly publicly rollicking the clientele for not standing closer. There are probably many-fold reasons for this, one being that many guys insist upon undoing their trousers and leaning backwards, either smoking or on their mobile phone or just being inattentive to life as they splash all around the place including their trousers and shoes. My observation is that this in part it is down to a combination of the urinals being full of urine due to the urinal being full of cigarette butts and other junk that has blocked the drainpipe but also the flushing mechanism which seem to work differently to most other parts of the world. I.e., it is typical in most western countries for the flushing system to work automatically when one has finished urinating and after stepping back from the urinal. Well in China it was usually set the other way around for some reason unbeknown to man, that is, as one stepped up to the urinal, the automatic systems flush it at overly high pressure and if it is already full up with urine, then well, one can imagine, but it is not only not good for the shoes, but the socks and trousers! Nor for the smell that is likely to be wafting around for the rest of the day. In nicer places this is improving, but there is a long way to go!

Just developing this theme, I have been to the men's urinals in some KTV places where not only is there a male toilet attendant trying to massage one's shoulders from behind whilst one is urinating, which is somewhat unsettling to say the least, but also there was another fellow crouched or on his knees trying to clean one's shoes at the same time, which never appealed to me as the sort of job that I would want! This also had the effect of inhibiting one's ability to urinate!

Around China I have experienced and had to endure a range of styles of toilets, none of which are recommended, and I learned to wish and pray that I never had unnecessary calls of nature or out and out stomach problems when traveling, especially as a large European, I have never really managed to replicate the Asian squat, which is a challenge.

At an engineering factory in Mudanjiang in the Hei Long Jiang province in the extreme north east China, I went to a loo where I was stood in a part open shed on planks of wood with a couple of full width plank gaps in it through which I was expected to wee into the cesspool many, many feet down below. This stunk! The situation was compounded when an office guy came out and dropped his trousers over the same gaps, squatted and proceeded to crap into the open pit below next to me, the time delay between his emissions and the plop in the cesspool was discernible! All whilst fighting off the flies!

This though did not fully prepare me for the car journey the following day to the provincial capital of Harbin in freezing conditions. Along the way we stopped for some lunch at what was a basic restaurant the small dining area which doubled as a bedroom, but which I was used to. Since it was a long journey after lunch I needed to loo, and we were told that the toilets were outside. Five minutes later my colleague came back ashen coloured, and I knew then that the facilities were not good. I followed out of curiosity and necessity and discovered that there was a small wooden outdoor shed at the top of a slope down to a stream, with no squat toilet, just a wooden floor with an opening at the back, but because of the frozen conditions nothing was washing away, indeed there was a large pile of crap on the deck, a frozen pile. The bottom of the toilet comprised a pile of frozen turds and when curiosity got the better of me and I investigated outside this frozen turd mountain extended all the way down to the stream; truly horrible! One of life's 'retching' moments!

Down in the city of Nanning in the south eastern Guangxi province, I was at the main bus station awaiting a trip down to Behai I believe when my accompanying translator suggested sensibly that as it was a long trip of many hours that I should use the toilets first, great idea in principle! I was not prepared for what I walked into, which was basically a large open tiled toilet area on a gradual slope with a full-length trench down the middle, a low-pressure water flushing line at the top which evidently did not work as the trench was full of turds and about thirty men all in a row one after each other, all facing downhill in the same direction, squatting and doing their thing, most reading newspapers and smoking. As I walked in there were murmurs and everyone looked up, surprised to see a tall foreigner in the midst in this then remote place. At that moment in time, I made an instant decision that I did not need the toilet and would cope!

In 2002 China suffered its third plane fatal crash in a brief period and the government clamped down heavy handed and demanded that maintenance improve. This was an immediate decision as ALL national flights were grounded with immediate effect pending more detailed structured safety checks. This caused chaos and the upshot was that I was stranded in transit in the old Xian Airport terminal in Shaanxi province along with multitudes of others. The place was a packed mass of humanity, and the airport was naturally not geared up for these numbers. It was simply horrible as toilets blocked, urinals overflowed, one waded through rivers of urine, there was no paper to be found and the place stunk in the warm climate; truly horrible! One of the vilest moments that I have ever experienced!

In factory office toilets just outside of Jinan, the capital of Shandong province I once walked in to find six squat toilets on the three sidewalls, all taken, no cubicles, no nothing, just six men enjoying their daily functions, all squatting or chatting, all smoking, all reading newspapers and not a care or modesty in the world. I seem to recall that it was a windy and noisy moment as well! I did not stay.

Airport loos, certainly in the old airports had incredibly low stall sides and no doors, the same as in so many factories, so basically there was no privacy.

In many office and factory toilets where there were doors no one seemed to bother shutting them, leaving them wide open to the view of anyone who may be passing.

Manual flushing toilets after use seemed to have been an arbitrary option shall we say.

At one of our company factories and something that I have experienced elsewhere, was the open window just above the urinals, with a corridor or public walkway outside. One is therefore faced with urinating whilst the world passes by, usually female and looking at one, albeit without reaction, never a comfortable moment though.

In Anhui province we once stopped at a countryside restaurant for lunch and for the most it was good although basic. It was not until we went to the loos afterwards that we saw that the kitchen, toilet, and all the hanging dried meats awaiting to be cooked were all in the same open area, with the same communal flies and mosquitoes enjoying the best of all that was on offer in all three locations and sharing it around! This was not atypical.

It is still common, just like in France when I was a teenager, to see men stopping and urinating on the side of the road, many immodestly, some not even bothering to turn away!

Where there are western style toilet bowls with seats then the Asian squat still prevails at times. I have been to my home loo after inviting work colleagues around and found multiple footprints on the loos seats where folk had obviously stood on it and squatted, and different footprints on the bowl to below it where someone has at least had the decency to lift the toilet seat and squat, but in neither case did anyone think to wipe away the foot marks! I enquired about this, and this is common even in the new colleges and universities where new western toilets have been fitted. Lecturers have been known to shout at students to use as designed as part of the educational processes.

There were far more instances than the examples here, but I suggest this is indicative of how things were.

Domestically, most of the middle-class apartments were fitted with western style loos, although the standard entry level apartments and restaurants were fitted with the old-style ceramic hole in the ground.

This of course is a changing and improving situation and in large, westernized cities the toilets are world class, but..for all of China's real developments it must get over this one! The growing middle classes are helping to assist this transition but the dominant county side folk despite the mass migrations to the cities continue to practice basic habits and hygiene.

The facilities are increasingly there in place, the educational processes and awareness are improving, the younger generation are far better educated than their parents and grandparents and it will change – just a question of time.

Just saying!

Chapter 20

The Family

Throughout my time I was impressed with the togetherness and role of the Chinese family in life. A bond and recognition of responsibilities that is not always the case in the West. In the widest sense, it is a question of family first, often the only ones to be truly trusted.

Marriage is encouraged by the government as the right thing to do in being a good citizen and traditionally there always seems to be considerable family pressure to get married. Hence with the marriages comes a greater sense of stability, responsibility, and control.

Like so many there is considerable ambition that comes with marriage including security (monetary wise) and status. It is usually the man getting married who must provide an apartment to live in for the married couple. This is the focus of his parents and his job to try and save up enough to secure a deposit for an apartment. Without that there is an issue! I was always aware of younger colleagues saving for an apartment.

When choosing partners there must be consideration of avoiding any form of close breeding, not necessarily easy given that the three most popular family surnames of Li (7.9 per cent of the population), Wang (7.4 per cent) and Zhang (7.1 per cent) accounts for 22.4 per cent of the population or about three hundred million people. The other seven of the top ten family names are Liu, Chen, Yang, Huang, Zhao, Wu, and Zhou.

Legally a man can get married from twenty-two years old and a lady for twenty years old. Until recently a child should not be born out of wedlock, although this is starting to change as a more tolerant view of this situation starts to emerge.

Weddings are impressive and certainly in Han China, increasingly westernized in so many ways although certainly not identical and grew and grew, many exceptionally large, and individuality although recently the government has introduced measures to ensure the scale of weddings are more modest and family orientated.

The official wedding ceremonies take place by registration and certification in the equivalent of a registry office, long before the 'main reception' banquet, certainly not on the same day. There was a time that both married couples needed medical inspection certificates prior and as a pre-requisite to getting married, with a view to disease control, but I understood that this requirement lapsed in the mid 2000's. On the run up to the wedding reception, the couple have their wedding photos taken in increasing innovative ways by professional photographers, the bride heavily made up with special hairdo in her white westernized wedding dress and the man suitably smartly attired, photos often taken in local parks and the likes, as well as studio poses, and these take all day. These will then be on display at the wedding reception, often as a series of photos or in video form throughout the proceedings.

The receptions vary but can be incredible. Attendees are greeted by a wedding line of the married couple and bridesmaids, best men team, where they are handed 'red envelopes' with cash donations to the young couple that contribute to both paying for the wedding and an apartment and start to married life.

Often large gatherings with most people turning up dressed informally, depending on up the people getting married of course. A series of many round banqueting tables, including the top table. Speeches by some dignitaries, often bosses of one of the married couples, or a political figure who says some kind words and sometimes a mock run through of marriage vows by the couple.

The banquet tables usually have a variety of alcoholic and soft drinks in the middle of the table, and these are attentively replenished relative to consumption. The tables are waiter served and dishes brought out routinely for the feast.

I attended many of these weddings, quite often in an official capacity as the boss of a company employee or joint venture board director and was asked to give speeches which I did through a translator. My presence was seen as good face as the wedding is supported by the head of the company and for me there was the added novelty of a foreigner, i.e., their child was working for a foreign company, which added credibility to the occasion. I learnt with time to practice this routine as I was finding early on, that due to nerves or mistranslation, I found myself getting laughs at times when I did not expect it and not getting them when I might have expected it. I recall one occasion when a young female employee was getting married, I said something along the lines that 'I recall when she was a young lady starting at work started at a similar time to me and over years has she grown into a confident and beautiful young lady that we see today' – all rapturous hoots of laughter. All hell let loose, and the bride blushed. As I sat down, I asked my translator why everyone had laughed? She replied, 'Well I said that when she joined us, she was a virgin and now she isn't'! Oh boy, just stick to the script!

These wedding receptions tended to go on for an hour or two with men drinking lots and then everyone went home, no official evening events like so often in the West. Certainly, no discos, although I did go to one wedding in the progressive Shanghai, where there was a dancefloor after the meal with accompanying band and dancing. Options though did usually include visiting the bride and groom's apartment, a traditional visitation for limited numbers.

Traditionally Chinese were not allowed to have a baby out of wedlock, which is without the parents being registered as married. Marriage minimum legal age for ladies was I understand twenty years of age, although this varied by region and certainly if there were issues, they had to be resolved by the backdoor (registration by illegal means) I understand that having a baby out of wedlock meant that the baby could not be registered and therefore e.g., could not go to school etc. Recognizing that there were a lot of children *off the radar* having been born out of wedlock, the government introduced an amnesty as a part of the 2010 census and allowed all children to be registered legally, drawing a line under this hidden population gap.

Much has been made of the much vaunted one child policy that was in place from 1980 to 2015 as a measure of state-controlled population control. I surmised that this policy related primarily to the towns and cities where it was enforceable, and indeed was, less so in the countryside and in minority territories, noting that five of the provinces were slightly independent due to the large minority populations. The penalties included large fines and were certainly not agreeable to the career of Party members.

This though affected the family in as much as the focus of both parents were upon one child, but also the combined focus of two sets of grandparents. The term for this that has been used is 'little emperors' and reflects the systemic potential for spoiling the child. As China developed and both parents got jobs, the child was usually brought up by one set of grandparents, usually the father's parents. This has the advantage of economic security for the family and grandparents as both parents can work, as well as the more mature parenting of grandparents to the child. This though at a time of high social change in China was impacted by many things including the fact that the grandparents were more culturally traditional, less educated, less worldly, and brought influences to bear that may at times differ from the parents.

The parents as well were often increasingly absent given the opportunities of an increasingly affluent lifestyle and the socializing that went with it. Indeed, with China's development there have been massive migrations of people around the country, working away from home, not officially on a permanent basis, but for a job to secure income to send home to the family who remain in their registered homes. In many cases both parents are living away and the child is brought up solely by the father's parents.

Modern life has started to take its toll on marriages though and divorce, once so uncommon is certainly becoming more common, and indeed was seen by some as a way for men circumnavigating the one child policy as they could remarry and have another child. Working away from home, wealth, business travel, more social opportunities all contribute for this. For a long time there has been the 'canary' syndrome whereby a husband kept a lady in an apartment in another city from the one that he lives in, but he remained married for the family face and the benefit of their child. Questions were not asked.

Women though are becoming more independent, ambitious, and often very career minded, happy not to be dependent upon and under the control of a man to provide income. This has resulted in delayed marriages and these women have often been defined as the left-over women, the *Shengnu,* and are not encouraged by the government and not understood by traditional society. This often happens in the big and professional cities and creates family tensions with parents expecting their daughters to get married.

There were many facets of the family to be admired and a stability that at times in considerable proportion of the western world is lost. From this stable base the family grows its ambitions and follows its dreams, in a country and generation where those dreams have the potential to be fulfilled, or at least one can have a darn good try.

A speech at a wedding, the daughter of one of our joint venture partner. Everything translated and I managed to reduce her grandmother to tears of happiness at this one!

Chapter 21

Language

Difficult! The Chinese language is a difficult one. I say this as I went to China aged forty-four years old and my main language was English with a little French that I learnt at school.

I was to learn that the main Chinese language was Mandarin Chinese, the standard version spoken by approximately two thirds of China, with Chinese Cantonese spoken by about fifty-five million who inhabit the southern provinces of Guangdong and Guangxi adjoining Hong Kong. I am told there are four different Mandarin variances – Southern, southwest, northwest, and northern. To compound this there are > 200 local Chinese dialects, not just differing accents, but in many cases like a different language. A few times away on trips in my early days my translator was to go quiet on me without explanation, when I prompted her, the response was a sort of "I don't know – they are speaking in their own language." Even at our Jiaxing factory at morning production meetings there were issues of misunderstandings between local Jiaxing dialect and employees from elsewhere in China.

My intentions were positive, to learn the language, but I was not to get too far with it all, never mind the reading and writing of Chinese characters. I did have lessons, indeed two or three times a week for 6 months, but at the end of the period my tutor suggested that I was useless and should give up despite having learnt a reasonable vocabulary.

Mandarin Chinese is officially the second most spoken language in the world (1.12 billion) behind English (1.35 billion), followed by Hindi (six hundred million) and Spanish (547 million). However, when it comes to native speakers, spoken as a first language, Chinese is spoken by an estimated 1.4 billion followed by Spanish (471 million) and English (370 million). Whatever the precision of these Wiki quoted estimates, Chinese in its various forms is a global leading language.

I was to discover that the interim language to Chinese was *"pinyin,"* the romanization conversion system to Mandarin Chinese. This is used for teaching Chinese infants' Chinese basics and used in their computer systems as well as by foreigners in learning the language.

At work I was privileged enough to have a young management team, most of whom spoke English which was a tremendous help. I had a translator during my working hours but was on my own during evenings and weekends to fend for myself.

My lingual inadequacy was made worse for me by the arrival of another foreigner in town not too long after I arrived, a German who at 18 years old had travelled from Germany on the Trans-Siberian railway to Beijing and studied a degree at a top Chinese University, appearing on National TV as a result. That was over twenty years before and he had married in China and was fluent, which was painfully embarrassing for me in comparison when it came to government meetings and events.

I did continue to work at it but like so many foreigners the four phonetic tones were the killer to westerners, a subtle tone change on the same word was significant. For instance, in Chinese pinyin, the westernized Chinese version of the language, the word Ma, could sound like either buying something, the mother-in-law or a horse – obviously in this context it was extremely important to have the right tonality in expression!

I learned to count in Chinese by playing the shidze dice games as the only foreigner in bars on Friday and Saturday nights. Likewise, I learnt the parts of the body, colours and phrases relating to age and nationality at the same bars just by pointing and looking inquisitive. This was not deep and meaningful learning, but it worked to a point on these fundamental parts of the language. I managed to get fed, get a drink, and order taxis home, albeit with an address card that I kept in my pocket written in Chinese to show drivers in my early years.

I branched out on my own, armed with the vocabulary that I had written down and tried to learn, but had a few spectacular fails. My confidence took a real hit when in a quiet bar I meant to ask for a beer and some sliced dried banana that I had just eaten. As I approached the bar the place was quiet and there was stunned silence and inhalation when I asked for this, followed by universal laughter when they worked out what I wanted. They thought that I had asked for a beer and to make love!

Another time I walked up to the bar and asked for a hot bottom instead of a warm beer with similar reaction. These instances dented my confidence it is fair to say. The biggest hits to one's confidence though were when I tried to speak Chinese to a Chinese person, and they did not realize that I was speaking Chinese; that is a real bummer!

At work I decided that it was too risky to try speaking but listened lots, went home and studied and came to understand certain words, phrases and meanings before the translator translated. I got to understand the drift intent of conversations and was able on many occasions to pick up when things had been mistranslated or misunderstood. As time went by it was evident that this happened far too often which worryingly raised many questions upon my communications at work and the detail of deals negotiated by company principals in translated agreements.

In a business environment it was essential to get the best understanding possible, not to offend and therefore required good translations to provide this service, something that I did not always get. That said, the additional benefit of translation was to provide time to digest what had been said and to provide considered responses, something that I found essential.

Socially I relied heavily in my early days on a couple of close male friends who I often had dinner with and went to KTV or bars with. They were good translators and enabled me to have a life and relax away from work.

Later, much later, I developed a relationship with a lovely Chinese lady who I was to marry and was able to take my basic language learning to another level, but it was never great and no reading or writing of characters except for my name recognition and my Chinese signature on Christmas and New Year cards that I sent to friends. I was okay with directions (right, left, straight on, backwards), numbers, addresses, food and drink, taxis, and a few other essentials, enough to get by with a degree of independence and enough pronunciation clarity to get me through.

Many foreign teachers who came to the schools seemed to do quite well learning the language whilst living in a learning environment, younger 'with time on their hands' as one put it. I was also to meet a few Americans and Canadians who had studied Chinese at university before coming to China, doing things the right way; fluent and quite impressive.

I survived fifteen years with an extremely basic understanding;

I suppose I should be ashamed of myself for not doing better, partly inhibited though mainly because I really did not expect to be there long!

I was effectively a baby at times in this respect, especially my first couple of years.

Chapter 22

Chinese New Year (Spring Festival) and Fireworks

The Chinese New Year, the named Spring Festival, or the Lunar New Year, celebrates the start of the new year and occurs annually. As a Brit I can only describe it as something like being a Christmas time event combined with New Year and some more! The date moves each year due to the Lunar calendar in either late January or February.

Each New Year is given the name of an animal on a yearly rotation, hence the years of the Rat, Dragon, Monkey, Ox, Snake, Rooster, Tiger, Horse, Dog, Rabbit, Goat and Pig on a twelve-year cycle. These often get slightly mistranslated, such as the goat being translated as a sheep or ram, and so on.

It is not an enjoyable time for animals given all the associated fireworks that incessantly filled the air and the eardrums. When I was in China fireworks were everywhere and used routinely throughout the year, although towards the end of my time controls were being introduced especially in the cities to restrict usage and improve safety and environmental performances.

It is the biggest holiday of the year for the Chinese and a time for families to be united. Given the migrant populace this then becomes a major migration home of the masses, with cities emptying as their temporary residents disappear, sometimes date of returns unknown. Each year, folks seem to start traveling earlier and returning later. It is an incredibly special celebration indeed.

The increasingly wealth of middle classes has also made this a time for tourist travel both within China and overseas adding to the travel chaos.

First though is the run up towards the Chinese New Year, the company celebrations, and dinners, visiting customers to present New Year gifts, getting together with friends, past and present. Restaurants fill to capacity with much merriment and business is good. Fireworks companies fill their boots.

Holidays are meant to last seven days, but somehow with travels and entertainment it often seems to encompass up to a month of disruption from the norm.

It became apparent very quickly that the Chinese have a love affair with fireworks, setting them off at every opportunity, at any time of the day or night as suited circumstances. I had long known about the power of some Chinese fireworks from UK firework displays where a friend demonstrated very proudly his Chinese specialities that went higher, were louder and more thunderous than others.

Fireworks became intertwined in the culture and apart from major celebrations and city firework displays they were used at National holidays, weddings, shops, offices and restaurant openings, birthdays, moving into new apartments, new births and so on, any excuse. Given that there were so many new apartments being built and then moved into, given the new shops opening, the high propensity of weddings given the population, rarely did a day or night go by without fireworks going off somewhere in the background. Sometimes it was just drunk folk setting them off on the way home as a clever idea.

Firecrackers can go off at any time, night, or day when somebody has something to celebrate. The only rule of thumb is that the bloody things go off when you are least expecting it! Not for the feint hearted. They are very, very loud!

Health and Safety awareness and regulations were not in evidence usually. When I mentioned this at a company safety committee as an example of awareness, they laughed at me, looking incredulously at me that I would suggest that anyone got injured by fireworks. Afterwards my translator quietly pointed out to me that I was right and the stories of accident patients at A&E in hospitals were legion.

Diary recollections:

w/c 25th January 2003 - As the week ends we relax in anticipation of our first Chinese New Year. Tonight we have no plans; just to walk around and avoid the firecrackers, fireworks, and fires that we are told will be lit on the pavements tonight. My secretary's genuine cautionary words of "Jeremy, keep your windows closed tonight," which were said in all seriousness and for good reason. The evening was like being in the middle of a mortar attack.

w/c 1ˢᵗ February 2003 - My walk to work was mayhem and carnage, the deserted streets littered with the red aftermath of firecrackers. On every corner and as shops slowly open, people continue to set off more and firework sellers are in abundance. As I get closer to work, two shopkeepers are setting off these things on the pavement, stood amongst their exploding firecrackers so I hastily crossed the road. As I did, I watched as they started setting off 'mortar bombs'; the heavy type that starts off with a 'whoomph' and moments later explodes overhead with a deafening and deep 'boooom'. I note that they are standing very close to these things and that there are no real precautions especially as these weapons regularly seemed to fall over as they are trying to light them. Then came the comic/tragic bit as they set off one mortar and were about to light another when they realized that there was no 'boooom'. I watched in horror as this thing got to its maximum height and then started to fall to earth.... Directly back to where it came from! It is amazing how fast humans can move in moments of panic, unfortunately this was not one of them. The mortar exploded between the two men who were stood just some four feet apart, who had just enough time to turn their backs. Luckily no apparent burns or the likes, but I suggest they will be deaf, if not permanently, for the rest of the day. My translator phones me back later in response to a question I had about gifts and informs me that there are always many serious accidents with fireworks. I am not surprised. Later my secretary was to deny this fact, no, no, there are not many accidents leaving me wondering why she changed her statement, presumably briefed by someone to do so.

The visit to my secretary's family apartment for a New Year celebration was an interesting, curious, and pleasant event that lasted all of five hours. I arrived at 14.15 hours in an aging and drab block of apartments set within gated walls, which are owned by our JV partner. This is no surprise, as they own everything else around here – hospital, three schools etc. The apartment, on the first floor comprised of five rooms (two bedrooms, small kitchen, small bathroom/toilet, and limited front room/sitting room/hall. If I stretched out in the front room I am sure that my span could touch each walls, or close to it anyway. The apartment was freezing and the one air conditioner (Labelled 'Hi Efficiency', Hi Quality, Hi Performance') was broken, the replacement electric heater wholly inadequate, so after eating some tasty homemade spring rolls, we headed out for a walk around the block, a chance for my secretary to show me off to the whole community in which she lives; big status issue, especially as most of the residents are from our partner company or from our JV. We returned for more discussion, dodgy music (Richard Claydaman) and then a large dinner that they really went to town on and which I was most honoured by; even had a bottle of red wine, opened by the practical father without a bottle opener – he must have been a student at some stage; he ended up pushing the cork into the bottle. The table was a small wooden table and they managed to muster five seats of different varieties from around the apartment and enough paper cups to provide drink for all of us. I note that there is Perspex covered laminate up the bottom five feet of the front room walls – as washable protection, but more likely to hide the damp. Then it was launching a large box of fireworks just outside, about 6 feet from the apartment, dad with cigarette in mouth, lit with a match, stood back five feet and watched the impressive array of rockets explode directly overhead of us, with debris landing on the roof of the apartment block's sixth floor and showering all of us, before we disappeared in smoke; no need to check the box when they finished, just abandoned it where it lay – in the middle of the pavement; course it's safe, don't fuss Jeremy. Then afterwards I decided to walk home to walk off the feast, but found myself accompanied for several hundred yards by my secretary, her Mum, and Dad, in extremely frigid conditions, but another chance to show all and sundry who they have been entertaining today on New Year's Day, whilst she pointed out the apartments of many of our work colleagues. I feel very honoured, they have worked hard and entertained us Royally on limited resources, they are a good people and a good family. My secretary has been an immense help to me, and she will be happy with today also; except being nagged by her mother to find a boyfriend, i.e. get married!

*Sunday at my driver picks us up to take us to my deputy's in-laws 'in the Countryside' for a New Year celebration. I understand that my deputy's wife and twelve-year-old son will be there, as well as my driver's wife and sixteen 'ish' year old daughter and my deputy's Mother and Father-in-law. Although the weather is much brighter, we expect it to be another cold day and we will be at the sole mercy of my deputy's translation skills. I am excited.........
another new experience in life; why not, you are only here once, and I am led to believe that my sidekick is on the wagon, especially as his wife will be there.*

The 'countryside' as defined turned out to be about a twenty-minutes' drive away to the outskirts of Jiaxing, although it was certainly rural and surrounded by flat fields, it was hardly the countryside that I had expected. We parked the car by a rustic bridge and then walked for about five minutes along a waterway that was none too clean, distinctly stagnant, and full of rubbish and abandoned boats, the effect of water flow being isolated to this canal upstream. As we walked by the many houses that shrouded the canal, it was evident that we were among relatively poor farming (market gardening) community – old style 'haystacks' and vegetables in abundance. When we reached the house, I sat outside in the sun on basic wooden chairs with my deputy and driver, which offered at least some warmth to this otherwise cold day. My driver's family had not come, but my deputy's son entertained himself by letting off a deadly collection of small rockets from his hands; sending them off in any direction – into the water, through trees (somehow disproving my golf ball theory as they all went through the branches), towards haystacks, over houses, at houses, you name it and who cares, often scolded by his Dad typically, but no corrective action taken; must have broken every rule in the book but survived. The nearby sewage station apparently stank (My driver simply laughed, whilst I was grateful that I have no sense of smell), although maybe the canal stank more, and we were the centre of attention for the local passersby. My deputy's wife, a dance teacher, was delightful, but spoke no English and my colleague sadly did not translate too much, which restricted the conversation somewhat. Her parents were also delightful, good, and honest types and the whole situation let me make comparisons to our experiences with my Grandparents in St. Dennis, Cornwall – cold hands, cold house, fresh vegetables, and relatively frugal lifestyle, except this was Chinese style, which made it distinctly poorer and distinctly dirtier around the edges. Lunch was a mixture of local vegetables, fresh fish and chicken and the likes (or dislikes), whilst accompanied by homemade warm rice wine, of which I later wished I hadn't. To start we were offered a warm bowl of sweet soup resembling the 'frogs balls from behind the ear' of the other night, but I later discovered that its contents was simply something out of a tree, a fungus. However, I got merrier and merrier, as did my deputy, and I thoroughly enjoyed these kind peoples hospitality and the experience was just quite different to any other that I had experienced in China to date. I like the comparative solitude of the countryside. The entertainment of the day was the next-door neighbour trying to kill and gut an eel just caught from the local waterways. Armed with scissors and a plastic washing up bowl, she started disemboweling this creature. Many minutes later, covered in blood, the eel was still wriggling well and unaware that its throat had been slashed and its guts ripped open, she carried it away still demonstrating strength in life; the animal rights mob would love this stuff I muse. Somehow, I managed to come home with a large China flagon full of this homemade rice wine and then headed out with my deputy to Milo Coffee to meet his 'classmates', most of whom were 30/40 ish something professionals who had been successful in life pursuing their careers in either Shanghai or Hangzhou, one of whom was MD of an Investment company. Discovered that the Chinese rice wine comes with a delayed reaction, not a pleasant one; thank God I hadn't drunk too much!

I was aware that the fireworks would continue but weren't ready for the extraordinary launchings that followed. Massive firework launches were set off directly outside at midnight, 02.00 hours, and 07.00 hours, but were inter-dispersed with many others and more in the not-too-distant streets. Many bounced off windows and walls. Must have some significance, but I know not want. Sleepless night guaranteed and a lie-in required. Maybe it's the advent of the "Richman", a wild looking menacing and mythical Chinese character who visits folk today to bring them good luck with money in the next year. On this basis I should become a sodding millionaire! The fireworks continued throughout the morning in earnest. As I walk to work, I observe that more shops are open than prior days despite still being a designated holiday and that the streets are often littered with the aftermath of firecrackers, the pavements literally strewn with the stuff.

w/c 17th January 2004 – Sunday and true to the festive spirit the firecrackers start, together with the mortars. They are annoying, but I realise that I am more immune to them than I was last year.

In line with my exercise regime I walked around the town again and noted that Jiaxing continues to change at pace, with lots of middle-class folk out for the evening with their cars in tow, parked outside of the big bars, which were heaving for the night, whilst in contrast the small bars seem to be dead. My Scottish colleague and I eventually landed on a small bar, where we know the folk a little, but were very quiet upon our arrival; that changed though!

Now I have witnessed many New Year's celebrations in the UK and the odd Hogmanay in Scotland, but I was unprepared for the events at midnight. It was like being a part of an anarchic war zone as everyone rushed outside with their fireworks appearing from everywhere to see others appearing from every available apartment, whilst others just decided to launch rockets from their windows. Apart from most folk being drunk, some very so, there was no safety awareness at all, lighting fireworks with cigarettes whilst leaning over them, not withdrawing too far, and ignoring ones that they had lit but had not gone off. Twenty minutes of pandemonium and carnage followed, but plenty of excitement and atmosphere that set the tone for the next hour's celebrations. A very weary colleague and I decided that a taxi was the best way home, not walking – safer too as fireworks continued to ignite throughout the night.

w/c 24th January 2004 – Monday, the factory is still on holiday. I had planned to go in for work today, but had forgotten that after the New Year's Day, last night/this morning was the next biggest celebration, the advent of the fellow who is meant to bring everyone money; the 'Richman.' All hell let loose again, indeed I suspect that celebrations were even noisier; and went on all night and all morning. I am no longer immune to the incessant noise, that only seemed to abate for about an hour or so overnight. I was certainly aware of the mortars and firecrackers going off directly outside my apartment at 04.30 hours this morning. The mortars seem to set off car alarms everywhere and even the odd small shops that have them. I hate to think what the damage rate is like, but notice later that my Bank has a large glass window panel smashed.

w/c 12/2/2005 - Tonight I went out to 'a government friend's' apartment for dinner with her, her husband, her daughter, a fellow government department head and his wife. She works in the Judiciary Department of the Jiaxing government, and I have met her a few times at various events around town and feel comfortable going to her place overlooking a park for what turned out to be a great evening. The government fellow was the one and same who presented me with my West Lake Friendship medal in my office and together we had our photos in the newspaper together at that time. What I didn't know was that he was also a basketball nut and Chairman of the Jiaxing Basketball Association. On top of all that his wife used to work for our joint venture partner, and he is a thoroughly decent and sociable fellow, making for a lovely evening despite our host's only intermittent translations – this being an informal evening and the fact that despite her excellent English, she was not a translator, a senior professional, and I am reminded that translating is a skill beyond the language. It was not a late evening either, which would have been wonderful except the night was ruined by the incessant and virtually continuous bombardment of mortar fireworks and firecrackers, most of which seemed to be outside of our building reminding me of the geographic proximity of my apartment to the town centre. I really do wonder what is the matter with all these people – do they never sleep? The noise pollution this year is the worst by far of my three years here at Spring Festival time, maybe also reflecting that people have more money to spend on these things.

In 2013 I decided to drive to a family home in central China for the duration of the New Year holidays, approximately 1,150 miles each way, the vast majority being on the excellent motorway system. The sad news that this was the year *before* the government decided to open the motorway toll booths to free access to keep the traffic moving. The result was that this was pure folly and madness, as every man and his dog who owned a car seemed to be on the roads and the toll booths created huge log jams along all motorway lanes and the hard shoulder. A 1,150 miles long traffic jam, with services unable to cope, much frustration as China came to terms with the magnitude of its car driving population going home for New Year. Long, long journey, mayhem but again illustrated the mass migrations at this festive time. Airports are fully booked, and pandemonium often reigns at train stations at these times.

I was to witness a very serious fire in a relatively new and prestigious apartment block next to our block and caused by a firework being set off by happy folk returning from a party. Unfortunately, it tipped over on ignition and the rocket went straight into the open balcony of a second floor apartment, which in itself should not have been a major issue, assuming no one was stood there, but unfortuantely the deocrators had left all of their paints, solvent based liquids, and materials outside on this balcony and the whole thing ignited with flames lashing the entire side of the high rise apartment block as a raging fire contnued. Truly terrifying, but a grandstand view of the dangers of fireworks unregulated in modern China.

In recent years, the government has legislated to reduce the use of fireworks especially in cities at major holiday times, often complete bans, recognizing not only the health and safety risks to people and property, reduce the effect of air pollution, but also the significant and wasteful cost of all of this. This was a big step culturally.

The opening of a new restaurant – like shops and apartments – always a time for flowers and fireworks, including firecracker strips set in figures of eight, a lucky number. The smoke is evident, but this does not convey the noise.

Chapter 23

Information Technology

In 2002 the technology systems available seemed basic but functional. Gradually we were to increase the number of computer users at work and develop the systems. What astounded me was the endemic copying of, unlicensed software, with virtually no one having paid for user licenses from Microsoft, something that was described to me as 'normal in China'. When I asked about the policing of this folk did their best not to laugh and shrugged, which could have meant a few things but basically no one was trying too hard to ensure compliance, focus being on avoiding raising costs. When I discussed complying with license requirements there was general disbelief and why the stupid foreigner would want to increase company costs when there was no need to in 'Chinese China' away from the main cities. The IT guy that we used said it was okay. Over time though compromises were made and sometimes one license was bought and shared a few ways, then several licenses bought, but still shared as China started to face up to its need to recognize and protect some of the IP. Eventually we achieved full licensing compliance, but it wasn't easy, including justifying this to the Chinese joint venture directors who questioned the need whilst smiling.

Internet access was sometimes dodgy, but I could connect at work and from home. Visitors early on would tell me that my access to the internet was monitored, and I could not access certain western accounts, the second of which was totally untrue at that time, the first of which I don't now, but there was nothing too sensitive and I was obviously never aware if my emails and systems were monitored, noting that I was hardly dealing with State secrets.

Over time China developed its 'great firewall of China' in its attempt to control and regulate the internet, which at one level is quite sensible given what we know today about the dangers and unsuitable influences of some websites. Unfortunately from my viewpoint China did eventually prevent access to Facebook, Twitter, You Tube, Google, and the likes, initially stated as a need to control terrorist activity and messenging in Xinjiang using an overseas language and escaping the Chinese monitoring and control systems. Maybe and valid perhaps, but it also enabled China to develop its own social media systems that given the numbers of users, like WeChat, became huge, a Chinese sort of equivalent that delivered commercial benefits and enabled a degree of State control. Disappointed that I couldn't get Facebook, I was comforted that I could access most other western websites such as my newspaper, the Daily Telegraph, and western news was not for the most blocked.

Over the next decade and a half China was to wholly embrace the new technologies available. Everyone seemingly had a new smart phone, noting that data usage costs were much cheaper than in the west and I seemed to be able to get a phone signal anywhere in China no matter how remote (A stark contrast to the UK even today), something that many others have confirmed as China built the telecommunications structures to support future developments and growth with its forward-looking plans. I used to joke that Chinese babies were born with a phone to their ear and the masses used phones constantly and hence developed understanding of the capabilities. Far before the West seemed to fall under the spell Chinese were constantly on their phones everywhere. Too much it must be said!

Restaurants started using ipads as menus for direct order placements and I recall one instance, having put the iPad menu down in a Korean restaurant, that my two-year-old daughter, familiar with my wife's Apple iPhone technology, picked up the menu, came out of the menu software and started playing games on it! A damning indictment perhaps, but indicative of a generation immersed in technology from a young age.

Once a cash society, China quickly adopted Alipay, a Paypal equivalent, for its payment systems. In airports I was to see people paying coffee shop bills with their new watches and so on. China embraced technology.

Security monitoring systems abounded with security cameras, and vehicle speeding cameras appearing everywhere, all linked through technology to the owners and their personal details.

Environmental emissions were monitored online, and any non-compliance auto flagged on government computer systems for attention and action; no chance for any illegal local interference on not compliance data as had occurred previously. The companies knew about it and so did the authorities in real time all part of its genuine intent to implement, monitor and control its policies relative to the environment.

Didi, the Uber equivalent taxi firm appeared with similar type software, creating havoc controversially with the established taxi systems but improving the customer opportunities to get a taxi quickly. This system for the customer worked incredibly well with taxis seemingly available immediately despite adverse conditions, and cheaper. There were though issues, security being a key one reported.

A diary note:

w/c 24ʰ October 2009 - Wednesday and for the second morning in a row I cannot get onto the Daily Telegraph page on the internet leading me to conclude that this is being censored by the local server in the town. Facebook never, ever, re-appeared, nor did Twitter and You Tube, and others and one can't help feeling that the government is getting confident about interfering in such things. I did eventually manage to get onto the Telegraph at work yesterday, it had obviously been cleared through policy as safe, but this sort of censorship is affecting my routines and my ability to stay up to date with news in life.

Anyway today was a positive day at work, except for the fact that our erratic IT guy has updated my computer software to be able to access new Microsoft Outlook and Office software attachments coming in, genuine software on my computer, licensed and paid for, only to find that I am now not compatible with the rest of the organization internally! I times I wonder where I get these guys from, but this needs sorting urgently and will be.

The Great Firewall was to remain in place from certainly 2009 onwards. Foreigners were able to get through to foreign blocked websites using VPN's, but it was obvious at times that screening authorities were on the case.

China with its huge populations does have a lot of differing opinions in life and these are openly expressed online, although if things step over the line of stability or strongly anti-government then there are people who enter systems and delete these comments. That though still leaves room for some controversial opinions to appear routinely.

China has fully embraced the modern technologies as an essential and central part of its strategic developments at every level. It has huge companies in technology centres and is exporting to the world, sometimes as reported in the western press, in suspicious circumstances as threats to National Security. Whilst WeChat develops, sites like TikTok are hugely global.

Chapter 24

My Personal Life Changing Events

There were good reasons that I stayed longer in China for what was to be another ten years from when I first handed in my formal resignation from my job. Yes, my company encouraged and incentivized me to stay and that was an essential factor for rescinding it, however, the other dominant influence was in my personal life which had resulted in life altering moments, so much joy but in many respects more difficult and painful than one could imagine. In parallel, work issues were proving incredibly challenging and telling, so many factors outside of both my and our company's control as we battled against the loaded dices. By way of explanation I refer to extracts from my diary:

w/c 8th August 2009 - Circumstances in life contrived to keep me in China and the consequence of this is that I developed a relationship with a wonderful Chinese lady, and we have two beautiful daughters.

Over the last two years I have had numerous works issues and pressures so intense that I cannot describe, leading to serious uncertainties.

I am comfortable living with the way that my life has evolved, one that developed out of loneliness and distance, but wishing that my older kids continue their progress in lives in the fullest way. Maybe when they are older, they will understand better and recognize the sacrifices that were made in life for them, their lifestyle, and experiences. Their father's love does not diminish whatever changes occur.

I do not know how things will ultimately pan out, where I will end up living, working and to bring up my younger family.

Apart from close confidants, China did not know about my private life and personal circumstances that had remarkably been kept confidential as I sought privacy and solitude away from work's challenges, however the accidental 'coming out event' that was inevitable, it was just a question of where and when, I refer to my diary extracts:

w/c 17th October 2009 - Out walking this morning we passed a car fair at the Tongxiang Exhibition Centre {A city in the Jiaxing counties} and out of curiosity we duly popped in to see what they had, only to be photographed by many professional photographers, and a few amateur ones for that matter. One handed us his card and announced that he worked for the Jiaxing Daily Evening News! The irony of this is that the 'news' is probably just the fact that we were a western style family out together with the push chair and with me carrying my eldest toddler on my shoulders, something that most Chinese would never do. Equally as ironic was the fact that just a few hundred metres down the road there were about 100 foreigners, Americans with wives and in some cases older children, of all sorts of origins, just killing time around the centre shopping as a part of their visit to a local large fibre glass factory from Shanghai; they could have had a field day of photos.

Monday at four o'clock I got an urgent phone call from a close trusted Chinese friend 'Have you seen the Jiaxing Evening Newspaper'? 'No, why'? 'There is a picture of you carrying a young daughter on your shoulders along with your partner pushing a push chair with your baby'! He is most concerned at the consequences, more imagined than real I think, and we agree to see each other to discuss over dinner. He is convinced that tomorrow that everyone and anyone will want to know about this and that they won't call me directly to ask, but that they will call him as a first port of call as he has been a prime contact over the years. Anyway we agree a story, just like a media press release – the truth though! Better to make clear statements than leave any gaps I decide; gaps provide scope for a vacuum in into a vacuum anything can be said and made up, better to be clear.

Anyway, now anyone who may have an interest in the situation will have a chance to know and it is out in the open good and proper. The way that it has happened has been a little bazaar, but I guess that this time I wasn't consciously hiding from cameras when they approached or indeed staying away from public events and just keeping my head down as I have done for three years; I was just going on about living a normal family life and it seems that this is what appealed to the camera man and the newspaper. The photo, set in the middle of the paper, had its own lined box around it and said something about **'Jeremy Bazley, an Englishman, goes to Tongxiang Car Fair**

with his wife and daughter'. *One can't get must more of a giveaway than that, although it did say daughter and not daughters, my friend estimates that there is a daily circulation of this paper of at least 500,000 per day, probably higher, as the paper goes to the wider Jiaxing area with a population of over four million people, to every business and many households, and that people still read these things avidly, as well as being posted on the internet for those who pay a subscription.*

Tuesday, I awake in a little trepidation. Strangely no one appeared to latch onto the photo according to my driver except somebody at our plastics company who called him inquiring more information having seen the photo. He expects more to hear about it tomorrow but informs me that he took the pages out of the two newspapers delivered to our companies directly so that no one could read about it whilst at work.

My friend phoned to say that he has only two phone calls this week about me, one from our main joint partner and one from someone government, but nothing to worry about.

So there I was, life changing circumstances and a huge raft of challenges for me to deal with in my 'new life'. My focus switched to how best to bring up my two youngest daughters, ensure the best situation for my family whilst trying to minimize the impact and the hurt that I had caused.

Initially I was distanced by some close government contacts for a year or so when this all emerged, but over time this softened, and the situation accepted. In the event I was to remain living in Jiaxing for another eight years, the girls attending kindergarten and leading schools in the city until our return to live in the UK in 2017. I stayed with the company out of respect and loyalty to the principal's family and work colleagues despite to challenges supported by various re-assurances, to try and best find solutions. It was never going to be easy.

Part 3

The Travel Experiences

Chapter 25

Jiaxing

The city of Jiaxing in Zhejiang provinces was the epicentre of my world – my home for fifteen years of my life and indeed it felt like home. In a terrific location about halfway between the Zhejiang capital city of Hangzhou and the vast metropolis of Shanghai, set just off the Grand Canal, it was a late developer, but develop it certainly has. When I arrived, it was clearly underdeveloped, with the possible exceptions of the impressive and newly built government building by Nanhu (South Lake) in the centre of the city, a twenty-six-story hotel, The Diamond, which had a revolving restaurant on top, the Sunshine Hotel, a pseudo westernized type hotel on the main street and some smart new large police headquarters. There were other developed aspects but were small and hard to find.

Just out of the then centre was the state-owned paper mill, the main industry of the city traditionally, and with that I was to become intimately familiar, with its effluent issues and power station nearby as well as a host of decaying typical 5-6 story apartments for its employees, which was the norm around the much of the city. There were also some large textile factories. The papermill was starting to modernize and invest with new plant and machinery, new office buildings, landscaping and so on, but like so much of China's old industry, it was in the wrong place and longer-term plans were drawn up to move such industries away from the city centre areas and into the surrounding countryside or even just cease to exist, with lucrative compensation to do so, for some!

There were though signs of aspirations, like the early day attempts to landscape around the Nanhu Lake, but it was early days, some wide and modern roads being constructed, tree lined and having, as always, wide bicycle lanes in parallel each side.

Nanhu, South Lake, though was the jewel in the crown, unfortunately unlike Hangzhou's West Lake, there were no beautiful surrounding scenic hills, but this lake, in the Zhejiang flatlands of the wider Yangtze delta in amongst a maze of canals, had real history.

It was on an island in the middle of this lake, on the famed 'red boat' that the Communist party in China was formally born in 1921 at the conclusion of its 1st CPC National Congress. The story was that the communist leadership team had met in Xintiandi in the old French Concession in Shanghai, but their talks were discovered by a police officer, so they fled Shanghai on a boat, along the canal system, some eighty kms or so until they found a safe spot to continue their debates, a tranquil island in South Lake whereby they completed the discussions and signed the necessary documentation. More formally this was the Communist Party of China (CPC) formed by a Chinese leadership team including a Russian and a Dutchman. Thus, China's history was made, and it was in Jiaxing! And that was it really, Jiaxing's claim to fame although it was not really marketed in a big way as I would know it for a long time but was to come to benefit from the state encouraged travel industry developments and the ongoing investment programmes that evolved, a mecca for Party members and the normal folk to visit, often as a tourist stop off traveling to Shanghai from Hangzhou or vice versa.

Over my time there, and continuing, the city planning officers applied their trade building whole new areas of modern apartment blocks that were of a much higher standard and many high rise, as well as the more expensive villa's, splitting the city government into two (Nanhu and Xuizhou) widening the city boundaries considerably and creating a whole new park, based in size and aspirations on New York's Central Park, with large apartment areas and hotels built around it including new high quality schools, Exhibition Centre and an Opera House. Building new apartment complexes in foreign styles such as French, Paris City, Italian and others, worked outlandishly hard to attract new investment from overseas as it allocated huge swathes of farmland on the outskirts to new light industrial factory development zones; truly vast areas were built upon. With all this building comes wealth – new apartments constructed, sold, furnished, decorated and so on, with huge design and installation industries developing around that. Restaurants boomed and offered wider in choice and tastes, whether it be the hot and spicy foods of Sichuan and Hunan, the Korean restaurants, Japanese, Xinjiang lamb barbeque restaurants, westernized type restaurants and so much more, all competing. New shops opened everywhere and huge new shopping malls like the Wanda centre were to be built, so popular. The city was planned and developed in large 'blocks' ala the US style city structures.

Nanhu was given its own Red Boat Museum, a truly historic reference point and the landscaping around the lake not only improved but became established with walks and parkland with a new vibrant area for restaurants and relaxation currently under construction based upon Shanghai's Xintiandi.

The canal systems were cleaned up, free of industrial effluent, they were tree lined with footpaths and cycle paths added, the not so old buildings demolished and replaced with grassy areas and modern housing and old towns redeveloped, capturing ancient cultures and a feel for these Zhejiang water towns that opened both social and tourist opportunities.

As the city modernized so did its people and their demands to improve every aspect of life. Increasingly western foreigners were to appear from 2010 but not in droves, some working for foreign companies, several English teachers, appeared from various parts of the world including Africa, although it was not an expatriate city as such, it was becoming far more internationalized and quickly.

New supermarkets appeared including some foreign owned ones, bringing new goods and foods for consumption, many of the older open fresh food markets being closed and restaurants including small ones being far more tightly regulated. Ad hoc Street food stalls all but disappeared in the drive for food and hygiene improvements.

The new wide motorway systems, toll roads, served the city well, this transportation improved further by the arrival of the new high speed train system which made travel to Shanghai, Hangzhou and indeed all over China, so convenient, comfortable, and affordable from the Jiaxing South Station, providing commuting opportunities. During my time there was no airport there, but there was an air base outside in the counties, which is gradually being converted into a public use facility.

The wider Jiaxing area, controlled by the Municipal government in Jiaxing, the counties, Tongxiang, Haining, Haiyan, Jiashan, and Pinghu, were likewise developed, some running just as fast in terms of development with their own specific advantages and industries, traditional, such as silks and leathers as well as new ones. The old town at Wuzhen was to play host to many international conferences along with the other old main water town, Xitang appearing as the backdrop in many high-profile international films. Its own port, Zhapu, a natural deep-water seaport on the Hangzhou Bay was heavily invested in and developed for international trade.

The police modernized, new police stations, smart new vehicles replaced the outdated transportation and modernized approaches. Passport offices appeared to speed up the efficient issuing of passports and likewise with visa centres.

Schools were rebuilt on larger new campuses and new schools formed, private schools such as the Peking University Experimental School (Jiaxing). Modern facilities to supply the city's demand for educational excellence and a stepping-stone to an overseas education or university entrance at a good Chinese university. Schools such as this also would assist attracting foreigners with families who so often had previously lived in Shanghai and husband travelled to and from daily.

Bikes were replaced with cars, a downside given the congestion and environmental issues that come with cars, but useful in getting around the much larger city and accessing all that it has to offer. A car became a necessity and plans for people moving trams around the city came to be implemented.

Jiaxing now boasts a futuristic overland railway to move its population around.

The speed and efficiency of these transformations were simply incredible and continue apace. Having been brought up in Devon and living in the UK it is difficult to describe the transformation that has happened in Jiaxing, Hangzhou, Ningbo and indeed throughout China; there is simply nothing comparable in the West, irrespective of the sheer scale of things.

Whatever criticisms there may be of government in China at times, the leaderships teams did an excellent job at modernizing and transforming this city and its counties. The Jiaxing government leadership successively have done a fantastic job in modernizing the city and improving the lives of the people who live and visit there. Jiaxing, a wonderful place to live, where two of my daughters were born and one that I am proud to have been associated with.

Nearby Hangzhou is about sixty kilometres away, another city with real history, set upon the beautiful West Lake. It is also the provincial capital of Zhejiang. It was said to me and widely reported that Marco Polo once visited and described the place as the most beautiful spot on the planet. The West Lake and its immediate surrounds are truly wonderful, peaceful, and mystical. I had the pleasure of visiting on many occasions pre the huge development of Chinese tourism when the hordes descended and detracted slightly from this, but still magnificent as were the tea hills outside. The city though has grown and beyond the lake it is now just a vast metropolis.

A snapshot reference to Hangzhou from my diaries, a city that I was to visit many times:

w/c 11ᵗʰ December 2004 - Saturday I decide – I am going to Hangzhou, an unusually spontaneous decision by me on such issues, exploring a city that has some mystique in the Chinese psyche, but about which colleagues knows comparatively little. I summon my driver, to take me and sort out a hotel via the efficient Chinese hotel booking system – it must be as everyone books at such short notice! Not a good start as the fog is dense and the journey there takes two and a half hours, oh those Zhejiang delta fogs – trip all off motorway.

The Hotel Xinxi is a very pleasant hotel in traditional Chinese style and in keeping with the local environment, only about fifteen minutes' walk from the Shangri-La Hotel around the top end of lake and, as a three-star hotel is cheaper. Low level and set with the lakeside landscaping around, it turns out to be very clean and very adequate.

First it was a taxi up to the Linling Temple and the active walk up 'The Mountain that Flew In', which is just the sort of exercise that I needed for my body, and subsequently recovered enough to walk down again and feel the benefits. Then it was hiring a taxi to go out towards the tea hills, a trip that I made when I first visited Hangzhou for my induction medical some thirty-one months ago. Much has been done to improve the landscaping along the way making the route virtually unrecognizable, but a pleasant drive through the tea plantations although as before the actual tea houses were a little disappointing, despite the opportunity to lift a bucket of water out of a stone well and wash one's hands in the freshwater before taking the fresh and famous Longjing tea, a local tradition. On the wall of a very basic tea house was a photo of the Queen Elizabeth and Zhang Ze Min on a trip which was said to be in 1992, but I think perhaps seems more dated; it certainly wasn't taken in this place, but as the only photo on the wall, it was nice to see.

On the way we had stopped at the taxi driver's advice, at a silk shop, where there were some magnificent silks at very good value, but I resisted the temptations, although I make a note of these two places for future tourists visits to this Chinese Mecca.

Having returned to the Hotel to drop off a newly acquired tin of the famous Longjing tea, I then walked through the newly and effectively developed Lotus Pavilion and park along to the long Causeway and around to the other Causeway, noticing very few westerners in comparison to past visits, maybe the time of the year. Dinner was at the self-described 'world famous' Louwailou restaurant on the shores of West Lake, which was started in 1848. I note again for future reference that they do have an English menu and in amongst a packed restaurant including Chinese 80th birthday parties and weddings, whilst I enjoyed some superb local specialities of the restaurant such as the excellent beggars chicken, sweet and sour soup, sweet and sour fish, and a couple of other less memorable dishes.

Then it was time to really explore, firstly to the Old Town, a place that I had never been near before and was 180 degrees around the other side of the Lake from where we normally go, located near to a large pavilion at Wu Shan, which we can always see across the Lake. This place had a great atmosphere of old China, including teahouses, shops, including minority goods from elsewhere in western China, restaurants and so on. Great place and it some ways more attractive to me than the Yu Yuan Gardens in Shanghai. I shake my head wondering why we have never been here before but realize that it has probably been redeveloped after our guidebooks were printed; such is the pace of change in modern China. Then it was a short walk down towards the Lake to a lakeside park and a walk along the road where there were several new western style bars, to the Xi Hu Tiandi, not like the Shanghai's Xintiandi, quite, but a smaller version and done along similar lines. Yes, Hangzhou is way beyond Jiaxing's standards, a fact emphasized as we walked past a Bentley showroom and a Porsche one nearby. This is a flourishing city, and I am reminded that Peter Ma, the China Internet king comes from this City. This is a successful and westernized place in a Chinese sort of way. Walking further we discover the stretch of lakeside where I went together with the ICBC Bank visit last year and notice the newly developed and tree lined shops long another stretch of Lake, including new Giorgio Armani shops in among the Haagen-Daz, new Grand Hyatt hotel and the Starbucks, McDonalds being relegated to a position away from the Lake. This is a walking boulevard area, a combination of Lake Geneva and Cannes or Nice, perhaps with a few more Chinese folk around though. Not quite walking all the way back, we treated myself to a nightcap in the Shangri-La bar before retiring for a good night's sleep, tired by the day's events, but a good day, leaving me with a feeling that I now know Hangzhou somewhat better.

But it was Jiaxing that was my town, remember the name as it is a coming city within China.

Stood by one of many canals in Jiaxing just before this old town was starting to be bulldozed and was later redeveloped as an old town. 2002.

Chapter 26

Beijing

Considering the length of time that I was in China I visited Beijing infrequently. My initial visit, early on in 2002 was to go to a large Tobacco exhibition there. This was followed by a family holiday there later the same year.

Further visits included two trips to the Great Hall of the People, once to receive an award and once as part of a UK government delegation. I was also privileged to go to the Beijing Olympics Finals in 2008. Other trips included a customer visits for annual sales tenders, a visit to see lawyers there and trips to see customers.

Unlike Shanghai, Beijing with its population of nineteen million people is far more spread out in size with long distances between key parts of the city, journeys that take time given the nature of traffic congestion. Beijing is obviously the home of central government and is more strictly managed as a result; less open and more formal! It is very traditional and the buildings less flamboyant in their architecture. Being geographically north it is a colder climate.

My first visit was special in many ways, I was new to China, the weather was lovely and there were less people around as at that time domestic tourism had not taken off and there were comparatively few foreign tourists as well. The purpose of the visit was to represent the joint venture that I was running making cigarette paper at the Chinese State Tobacco Monopoly's cigarette and tobacco exhibition, and I wanted to understand the markets and products better. This was important as cigarette manufacturers from all over China had stands there as it was the largest domestic exhibition. I was informed that I could not go as it was for Chinese nationals only, thereby shutting me down. I decided to push back and point out that I was running a joint venture, in China, making cigarette paper with innovative technology, living in China, and supplying the Chinese markets, logic that could not really be argued with and eventually I was granted special permission from someone up high in the CNTC apparently. Having got there what happened on the day was "rock star stuff" as I was the only foreigner attending.

Below are diary excerpts of certain visits to Beijing.

w/c 28th July 2002 - Sunday morning starts with a trip to Shanghai Hong Qiao Airport for the flight to Beijing. I am not actually comfortable carrying ¥20,000 plus in cash (£1,900). This is still a cash society, but the two thick bundles of 200 x ¥100 notes is a strange and bulky feeling – and not easy to carry; my briefcase remains locked and close to me.

We are booked into the five-star Wang Fu Jing Grand Hotel in Central Beijing, a few blocks from Tiananmen Square. The weather in Beijing rainy on arrival, hotel very pleasant, with a decent sized swimming pool in the basement and the usual five-Star facilities, although perhaps not as opulent as some others in town. With room rates discounted from about £180 per night to approximately £55. The only perceivable downside turned out to be the hard beds.

Breakfast on Monday was at a Deli France; five minutes' walk away in the new shopping precinct on the 'Walking Street'. Well eaten, we then headed off in the burning sun towards Tiananmen Square, which was disappointingly busy with tour parties. Trying to explain Chinese history to the younger generations is harder work than expected as they obviously don't remember Mao, the uniforms, Annual May Day parades, or even the 1989 Tiananmen Square incident – which I recall to them in hushed tones. Then it was into the magnificent, but equally busy Forbidden City. We follow the crowds, do the usual tourist stuff before heading off to a local Baihai park, going around the lake on a boat trip to cool down. Then it was another hill park, Jinshan Park, next to the Forbidden City where one of the Qing Dynasty Mandarins once committed suicide and were we discovered that the hill was made from the earth dug out to create the moat around the Forbidden City. Some feat, especially if the poor workers had to dig it out in this humidity!

I reflect on the odd feeling that this was the second time that I have been here within two months. Then we head out to the city's "Hard Rock Café – Beijing".

A comparatively expensive, but genuine western meal followed, and got the feel of much Rock History. Pictures of all sorts of 'old folk' and funny guitars everywhere around us that I had to justify and explain. Afterwards before we walked around the leafy and guarded Embassy district and the expatriate bars in a 'western entertainment street'.

Tuesday, we piled into an air-conditioned minibus together with driver and personal English-speaking guide for the two and a half hours trip to see the Great Wall at Si Ma Tai, which is considerably less touristy and more rustic that Badaling – This was correct, indeed an understatement. This was further than my previous trip to 'The Wall' and was made more interesting by driving through very green and fertile fields surrounded by picturesque hills and dotted with peasant farm compounds. We also went through a Town that is either a new town or being constructed in preparation for an Olympic event – it is just a building site of plush and modern buildings.

Si Ma Tai proved to be an interesting experience, underdeveloped and very quiet, despite the usual presence of souvenir shops and cafes. The walk to the wall was a challenge and feat in itself – a good half mile, probably more – 'upwards'. The first two sections of the Wall out of the valley bottom were as steep as one could imagine – all in searing heat and humidity. Unofficial local farmwomen were making a nuisance of themselves as potential guides. By the time that we got to the fourth section, it was time for a rethink and had an angry exchange managed to clear off the 'guides'. In the event my, we kept going to the top (thirteenth section) and then down a steep path, returning the last section by cable car.

On the way back we visited 'Dr. Tea' on the outskirts of Beijing, which included a demonstration in English of a variety of different Chinese teas and how they should be drank and prepared – basically the more slurping and funny faces made, the better! Then they tried to sell us everything in the place. We escaped with a couple of mugs! At least I know what I should be doing with all the tea and tea sets that I have at home in the apartment now.

I dined at the hotel's seafood buffet restaurant, which was fairly priced and included such well-known seafood delicacies as beef goulash soup, chicken pieces, beef slices and lamb. The rest of the seafood was quite standard, including Japanese style dishes.

Wednesday started with a three-kilometre walk to the Temple of Heaven, in what must have been the most humid conditions that I have ever experienced.

The gardens and Temple were wonderful, but not as heavenly as the ice-lolly and ice-cold drinks we had there.

Then it was back to the hotel, getting truly ripped off by the taxis drivers who took us on a tour of the city's congested ring roads before returning us safely. After lunching I went to the Summer Palace about twelve kilometres from the city centre. Truly wonderful, a 'Chinese Versailles'.

I am starting to get a feel for Chinese entrepreneurialism, when I, quite out of character, decided to by a cheap Rolex watch on the street. I managed to get myself passed what we suspected to be a dud ¥100 note, although I managed to get clear of it later; however, getting rid of the Russian '50 ruble' note he also gave me in the change will prove harder! I really must pay more attention in future.

Dinner was at the American/Aussie 'Outback' restaurant at the famous Beijing Grand Hotel just along from Tiananmen Square. To my mind the best food yet, proving the point that Americans do produce and present the best steaks. I escaped the shopping afterwards (Burberry handbag, Chinese style shirt and a traditional Chinese silk dress, which is in keeping with smart restaurant waitresses and ladies at the front door of massage parlours) and preparing for the journey to Xian tomorrow.

Leaving Beijing, I realize how much we have enjoyed our trip to Beijing – a wonderful mixture of 'old', tradition, and 'new' and different cultures, albeit bloody expensive.

W/c 14th December 2002 - Tuesday morning I was up fresh and early to head off to Beijing with sales colleagues and a German other JV colleague who is travelling with us to Beijing. These annual meetings are where the Chinese State Tobacco Corporation allocates most of our sales volumes for the forthcoming year. Oh the joys of a well-run Monopoly and this one is a well-run one. These are the most important sales meetings of the year, although a lot of preparation has gone in over the previous months as the sales guys have sacrificed their livers for the good of the company. I ponder what lies ahead of me? I wonder; this could make or break us, and the competition is getting fiercer and fiercer. I am told that the weather is flipping cold up there and all that I have dug out is the old red Helly Hansen ski jacket, which is not that

old and is quite smart but is very bulky and is not standard business wear. However, I am a westerner, and it is cold, I conclude that I can get away with anything. Has the dual effect of making me look like a fat! Like many Americans out here.

Not a good day. Journey delayed, had my scissors removed from my wash bag at the airport security, arrive in Beijing hot and sticky despite cold weather and hotel room was a comparative fleapit Chinese style – cigarette burns and stains on the carpet etc and all, oh yes, and no windows, very claustrophobic, but at least the bed is comfortable. Beijing was cold, very grey, and miserable and the traffic worse than that. Tired after a sleepless night and uncomfortable journey, we had a terrible meal, whereby my moody translator translated absolutely nothing, as she did not understand the dialect of the customers, we were entertaining from Hunan Province, and I drank too much to toast everyone but got to know no one really. I am tired and the effects of my cold, and the cold weather are taking effects on my face but looking around many of my colleagues' complexions have also changed; reminds me of the benefit of living in a warm climate.

Wednesday morning, I felt a little better in myself despite the 60 per cent proof baijiu being consumed the previous night. The CNTC had the wisdom to move all the morning's meetings to the afternoon, I surmise on the grounds that most of the delegates were either dead, dying or in a condition somewhere in between. I base this observation upon what I witnessed the night before. Took the opportunity to meet a few 'old friends', which in China one tends to do in their hotel bedrooms; all very sociable but included one where we walked in to find the guy half dead from the prior night's activities and lying there totally immodestly in his underwear and with the door open. He showed some slight embarrassment at my presence, but nothing compared to the colour of my translator's face.

Gordon Brown

w/c 12th January 2008 – Tuesday was one of those strange days in life, although given what I had gone through in China I am rarely surprised or phased by developments. Out of the blue I received a call from our UK principal and effectively puts me on standby to meet with the UK Prime

Minister, Gordon Brown on Thursday along with Sir Digby Jones, formerly the Director General of the CBI and now Minister for Trade and Industry and I recall hearing him speak somewhere in the UK a decade or so before, maybe at the Grosvenor.

Returning from a routine banking trip to Shanghai I get a follow up phone call from our principal to inform me that I am now joining Gordon Brown's delegation tomorrow and going to Beijing to meet him there. "It is all arranged, and Digby has your mobile number and will call you" End of call. Somehow, I was sceptical that this would happen, but..........

Digby is indeed Sir Digby Jones, also a Labour Peer, otherwise known as Digby, Lord Jones of Birmingham as well as being the former director of the CBI for seven years. He was fifty-one years old and now Minister of Trade Promotion and a slightly controversial appointment apparently by Brown to the Cabinet. He is the Vice President of UNISEF, a member of the Commonwealth Education Board, Commission for Racial Equality and the National Learning and Skills Council.

Gordon Brown, the UK's new Prime Minister is seemingly visiting Beijing and Shanghai in China with a trade delegation from the UK for three days starting this coming Friday, following a similar visit to India, where he met our principal. This visit is getting a fair amount of attention here with the Chinese government declaring that Sino-UK relations are at an all-time high, which is great given that there has always been an uneasiness with Britain given the fact that it pinched Hong Kong for 100 years as well as developing the opium trade in China at the same time which made the British a lot of money and had a proportion of intellectual China wondering around in a drug enhanced state that eventually resulted in a war.

Thereafter there was lots of confusion, but I eventually managed to contact Digby Jones' private secretary who was aware of me and expecting me in Beijing, basically get to the airport asap and fly to Beijing. Work it out yourself Jeremy – this week's management challenge.

Another short call identifies the hotel, the China World hotel in Beijing, a Shangri-La hotel, that I need to check into and that Gordon Brown himself has agreed to me joining his delegation on behalf of our principal and that he has my CV (resume). Then another call from him – Dinner at the British Embassy, flying back with Gordon Brown to Shanghai on his privately chartered Boeing jumbo jet and so on, but behind it all I had a sinking feeling of not being included and a return trip back from Beijing having wasted a day or two.

It was snowing when I arrived in Beijing after the flight, and it took a slow taxi journey into the 3rd ring road and around past the distinctive Lufthansa Center and the Hard Rock Café onto the World Trade Center. As I had predicted this is when things started to go a bit pear shaped, as due to security reasons and over subscription, the events at the Great Hall of the People and another at the hotel, were very high security and very sensitive with all attending delegates cleared a month prior as Digby's private secretary and official from the British Embassy explained to me. This had all the trappings of a total cock up and I was told to wait so with time on my hands I went down for a dinner alone and noted that this hotel had all sorts of awards such as Best Luxury Hotel in Beijing, Best Business Hotel in Beijing, on the Gold List of Best Hotels in the World and so on.

Just when I was starting to think that this was all total waste of time, I got a call from a British Embassy official who told me to get myself up to the seventh Floor of a nearby Sofitel Wanda Hotel, a ten-minute walk, to register myself for the China-UK Business Summit of 'Partnership Through Innovation'. It seems that I am indeed invited to tomorrow mornings Plenary Session at the Great Hall of the People where a shed load of important people, both British and Chinese, will be giving speeches, including the Rt Hon Gordon Brown MP, Sir Digby Jones, Sir Richard Branson and of course Premier of the State Council of the People's Republic of China, Wen Jia Bao.

Then in the afternoon it was lunch back in the Sofitel and an afternoon of business matching and informal networking, hosted by Lord Jones. Sadly, I was not invited to the formal dinner this evening, too tight for numbers at short notice I was told.

Friday morning I joined a delegation bus trip to the Great Hall of the People just off Tiananmen Square. Deja Vue for me, my second formal visit here, my first being in 2005. The event was a long winded three-hours of speeches, with Digby Jones making a very good speech, selling the virtues of the UK and he seemed like the affable sort of bloke you would meet at a rugby match or downing a malt whisky in a cigar lounge.

Conversely Gordon Brown demonstrated that he had certain lack of charisma despite his talents! He managed to get himself 'out charisma-ed' by a Chinese leader which takes some doing, but he sounded competent enough.

Wen Jia Bao as always, had a good story to tell, told it well and was ever the polished diplomat and courteous.

Richard Branson is not known as a great orator, more a visual presence, although in contrast to Sir Richard Brower, Chairman of the China-British Foundation, he does have the most wonderful tonality of voice and a great story to tell, referring to anecdotes about how the Virgin brand came about, either that or 'Slipped Disc' was the choice of name by his account. And how he started his first airline company – a charter from the British Virgin Islands to Puerto Rico after he and a lot more were bumped off a flight – he chartered a plane and charged all the bumped off passengers to fly with him......and made a profit!

The Brits sat in our row were typically mischievous as ever in these situations, with that Brit schoolboy type humour, like how to get photographed for tomorrow's world news? Simply produce a picture of the Dali Lama or unveil a t-shirt with 'Free Tibet' written on the front and so on. Brave or fool-hardy saying such things in the centre of power of the Chinese government in respect to such sacred topics! Dangerous humour!

Thereafter it was back to the hotel for more networking and thereafter the day fizzling out somewhat. I didn't really get that close to major politicians and, never would have given the Chinese security provisions in place that were even stricter for the Shanghai visit I was told.

It was an experience non-the-less, and I was proud and honoured to represent our company, a significant British company investor in China at this event, even in a peripheral capacity.

The Beijing Olympics

I had the privilege to have been invited to the 2008 Beijing Olympics as part of the PICC's Zhejiang Province delegation of major clients. The PICC being the largest Insurance company, a state-run institution.

w/c 16th August 2008 – Friday the arrival at Hangzhou's Xiao Shan Airport was another first for me, entering through its VIP gate and VIP check in, not that it was anything special, but there were lots of comfy seats and everything seemed to have been done for us. Now I know a bit more about how the other half live out here – later appearing in Departures through glass lifts that arrived up through the floor in the centre. Traveling with this party is proving a little difficult, as I don't have a dedicated translator as such as they are also the tour organizers, so I am left to fend for myself in silence, frustrated that I am unable to communicate with anybody as the only non-Chinese in the party, but enjoying the moments of peace and isolation.

The arrival in Beijing was good – the weather was fabulous, hot, sunny, not too humid, clear blue skies, none of the torrential rain of yesterday, nor much of Beijing's much vaunted smog! Indeed the place was looking great and the new airport simply fabulous. The coach trip into the city was quick and we were taken to the Beijing International Hotel, I guess a Chinese five-star hotel and I had a very pleasant room on the fifteenth floor having entered the hotel and noting that we did not have to go through the airport style security checks there as we were VIPs! Nice buffet lunch but I am again frustrated that I was not able to talk to anyone as I still don't have a translator and the young male student on the bus was frankly worse than useless. At this moment though was the only downside. The hotel was quite central set on the main road into Tiananmen Square and the Forbidden City, which are only a couple of blocks down from us – although in Beijing a couple of blocks is still a good walk! I note that the Olympic Village and park is set in the north of the city centre. It also must be said that the traffic was remarkably light compared to the normal Beijing road congestion, so whatever measures were being applied were working, at least for the duration of the games.

Sebastian Coe has stated that these Olympics have been planned with forensic detail for a long time and that is very apt and is evident everywhere. On a smaller scale, the PICC have been very good providing us all with a commemorative dish, two PICC t-shirts (the only downside being that they are far too small for me), rucksack, baseball cap, umbrella, fan, sunscreen and basic medications, introduction booklets and more. Excellent, but a real shame about the shirts that are unwearable.

This evening we had to attend a large banquet in the hotel, hosted by the PICC. It suddenly dawns on me how privileged that I was to be here. This is not the only dinner that the PICC has had over the last fourteen days here, but it is big, 400 people in a large hall, hosted by the Chairman and Chief Executive of this massive insurance company that was a part of the Bank of China until about twenty years ago. Guess what, I was the only foreigner present, and it became quickly evident that the guests were selected handpicked senior guests from all over China given that this was the 'finals' season. Great occasion and throughout there was stage entertainment – basketball spinners, magic, the lady with the changing faces, singers, gymnasts, electric violin players and the likes – great event and back in my room by eight o'clock to watch the basketball on TV. I suddenly feel extremely humble and privileged again – here at a time like this, a global showcase, the only foreign guest on this night of the PICC Insurance company, a state icon, the official sponsor of the Olympics and one of the biggest companies in China, at least for now, that is the pinnacle of China's development. Tonight I was photographed A LOT, even if Beijing has lots of foreigners living here now – I was the only one in this place! I just hoped that I could get a photo with the Chairman and Chief Executives toasting me at the banquet – it would be good company PR.

Looking out of my room tonight Beijing looked great, all lit up, clean and brilliant and it dawns on me that I am here right in the middle of it all – all the stars and dignitaries are around and nearby, privileged times at an historic moment. I remember that I had once been to the Sydney Olympic Stadium in 1999 to watch a Centenary International rugby match, ahead of the Olympics and hope perhaps to get to the London Olympics in four years' time.

w/c 23rd August 2008 – Saturday was another lovely morning, looking out upon quiet streets, blue skies without a cloud in the sky and only the merest trace of a minor fog haze. Indeed half the moon was visible in the bright blue skies for much of the day, all of which boded well.

Having attended breakfast in the presence of several hundred other people all wearing their nicely styled PICC red T-shirts, I somewhat self-consciously decide that I will have to wear mine, as tight as it is, as I would probably feel less self-conscious than wearing a non-team shirt, but also not wanting to risk upsetting my hosts. I do though feel somewhat like one of those certain type of British tourists in Spain with the big gut wearing a football shirt that is many, many sizes too small. As a compromise I put a spare comfy shirt into my rucksack for the day just in case but console myself that with Chinese politeness that my fat will disappear quickly into the crowds and that no one will notice that my shirt is ridiculously too tight around my chest, a real effort to put this on alone. I note an air of excitement amongst the rest of the delegates and observe that most of the attendees at the games were people from the State and Provincial governments, Bank of China, PICC Insurance Company, Lenovo, the computer manufacturer, Coca Cola, Volkswagen, Visa, Sinopec,

*Samsung, Adidas, GE, the State Grid, Panasonic, and China Mobile.........
and of course friends and families. I reflect that there won't be much chance
of 'common folk' in attendance.*

*At eight thirty we all congregate in Reception for our coaches and our
adventures of the day. What a fabulous day and experience that it turned
out to be, albeit a tiring one. The first thing that happened when I arrived in
reception was that the Chinese Beijing PICC organizer burst out into fits of
laughter at the sight of my shirt commenting that they didn't have any bigger
sizes, and other members of our delegation politely commenting that it was "too
small", whilst stifling their obvious inclination to laugh too; but I am doing
this. Bring on the Sport!*

*Firstly we arrived at the Olympic Park, about twenty minutes' drive to
the north of our hotel and I still can't quite believe how clear the Beijing traffic
is. Then it was a good chance to wander around the extensive Olympics park,
taking photos of all and sundry, albeit me with my new camera phone – The
"Birds Nest" Stadium, the TV Tower, the "Water Cube", the adjacent reputed
'7-star' Pang Gu hotel, with the massive external TV screens on the outside of
the top of this uniquely designed building, the sculptures and many others until
decamping to the PICC hospitality centre for a rest and more photos from the
building's third floor decking shaped like a boat and pointing directly at the
"Nest". The mood is now full swing party mood, and I am feeling the Chinese
nationalistic pride starting to emerge.*

*Then it was to the Nest itself, an amazing experience and certainly not a
disappointing one, along with 89,099 others, to watch the Olympics Football
Finals, which Argentina won by beating Nigeria 1-0. Not the greatest match
of soccer ever played, but the second half improved, and the world class Lionel
Messi was fantastic. I was left wondering why GB never enters a team for this
competition and was later to discover that there was talk about GB entering
a team for the coming London Olympics in 2012. 89,100 people – that is a
big crowd by any standards, but this though was about the stadium and the
atmosphere inside, which it was impossible to try and describe the magnitude of
it all. What I would say though was that it was extremely well supervised and
planned out – none of the crushes associated in my mind from my youth of the
pushing and shoving and queuing to get in and out of grounds, no hooligans,
just a great atmosphere and everyone seemingly proud and honoured to be here.*

Then it was some rest in the Olympic Recreation Center, in another PICC hospitality restaurant and some light refreshments before heading off site for dinner, a luxury international cuisine restaurant and one of the best that I have seen in China with western, Chinese, and Japanese specialities available – excellent. Still virtually no traffic and the word from the translator is that the Beijing residents have been paid significant amounts of money not to take their cars onto the roads during the Olympic periods; money always works here.

Then it was another twenty minutes bus ride out of the centre to the Capital Gymnasium, the venue for the Olympic Volleyball and the woman's finals. This was a fantastically exciting match as Brazil beat the USA. I guess about 20,000 folks were in this refurbished auditorium, with Wu Yi present in the VIP box, she who had overseen my national friendship award three years prior and an amazing atmosphere inside fueled by the Brazilians zest for life and a party.........and boy did they have one! Great game and great evening. After the medal ceremonies we eventually got back to our hotel at midnight, tired and exhausted, but a day never to be forgotten, the Olympic Finals in Beijing! The biggest cheer of the evening though had been when the Chinese National team who finished 3rd, sneaked discretely into the stands to watch the latter half of the volleyball match. I have discovered that the Chinese equivalent of 'let's go' combined as a sort of nationalistic chant, was "Jai you", pronounced 'zhai yo', and when China, or 'Zhong Guo' is put in front of it, then there was a spontaneous crowd reaction that was passionate. So when a foreigner in a tight red t-shirt stands up and shouts "Zhong Guo jai you", the stadium instantly starts a chant of 'China lets go' – and that is how I did it, getting into the spirit of things, and smiles all around me along with thumbs up signals of appreciation.

Sunday I was up at seven o'clock, and we were afforded some rest time this morning congregating at 10.30 hours for lunch and our trip to the boxing finals. I used my time by walking for an hour and a half along to Tiananmen Square, a place that still fascinates me. After a very nice Beijing speciality lunch it was out on a coach again for about twenty minutes to the Workers Gymnasium, the venue for the Boxing Finals, along the way passing the impressive new CCTV Television station building, and the tallest building in Beijing opposite, along with many other newly finished or new finished modern high-rise buildings nearby. These were right behind the World Trade Centre hotel that I had stayed in when last here in January and noting that Beijing is looking far more modern than I have noticed in the past, still vast, but its array of buildings seems more stylish, although Shanghai it is not.

The boxing started well for China as it won a gold on an early retirement by a Mongolian boxer for a clearly injured arm in round 1, but thereafter it was good entertainment with China winning a storming light heavyweight gold again a feisty and well supported Irishman. Deontay Wilder won a bronze.

Then it was off for another excellent meal and an informal banquet of sorts, but nothing heavy. Then it was back to the hotel to watch the closing ceremony for the Beijing Olympics as we didn't have tickets for this. Long after the event finished there were fireworks going up all over Beijing for a long time, keeping me awake long into the night. I had thought briefly about trying to scalp a ticket for this event, but after hearing a large American guy on his phone at the boxing arena saying in a long drawl that he would 'pay anything' to get a ticket from a scalper, I decided against it.

Call me old fashioned and a sceptic, but as I watched the finale to the most fantastic Olympics ever staged until that stage, Boris Johnson, as mayor of London must have been sat there thing 'Oh Fxxx, how do I follow that'? And 'How the hell did we manage to come up with a GB presentation for the ceremony like that?' The event seemed to be a phenomenal show except in my mind for the British bit – a London Bus, an aging rock star who looked terrified, a hot and embarrassed female singer who I didn't recognize, but I was sure must now be famous in the UK, crap sound effects from a TV viewing point of view on the guitar rift, amateurish routine by a little girl who got there by winning a Blue Peter competition I gather, three cyclists and a weird collection of pink haired punk street entertainers, a British Airways step ladder and of course David Beckham, who I do admire, and so does China......oh yes, and one of the weakest renditions of God Save the Queen that I have heard, an apology for being British by a scruffily attired choir. Maybe it was a sound effects issue? Somehow, I could not help but be embarrassed, embarrassed for our country. London Olympics won't be Beijing, and will try to emulate it, but surely this presentation could have been better? It was an attempt to reflect the modern all-inclusive Britain but somehow seemed to miss out middle Britain. Boris Johnson did offer some light relief and his presence was in stark contrast to the overly formal and stuffy Chinese hierarchy though, who were just a bit too formal for me, maybe nervous, but their impression I thought on this occasion was not so good until the ever smiling Premier, Wen Jia Bao, turned up. All in all it is no wonder that the world sees us as mildly eccentric at times, and then there is that bloody London Olympics Logo, that I still can't work out and certainly would not start to create anything like it if handed a pen, although I am sure that in time that I will come to love it.

Conversely to all of this I was stunned when later a CNN commentator said that London had used its eight minutes well enough to 'steal the show' and ended on that note. I need to re-calibrate myself. The CNN anchor following that comment did not react with the same enthusiasm looking a little stunned though. Then next morning when one of our Chinese team translator asked me what the British presentation was meant to depict, I must confess that I struggled to enlighten them beyond being a typical street scene whereby British threw their newspapers on the ground as rubbish and a London bus that was overcrowded and occasionally gets blown up! She conceded that she found the presentation a little strange (translation of 'a little' being 'very'), rather too directly for the normally polite Chinese, but it seemed that Beckham saved the day, he is one of the two biggest sporting icons on the planet along with Kobe Bryant.

After this lot is the world still calling China backward. Possibly the Yanks, who made a major criticism today on Chinese Human rights, but I noted that despite China's success, that the USA also had their most successful games ever and GB its best medal count this century. I keep reading about human rights violations in China and I am sure some of the facts are right, but on a personal level I am not sure that some of the personal freedoms and rights are so great either elsewhere in the world. I should note that at no time have I felt threatened, for the most haven't been hassled, wasn't mugged, was ripped off, wasn't delayed by protestors, wasn't delayed by traffic, didn't queue anywhere for any meaningful time, everything was clean and free of rubbish and the atmosphere generally great, as was the weather.

My only negative? Not getting a ticket to see the basketball finals, the hottest ticket in town!

Inside the "Birds-nest" stadium in Beijing ready for the 2008
Olympic Soccer Finals with Argentina starring Lionel Messi beating
Nigeria. Later I got to watch the 2008 Olympic Boxing Finals
where Deontay Wilder was to fight and get a bronze medal.

Chapter 27

Shanghai

Shanghai to me is the most exciting city in the World, or at least certainly right up there in my top three. The modern Shanghai has everything, from the beauty of the 1930's European building influences on the Bund and the former French Concession, the dominating skyline of the new Pudong area, the tree lined roads, huge malls, traditional Chinese influences as well as authentic restaurants and bars to cater for tastes of expatriates and visitors from all around the world. Always with international exposure in its history, it has a certain style that many Chinese aspire to. It is rich and getting richer and despite its growing boundaries, it is still relatively compact for a population of its enormous size, with key attractions closer and more accessible than some other cities such as Beijing. It is also more relaxed and 'open,' less strict that Beijing.

Sure, there are a lot of people there, estimated at 27.8 million and climbing in 2021, plus all the migrant labour that is in the millions, but that adds to the character, the hustle and bustle of the place. The largest 'proper' city population anywhere in the world I gather, with 99 per cent being Han Chinese although minorities growing quickly. It combines a modernization of the new China with the influences of the western world, both old and new. It is a place that young Chinese lust to get to work and enjoy the wealthier lifestyle there. There are over 150,000 foreigners registered in Shanghai, the largest of which is Japanese followed by Americans and Koreans. In such environments, opposites attract, relationships develop, and I understand that about 3,000 mixed blood or foreign babies, are born each year out of relationships.

The comparatively new Pudong region has grown out of flatlands, a marsh on the other side of the Huangpu River, which was once home to a power station, coal dump and a paper mill and now boasts one of the globe's most famous skylines.

I cannot compete with tourist travel guides, but this is a truly fascinating city – the history on the foreign banking investments and racecourses, the divided city with American, French, Japanese and British influences, the lockdown under the communist revolution, the decadent 1930s, and of course the traditional cultures. So much to see from the Buddhist temples, the markets, scientific museums, the impressive city planning hall showing small scale models of the city, the airports, extremely tall buildings (Some of the world's tallest), restaurants, orchestras, foreigner streets, bars, simply everything it seems set around the flow of the Huangpu River, still a working river with barges appearing in amongst sightseeing boats. There is so much entertainment at so many levels.

The temperature is great, albeit a tad too hot at times in summer. It is where many of the Chinese populace aspire to live, although hukou's, the registered permissible homes of people, is obviously strictly regulated.

For the international tourist who has travelled all around China's key tourist sites from the Great Wall and Forbidden city in Beijing, The Terracotta Army in Xian, and those hills in Guilin, this is a wonderful place to end the trip, weaning off Chinese food for western luxury and authentic food and drink in the relaxed areas of Xintiandi or overlooking the Bund or Pudong. The economic powerhouse that has everything.

With China's and the city's development came new events such as the prestigious 2010 Expo, an enormous success, and another Chinese showcase.

In 2004 Formula 1 grand prix events arrived on a brand-new purpose-built circuit – over the years I was to attend most of the annual F1 events at the Shanghai circuit. I did though also have the pleasure of attending the very first F1 grand prix held in China on 26th September 2004 which captivated the nation's interest with huge attendance.

Shanghai is a must visit, one for life's bucket list of things to do. I cannot adequately do justice to the city and its progression and most of my experiences there centered around tourist visits, medical visits, weekend relaxation breaks and shopping.

It is now perhaps the more authentic *"East meets West"* than its predecessor, Hong Kong, although some may liken this statement to comparisons as to who was the best James Bond actor.

After lunch photo on the terrace of a Bund restaurant overlooking the Pudong skyline and Huangpu River including working barges 2014 - The four tallest buildings are the Pearl Oriental Tower, Jin Mao Tower, Shanghai World Financial Centre, and the Shanghai Tower that was nearing completion.

At one of many annual pilgrimages to the Shanghai
Circuit to see the F1 Grand Prix.

Chapter 28

Tales from My Travels –
Provinces and Regions

In this chapter I share some of my first-hand experiences and observations of them from various visits around China during my first few years, as thereafter my business responsibilities were constantly changing, and travel then became international in nature. What follows are extracts from my personal diary notes highlighting the lifestyle and differences. Many of the experiences were before the Chinese domestic tourism took off so venues were often quieter and less commercialized than they would be today.

Most of the trips were business related although there are some private ones as well. In China, business trips at the time that I was there were different to those in Europe, where I may fly into a city for a meeting, stay overnight and fly back. In China, as per State policy, to encourage guanxi and to learn new experiences, business trips were more akin to short holidays, no chance to fast track these trips. I found myself in the hands of the joint venture partners who initiated the trips in the first few years and indeed our customers who would have been offended if these visits had not taken place or had been rushed.

As I was involved into the tobacco industry, the biggest cigarette smoking market in the world and a sizeable proportion of China's GDP at that time, I was privileged to be treated accordingly and to meet many senior regional folks along the way. I should comment that when I was appointed by the Board to the position of GM of the joint venture making cigarette paper, our Group CEO said, "Congratulations Jeremy, you got the job, but it looks like you won't have any sales as the joint venture partner is taking them away"! Hence there was added method to my madness, meeting as many customers and potential customers as quickly as possible, promoting the advantages of our products, our western orientated business, and our cause under challenging circumstances.

These diary notes are not inclusive of all my visits to provinces and cities, and they are shown in alphabetical order, except for the last two due to time variations and changes in personal circumstances, and calendar order within provincial visits thereafter.

28.1 Anhui

w/c 6th September 2003 - I had not been to Anhui Province before and don't know too much about it apart from the fact that it is relatively close (10 hours by train), in a Province adjacent to Zhejiang, often floods very badly in places and is also quite poor in places. We are firstly heading towards Hefei, the provincial capital, then later onto the more remote city of Fuyang in the northwestern area of the province.

The train left from the Jiaxing Train Station at ten o'clock in the evening, and I am travelling with my translator and a joint venture Sales guy who I realize that I don't really know at all. Suddenly I could do without this trip and the thought of ten hours or so on a sleeper train does not fill me full of glee, neither did having to leave my apartment with two cases trying to find a taxi in the middle of a thunderstorm. I am glad in these circumstances that I had decided to travel overnight casually – donned in shorts and short sleeve shirt, although I am not sure what my travelling companions made of it; shorts not being a norm at this time.

On the way into the station I had to put my large case through a security check scanner, which I always find highly amusing as at train stations during these times they never check any of the large hand luggage, no matter how many pieces one carries, and I was just joking with my translator about it when the security men demanded me to open my suitcase. The x-ray cameras had spotted my underarm deodorant aerosol, and this threw them, as they don't use this stuff in China. The fact that it has a flammable safety sign printed on the side of the can throws them into a panic and they want to confiscate it, thereby throwing me into a panic and a mild rage at the thought of travelling to customers without any deodorant in hot and sweaty conditions. One of those heated 'Chinese moments' followed and in hindsight I am again pleased that they didn't speak English. The situation was only resolved when my normally mild mannered and polite translator grabbed the can out of the security guard's hand aggressively, snarled at him and I suspect told him not to be such a silly boy, but I didn't like to ask. I proceeded still mumbling Anglo-Saxon to myself about Chinese rules and procedures.

The train journey was another one of those Chinese new experiences, primarily as on the first leg of the trip to Shanghai we were not allowed into our 1ˢᵗ Class soft sleeper cabins, even though they were empty and the fact that we had ticket numbers allocated to them, because Jiaxing Station was not authorized to issue tickets until Shanghai – Chinese rules job! This exposed me to the virtues of travelling in Chinese 'cattle class' – overcrowded, poor air quality, being gorped at, giggling girls, funny smells and Chinese arguing, leaving me feeling a little nauseous by the time we reached Shanghai station at eleven o'clock. Having transferred carriages though, things were much better and remarkably I slept solidly from midnight to seven o'clock next morning in my cot.

Monday morning was grey and overcast in Hefei, as we exited the station out onto one of those large concrete 'square' expanses with a large non-descript sculpture that seem typical at most Chinese train stations.

The Wencai International Hotel there gave us a chance to rest ahead of a trip to see the provincial CNTC bosses. These meetings went well as did the lunch in the CNTC's own restaurant accompanied by a little too much baijiu and a dinner with a sensitive amount of red wine; the food in both cases being excellent in quality and variety.

Whilst here I discover that Hefei has a population of over 2.6 million and that the biggest local attraction, some three hours away, is Huang Shan Mountain (Yellow Mountain), an impressive large hill of some type, one of the most famous in China apparently and after which one of the province's most famous brands of cigarettes has been named.

Tuesday starts early as we head off by taxi for our four-hour drive to Fuyang, where one of our more significant customers operates. These four hours were one of my most interesting since I have been in China.

The road up to the northwest of the province was lined virtually all the way by houses, some in small towns, but mainly agricultural in nature, indeed sadly many resembling farmyards, not assisted by the recent heavy flooding in this area. This is a side of China that I haven't really had extensive exposure to before and reminds me that China really is still a developing country, with many of the scenes that I am watching reminiscent of my visit to Kenya four years ago. In contrast though, there were vast areas of flat and fertile plains, framed in many parts by hills silhouetted against the skyline, one set of which had a big sign up in English proclaiming these are the "Woolong Mountains", which I must confess I had previously assumed that they had been in Australia. The scenery was quite beautiful, but spoiled by the squalor, dirtiness and untidiness of the residents and their accommodation. I don't believe that I have ever witnessed so many people over such a long stretch (a four-hour taxi journey being the equivalent distance of Exeter to North Manchester), but on distinctly average roads, they seem to be everywhere – walking along the roads, working in the fields, hanging around outside of shops and generally hanging out. Nor have I seen so many dogs running around loose, nor goats tethered by the roadside, nor for that matter so many oxen slumbering around. This area is truly rural, and many the roads were raised out of necessity above the flats reminding me of the dykes in northern Holland.

It is also quite evident that they do not have too many western visitors to this region, judging by the attention that I am getting when the taxi slows down, and indeed when we had a puncture. It was apparent as we passed through a small town, where the roadside markets encroach right across the road, that we had a 'flat tyre'. Enquiring whether the taxi has a spare, my translator informs me abruptly, 'of course, but it doesn't have any air in it'! So for some reason the taxi takes off with our sales guy leaving Sindy and I stranded on a grubby roadside being gorped at by all and sundry; lorries stopping, tractors stopping, kids and girls laughing, men crossing the road to look and so on. Yep, they really don't have western visitors here I conclude. I can visibly observe the jungle telegraph operating in front of my eyes and I wonder whether news of my presence will reach Fuyang before us.

As we close in on Fuyang, the ravages of the recent floods become more apparent as the main roads have broken up extensively, the large concrete sections having been undermined in the foundations by water. The road becomes an obstacle course as well as having to cope with the local driving techniques, which are way below the standard I am used to in Jiaxing. At one stage we drove the wrong way around a large roundabout, I kid not, at a reasonable speed too and I could only watch in disbelief as the oncoming traffic just avoided us, apparently without batting an eyelid, certainly without visible anger.

Fuyang's main street itself was not so bad and indeed was not dissimilar to

Jiaxing's main street, but beyond that there was no hiding the fact that this was a very poor area. At the hotel I got out of the taxi, wondering why my trousers fronts were covered in dirt, only to realize that this dirt had transferred from the taxi's front seat belt into my lap!

The factory was basic, consistent with the rest of the town and remains an old-style communist garden factory in many respects, with apartments and vegetation inside of the factory compound, but the people, as so often in such circumstances were extremely hospitable. We have booked a very nice shark's fin restaurant for dinner tonight, but the deputy factory manager insisted that as a first-time guest, I must dine in the hospitality of their own factory private rooms, which had the effect of turning my sales guy's face white. I found out why when I went to the loos before dinner, basic perhaps being an overstatement and clean not being an appropriate description. However, the excellent food and equally affable company compensated, associated by far too much baijiu; far too much; I mean far too much. We made friends and that is all I can remember between 21.00 hours and 07.00 hours; embarrassingly awaking still fully dressed and having not moved from where I had planted myself on the bed the previous night. I felt awful and a learning experience with baijiu.

So, Wednesday started on a somber note compounded by the fact that I had a mother of all hangovers and was not looking forward to my four-hour car journey back to Hefei (Fuyang has no airport), the subsequent one-hour flight back to Shanghai, and the hour and a quarter car trip back to our factory.

w/c 10th December 2004 - Wednesday morning is a very early start for us, four o'clock precisely, for a trip to Hong Qiao airport and the forty-five minutes hop into Hefei. That was the plan anyway! Firstly, it turned out to be extremely foggy in Jiaxing, resulting in the motorways to Shanghai being closed and us having to take the back roads. Having made take off on time though as we were descending into Hefei in fog the plane suddenly ascended steeply, apparently deciding that it was too foggy to land and promptly returned to Shanghai, where we sat on the ground for half an hour before taking off again and heading back to Hefei, by which time the fog had cleared. I am sure that they would have made this landing normally, but hot on the heels of the recent air crash, no one is taking any risks it seems.

Late in the day we went to the local Tobacco Monopoly offices where we had to wait for a while, but which gave me a chance to talk to a delightful fellow, speaking almost fluent English, who had spent a year in Liverpool in 2001 studying for his finance master's degree. Dinner with other guests including another supplier was excellent, with our customer services assistant obviously very popular with the customers, before returning to the New Wencai Garden Hotel that I stayed at last year.

Thursday, after a long night's sleep I awake to the coldest and most miserable weather that I have experienced in China this Autumn, before getting picked up for our three-to-four-hour trip up to Fuyang, which included a miserable lunch in one of the coldest and most miserable restaurants that I have been into and with what must be one of the most miserable toilets that I have been into – the male urinal was obviously used for more than just its intended purpose!! Miserable!

We have good friends in Fuyang, having met there last year and subsequently in Hong Kong, Macao and Jiaxing on more than one occasion. The key guy had also just returned from England and was excited by his visit to London and the Lake District. The worrying thing is that they like to drink a lot of baijiu here and I became very worried when I saw the large turnout, with seventeen people around a large banquet table, but restricted by their leader they treated me with respect during a wonderful dinner. Thereafter it was back to the large and modern hotel, proudly named 'Buckingham Palace'. No one believed that I had been to the actual Palace and had shaken hands with the Queen and Prince Philip though. When they realized that I was serious they were mightily impressed, even more so when I offered to take the leader of the party to India next year and phoned our principal on the spot to confirm it. Maybe the baijiu had something to do with it!

Friday morning we had an early lunch at the factory restaurant before taking a long twelve-hour train journey all the way back to Jiaxing in an open hard sleeper carriage, which turned out to be nearly thirteen hours of purgatory. These trains are always well organized but was very congested and noisy and was late meaning that I didn't get home until after midnight and very tired; indeed exhausted. This however was a good trip and may pay dividends for next year's business, indeed we are sure that it will.

w/c 11ᵗʰ November 2006 – Friday we depart for a long car trip to the city of Huainan in Anhui province, a trip which including a lunch stop, of over seven hours by car. The journey reminded me how big China is as we only just ventured up the Yangtze River delta, through Jiangsu, past Suzhou, Wuxi, and Zhanjiang, then onto Nanjing, Hefei and then north to our destination of Huainan. The weather was grey and miserable, but we left the heavy rains behind us, although the greyness did not help the impression of the poor Anhui countryside with its low-grade housing and agricultural background with haystacks seemingly everywhere including be transported on bikes. We stayed at the excellent Xin Jin Jiang Hotel in the city centre, and my room on the twentieth floor. Dinner was at six o'clock in the wonderful banqueting room, bedecked in traditional Chinese red, carved wood and gold and containing a large banqueting table for sixteen people, with a large and impressive gold Emperor's Dragon Chair at the head.

There were three simultaneous dinners related to our event going on, but things remained very sensible as we had a meeting afterwards, which continued until ten thirty, not actually finalizing the deal, but doing enough to get it very close, although a call to our principal nearly scuppered things good and proper.

w/c 18ᵗʰ November 2006 – This Saturday was one that I will remember in my life for many reasons, although a main one was that my son, here on holiday, was there to share the experience together with me. I awoke early looking out to a wet and grey day and overlooking quite a pleasant looking park opposite. A moment of levity at breakfast was when I was looking for tissue paper napkin for the breakfast table and I had some trouble for some reason making myself understood to the waitress in Chinese, but glad that she understood 'paper' when I said it in English, instant recognition. A minute or so later she turned up at the table armed with 'salt' and 'paper' (pepper) pots; never mind, we coped.

In China there is always a positive side to everything and the fact that it is pouring down with rain I am told, means that it will be a lucky day. I was though disappointed when I arrived at the twenty-first-floor official reception room at nine o'clock to find that it was hot. Anyway, we met the city's Party Secretary (the city's top man) for about half an hour with him breaking out into a major sweat in the heat and he demanded lower temperatures which made the whole thing easier. The room was set out formally in traditional Chinese fashion with me and the Party Secretary next to each other at the far end of the room away from the door, with respective translators tucked in behind us, and the large armchairs down each side of the room. Everybody commented on how handsome my son was. The Secretary then went into a narrative that didn't half go on about the place, the vast coal mining area and iron and ore resources, its partnership with the Ruhr area of Germany and the significant power generation facilities that supply much of China. It was though an excellent introduction accompanied the whole time by TV cameras and photography. Anhui province describes itself as being in northeastern China, although I would say that it was more east than north. Its lies in the Yangtze Delta, but also boundaried by the Huai He River, which is presumably why it floods so much, its average land height being only twenty to forty metres above sea level. Huainan is the seventh largest of sixteen cities and districts in Anhui province and is keen to develop other industries and encourage foreign investment. The population of Anhui was quoted at 55.6 million, which seems about the same as the UK in total and its area covers 139,600 square kilometres. The main tourist attraction is in the south at Huang Shan, which I still haven't been to and would really like to visit; must find time one weekend.

A little later we all went down to the very large and grand reception area for a 'signing ceremony' for our deal. Incidentally I am not too comfortable with the merits of this deal, but we are going ahead anyway it seems, but just signing a 'letter of intent' on the day, which is not legally binding.

The place was set out with big signs announcing the joint venture, unusually in such circumstances being all in Chinese with no English, facing the main reception area denoting the formation of our new joint venture, with about twenty dignitaries stood in front of it from Huainan, ourselves, and our joint venture partners, who are from Pinghu, one of Jiaxing's five counties. There were four or five speeches, one of which was by me being translated and my son was sat in the front row of a group of folks lined up and watching proceedings and then there was the formal ceremony and handshake. In total there were about 100 folk mulling around including the TV cameras and photographers, an educated old boy from the Beijing Stock Exchange and an old friend of mine from the Anhui CNTC, which means that the cat is out of the bag and that this deal, whilst sensitive with our original joint venture partner in China, is now public knowledge officially. The whole thing went well, toasted by a glass of red wine at the end before we set off in convoy to the new factory site, which at this time was a muddy field, for the formal 'stone laying' ceremony.

This ceremony was unfortunate because of the rain and there was all the normal associated stuff – red carpets, stage set up and red carpeted, big red signs, speeches, tall models in long red dresses, fireworks, and the spading of earth onto the main commemorative foundation stone, for which I was centre stage along with the old boy from Beijing. Great experience, and one which I am pleased that my son witnessed; I was proud having him there, but not so happy at the thick layers of mud on my shoes as the model who had led me onto the stage had taken me via the cross-country route, possibly thrown for a moment at having a foreigner in her presence. Afterwards it was back to the hotel for an excellent and high-powered banquet with excellent food and even more high-powered company, whilst my son and finance director went off to another banquet in another restaurant with 8 large tables of which he was one of fifteen on the top table which was kind. My son had been impressed by the 'convoy' of black cars to and from the hotel and the new site, which ironically was one of the worst organized that I have come across in China, despite all points police escorts, perhaps made worse by the heavy rain and city centre traffic, but included our driver jumping red lights, regularly crossing central lines into oncoming traffic to keep up and only very narrowly avoiding a couple of head on accidents. My son was even more impressed by the girls at the wedding reception back in our hotel, getting all excited at seeing him and shouting "marry me, marry me" to him. I discovered that Anhui is apparently the home of 'dofu', tofu to us, and we experienced many differing and very tasty types, but as always with these things they are much better in the environment that one is in at the time.

After lunch and formal goodbyes we headed off by car towards Shanghai for some relaxing father-son relaxation ahead of his flight back to the UK the following day.

28.2 Fujian

W/c 21.6.2002 - Wednesday was a pleasant drive to the very impressive Hangzhou airport another splendid airport in a splendid setting. Quiet, as most of the new ones are, but geared up for future growth. Flight into Xiamen on the south coast upon descent revealed a very pleasant looking set up, surrounded by water on three sides and lots of investment from apparently Chinese expats (re: Taiwanese, Philippines etc) returning to the mainland.

We grabbed a taxi for our four-hour trip inland to Longyan, but immediately it felt dodgy and uncomfortable. Fumes were awful, there was a bell hanging from the mirror which I knew was going to drive me mad only thirty seconds into the trip, the driver's photo must have been forty years out of date (or perhaps it was his dad moonlighting), electrics looked terrifyingly shocking (this is not a pun), I also found out later that it leaked water from just about everywhere imaginable. The roads initially were basic and rough, before we had a 40-minute total stop for road works – market time. Bought a bundle of delicious Lychees from local entrepreneurs who were lying in wait as these road works will be going on for many months.

Beautiful mountain area, very fertile with banana and lychee trees everywhere, valley bottoms with large boulders – reminded me of St. Lucia, although I feel a lot safer here! Then it was off. We could go along the one lane stretch. It was like an old Le Mans start, where everybody rushed to their cars or lorries, jumped in and then everyone for himself. Bedlam and chaos, no order here as overtaking was sometimes three abreast with no quarters given. Dick Dastardly and Penelope Pitstop come to mind, I just feel like Mutley! Then it was foot to the floor along old roads until the new toll road booth, where we got stopped and our driver fined by the overzealous local policemen for not wearing his seat belt.

The trip continued through wonderful scenery reminding me of mountains in Italy or France, but more fertile and more beautiful (and more banana trees!), through valleys and tunnels. However, by the time we arrived in Longyan, it was dark though and there was a serious thunderstorm in full flow. I said serious. Rod lightening, fearful thunderclaps and instantaneous flooding, car alarms going off everywhere. The hotel room was surprisingly good for a room rate of £23.00 for the night. TV not working as transmissions mast was down because of the storm, but still got one channel – Wimbledon via Hong Kong Star channel.

I have arrived again knowing nothing about the customer, nothing about the agenda, who we are meeting or why we are here? "This is normal, it is okay" is all that I seem to get if I ask questions. This is China and I make a note that this must change, although for now I must go with it and see what materializes. Oh yes and the hotel is also owned by the cigarette factory. Our meeting is delayed because "the rain is too big" …he is not flaming joking, I have never, ever, seen a storm like it!

What materializes is a piss up under the guise of a banquet dinner at a new restaurant in the city. Dinner was incredible. We were taken to this new restaurant in the company of the factory 'dilector', who had been on TV for most of the day; its speciality is snakes….'Do you like snake?', 'Well'………..'You will love this'. Fxxx (Sorry, but it summed up the moment!). There was snake, snake, snake, and snake, interrupted only briefly (too briefly) by wild turkey. Snake's skin, poisonous snakes, multi coloured snakes, snakes' soup, drink of snake's blood, snake's spine, snakes' flesh, snakes' tails (the worst), snakes heads (I lied – even worse) and snakes' livers…I am totally happy by this stage and don't care anymore, you would be if you had to eat this muck. The red wine saved the day. These regional varieties are becoming wearing.

Thursday was a stuttering start. Breakfast was the pits; I thought the noodles were safe but had something in it too close to snake for my comfort. Late meeting, nice coincidental introduction to factory manager who is off to Edinburgh to do an MBA, then a poor lunch. These people are ruder than I have been used to, ignoring their guest, despite toasting me a lot. After an afternoon sleep its dinner. I am angry because of the wasted time. At home this lot would have been sorted quickly, here it is two days! Dinner again, and I meet the Director of Purchasing who was a tiny man and who was an ignorant little so-in-so who was loud and had the table manners of an ill-behaved dog. My translator dismissed this as typically Chinese, but I am increasingly fed up with advice from a translator who is twenty-three years old and increasingly translating less and socializing more. She is there to translate, not for a break! Dinner included alligator - remarkably good (I have had this in Kenya and South Africa before), something like a frog, but not a toad, and a wide variety of other stuff, including vegetables for which there is no English translation. Mercifully, there was no snake in sight!

Afterwards it is karaoke. A quiet large room on the fifteenth penthouse floor, so I tried to experiment. All the songs seemed about forty years old, and the background videos all seem to be the same – 1980's Cologne or somewhere on the Rhine with some woman walking up and down in a fur coat looking lonely and fed-up! I will never get used to this silly pass time, but as it seems to be a mandatory requirement so I must practice. Despite mobile phones going off, I murdered 'Feelings'; felt I couldn't do much damage to 'My Way' after the Sex Pistols version, although I suspect that I did. 'Yesterday' was my best attempt, whilst 'Bridge Over Troubled Water 'was my worst. I forget the others but resisted 'Tie a yellow ribbon to the old, old tree' and 'Wooley Bully' among other options. I hate this stuff, sounding at different times to match the extremes of Leepy Lee and Marvin (Not Gaye). I also keep forgetting the 'Flank You, flank you' saying as I leave the stage, that the locals always say, whether they have sung in Chinese or English – Well it makes them feel like Superstars and me like an embarrassed pillock. Other intriguing translations that I remember were 'It started with a foke!' (Sounds rude to me, but I seem to remember something along those lines); 'The Moring after'; 'Sugar Auger' (?); 'Bridgy of Troubled Waters'; I have had enough.

Friday first thing we head back to Xiamen, with my deputy suggesting that I should spend the weekend there. As we are leaving, I am encouraged to visit Guangdong and Shenzhen where apparently, they have even better snake restaurants…. really? If you must try snakes, avoid the tails! Oh yes, we will get more business – the smiling and snake eating was worth it!

I have noticed that the men in Fujian Province roll their trouser legs up to their knees when they sit down. A quaint practice, and very practical in the heat, but odd all the same, very 'un-British'. Some also un-tuck themselves and roll their shirts up under their arm exposing their midriffs.

Wow, Xiamen (Shaaman) is something else. Frankly, I had never heard of the place. My deputy produced a host of football mad 'friends' for lunch and another round of toasting. I started by splashing the contents of a large prawn 'all over' my white shirt, which is far more impressive than splashing noodles and far more humourous to fellow lunch guests, despite their protestations that it didn't matter. The shirt is a work of art, but I hope the orange stains come out. Our meetings at Xiamen with the 'customers' were simply farcical and unprofessional – I have some thinking to do. We do not have a good relationship here and as the Americans would say "We have an opportunity here". After a polite light meal at the Xiamen cigarette factory's own hotel, it was a look along the impressive frontage to the sea, beautifully lit up, then a look around the shops. I commented on the way back that I could do with a quick beer for a nightcap (very hot and sweaty etc), just a quick pint, no silly Chinese drinking I laugh. I was told to hang on for ten minutes 'have a rest', which always means hanging around 'waiting' for about forty minutes and by which time I was ready for bed. Oh no, a 'friend', another one, was produced who took us to a floorshow club. My night cap turned out to be a night toasting our new 'friend' with small glasses of Mexican beer, whilst watching an impressive array of singers, dancers, ballet dancers, comedians (which for obvious reasons were a bit lost on me), boy acrobats, fantastic classical musicians playing the bamboo recorder and flute, and finally a four-year-old girl in traditional dress in a high wire act, bike wheel and everything – very impressive and set in a huge club that resembled a jungle. When our 'friend' who was paying for everything for some reason suggested that we all go upstairs for a bath in milk, we suddenly decided that we had to get home early, it was midnight!

Saturday morning was a boat trip for two hours around the archipelago of islands along the coast. The front at Xiamen reminded me of Nice, but better, whilst the harbour and islands reminded me of an Auckland or Vancouver. I am mightily impressed, and it is more spread out, less developed and cleaner than Hong Kong. The highlight was an island a little way out, that had watchtowers, and heavily fortressed beach and a large sign in Chinese that I am reliably informed that said 'Republic of Taiwan', even though the main island is another 200 kilometres away. A lot of excitement and photos all around. I am also informed that there are 400 heavily armed Taiwanese in them there hills – a poignant moment as we were only fifty metres from the beach. The harbour is a strange mixture of a few poor fishermen (although better than Hong Kong), the rich and famous Chinese, of which there are lots, and a working port, which detracts somewhat. The backdrop, out of site is a huge investment programme that beggar's belief (Another large new airport and a large 'Dell' Factory adjacent among many others. Xiamen is an academic town with lots of overseas students (Canadian, Australian and U.S. Chinese), with an educated upper class. It is a playground to the rich. The beautifully lit island off the coast (Gulangyu), boasts an array of Old Portuguese and Dutch style buildings complimented by new ones that have been designed tastefully. The landscaping is magnificent and the climate Mediterranean. I get very sun burnt but am suitably impressed. We will come back here, although I am not totally convinced of the water quality, the beaches are very pleasant despite overlooking the shipping lanes and occasional large container port. The hotels look good. We drank green tea all day and I have an extremely pink face and red forearms! This place is special, confirmed by a discussion I had at the airport with an Aussie from Melbourne – his favourite spot – anywhere!

w/c 12th April 2003 - Friday afternoon at work and everyone in the offices is very excited, with comparatively little work being done as they are de-mob happy, ahead of this evening's traditional company trip away. The party, of twenty-three office employees, are excited like children at a primary school birthday party and perhaps reflects how few opportunities of this type that there have been in recent years for the Chinese people to travel, even in today's changing environment. Previous annual 'work trips' have been to Shanghai, Nanjing, Ningbo, or the likes, but this time is the first that we are going to a bonifide tourist destination, away from the large cities. Everybody seems very organized having been to the Supermarket to buy food and drink for the trip, paid for apparently by the local Communist Party's labour department. I ask our financial manager again if there are any Government warnings about SARS or any guidelines from the travel agency who have arranged this trip for us – the response was simple, there is no guidance and Fujian province is free out SARS; 'No big issue'! I buy this story even though there is suddenly a lot of coverage about SARS, although mainly self-congratulatory stuff that the spread is under control and no one should unduly worry, especially as it is confined only to certain areas.

Late afternoon we duly tottered off to Jiaxing's Central railway station, my first such experience. We are greeted by a representative of a local travel company, appropriately carrying a yellow flag for easy identification so that he doesn't lose any of us (reminding me of Asian tourist groups around London) and I discover for the first time that he will be traveling together with us. Not a great station and access is as per standard, not readily permitted to the platforms until ten minutes before the train arrives; you queue at a gate until you are told you can progress and then join the scrum Chinese style when the guards start collecting tickets and allowing you through. I notice that I still manage to attract a considerable amount of attention and general curiosity in such public places. The excitement among the party mounted as we entered the train, which was surprisingly good. The sleeper booths are directly open to the main carriage walkway and each open compartment contains six bunks, three on each side, with the bottom bunk having the most room and for which I was grateful that I had been allocated as the roof is much higher than that of UK trains and the top bunk seemed one hell of a way up. Given that everyone was in party mood, the alcohol flowed freely, and everyone ignored the lights out signal at 21.30 hours to keep talking until midnight, surprisingly not inviting *the chagrin of other travelers around who were trying to sleep; the Chinese are amazingly tolerant in these situations. With such a large population living in such proximity, they have obviously developed a patience and tolerance of noise. A night of little sleep therefore ensued, not assisted by the fact that we had to be up 'early' to get off the train at 03.30 hours on Saturday morning. The toilet and washroom are separate from each other, with two basins for the washroom and the door permanently open it seemed. The toilets were basically a large hole in the ground, albeit a stainless steel one, but nonetheless a hole. Those who know me well will know that I have no sense of smell, but in situations like this my imagination feeds a smell to my brain, and I find myself retching accordingly. S**t holes! In the morning (02.45 hours) everyone awakes and produces flannels from plastic carrier bags, which they duly take off to the washroom and return minutes later refreshed, made up and re-moisturized and asking why I have not washed? Simple – I will shower when we get to the hotel. At this I am informed that to save money we cannot get to our rooms until 09.00 hours and will have to hang around in lobby. I have a different view! In the end we all managed to get into rooms and 04.15 hours and welcomed our four hours sleep and a shower before the day started in earnest. It's amazing sometimes the effect of a simple comment that I make. And what a day!*

Our town was called Wuyishan, in Fujian Province and seems to be a long street, built up on either side for miles, but still very much a small town feel and set in a rural environment. The 'mountains' surrounding the town, mainly impressive sandstone hills, are a designated World Heritage Centre site for the last five years. I am struck though that I have seen no Westerners, either in the train or around the town. Possibly this is the effect of SARS, but also, I suspect that this is primarily a Chinese holiday destination and largely undiscovered by international travel firms who concentrate on the Great Wall, Terracotta Army, Guilin axis. The scenery is quite like Guilin and whilst it is evident that Guilin is near the top of destinations for foreign tourists to go in China, conversely until a week ago I had never heard of this place. The 'two stars' hotel was actually very good, albeit a little grubby around the edges. The first trip was to local hills, with wonderful names like 'Three Sisters' and 'Woman's Breasts' (A two lumped hill). This was an impressive and hard walk-through undergrowth, up stone steps cut out of shear sandstone rocks faces, past a large statue of a Buddha, over cavernous faults in the rock which seem to disappear to the centre of the earth and down again, only to walk through narrow and beautifully fertile flat valley bottoms at the end. The only real downside is that there are far too many people around making progress slow and hardly a relaxing walk in the country. There seem to be tea bushes everywhere, which is a giveaway to one of the area's other industries. Then we come across a place called 'Heavenly light shaft' or something of that ilk. As we approached the long queues emanating from a cave entrance made me nervous and I was actually very pleased when informed that there is a tight spot in the cave and that I was unlikely to get through it; those who know me also knowing how claustrophobic I am, and the thought of two hours (due to the queues) underground frankly terrified me. Interestingly, when I was pulled out, most of the party decided to excuse themselves as well.

A quick lunch back at the hotel was followed by something else, quite another unique experience. The afternoon was a quite magnificent experience, walking firstly through a lovely green and wooded river valley, then up a quite spectacular hill, far bigger that the two this morning and apparently a very famous 'mountain' in China (one of four 'famous mountains' in China). We are warned not to drift too far off the paths or into the many local caves as Fujian Province has the highest population of snakes and some of the deadliest in China. That worked! discover that mountains in the Chinese language are ill defined; the same word, 'Shan', being used for both hill and mountain. The climb was proceeded by mandatory group photos alongside of the beautiful riverbank, then up through a 'fault' in the shear face of sandstone rock, climbing steeply, and only slightly claustrophobically, to the first of many vantage points. The climb was truly exhilarating and breath taking with the scenery being like the ancient Chinese pictures one sees with rocky hills shrouded in fog and low cloud; quite beautiful, indeed stunning and mystic. This is snake country, and we were again warned not to venture into the many former troglodyte caves in the rock along the way, although a few brave folks had their photos taken with a large and very live snake at a teahouse near the top. As we neared the top, the humidity levels rose steeply and the skies got blacker, and blacker, and blacker. The descent was a swift one as a result, but as the thunderstorm struck, I was faced with a run back alongside the river for the kilometre or two back to the bus. I was third out of twenty-four and quite pleased with myself, despite the soaking.

The trip back to the hotel was delayed due to a detour to local teashops for a demonstration of how to prepare and drink the local teas, something that I have now seen many times around China and am starting to find boring but seemed a novelty to most of the group and in which they seemed fascinated.

A quick change and drying out session back at the hotel was followed by an extremely good quality meal at a local 'farmers' restaurant, accompanied to large quantities of red wine and much merriment amongst the party. Must have been relaxed because afterwards we ended up spontaneously going to watch one of the Thai 'Lady-boy' shows, which I note are becoming a curiosity item in China. This setup is not my cup of tea, with a bunch of Thai 'Danny La Rues' prancing around on a large stage in a new auditorium. After the show these lady-boys went to the auditorium's reception area to say goodbye to everyone watching and they quickly attempted quite pointedly to latch onto me as the only westerner present; overly so!

Sunday morning was a very wet affair as the skies continued to open. We all invested in the plastic capes with hoods which are prevalent throughout China at a cost of about £0.30, before heading off down the river for our two-hour trip on a bamboo raft, down through some of the most amazing scenery, past the hills we had visited the previous day along with many more. The rafts were basically long large bamboo poles strapped together and about two metres wide each and six to seven metres long and somehow bent up at the front. On the top were five wicker chair seats and came together with two fellows, one at the back and one at the front, kitted out in wellies and long poles, gondola style. All very beautiful, but a tad too wet and which unfortunately took the edge off the trip. Then it was back to the hotel to dry out have lunch before heading off collectively for a 'foot massage', a novelty to most of the party. This was okay except that I didn't have my translators anywhere near me. Probably Chinese modesty I console myself and therefore didn't understand the narration. Found out later that for instance they were talking about when they stuck their knuckles sharply into the bottom of everyone's foot. I remembered that it had hurt me. Disconcertingly this raised alarm bells as apparently the narration had explained that these 'points' in the sole of the foot related (aka acupuncture) to various other parts of the body; seems like everything is wrong with me! Wish that I hadn't mentioned it. This was followed by a shopping session in the local town where I purchased what I considered to be a lovely example of Chinese wood carving, although everyone else thought that it was horrendously expensive (£60.00), before heading off to the station for our trip back by train. The station was pure bedlam, the designer for which must have been drunk when designing it and brought out the worst in Chinese queuing – pushing, shoving, queue jumping, elbowing and the rest all very unashamedly. My party, or at least the more 'worldly' ones, are embarrassed for me in this situation. I am getting used to this behaviour in more rural parts of China, but it still unease's me, especially as I realized that even as recently as five years ago, I would probably have decked somebody in this situation; I must be getting older. Lovely evening followed on the train talking to colleagues and a solid five hours sleep for me before arriving back in Jiaxing at 04.30 hours where immediately the party being recognized by a railway guard as being from 'The State-owned Paper Company', because they recognized me! Ten minutes sleep before heading straight into work, strangely full of vigour and energy.

w/c 24th April 2004 - Tonight I packed for our annual company trip and ready for tomorrow's early morning alarm set at 03.30 hours. This early start is not a good portent given what I have ahead of me in terms of schedule over the next week and a half. Still by 05.00 hours we have picked up another twenty-eight employees in our package tour bus and are on the road to Shanghai's Hong Qiao airport for our long weekend break. Fatigue rather than excitement permeates initially, but that changes as we approach the airport, and it is confirmed that more than half of the team has never flown before; therefore everything for them is a novelty. A good flight and an hour and thirty minutes later we arrive in the southern Chinese city of Xiamen in Fujian Province.

I have been to Xiamen once before, in July 2002, and have very fond memories of the place. This is a refined city, one of the most refined in China, and was in the past the home of rich families, most of whom now live in Taiwan, some 300 kilometres away off the coast or elsewhere in Asia, but who have been heavily reinvesting here over the last fifteen years or so. The cities relationship with Taiwan goes back centuries.

We have a brief drop off at our hotel, before taking the opportunity to visit Xiamen's new cigarette factory, a customer. This was opened in August of last year and light years away from their old facility. This is truly world class and like the other modern cigarette factories that I have seen in Shanghai, Nanjing, and Liuzhou. Quite magnificent together with wonderful landscaping and foliage which befits a neo-Mediterranean climate by comparison. Then the surprise – they invited us all for lunch at their company hotel in the city centre. I feel a session coming on and suddenly feel uneasy!

My judgement wasn't wrong as two guys from the purchasing department host a wonderful lunch comprising mainly of delicious seafood, but also dropping in the fact that the purchasing department director would probably be back tonight and that it would be good for me to meet him. The drink was warm white wine – the type we have in Europe, just a Chinese version…. And very warm; Too warm! This reminds me though of the city's relative sophistication combined with the fact that they have wonderful seafood here. One of the great lunches, but far too much alcohol consumed by all.

Next was a boat trip out to see the 'Taiwanese owned' islands off the coast. I have done this before but did not relish the trip as we played and took photos from the beach, as the winds were high and the sea rocky. I declared that everyone must be mad wanting to go out on such waters, but they did and so we went. I can honestly say that if I had been sober, I would probably have been terribly ill, but under the circumstances I was fine, the only 'casualty' being my secretary who was violently ill as she disembarked the boat. Sea sickness is never nice anywhere!

Back at the hotel we are informed that we have an hour and a half's rest before dinner all together and I drift off into a wonderful sleep, only to be awoken by a call from a colleague, who in turn had just received an urgent demand from my deputy to join him for dinner together with my finance manager, for a dinner with the aforesaid director and other important colleagues.

The positive points were that I met two very important contacts and that we ate at one of the best restaurants in Xiamen. The bad news was the obvious – there was alcohol involved. I proclaimed my innocence immediately and declared that I was physically unable to drink, which seemed to be accepted by and large and our finance manager was duly nominated to drink on my behalf.

The director was relatively sensible as was the business contact and his wife, whilst my deputy and one of the guys we had met at lunchtime, just kept on going. Silly boys and I have concluded that he will never learn now – this is just stupidity of the highest magnitude.

By the end of the meal, my deputy and this fellow were just like the proverbial bookends. He is shouting loud, making no sense, and speaking only in English having seemingly lost any ability to speak Chinese, whilst the other guy was all over the place. My finance manager was nominated for the second time tonight, this time to get my deputy home safely, which he failed at immediately as he didn't prevent my deputy from falling headfirst down the last 6 flights of stairs and falling directly onto his head with a horrid thud, whilst his colleague in drinking was dropped off at the company's hotel, dropped at the feet of the doorman who was ordered to 'just get him home somehow'.

I meanwhile had been told by the director that we had to go to karaoke to meet some friends of theirs; bloody brilliant, but no option and at least I hadn't been drinking tonight. Late night but ended up by meeting lots of his friends and their wives and girlfriends, thereby adding to his credibility and hopefully developing the friendship some more. I suspect that it wasn't their real wives I met!

This wasn't the end to the week that I had envisaged, but customers pay for our costs, such as the trip we are on to Xiamen; we must do it but wish that it could be a little easier sometimes.

The only downside about Xiamen at present is that the weather isn't brilliant, being grey and overcast, albeit warm. This is a wonderful city though and we set off to a small island not too far from the city centre along the green and fertile palm tree lined roads with the orange soil very much in evidence, to a town called Jimei, which was set up at the beginning of the century by the fabulously wealthy 'King of Rubber', who left all his money to the education of the Chinese people and apparently very little to his seventeen children, although I remain skeptical. At Jimei, there is now a thriving town and the Chinese equivalent of an Oxford, Cambridge, Yale or Harvard style campus, the difference being that the facilities cover educational requirements all the way through from primary school to a university for the wealthier element of the Chinese nation. This was impressive, cultural and an intriguing mixture of east and west, with many western style buildings apparent, combined with Chinese trimmings. I am not quite sure how this lot survived the Cultural Revolution but suspect that many of the leaders' kids were educated here. Lots of photo opportunities with some overawed colleagues before setting off for Gulangwu Island for lunch, which turned out to be somewhat disappointing in terms of quality and setting but reminds me that we are on a basic package holiday and that I am generally somewhat spoiled by the standards that I enjoy in this country.

This island, which I have visited before in July 2002, is wonderful – educated, cultural, peaceful, a balance of buildings and vegetation, some magnificent views and something more; it is also known as the 'piano isle'. We traipsed all over this beautiful small island viewing the old colonial influenced houses – Dutch and Portuguese influences to the fore with the terracotta coloured tiled roofs, the narrow streets devoid of any cars, through a large netted aviary, to the large rock formations in the centre of the isle, providing wonderful views of the other islands around and over towards Xiamen's growing city centre, over a small valley by two person cable car, which created huge excitement for most of our party who are experiencing so many of these things for the first time in their lives, to a museum and then lastly to the mandatory Chinese dried food gift shops.

Then it was back to the mainland by the ten-minute ferry trip, reminding me of the crossing in Hong Kong, albeit with distinctly less sea traffic around, and then back to the hotel for a rest, which turned out to be anything but as I immediately get a phone call from our principal who has just landed in Shanghai and who immediately demands mine and a colleague's presence in the northern city of Binzhou tomorrow morning, although he did put it nicely. This was a total cock up in the organization really. This is my weekend peace shattered and there is a mad scramble to get plane tickets and make other arrangements before the morning. Darn it, there goes my Sunday morning lie in tomorrow, although I am not too saddened about missing the visit to view the 'Canons' along the coast tomorrow morning with the rest of the team, the largest coastal guns remaining in China from the wars of past centuries against the invading westerners.

Tonight we went for a seafood dinner is a very large restaurant, especially geared up to tour package parties of which there are lots in Xiamen. This is a different break for us, as last year we were in a poor country area and our money went a long way; this year we are in one of the richest areas in China, and the money does exactly the opposite. I was just looking forward to an early night, which I duly got, although I didn't sleep well, disturbed by the twenty-four-hour passing traffic on the main road outside.

w/c 2nd July 2005 – Thursday we were up early and dashing for the airport for our flight to Xiamen in Fujian province, via a short stop off at Fuzhou International Airport, along China's south coast. The climate in Xiamen was entirely agreeable as ever in the semi tropical type climate and we were picked up by our business contact personally, who used to be a rural village leader and to make a point we are being driven by the current village leader. There after we had a one and a half hours drive northeast and inland through gentle and extremely well foliaged hills, indeed in some places it could be called dense jungle, to a town called Anxi. This county of 1.1 million people is a real mixture of history and background, not least being geographically right across the straits from Taiwan and that one in ten Taiwanese apparently have their heritage homes here and last year as China relaxed its rules, about one million returned from Taiwan to pay homage. I note that Fujian folk also emigrated all over Asia over the last 100 years or so. It has also been very poor and whilst it is only a relatively short way from the sophisticated Xiamen, it really is light years behind in terms of development. It is also one of the major tea growing centres in China, producing the famous Oolong tea, which is why we are here, to talk business.

We arrived at the only decent hotel in Anxi, the Ming Guan Hotel, this nine-story hotel set centrally on a bend in the river, which turns out to have been dammed to create a lake due to low flows for much of the year. Then we went to the "Tea Capital" for a brief meeting with the Director of Investments from the government, including a tour of the tea museum that included a collection of 30,000 tea pots, which were donated by a wealthy expatriate collector. Next, we went to see a location alongside the river which we may consider buying along with a small tea hill nearby overlooking the river and the city centre. Finally we had an hour-long trip out to our contacts village through more and more beautiful tea hills, towards what was a genuine mountain range, the only shame which was at its foot in the town of Huto, there was a massive and unsightly steel and cement works, and that's ignoring a huge new power plant, belching emissions quite worryingly. Still undeterred, we climbed to near the summit and turned off onto a three km unmetalled track to go to a 500 acres piece of land at the summit that was for sale. Our principal is interested in this and hence we are here, for what is likely to be one of the more speculative investments in life. It comprised a Tea Hill, a large house that would need some work, a lake, a pig farm, and peach trees with ten peasant workers, lots of snakes one of which I saw at too close a quarters for comfort, wild boars, and some scratchy dogs. Beautiful spot, maybe deliverable as a pleasant retreat away from it all, but the business plan will be an interesting one. Oh yes, and there is also a tea processing plant included which is back in Anxi as well as a shop.

This evening's dinner at a restaurant alongside the lake was with the Head of government, deputy county mayor and town mayor along with a cast of others from the foreign investment departments etc, and was pleasingly sensible with lots of local dishes, the likes of which I had never experienced before. These folks were willing, but appeared naïve in their dealings with overseas folk, a long way to go in that respect, but as ever in China, I suspect they are very shrewd. The restaurant itself, apparently the best in town, was nothing too special and the lighting alongside the lake and hills outside, which they described as "a mini-Hong Kong" was really stretching the trade description act somewhat. Apparently, there is to be a major water sports event here soon and they plan for this to be a mecca for fishermen at some stage in the future. In conclusion, the place has potential, and it may well be a good time to get in, especially with Taiwanese and their money returning to visit in their droves, but...

Friday was to be a frustrating day hanging around the hotel, whilst a colleague prepared all the agreements, agreed by our principal, and translated them before hundreds of pages were checked in more detail. At one level this is really seat of the pants stuff, but it is the entrepreneurial way I am told. We broke things up with a visit to the new potential joint venture partner's office reminding me how basic the place is. The owner's office is adorned with photos of himself with people who I am told were very famous folk, and this collection will soon include pictures with us foreigners we are advised. Our colleague had previously mentioned his vanity, maybe because he let's say looks like an average guy, but he had shown the photos of himself and the famous that he carried around in an album, just 10 minutes after leaving the airport yesterday. He had worn a brown loose hanging shirt with yellow traditional Chinese patterns on it. This was obviously his favourite, or lucky shirt as we noticed that he had worn it in almost all the photos he had shown us, but we managed to stifle laughs.

The news that the owner did not actually own the land himself, but that he had power of attorney for a villager that did own it raised obvious alarm bells, especially as it was explained that the actual landowner was in jail, but we were advised to progress.

Finally, the agreement was signed at 20.00 hours followed by a late dinner with some mayors present. There was an embarrassing moment as it turned out that we had been expected at the owner's office at 10.00 hours this morning and that he had an office full of family, friends from government and banks present to meet us upon arrival, but we didn't know and were tied up with agreements. The deal was eventually signed at 01.00 hours Saturday morning with handshakes all around and our company now being the majority owner of a tea processing business and some land on top of a mountain with an option to buy three kilometres of a riverbank for development in the town centre. Hum!

w/c 3rd February 2007 – Sunday we had a two-hour flight to Xiamen in southern Fujian province from Jinan. Followed by what should have been a one-and-a-half-hour car trip to Anxi. Unfortunately the company car broke down coming out of Xiamen, so our journey was extended by an hour and a half whilst it received some running repairs at a local garage – another cultural first for me hanging around in a backstreet greasy monkey environment with lots of broken cars, lots of car bits everywhere, no queuing and lots of dirty oily rags, and mechanics, everywhere! The description of the car was indeed a loose definition. It was the company's car/delivery vehicle and was somewhat battered and not big enough for the five of us unless one of us wanted to be over the back with the luggage. My three colleagues, including our UK based CEO, kindly agreed to wedge into the back, but in truth the front was not much better. The company there is not doing well, and the location was very rural, but we really shouldn't have been picked up in this vehicle that was barely roadworthy. We arrived very shaken................and somewhat stirred for that matter, feeling that someone down here was trying to make a serious point to us!

Eventually arriving at the hotel in Anxi where I had previously stayed, noting how much busier Anxi had become over the last two years. Hotel was dreadful, blocked loo upon arrival, and it obviously hadn't been checked properly prior to arrival, internet incredibly slow, i.e. we couldn't get a connection. On top of that the rooms were like fridges and the centralized air conditioning – that could be set for heat or cooling, was switched off as the climate around here is meant to be twelve months springtime; today though it wasn't, or at least this evening, it was darned cold. We had a quiet alcohol-free dinner, again we warned against any banquet activities much to the disappointment of the joint venture partner.

Monday, we went firstly to the company's shop at the "Tea City" in Anxi, venue of China's largest tea market we were told, where lots of photos were taken and where interestingly there was a photo of me receiving my friendship gold medal framed and hanging on the wall. My colleagues decided to go shopping and wasted time buying tea sets as Chinese New Year gifts. Next were the tea processing buildings and company offices before heading to the tea plantation in the mountains for a meeting, or would have done, but for another delay when the 'hire car' broke down. It must be said that this was the worst condition hire car that I had ever seen, but the issue was a simple isolation switch, another hour wasted and didn't help anyone's moods in a situation where the company is already far from happy about the partner's activities. This is the countryside in China, a world apart.

First though, upon arrival at the tea mountain, we had to have lunch in what was a very basic environment at the tea mountain dormitory, but we all survived without consequences. Thereafter the meeting did not go well. The lake that had previously been an attractive feature now was an environmental disaster, with all the fish stolen by the locals, the planting of the tea terraces around the lake had wrecked the aesthetics and filled up half the lake with silt and the lake considerably drained from previous levels. Waste was everywhere and walls built across the entrance steps, due apparently to feng sui, that made the approach look ridiculous to what was obviously a 'Jerry built' building. Security was a joke as countryside folk from the village were swimming in the lake when we arrived and the dogs that were guarding the building and land previously had apparently been eaten! As had the pigs! The local management was worse than a joke and the locals were just helping themselves, claiming land use rights by law. The management team have proved challenging as the money provided wasn't in evidence as being spent on any of the assets, raising concerns about how it had been used. This is pretty much what I had expected, probably worse in fairness, and I am left wondering why we are in businesses like this distracting our attention from core businesses.

This evening we had a dinner in the hotel with one of the local deputy mayors and an early night. This just isn't right!

Later that year, two company directors, one Chinese, another USA based, were literally chased off this land by local populace – such is life in China at times!

28.3 Gansu

W/c 27th May 2002 - I had a plane to catch to Lanzhou from Shanghai. A little research has revealed that Lanzhou is the capital of the Gansu region. It is statistically the most polluted city in the world, is the oil capital of China, is the centre of its nuclear programme, has its space launch programme nearby and is on the edge of the Gobi Desert. Therein ends the geography lesson.

At Hong Qiao Airport, I had an interesting experience. I 'bleeped' going though security, despite having no metal on me whatsoever. Thereafter, I was checked by a smart looking security woman, who used the standard hand detector and her hands, literally all over – And I remain unsure of exactly what she may have been looking for! No political correctness here. The flight was different! Shortly after we had climbed to cruising height, I decided to go to the loo before dinner was served. A nice steady flight, until I was stood unzipped in the loo. At this stage the turbulence hit us, unbelievable turbulence, I walloped the door hard, was thrown around violently. You can imagine the consequences. I quickly got out of there, still being thrown around only to be scolded by the white knuckled stewardess sat down outside for not being in my seat and strapped in! We all had a bad half hour, after which the food was again truly awful. One nice touch, however, was the issuing of a nice little notebook to everyone, leather bound, which I thought was a bit over the top. Upon investigation one of the little diary bits at the front showed the calendar dates for every year from 1867-2066; I racked my brain to find a use for this but failed miserably. Joined the Chinese Northwest Airlines' Frequent Flyer Programme.

I found out when we arrived that our sales guy for this region doesn't like flying and normally does this trip by train – all thirty-three hours of it! Poor fellow, what must he have felt like during the turbulence, which was genuinely frightening and following the three recent air crashes – he was a strange colour.

The journey to Lanzhou from the airport was an interesting late-night trip. For a start Lanzhou airport is nowhere near Lanzhou, it is eighty kilometres away. This is apparently because Lanzhou is very mountainous, and the nearest flat area is a long way away. I was immediately informed by the taxi driver that the main highway is still being built. It is evident that when it is built, it will be wonderful, however, at present it isn't, mainly a wide, bumpy dirt track, with a million obstacles, no warnings, no lights, no cones, no anything, and a bunch of idiots driving very fast on it! My driver thinks that he is Michael Schumacher with a touch of Colin McRae. My stomach suddenly takes a turn for the worse. I am struck by the number of women labourers working on the roads at this time of night. When we arrive in Lanzhou we find a modern city with awful roads, located on the infamous Yellow River. It was a major trading city on the 'Silk Road', but at midnight it was too late to appreciate. The hotel was officially a four-star but going on a five-star; so much for the roughing it bit forecasted by my Deputy and was located looking out over a huge square. Interestingly, in this hotel knives and forks were standard, not chopsticks – we are moving west!

Discovered that Lanzhou also is a centre of gold mining, vineyards, fruit growing, sheep farming, cattle breeding, stepped/layered terraced fields in the hills, large wheat plains, and that a key local attraction is Buddhist statues in caves, although later discovered that they were 1,300 km away – this really is a big country. There are also 50,000 Muslims here, together with respective Mosques, who my companions kept referring to as "Bin Laden's" and then bursting into hysterical laughter. Didn't really understand the joke! Very, very hot! Enough tourists around to suggest that there is stuff of interest around.

Tuesday, I was slightly apprehensive about meeting my first 'live' customer. I needn't have been. They were a delight. Good meeting and great lunch that went with a swing, fabulous food, and lots of (local) red wine. Any minor quality issues quickly dissipated as we all toasted each other (seven of us) at least three times. The lady vice president warms up nicely and was delightful company. She suddenly 'remembers' me from the Beijing exhibition last week – I was the guy being mobbed and photographed, oh no not me, really? Sadly, no photos were taken with my second biggest customer! We eat a range of local delicacies and the whole thing went like a dream. This was one of the better

371

customer meetings of my life, and we got an extra 20 per cent business allocated, with more promised. It was never like this at home! I notice that here the men smoke holding the cigarettes in a reverse 'erect' fashion, between thumb and finger and palm facing up – must be a macho thing, but they look strange!!

The afternoon was spent looking around Lanzhou, briefly meeting the Director of the local Chinese State Tobacco Monopoly and then heading off for dinner, which I wasn't looking forward to as you can spoil things by spending too much time with people. Our sales guy was doing an impression of a dying swan, having had too much red wine at lunchtime; we had to carry him in for dinner. It was a matter of honour, and everyone seemed to find the fact that we had a body lying in the corner of our private dining room 'normal' when the meal started. However, to my surprise, we had a lovely evening at the town's best restaurant right on the banks of the Yellow River. Basically, sheep are a speciality of the region, so we spent most of the evening eating just about every part of a sheep imaginable, except for any spherical bits, although I'm not sure that they weren't in there somewhere in disguise. Remarkably tasty except for the sheep knuckles, which had no meat on and were vile. Akin to chicken feet really, I just don't see the attraction. That all said, our hosts were wonderfully kind and genuinely hospitable people and I think we can safely say that we cemented the relationship. Boy did we cement it, with local 'yellow' beer flowing freely. Later, they sang Karaoke, I didn't!

After the evening meal we strolled along the heavily lit banks of the Yellow River, which was surprisingly pleasant at night. I drew a lot of attention during the walk, getting back to 'celebrity mode'. This culminated in a spontaneous photo at a riverside landmark with ten teenaged girls who I adjudged to be nice well-educated and 'westernized' Chinese girls. Two of them saw me and begged me to join them. I couldn't refuse and a photo was taken in the presence of about one hundred onlookers who decided to stop out of curiosity – 'Who is that big foreigner?'

I think that my deputy will bring the translator next time. He has done a fantastic job and been good company, but its hard work constantly translating – he is knackered.

It dawns on me that there are so many new experiences that are both exciting and exhilarating, but I cannot recount them all or do justice to them, whether it be the old Chinese Muslims, the scale of the Yellow River, the buildings, birds in cages, temples, hills, countryside and so on. Just fabulous and very different experiences!

Wednesday was the slowest start I have had yet in China, although I was up early. It is all-true about the excesses of Chinese customers and the need to build strong relationships over alcohol. To cap it all, we must go and eat the 'world-famous' Lanzhou beef Noodles this morning at the City's best noodle restaurant before heading off for the trek to the airport. Apparently, the local beef is a speciality (hang about, weren't sheep the speciality yesterday?). I am not thrilled at this prospect! The noodles were okay, better than okay and better than my stomach; the flight to Xi'an went well. I noted that the countryside around Lanzhou had the most extraordinary hillocks, like giant golden molehills or bomb craters, which nothing grows on naturally. The only time I have seen anything vaguely like it was the old Johannesburg mine dumps ten years ago. The result is that literally millions of trees have been planted and in ten years the new highway will resemble a forest road. Thereafter the day went disastrously wrong! We were delayed six hours at Xi'an airport. A new terminal is being built, but for the time being we must use the old one, which is a tip. This is not good, compounded by the fact that six planes were seriously delayed, as an over-reaction to the recent air crashes. There were a lot of angry Chinese around, small, dirty Chinese toilets, exceedingly hot conditions, no restaurants and the three of us weren't feeling too well and very tired.

w/c 15ᵗʰ March 2003 - Wednesday proved to be a good day at work before heading off to Shanghai for the three-hour flight to Lanzhou. Whilst awaiting my driver to collect me from my apartment, I observe a woman going about cleaning the washing rails outside of her sixth-floor apartment window. Polishing away furiously, it seems that she came across a large piece of loose concrete on the window ledge (which is not untypical out here), which she instinctively tossed to the ground below, only belatedly looking interestedly out of the window to see if there was anyone walking along the pavement below; I have come to discover that this is just such a typical type of Chinese action. Just can't help themselves; something instinctive, about the stupidity at times. Upon arrival in Lanzhou, I am encouraged to see that the new highway has nearly been completed so that we had a speedy fifty-minute drive to our hotel.

The same hotel as before, was very hot and with no way of opening the window apparently, other than putting a chair through it. Surprisingly, despite the heat and the 23.45 hours arrival, I slept soundly until the alarm.

The meeting Thursday morning was another excellent one, highlighting the great relationship that we have developed, followed by a long lunch accompanied by baijiu, a brief afternoon nap and an excellent evening dinner in a restaurant on the riverbanks of the Yellow River. The only dodgy course during dinner was the sheep's feet again, that were also under cooked, and the novelty was having deliciously succulent lamb, covered in pepper, and eaten with raw garlic bulbs, a local custom apparently. The strange feeling during the day was when we got into the taxi after lunch to be informed that the 2nd Gulf War had started. It struck me that this was typical, as I am in the second largest Muslim City in China and looking around suddenly everyone looks Muslim to me. An early night followed, a chance to follow the war progress on Germany's international DW channel, with foreign 'German' presenters who are obviously second-generation Americans or Aussies. In the absence of CNN or BBC World this was the best I could get to follow progress of the first day of the war and was typically efficient. The warning to all American and Brits around the World also uneased me slightly.

Friday turned out to be a free day in Lanzhou having completed our business agenda and the fact that there is only one flight to Shanghai today, at 16.10 hours. Found a half hour or so and with enough courage to go shopping in one of those typically Chinese gift shops that sell all sorts of oddities from alcohol to gift souvenirs, to typically Chinese dried foods, fruits, and nuts etc. I declined to buy the packets of dried ants – good for the bones apparently, and my translator bought some large, dried flowers, which when I enquired, she directly told me that this would be "good for her periods", which in turn surprised me slightly and momentarily shut me up. Another example of routine Chinese directness.

After a pleasant lunch at the hotel, we set off in bright sunshine for the airport along the new highway, observing the old troglodyte caves, although occasionally the odd one looks to still be inhabited. These hills are on the edge of desert and have been extensively planted with firs of all things over the last two years; firs which are dying despite the protestations of the driver that they will green up when the rain comes. Nonsense, these fir trees are dead firs trees, ex firs, they are firs no more – millions of them, literally. I could be wrong, but the same dead fir trees in Zhejiang just never green up, because they are dead. The plane trip back was largely uneventful despite the mandatory turbulence on this route. At Shanghai though they are at it again, I just can't understand why certain Chinese insist on standing up and switching on their mobile phones as soon as the flight has landed, followed by an angry berating from the hostesses. Sheer ignorance but happens every time.

28.4 Guangdong

w/c 24ᵗʰ August 2002 - Tuesday and I am starting to learn from experience that a business trip can often be defined as a pseudo holiday for the Chinese who aren't used to such things, either at the expense of the Company or the Government. Somewhat embarrassingly, although useful from a business relationship and understanding viewpoint, Tuesday and Wednesday, the traveling apart, can only really be described as holiday! This was a good old-fashioned jolly and all paid for by the key supplier. I feel guilty but am please for our purchasing clerk and production manager, my travelling colleagues on this occasion.

A good flight from Shanghai to Guangzhou, in Guangdong Province, Southern China, was followed with a very pleasant drive to Panyu and then a delightful Thai cuisine lunch, which came as a welcome surprise. I am informed that Guangzhou is not a large city – only six million people – but is developing fast and with big plans. Panyu, where our supplier's factory is located is a developing suburb. The area is quite fascinating, extremely fertile and a mixture of flat areas and well shrubbed hills akin to those we saw last year in Hong Kong, which should not be too surprising as Hong Kong is only sixty kilometres or so away. I have never seen so many duck farms, located on man-made ponds, in my life, this is obviously the area for breeding them. Literally mile after mile and millions of ducks of all sizes.

After lunch, it was off to the factory for work, which turned out to be a nice chat with a good old boy British (Sorry, Yorkshire fellow, who has been a resident of the USA since 1961 and lived in Japan for two years) expatriate, for twenty minutes and then a tour of the factory, which we somehow managed to stretch out to forty minutes. Since there were no major items on the agenda, my two colleagues and I were then ushered back to the mini-bus and off to an

*extremely pleasant local leisure park, Golden Lotus Park, or something.........
set up with Hong Kong money, for Hong Kong people. Set high on the hill
with magnificent views over the Pearl River delta that runs down to Hong
Kong/Macao, this relatively new park had a pagoda, a huge golden Buddha,
wonderfully landscaped gardens, a Buddha with thousands of hands, and lots
of traditional Chinese buildings – lots of photos all around and very pleasant.
On the way back I was impressed by a new development – the 'Golden
Seashore' resort, which were nice apartment blocks, balconies on which to sun
oneself and to take in the sea breezes. Only problem is that the Seashore is some
60 km away, which seems to me a slightly important minor missing detail.*

*Then after a chance to rest at the 'best' hotel in Panyu, it was dinner in
a private room overlooking the new palatial Government buildings, which
cost 1.3 bn RMB (1 RMB for every person in China!) and then off to a
nighttime circus. Yes, that's what I said, but what a circus. Set in a superb
new outdoor Amphitheatre with partial covers it was fifty minutes of wall-
to-wall excitement, with artists that I guess came from Russia, or somewhere
of that ilk. Amazing stuff. Acrobats, magicians, elephants, high wire stuff,
bloody big white tiger et all, horse riders who all wore headscarves thereby all
resembling Axel Rose. Not like I remembered Billy Smart's circus – this was
a very modern production and very well attended. And a lot more exciting
than I have portrayed it, I suspect. Then it was back for a bit of shopping for
our purchasing clerk's entertainment before we all went for a communal foot
massage. This was an extremely relaxing couple of hours, the first hour of which
was anything but a foot massage, except that we had our feet in a large tub of
hot water each with some form of salts in it, whilst ours backs and arms were
massaged by young ladies. They eventually got around to the feet and the legs.*

*Wednesday was a nice relaxing breakfast then the one-hour trip to Zhuhai,
one of the three cities in special economic zones adjacent to Hong Kong and
Macao. Very coastal and very beautiful, I even saw my first Chinese Rolls
Royce, reflecting the standard of living in this area, which is managed on
a different basis from the rest of China and is being prepared for one day
integrating with Shenzhen, Hong Kong, and Macao (My colleagues needed a
special permit to go here). The drive down was through flat fields and ponds,
which were extremely fertile and there were more banana trees than I have
seen anywhere, including St. Lucia and Mauritius. The area is generally a*

mixture of new buildings, low level established buildings and what could only be termed as shanty houses/slums – odd.

Zhuhai was lovely with a few rough edges, but the seafront was green, well landscaped, palm trees everywhere, golden sandy beach and modern apartments, not unlike some parts of the south of France. A boat trip out around the bay to get a close-up view (and comparatively disappointing one) of Macao, confirming my view that it lacks the appeal of Hong Kong. Apparently, it gets > 65 per cent of its revenues from gambling, drinking and girls – well it was run by the Portuguese! I note that the Women's World Hockey championships are going on in Macao. China is doing very well, whilst England has lost all their games heavily! Then it was a quick drive along the Macao 'border' before some quick shopping and a quite wonderful seafood banquet overlooking the bay from the third story restaurant of another five-star hotel. Wonderful, but still lacking something, hard to put your finger on it, but something is still missing.

A stroll along the front was interrupted by the passing of some poor gent who would have made the elephant man look beautiful. This guy had a problem of the likes I have never seen before, again putting life a little more back into perspective. Serious, this guy must be a case study somewhere. Sad. Then it's a leisurely dash for the airport, observing all the new and palatial real estate developments as we go.

I take everything back about Xian being the worst airport I have ever been to; Guangzhou's is far worst. Old, poorly laid out, undersized, poor access by road (traffic jams), gate exits that are all adjacent and then herded into cattle holding areas (Chinese queuing systems) before being 'driven' onto a bus. Except of course the company is 99 per cent Chinese, and Chinese as I expected it – loud, hustling, bags, boxes, overloaded cases, presents, fruits et al, giving the air and organization of a riot in a street market. An awful experience and to cap it all, the plane was an hour late meaning that I eventually got home in the early hours Thursday morning.

28.5 Guangxi

10th August 2002 – Guilin. Wednesday was an early pick-up, followed by a lot of pratting about in Guilin city picking up folk from all over town before eventually heading out for our boat trip down the River Li (Li Jiang). Despite *the administrative issues, organizational issues and what was a dodgy lunch, this was amazing. The terrain ('those hills') is unbelievably beautiful and the sun got brighter and hotter as the day went on. The riverbanks were green and fertile with numerous water buffalo wondering around, cormorants, local fisherman and cultivated fields both on the flat and in places, some terraces. Must be one of the most beautiful spots on earth, although I'm not sure the kids fully appreciated the magnitude of being here. We all burnt in the sun on deck, but that was our choice, in preference to sitting inside other than for lunch. The trip on the river was four hours in duration and over sixty kilometres in length through paradise to the town of Yangshuo, which was far better than the warnings about overt commercialism, pick pockets etc had prepared us for and is the home of backpackers. One gets the impression that this could be a great atmosphere in the evenings with all the very reasonably priced bars and restaurants, all overlooked by those impressive hills! The town included a Hard Rock Café – Yangshuo, which patently wasn't, a Planet Yangshuo and even a Fawlty Towers. Get the gist?*

The downsides of the trip were:

> *All the boats go at the same time (09.30-10.00 hours), which means that you have a long convoy of boats that you could do without – this is typical communist organization though; but detracts slightly from the occasion.*

> *Everyone is trying to rip you off for an extra buck, which becomes wearing – I qualify this as taxi drivers and tourist operators, the shop keepers seem more patient than elsewhere in China, and they seem like 'nice' people.*

> *Trying to fit in 'extra' trips on the way back – the tourist operators try to get you at extra stops for which they try to charge extra, and they obviously also receive commission from the shops they take folk to; darn that and created a fair amount of emotion at the time, but I won't expand.*

> *Chinese food on the boat – not great!*

Chinese organization – supports my theory that there isn't any at times, but things do seem to happen.

Americans: we were on the same boat as an amazingly fat American who kept talking loudly and coming out with such observations as 'these Chinese haven't figured it out – they are not stupid, they are dumb!' 'The next World War will be between USA and China'. 'I don't like the Chinese people' – How to make friends and influence people! I am embarrassed and offended on behalf of the Chinese race.

More Americans: there were seven American couples on board with brand new Chinese babies which they all adopted. Most of the 'mothers' looked too old, and I guessed that they may have pursued careers first, but this was only a guess. Some poignant moments observing these new families and I am genuinely pleased for them.

Upsides – everything else!
Guilin is larger than I first expected and most of the development is limited by height to no more than seven-stories, (Our hotel is four stories, and that seems to be quite consistent with most other hotels in town) set around a main river and a few other waterways – surrounded by 'those hills', although not a touch on Yangshuo (except that it does have some decent hotels!).
Thursday was a day of relaxation and doing what we wanted. I walked around the local 7-Stars Park, which was pleasant enough, followed by an equally pleasant walk along the river, a look around the Sheraton Hotel and then the walking street. On the way up to the Sheraton we managed to fall out with the taxi drivers who were trying to rip us off, so we all ended up walking.
Friday and it's a trip to the country, this time to see the landscaped rice terraces at Longsheng. My feelings are difficult to describe – possibly the most beautiful landscapes I have come upon on earth, perhaps even usurping the Li River trip, certainly comparable in terms of impact, yet so different. We left Guilin in a mini-bus and quickly left the famous hills behind heading out through relatively poor towns that reminded me more of Kenya than China. Then it was lush and fertile valleys, well-manicured and developed – one got the impression that anything would grow anywhere. The journey was punctuated by the usual driving exploits, but also such events and a flock of young geese

walking across the road and four water buffalo walking up the middle of the road towards us, being driven by a local who just didn't care. Then it was past a road barrier, which for some reason marked another small and poor town before we climbed green and fertile hills, along some dodgy roads. Yet to me it was more beautiful than St. Lucia, with hidden river bottoms, some terraces and everything green – without any feeling of a threat to security. We then climbed and climbed on roads similar in style to those of the French or Swiss Alps, yet without any of the safety barriers or decent road surfaces whilst the landslides and road damage did not inspire much confidence. We arrived near the top of the hills in thick cloud at the famous rice terraces. Initial rain disappeared and we found ourselves walking along and up the rice terraces to the tranquility of a village that is over 400 years old, made of primarily wood, but also some bricks. Truly wonderful, 1,200 people live here at 880 metres above sea level and many of the 'farmhouses' have converted upstairs into hotels for the backpacking community. As we walked among the clouds there was this mystical and feeling of unreality; I loved it. The minority women wore traditional clothing (of the variety that I was never aware of in China before coming here) and had their hair wrapped up into what looked like black turbans. With a bit of encouragement, three of them let down their hair, which turned out to be over four feet long and was wrapped into their hair that had already been cut. This is the local style and an excellent photo opportunity. The people up here reminded me more of South American Indians than Chinese. As we walked further, we passed other crops apart from rice – potatoes, sweet potatoes, maize, tea, and lots of chilies – green and red varieties. The people of Guilin seemed very pleasant and unassuming – when you get away from the travel operators and taxi drivers.

Saturday morning was the flight back to Shanghai. Unusually, I broke my routine of having an aisle seat and sat by the window, even stayed awake. As we took off from Guilin the scenery was quite staggering and unique and I felt that I was leaving somewhere very, very special. I reflect that most people come here for one day and night for the Li River trip and 'those hills', but I can't help feeling that those who miss out on the Longsheng experience have really missed out.

Guangxi in the countryside hills near Longsheng –
minority young women with long hair

16th November 2002 - Monday morning was a stressful short time at work before heading off to Shanghai Hong Qiao for the three hours flight to Liuzhou in Guangxi. I am travelling on this occasion with my deputy, the sales guy, and my translator, this being the first time that she has translated for me and indeed the first time that she has flown. After the issues that I had with a makeshift translator last month I am a little concerned and although her grasp of English is good, indeed very good, translating with a live customer is often different; nerves kick in, customer dialects kick in, technical words kick in, but it is all part of learning. This customer is key though and we cannot afford any mistakes. At times like this I miss my previous translator, who 90 per cent of the time now reads me well; she has also heard most of the lines before! The remaining 10 per cent is generally there or there abouts, or at least I assume it is. However, no one still laughs at my attempted jokes, so there are some things being lost in translation. This worries me!

The plane was a small plane, but the flight was very stable, the food

381

remarkably good on the Shandong Airways flight and the views coming into Liuzhou were breathtaking – mountains, meandering large rivers, sugar cane plantations et al. The small airport was very refreshing, and we were quickly through it and picked up by the director's driver in a big old blue leather upholstered Cadillac. Thereafter it got a little disappointing, firstly greeted by four large and belching (and smelly) chimneys, two emitting thick black smoke, one pure white smoke of a density that I haven't witnessed for donkey's years and one somewhere in between. Liuzhou, despite its setting was also disappointing, with few new buildings, poor (dirt pavements in many places, leading to dirty 'garage' shops) and a few new, but uninteresting buildings, the biggest of which, whilst a nice bronze shiny glass round building, resembled a large liquid storage tank – all thirty-stories of it.

The hotel was okay, my room on twenty-third of thirty-three floors, although not prepared when I arrived and wanted a quick wash before dashing out – safe not working, no towels, no toothbrushes – 'sod all' was the expression that comes to mind, and I get mad! Got the adrenalin running nicely for the factory visit though.

A quick visit to the cigarette factory showed it to be an old factory quite close to the centre of town. Like all of China that is changing, it is being relocated to a modern purpose-built factory ten kilometres outside of town from next May.

Dinner with the factory vice irdector and other departmental leaders was fun and affable, tasting camel, which I seem to recall that I have had once before out here (Lanzhou I think), and goat's gristle (for want of a better description), as no-one else seemed to be able to define what it was, and I certainly couldn't easily recognize its origin.

Tuesday morning I awoke to rain and an unplanned bus journey to Nanning. I cannot recall when I last went on a decent bus journey, and this wasn't one, but it was an experience not to be missed, just from a general interest point of view. The bus station was old and messy, but remarkably well organized with allocated seat numbers for our three-hour journey being allocated. My deputy brought me some take away rice food, which I took and ate on the bus, but couldn't help wondering when I was going to develop problems as a result. I noted my deputy's meal was slightly different from mine, presumably to suit his taste, for which I am grateful, watching the muck that he is consuming. The other notable event was the public toilets, never one of life's greater experiences, but this was distinctly different. I said, distinctly or maybe I've been sheltered. As I moved to the packed and bustling urinals, I noted that there were no toilet stalls, doors, or anything, just a long-tiled latrine running the length of the back of the toilets, over which were squatting maybe thirty men, squatting, trousers around their knees, in a line with one foot either side of the latrine, there without a care or modesty in the World, except perhaps to watch me. We are really getting basic here and this is the first time that I have witnessed such open latrines in use; no paper in sight although lots of other things. I am glad that I don't have any problems in that direction suddenly, because I would never have coped with this without throwing up and everybody looking at me, because I am the biggest 'minority' around. This is one of the body's most natural and basic functions and perhaps we make too much of it. I chose not to wash my hands given the state of the taps in the sink and left quickly. The buses were in quite good condition, we were supervised and 'talked' through the 320 km and 3 hours journey by a stewardess. The countryside gradually got flatter as we moved away from Liuzhou towards Nanning, leaving the hills and the plantations behind, although the land remained fertile and green, and it was intriguing to see the peasant farmers in their 'Coolly' hats riding oxen across the fields. Despite very modern freeways, well planted and green, there is a lot of rubbish around and no evidence of domestic pride – this is a poor area. I discover that for some reason that Guangxi Province remains one of the five autonomously managed Provinces in China along with Tibet, Xinjiang Uygur Zizhiqu, Neimongol Zizhiqi (Inner Mongolia) and Ningxia Huizu Zizhiqu, all of which I note run easily off the tongue. It has a big influence from officially classified 'Minority' populations, but it is not isolated like the other autonomous regions, so I don't quite understand the situation, indeed it borders Guangdong (Canton to those of us from the old days – adjoining Hong Kong), but I note that it also borders Vietnam.

Nanning, although a mixture of old (poor, industrial, and grubby) and some very modern buildings, big cars, palm trees etc, is a relatively new city, only originating some hundred years ago and only properly developed as a 'new town' under the Cultural Revolution fifty years ago. It now has a city centre population of 1.8m people and another two million within proximity; one of the busier and more densely populated cities that I have been to in China. It is not the finished article but judging by the number of large black Mercedes cars around and a stretch limousine at the Hotel, there is plenty of money coming from somewhere. Our hotel is the very pleasant twenty-three-story five-Star Guangxi Nanning International Hotel, run by the Chinese National Tobacco Company. It's okay and hosting part of a major folk arts festival, which means that there are all sorts of minority people walking around in very odd, but very colourful and attractive costumes. It also has a strange glass spherical ball on top of it, which turns out to be a small revolving restaurant.

A good, but short meeting with the CNTC preceded an excellent dinner at a top brand-new restaurant in the city centre. I note that my deputy is very quiet and not eating. The food as usual produced the off the wall range of local specialities and delicacies including spicy pigs stomach lining (actually okay, if you have drunk enough baijiu before), the most disgusting speciality dish of a large seafood tentacle of some description together with a duck's leg and foot – the bits with no meat on, but on which everyone happily feasts – chewing noisily and spitting bits everywhere. I am informed over dinner that there are seven motorbikes for every ten people currently in the city, but within seven years cars will dominate. I try to imagine the chaos that will rule the roads at that stage. I note that this city also has a South Lake; it seems that every Chinese City seems to have either a South, East, West, or North Lake. If there isn't one naturally, then they tend to build one; that is the way things work.

Wednesday started with breakfast in the hotel with the guys from the CNTC again. My deputy immediately announces that he has spent the night visiting the loo every twenty minutes, much to the collapsing hilarity of the table's company. They have been very kind and hospitable to us and the dim sum breakfast was excellent. We noted that the big fellow had very red eyes, typical in the Chinese man after a heavy session the night before – he had gone on somewhere else. Of the other two one hadn't been drinking the prior night due to a range of drink related ailments and the other shouldn't have been drinking due to his health and his past drinking history but did anyway. I am truly honoured I am informed. This is typical Chinese of a certain generation. This was followed by a quick meeting at the Nanning cigarette factory then the four of us had a typical Chinese lunch, including an extremely large bowl of chicken, turtle, and snake soup (clear soup, but with all the bits in and which one is expected to eat). Now if there is one thing that I hate more than snake, it turtle; truly disgusting, being rubbery, all bones and bits of everything everywhere and equally as disgusting to look at. I also had the pleasure (matter of honour and all that stuff) of drinking four small cups of snake's gall bladder mixed in baijiu. My deputy informs me that this is extremely healthy for you, particularly for one's eyesight and skin; he makes his child drink it every year. I made sure that we all drank it; I am not doing this alone.

w/c 4th January 2003 - Thursday and I departed at midday for Shanghai's Hongqiao Airport for the flight to Nanning. As we landed, I noticed the large number of military jets at the airport together with grass covered jet parks to hide visibility from the air; reminded me that Guangxi is not changing at the rate of many other provinces.

We ended up having a sensible and sedate dinner with a couple of customers in the hotel that we are staying in – the Guangxi Nanning International Hotel – before going out for a walk around the town and a little shopping. At dinner they had offered me a local speciality, but for once I declined on the basis that we already had plenty of food – "dog meat", which seems to be prevalent in my life at present. I politely enquired what breed of dog that they had in mind, but they laughed; could be anything apparently! Dog is very big in the southern provinces of Guangxi; Yunnan and Guangdong I am told.

Friday turned out to be one of those remarkable days in life, both from any enjoyment and experiences viewpoint, and was even more remarkable in that it was totally unexpected. The day started with breakfast with the head of Guangxi's CNTC and his colleagues at a private dining room in our hotel, which was sociable enough, despite my fatigue and I managed to resist their suggestion that we should have red wine with breakfast. Then there was the reason that we were here; we had to polish off a formal agreement between each other.

Lunch was done in style at the city's tropical restaurant. We were lead through mock tropical environments to the large private dining room at the far end, which had one of those delightful large round tables and places laid for sixteen people. The room was tastefully decorated with a large variety of typically Chinese ornaments as well as the mandatory large TV and karaoke set up. The room was also adorned by eight glamourous women dressed in traditional 'minority' costumes which are bright colours – red, light blues, yellows etc, which are attractive and add to the sense of occasion. The food was a variety of delicious local specialities (despite the odd dodgy one; on this occasion being baby chicks cooked whole and presented sat up on a plate - one simply picks them up by the head and bites of the body etc, eating soft bones and all – Uhmmm, just keep smiling Jeremy….) and the CNTC Director has obviously decided that he likes me, bringing a significant number of colleagues along and drinking a fair amount of baijiu that kept events going with a swing. During lunch I was treated to having songs sung to me by the 'minority waitresses' that included toasts, girls singing songs on the karaoke machine, one or two of the men singing songs, a toast whereby I was sat down with two girls either side of me whilst both were standing on my feet, holding my ears back and pouring a drink down my throat; don't ask but its local custom and all above board I'm told! At the end my translator and salesman and I were all presented with traditionally colourful cloth 'embroidery balls' for want of a better description and hand woven black 'handbags' with colourful patterns on them, again made by local minorities, which we had to put around our necks and leave the restaurant wearing that had the effect of making us look like total Wally's, but who cared, everyone was happy and merry. This in summary was one of the most enjoyable and noteworthy lunches of my life based upon the quality of food and alcohol, company and the events and circumstances that surrounded it; certainly in the top ten-twenty and comparable with memorable lunches that I have had in London, Los Angeles, New York, Paris, Auckland, Sydney, Lisbon, Cape Town, northern Finland and Helsinki, Laval, San Sebastian, Avignon, Southern Spain and Geneva, all of which were very different, but special in their memories.

Then it was the awaited three-hour car journey to Beihai, which I have become quite excited about. Our driver is a total nutter – foot to the floor and drive more than 100 mph along the wonderfully quiet motorway through the gentle, but very fertile hills. Our journey was accompanied by sun and increasing numbers of palm trees that lined the road, getting me in the mood for our topical destination on China's southwest coast. What followed, in one sense could not have been more disappointing, but in another sense was made more enjoyable by its uniqueness and experience.

Beihai turned out to be something of dump for the most part. Set around an old port and beautiful large light golden sand beaches with a good climate, it was developed in the early 1990's into a holiday resort; one could not imagine anyone getting this more wrong!! Great idea, but terrible implementation. Our hotel was quite good, but the approach to it had demonstrated a shabby city exterior, noteworthy by some very poor dwellings and the very high number of building developments that had simply been abandoned midstream as the developers had run out of money, this included three high rise buildings in prime sites directly opposite my hotel. The Friesian cows grazing on the verge outside of our Beihai International Hotel Jiatianxia, should have given me a clue to some of the local poverty. The ten-minute taxi trip to the beach and back had the effect of turning my blood cold and reminded me of some type of anarchic 'other world'. The flat hinterlands from the beach to the old town are simply littered with abandoned shells of buildings and large wide highways that have simply been ignored and have weeds growing through the asphalt as they go nowhere and come from nowhere as the city plainly has not developed as originally planned. There is no evidence of wealth, despite the palm tree lined main boulevard, until we get to the seaside, where there are very large old 'new' houses, gutted and left as they were never sold. One had to pay to get onto the beach and be immediately confronted by decaying and seedy facilities reminding me of a 1970's holiday camp, only to then progress to palm trees a quiet and quite beautiful beaches spoiled by large rusting 'Baywatch type' towers along the beach. I am saddened, as this proposed paradise has turned into a nightmare. Although I am informed that it is busy in summer and I recognize that beach resorts never look their best in the middle of winter (the sun is still shining and I am walking around comfortably in a light shirt and jacket), the expected visitors have never materialized, preferring the more refined climes of Hainan Island or Xiamen or the likes. I am left wondering where this town goes, and I conclude that it should start demolishing and start again from scratch.

My views were not changed as we drove back to the old town which was dirty but had beautiful old arched walkways like Italy or Spain and must have had European, probably Portuguese, input to their design, but were decaying almost beyond recognition and in many cases have rubbish or huge piles of rubble up against them or coming out of the doorways resembling the photos of wartime London or Dresden in the aftermath of bombings. I started to ponder about my security in this town, as outside of the hotel I have witnessed no evidence of wealth, despite the number of large apartment stores selling primarily local pearls, which are famous throughout China. Despite my disappointment, this city is fascinating me, and despite my struggling with my ability to comprehend what I am seeing before my eyes or indeed describe it adequately. This is unlike anything else I have witnessed in China, and I reminded myself that this was in Guangxi Province and as such was an 'autonomously managed region' within China.

Then everything changed again as we arrived along severely damaged or simply destroyed roads to the bay front port of the old town, which was partly a building sight, partly wreckage, although of what I am unsure. The restaurant that we were going to for dinner was unsurprisingly a seafood restaurant and turned out to be simply wonderful for its experience. The restaurant was a series of wooden/bamboo huts on stilts by the bay surrounded by sand, an abandoned boat, and series after series of large fish tanks, from where one selected dinner. Large turtles, sharks etc, all live, were on offer. Turned out to be a fantastic seafood dinner of the quality and variety that I have never had before, all for under £20. The cooking could have been better maybe, but the food was fresh and thoroughly enjoyable, including large shrimps, wine which had seahorses marinating in it, a tiger fish, clams, sea creatures in their beautiful shells, beach worms in salad, crabs and so on. Excellent and a special type of setting. Early night and slept like a log assisted by the day's alcohol consumption avoiding the temptation to go and see the lady-girls in the town; 'just like Thailand' apparently.

Beihai is a tourist town, but apparently without any tourists and given China's pride, there must be a real dichotomy as to whether they want anyone to see the city of 300,000 people in this state. Beihai is also famous for its pearls that seem to be in abundance at many shops, maybe we will go looking tomorrow. The only downside of the hotel was the toilet paper, best described as sandpaper.

Saturday was a nice lazy start on a sunny and warm Beihai morning. We had a lovely dim sum steamed breakfast at the hotel before wondering off to a large pearl shop to find some pearls for my translator, oh yes, and some cow horn combs that are also a local speciality.

The airport is about half an hour out of Beihai along a major highway that somehow fizzles out into a roughshod road through fertile green and sunny fields and a few more abandoned apartment blocks. The airport itself was very small and old time communist in style, pertinently being an ex-military airport. When I say small, I mean small — one China Southern airplane neatly parked out front of the small building adjacent to what I could be describe as a grassed roundabout, to which we all trotted out to. Next door they seem to be starting a new terminal, but I am not sure whether this is abandoned either or just new but looks a little rusty already. This is one of the reasons that Beihai is not a successful tourist centre; in a country of this size the airport facilities here are naff, not assisted by a lack of computerized systems so they couldn't enter frequent flyer points, handwritten boarding passes and overzealous security guards scrutinizing documents in extreme depth and with suspicion – not user friendly and flipping slow and frustrating. Sort of a sales prevention officer type that made me feel distinctly guilty before I had started. Shame, as the climate is wonderful. Found out on the way that it was the Chinese Triads (re: gangsters) who put money into these developments and then pulled it all out late in the day for reasons unknown, thus collapsing the town and leaving a lot of local folks broke, whilst the town simply decays.

22ⁿᵈ November 2003 - It was a two-hour flight to Guilin. On the way into the city I noted that the road upgrades have been completed since I was last here, and large villa parks were being developed.

We had a local speciality lunch in a restaurant in Guilin city centre with the Deputy Factory Manager and a couple of his colleagues from the factory at Zhongshan, some 200 kilometres to the North and is the main purpose of our visit on this occasion. I didn't really need lunch, feeling stuffed from a meal on the plane, but the local dishes, were pleasant enough. Our host informs me that tonight will be much better when we can enjoy the local speciality...........dog meat! I try to distract this thought by establishing that there are 670,000 residents in Guilin, but 2.8 million if ones includes the neighbouring agricultural districts. Dog meat?! Unfortunately, there is no way out of this one I conclude!

Then we set off in a large people carrier for one of those four-hour trips through the countryside, which seem to be becoming a feature of my business trips. The first thing that I noticed was how many darned dogs there were running around! Secondly though, I was seduced and distracted by those wonderful hills again which rolled on for mile after mile until we reached the town of Yangshuo after an hour or so. Yangshuo was bigger than I remembered and is and distinctly ragged around the edges, symbolic of rural and poor China. The countryside here is like the countryside in much of China, extremely fertile, lots and lots of people along the way working the fields in coolie hats industriously trying to earn a crust, lots of fruit on the side of the roads for sale, scared countryside hills from shambolic mining over the years, untidy and waste randomly dumped and so on. There were also huge numbers of carts pulled in this case by the Chinese water buffalo which are prevalent in this area, and lots and lots of, well....... dogs, along with the mandatory three-wheeler motorized bike taxis. A loo stop confirmed the worse, although nothing as bad as my recent experiences in Heilongjiang, but these were tiled open troughs, available for all bodily functions, no doors, although there were tiled walls, measuring an approximate two and a half feet feet high and as always – no paper.

One thing that I saw which was new were live pigs and piglets encased in small packages that seemed to be made from bamboo leaves or something akin, but which allowed them to be tied to the sides and back of motorbikes to facilitate transportation. Generally I note that you can hang two quite large pigs either side of the back of a motorbike, whilst one could get up to twelve piglets around the joint with studious stacking and suspension. This could not be described as an overly humane practice and the animals managed to look distinctly drugged, but were alive at present, perhaps resigned almost to their future. Apart from a lots of stone masons, bark driers, the other main features were the architectural ones, with one drawn to the style of the houses that around the towns are made of brick, are the width of a garage, can be quite deep and up to four floors high; strange and that is the best description I can give.

We immediately went to the paper slitter factory, our customer. This is being converted from an old run-down cigarette factory that has been closed earlier this year into a modern slitting and paper conversion factory. The town is poor, but the factory upgrade, although not yet completed is looking good and we headed off to the factory's own 'restaurant' for dinner in the old guesthouse that has not yet been upgraded. They are delighted to see me here, stating that in their recollection 'no westerner' had ever visited, which I can believe looking around and noting the attention that I am getting along with the constant flashing of cameras. The restaurant was a rundown tip and the toilets which they opened especially for me were no better. The people though were great, thoroughly nice, and hospitable folk and I find myself getting into

'Bill Clinton mood', pressing the flesh and having photos with all and sundry including the cooks, whilst drinking local baijiu and trying to forget that the main course speciality was dog. It was awful, the hide tough, the tail dreadful, which I assumed was the tail, although when one did eventually find meat, it was quite tender and edible, but is best taken with spicy sauce and as much alcohol as required to forget what one is doing. I did though find the need to enquire about the dogs and was informed that these were not family pets but raised on professional dog farms. The food was generally not great, but the company good and we eventually headed off to check into an unexpectedly good hotel in the middle of the town before heading out to local tea rooms for a tea demonstration in what would have been a relaxed environment had the young girl demonstrating sat next to me not started sweating profusely, forgetting what to say, dropping cups, spilling tea and screwing up just about everything that she was meant to do; it was explained to me after much debate that she was nervous – she has never seen a westerner up close before! More photos followed.

Back at the hotel, the Grand Global Hotel (The only English that I could find written anywhere) the room was good, a small suite, but was noisy despite being three floors above the disco and KTV rooms. Whatever, I slept extremely well, maybe re-assured by the large number of military and uniformed senior looking soldiers wondering around the place, or maybe it was just a good balance between the baijiu and tea for a change.

I awoke with the alarm at 06.30 hours on Wednesday to look out of my seventh-floor bedroom window at the back of the hotel to confirm that this was a poor town, with most of the new buildings being of these Japanese style tiled designs and the rest much scruffier.

At breakfast I am informed that the business had been completed the prior night and this morning we would set off for an hour's drive through the countryside, to a local mountain that was beautiful. Guoposhan mountain was a lovely country area, with the air fresh, a distinct lack of any westerners, 'they don't come here', and miles of hilly and fertile land to walk in, along boulder lined rivers, through green forests, to a waterfall, to a local rice wine brewery, the compulsory Temple and so on. I was encouraged about future tourist opportunities. Lunch and the food was not good again and I recognized the fried stomach linings with vegetables, fish skins and so on, but not the 'something' described as 'it eats insects in the fields', but no better translation; seemed more like turtle to me but could have been anteater perhaps. Halfway through the meal I thought we were being bombed as there was a dreadfully deafening racket from downstairs that seem to engulf the building, followed by arid smoke; it materializes that a couple were having their wedding ceremony here and that the racket was all the firecrackers being set off in the garage entrance. On the way out the proud couple were still standing outside and who apparently were not yet deaf, got all excited at the sight of me and I ended up joining them for photographs and inclusion in their wedding video, apparently making their day I am informed. Jesus, life must get more interesting than this for them and I wish them well.

Next it was the five-hour trip down to Liuzhou, the red/orange soil seemingly incredibly fertile, before arriving at the cigarette factory.

It is a city developing fast and evidence of its increasing sophistication was witnessed in some of the villas being built on the outskirts as well as an increasing degree of tidiness noted as we approached the city along the new toll road. The road into the new industrial area seemed to be a demolition site as the government obviously has plans to radically redevelop the area. I knew that our customer had recently relocated into a new factory but was unprepared mentally for what I witnessed. It is set with a backdrop of beautiful hills silhouetted in the background, quite close and like those at Guilin. The factory itself was enormous and the exterior virtually all polished tinted glass, the front resembling a 5-star hotel and the basement car park facilities resembling a modern airport car park as the plan has allowed for 800 car parking places for its employees, which is virtually empty at present, but has an eye to the future for the affluence of its 1,000 employees. Upon arrival we immediately headed out for 'a walk' and found ourselves walking through newly landscaped gardens past a swimming pool to newly formed 'rocks and waterfall, behind which was the company's new coffee shop for welcoming guests. This contained mini-grand piano, electric guitars, high quality coffees from around the globe et al. Impressive, reminding me that this is modern China and that it is building world-class factories that will set the standard for its competitiveness for the coming generations, benchmarked against the best in the world. Oh yes, and how well the tobacco industry lives.

The hotel was the same one that I stayed in when I had visited here last November, my eighteenth-floor room looking out over a mixture or new and old apartments in the foreground, but out to the panoramic scenery of those beautiful hills in the distance. We headed out to dinner at a local up marketplace for a sharks fin speciality meal.

Thursday morning I get a lay in, prior to breakfast in the hotel, before setting off for a local lunch and then another four-hour trip down to the province's capital, Nanning.

It turned out to be a good meeting, confirming our continued business for next year at higher levels, then dinner at the restaurant where to date I have had my favourite business lunch in China, a 'minority speciality restaurant. I was not disappointed by my second visit either, joined again in a large banqueting suite by sixteen others and treated with excellent hospitality and wonderful food and singing minority girls.

Nanning has developed significantly since I was last here as there has been a significant demolition programme in place as well as continued building projects and new parks constructed. Its warm climate and palm tree lined roads lend it well to the planting of trees and parks around the city's central lake and boulevard. This has the potential to be a magnificent city. I note that in our Guangxi Nanning International Hotel, that there are many Americans. Apparently, during the 2nd World War this Province was the site of aggressive fighting between the Americans and the Japanese and during this there was a large American plane crash into the hills around Guilin. Surprisingly, this plane was not actually "discovered" until the year 2000. Since that time there has been something of an annual pilgrimage from descendants to the site of the crash and these Americans are a part of that visiting party. I can't help but notice that it seems far busier than when I previously stayed here and more vibrant.

The people are magnificently friendly, although the majority still poor; I would like to see this place in ten-years' time, indeed this applies to the whole of China.

20th March 2004 - I set off to Shanghai's airport for the flight to Guilin. I have already done this trip some four months or so ago, but I am compelled to come again, as it's the conversion factory's opening ceremony tomorrow and they are our second biggest customer. Today is miserable weather and we land in Guilin among grey clouds and wet weather. The driver who collected us

hasn't improved his driving skills any since my last visit and we headed west on the four-hour drive to the factory through the hilly and impressive Guangxi countryside.

Lunch was in a small town along the road about two hours out of the touristy Guilin and half an hour past Yangshuo in a small and very dirty restaurant for want of a better description, but it did give us time for our nerves to recover from the drive to date, most of which has been at high speed, very bumpy and conducted upon the wrong side of the road. Upon stopping we discovered that the front left tyre was flat, perhaps explaining some of the swerving that had gone on, but we were lucky that there was a garage repair shop only three shops up the street from where we were eating. The food was okay, but very rural China, as we sat on small ten inches high wooden stools around a dirty and battered circular table perhaps fifteen inches in height with a hole in the middle for a spicy fish hot pot, which was quite good along with the fresh countryside chicken, soup, and fresh greens. I am getting quite used to China and perhaps would have been phased by this situation in my early days but got stuck in in typically Chinese fashion along with the countryside peasants on the surrounding tables. The downsides were all that comes with rural life in China – filthy toilets, without a tap to wash your hands or anything else, shared by the adjacent kitchen; dog wandering around barking intermittently and eating the scraps of food left either on the floor or on the table tops; seaweed drying from a balcony on the roof for use in soup at a later stage, indeed of the type that we had just eaten, together with another dog urinating in close proximity; chipped spoons and China bowls from which to have your food; dishes being washed in water that looked non too clean; rubbish outside everywhere, in amongst the mud. And of course everyone staring at me.

At the hotel I am segregated from all the other guests and shown to a suite on a separate floor, which didn't prove too advantageous as we were immediately hit by power cuts and noise from building work outside, demolition. However, I am impressed that in few months since I was last here that the local park opposite the hotel is being upgraded and landscaped although it will be a while before it is the finished article. The power cuts continue throughout the afternoon with such regularity that the lights are flashing on and off like a darned discothèque. I am informed not to use the lifts and that this is normal as there is insufficient power in the town to satisfy all the needs.

I reflect that I have some very good friends down here in the rural and relatively poor corner of China. They are good and honest people, and we have an excellent business and personal relationships. That leaves me worrying about what may happen over the next couple of days.

The dinner was held with five large banquet tables in a private room with special guests from the provincial state tobacco company, local politicians, and Party folk. In this part of the world the first dish was the delicious local speciality – spicy dog meat, which turned out to be very good this time. The meat was very tender and succulent and when the hide and bone is discarded was quite enjoyable, as was the local baijiu and the sociability of the evening set amongst friends and competitors. The meal was over at 20.00 hours, but we then had a very frustrating evening waiting around until 23.00 hours for a private audience with the head man from the local tobacco company to formally introduce ourselves and to leave him gifts; all very Chinese and a little odd to my mind, but I am informed by deputy and the joint venture sales guy that this is the way things are done around here. So be it, but I really don't know what is going on.

After a good night's sleep we had a communal breakfast before being taken to the factory for the opening ceremony. I felt proud for my friends and what they have achieved with the place. I felt sad for them though about the weather, unseasonably cold, grey, windy and rain in the air, although mercifully it wasn't raining at the time of our visit. This was a very Chinese style event – big red inflatable balloon tubes arcing across the front gate, red carpets, speeches, 'lion-dragons' dancing, girls in long red dresses welcoming and guests signing in, drums, brass bands, firecrackers, helium balloons tied to the ground with slogans hanging from them, numerous photographers, TV cameras and videos. I am convinced that they deafened all the employees behind us when they set the firecrackers off within four feet of them.

Although not one of the official dignitaries, my friends ensured that I was always in pride of place at the centre of all photographs and just behind the main party and I was the only one caught for a TV interview discussing our cooperation with the local Mayor and the Party head. The female presenter for the day's events was a local TV anchorwoman and I was formally presented with a foreign coins and stamps collection, which is quite impressive although I was surprised to find the Queen's head (Elizabeth II) on the back of a Spanish coin! These will need further inspection. There is no doubt now that in this region I am a distinct novelty and celebrity status is accorded to me in these circumstances.

The brass band was a real ramshackle mob, reflecting perhaps the poor living standards in the area. Yes, they had matching faded light blue suits and peaked caps, but that was where the smartness ended. A few had red ties, they all had very visible underclothing to keep the cold out, multi-coloured shirts and some of the men's hairstyles were more like rock pop, with long hair down their backs in evidence. Nevertheless, they played well enough and did a good job.

This was fun, followed by lunch. These are friends and I am thrilled, although this was not the case of two of our industry competitors who were apparently really fed up with my close friendship and high profile and showed their disapproval, one of them by departing events immediately. I am told that this is typical, a sort of demonstrable Chinese sulking, down on their luck. Let them sulk!

The lunch food was not good, food not being one of the strengths of this region. It included more dog meat, very fatty (and hairy) pork rind, grubs, a delicacy that I am informed that I am honoured as I have just caught the only two-week season in the year when they are available, and nothing much more that was too edible.

The afternoon was a visit to local hot springs an hour and a half away in the Guoposhan National Park. Set in beautifully stunning surroundings, I had naively not realized that we were going to bathe in these springs, as all the other guests did. I declined on the basis that I am not 100% and that I would keep my translator company, who had in very Chinese style come out and stated that she was on her period! I was dissuaded by the thought of exposing my flesh in an environment where I am going to be stared at by literally everyone....... and those very, very tight brief black swimming trunks that they were handing out with associated very thin and flimsy material......and the fact that they go see-through when wet, despite being black. The Chinese have odd standards of modesty sometimes, with the fellows wearing these things and the women wearing very large and un-trendy costumes and the bikini versions coming with modesty skirts – no topless sunbathing here! Sorts of 40's style, I guess. This was an interesting and very Chinese experience set amongst mystical, green, and fertile hills.

Then it was a dash back for dinner in the factory's employee canteen. This was a basic set up and many of the dignitaries had departed earlier, thrusting me to the position of No.1 guest status at events along with the multimillionaire businessman from Hong Kong. We got a standing ovation as we entered, were dismayed to see that dinner was the same dishes, to the dish, as what we had eaten at lunchtime and consumed large quantities of baijiu, with my deputy, sacrificing himself and falling over at the table; literally. All very Chinese – he was a very good friend tonight, although I have a different definition for folk who cannot hold their drink.

The evening events were taking place upstairs in the company's ballroom from an era gone past, built for more like 3,000 employees more so than the remaining 200 or so! Then they dropped it on me – they would like me to make an opening speech, have a dance and sing a song; bollicks! My brain is not working due to the alcohol; I can't dance (as in ballroom) at the best of times and can't sing a song without a karaoke machine and not at all well with one! In the event, I made quite a good speech to big rapturous ovations at the start, just by saying things like 'Hello', 'I am very happy' and 'My good friends in Zhongshan' all in Chinese. Five minutes later I left the stage to a chorus of 'Hellos' and 'I love you' in English! The dance was a nightmare as I tramped all over some poor lady's feet and seemed to lose all sense of coordination during the excessively long music piece. Her face was a picture, a mixture of nerves, excitement, pain, embarrassment and occasionally bursting into fits of laughter as all eyes were on us for this solo dance. I managed to avoid the singing, but instead got involved in a couple's party game whereby the men were fed cream cake by a lady (in this case my translator) and had to eat it on the shortest time. Unfortunately, I didn't win, but I suspect that close video pictures of me stuffing cake into my mouth and up my nose and cream all over the place, will run and run in Zhongshan. They are happy and I go home happy until I come across my deputy who has recovered enough to go to karaoke and wants me to go. We have a serious, serious conversation about his future conduct and drinking habits. Probably not the right time or place, but which is wholly appropriate given his condition in the circumstances and I make my point, about five seconds before he passed out; silly so-in-so.

Next morning my translator informs me that she saw us both in several shots on the local TV news.

22ⁿᵈ May 2004 - Monday morning I set off for Guangxi.

Liuzhou was warm at thirty degrees and was looking at its best. I am amazed at the changes that have taken place here over the last eighteen months; they are phenomenal, with some serious demolition taking place along the main roadways, associated landscaping in its place and an array of new buildings and factories in various stages of construction.

After a brief technical meeting we join the deputy factory manager and the technical team for a western dinner on my behalf in their new factory coffee bar, the place situated behind a manmade waterfall. My heart sunk somewhat as I have repeatedly discovered that western meals outside of Shanghai or Beijing can be a bit iffy.

Started well enough, with an ice-cold beer, but the small coffee that came with it was strong and obviously out of place timing wise. The sweet corn soup was sort of okay, but far too sweet, although it complimented the sweet bread and Lurpak butter. The peppercorn steak and chips were quite good despite the thinnest of the beef; the funny bit here was watching everyone come to terms with a knife and fork and there definitely were not enough chips. Then an anomaly – fried rice, before a large plate containing two fried eggs and bacon turned up, for which they gave me seconds for some reason.

Then there was time for a walk around their brand-new purpose-built factory, which resembled a showroom more than a factory, before heading off for the compulsory karaoke.

Tuesday morning we left the hotel for our four-hour car trip to Nanning. I noted a big sign along the way informing me that we have crossed the Tropic of Cancer, which I hadn't realized on prior trips.

At Nanning it was immediately apparent to me how much it has developed over the last year or so. I am informed that the population will over double by 2010 and that the infrastructure for this is currently being put into place. The pace of change is staggering and difficult for me to describe.

The city has also had an extraordinary amount of demolition, but the rebuilding programme has by and large been done quite tastefully, befitting the natural vegetation surrounding and making the most of the wide river expanse and the hills that prevail. This is a relatively modern city also, with large numbers of people wearing shorts, something that Jiaxing folk rarely do, befitting the climate and reflecting perhaps more advanced development processes, resulting in its neighbouring proximity to Guangdong Province, and therefore Hong Kong.

Dinner this time was at another minority restaurant on the sixteenth floor of the Nanning Hotel. The meal was impressive, made more so by the waitresses bedecked in brightly covered minority costumes and hats, the likes of which I hadn't seen such variation. The meal was accompanied by the usual white spirit but was controllable and the food was very good if you excepted the sharks stomach lining and the pigs' ears, sliced that is, and presented on thinly sliced cucumber to compliment it. This was with a group of old friends and a pleasant evening. Then another first, a Korean style massage followed for two hours with oils and folk walking up and down one's back and massaging with knees a lot of the time which was quite good and more positively meant no karaoke.

I remember that new transport regulations came into force this month and are wide ranging with a view to addressing the significant issues that China has on its roads with poor driving standards, old polluting small vehicles have been banned from city centres, overloaded lorries are being addressed and accidents reduction is paramount. The most visible effect, apart from the fact that there are policemen everywhere, is that drivers and front seat passengers in vehicles now must always wear seat belts or risk a ¥50 Yuan on the spot fine (about £3.50). This I find funny as I have been preaching this for two years and folk have often laughed at me when I have buckled up. This reminds me of the 'Clunk, Click, every trip' campaign in the UK some twenty-years ago that is widely recognized around the world as having been so successful in changing car drivers and passenger habits. There is a challenge out here though, and God alone knows what clunk click translates like into Chinese?

Wednesday we were taken by one of our key contacts, to take us to nearby Qing Xiu Mountain on the outskirts of Nanning.

This turned out to be a good idea, despite the heat. The mountain is really a series of hills but has been developed tastefully befitting the tropical type of climate with palm trees and other wide leaved vegetation everywhere. It materializes that we have arrived on the first day of the 'water spraying' festival, which pricked my curiosity a little, but came with the associated usual lack of facts. Firstly we attended a temple packed with the Buddhist equivalent of monks and nuns, being sprayed with water, a bit like a baptism ceremony, which was fascinating and had associated large numbers of photographers in attendance, who were equally curious about me as the only westerner present.

Then it was up to the top of the hills, for beautiful 360-degree views of the area – the fast-developing Nanning city, vast river, golf courses and the likes, before going down to a courtyard and temple for the water spraying ceremony.

I was warned that there may be a little bit of water around as the ceremonial drums started booming away at the entrance of glamourous young ladies in brightly covered minority style dresses. Their looks remind me more of that of Vietnamese women that I remember from the TV during my childhood, reminding me how close we are geographically to their border. About ten seconds before the spraying started, my translator said that she was moving away from me as 'I may be dangerous', the meaning of which I was still trying to comprehend when the first bucket of water drowned me. No shit Shylock! Thereafter all hell let loose about forty-five minutes of the biggest all-out water fight that I have ever witnessed. Miss wet t-shirt competitions had nothing on this lot; this was war in the good old minority traditions in Guangxi I understand. This is one of those moments that I was privileged to have been a part of in China and a fun one, mainly at my expense, but several hundreds of other people were also into the swing of it, most of whom must have drenched me at some stage!

w/c 29th January and w/c 5th January 2005 - Thursday I finally got off for my re-arranged trip to see our biggest customer ahead of the Chinese New Year. I am travelling with the excellent sales guy down here and a customer service team leader. This is also her first time to Guangxi and to meet these folks.

We were greeted by two old friends. A quick stop at the Jin Du hotel and a big but soulless twelfth floor room reminded me how disappointing this hotel is compared to its potential. The hotel also kept having power cuts all night, after which when the electricity was turned back on, the air conditioner kicked in with a large ping sound and the lights flickered on momentarily, awaking me several times.

In the restaurant I noticed a lot of westerners, a couple of western kids, but mainly excited couples and then I twigged, they all had Chinese babies, something that the family and I noticed in this Province once before when we were in Guilin. This is the baby capital for westerners who want to adopt!

Friday morning after a pleasant breakfast it was a three-hour drive in the rain down to Liuzhou, this time to stay in the four-star *Liuzhou Hotel*, which in contrast to last night's was a good hotel, apparently the 'Party' hotel in town.

Saturday, I awake after a wonderful night's sleep in what must be one of the most comfortable beds and pillow sets in China and I make a note to stay here again in future.

This is a relaxed trip, all except for the travel, which given the long distances in a small minibus, is often challenging on the body and the nerves, but especially my neck as the headrests in Chinese aircrafts and cars alike are too short to provide adequate support and I always come away with problems. This drive took us far longer than expected, nearly five hours due to a lot of heavy traffic on the narrow and winding roads, slowed by the rain and mud, and masses of peasants along the way and in the towns that we pass through reminding me that this really is a poor area. This is also compounded by a lot of people travelling home in readiness for the impending festivities.

My friend there is a happy man, proclaiming me genuinely one of his best friends. Alcohol consumption was modest also and new translator proved very popular with them. Intriguingly they did not seem to want to go home, reminding me that they don't have too many visitors out here in the sticks, never mind Westerners, and they opened up, talking about Mao Ze Dong and about how he compared to Zhou Enlai, perceived as the real leader at that time, but who did not have the strength of Mao. Thereafter there were all sorts of open discussions about how Mao was for China, the country's development, poverty, minority peoples, anything educated or intellectual, family lives and so on. General constructive discussion around the table. This is the first time that I have discussed this openly and with trust for me as well as a sign of the changing political climate in China.... I was reminded that this is a minority population area.

Sunday morning, we set off back to Guilin to fly home in that damned minibus again, also knowing that we must make an hour's detour as a bridge at Lippu is in imminent danger of collapse and has therefore been closed. We were hardly out of the town when we were stopped by a police roadblock checking vehicles, obviously and blatantly intent in collecting money (bribes) for themselves ahead of the Chinese New Year and finding that one of the vehicle's brake lights wasn't working. Unfortunately at the next town the same happened again, so for the next hour and a half we stopped at every Tom, Dick, and Harry 'garage shop' that may sell such lights, but to no avail, but luckily *no more fines either. This did delay the journey and I noticed that for the first time that petrol stations, at least around here, don't sell auto parts, just petrol; a commercial opportunity for the future.*

w/c 9th and 16th July 2005 - Friday morning is a flight to Guilin.

Then it was on to the five-star Li Jiang Waterfalls Hotel in the middle of Guilin. This is an excellent hotel and is named because it has a manmade waterfall cascading down the whole side of the hotel. The hotel is excellent with swimming pools, leisure centre, large shop, a variety of restaurant and bars etc and a great setting surrounded by water and the town square with great views everywhere.

First a trip to the Red Flute Cave, which was far better than we expected.

After a brief rest we were out again, this time for a passenger boat trip around Guilin's increasingly impressive waterways with four lakes and two rivers included in the trip, viewing fountains, impressive multi-coloured lighting around the shores, three or four pagodas, going up a canal lock, seeing a newly created old town and enjoying various shore side entertainment from comedians, musicians, actors, and a Peking Opera.

Waking up Saturday morning was wonderful after a glorious night's sleep in the comfort of a large Queen size. Opening the curtains the weather is glorious and the views magnificent. A lake is below us containing two pagodas in the middle of it, with another lake away to the right with traditional Chinese humped backed bridges, both lakes being surrounded by trees. To the left is the winding Li Jiang River with fishermen on traditional bamboo rafts already out fishing with their cormorants and bathers already wading in. In the distance, some not actually so distant, are those magnificent limestone hills including Elephant Trunk hill, which is less than half a kilometre away. This hotel is the best in Guilin and a magnificent central location in a city of 600,000 people that I realize has improved dramatically from an aesthetic point of view since my last visit some three years ago.

The trip up to the minority mountain village of Ping An in the Long Shen Valley area was just over two hours by minibus and again there were several places where the mountain road had been washed away over the last two months by torrential rain. Ping An was the place that I had all been to three years ago and whilst wonderful. Today the weather is wonderful, and we walked the kilometre or so up to the wooden mountain village and beyond, avoiding the calls to be carried up on chairs supported by bamboo poles and setting a pace far too fast for my Chinese colleagues. After climbing to a great vantage point for lots of photos of the mountain terraces for which this area is famous, it was back down to the A Meng Hotel and Internet Bar as it described itself for a rest on what is best described as a sun terrace for a couple of hours and then inside for a lunch of dishes including bamboo rice and bamboo chicken, dishes that are cooked barbeque style with the food stuffed inside of bamboo cane.

Thereafter I walked back down to the minibus again through the terraces and then down to another village in the bottom of the valley where we were treated to traditional Yao minority dances by a dozen women or so, who then wrapped me, much to the hilarity of the others, dressing me in local garb and getting me to perform a marriage dance with an unmarried girl, providing lots of photo opportunities for everyone. The local thing to do is to pinch the bottom of the one you like, all very touristy, but I had lots of pinches. Thereafter it was out to see the girls let down their five feet long hair and wrap it up again before departing back to the hotel in Guilin.

Sunday morning we started the four-hour boat trip along the Li Jiang River to Yangshuo, our destination for tonight. I discover that not only is it my translator's first time to see a lot of the local tourist spots, but also our salesman's even though he comes down to this part of the World about twelve times a year.

The trip along the Li Jiang was as spectacular as ever drenched in wonderful sunshine, and although was naturally not quite the same impact as my first visit, remains mightily impressive. Arrival in Yangshuo was hectic and chaotic as all the fifty odd boats in convoy seem to arrive within half an hour of each other and we run the gauntlet of souvenir shops up the main street to the Paradise Resort Hotel, a four-star hotel, but the best in the town, even if in truth it is slightly closer to a three-star in Shanghai terms. The reception area has all sorts of photos of past patrons, including President & Mrs. Bush senior, President & Mrs. Carter and President & Mrs. Clinton along with a range of others such as former Chinese Leader Zhou Enlai and the Vietnamese leader Ho Chi Min as well as others like Perez De Cuella and so on.

The hotel whilst the best in this country town is distinctly average, but it has a half decent swimming pool, which is much appreciate by all of us in this high heat and humidity climate soon after we arrive, allowing us more sun as well as a chance to cool down. Later we went down the famous main street next to the hotel that is full of bars and small shops, a back packer's heaven, but has quite an atmosphere as we head for one of the air-conditioned bars looking for coolness and food. This evening we set off for the 'performance show' called "Impressions" by the apparently famous show director Liu San Jie. We weren't particularly looking forward to this and when we saw our plastic seats at floor level our hearts sunk somewhat, but the next one hour and twenty minutes was one of the most impressive and certainly unique performances that I have ever witnessed anywhere, the setting far outweighing anything that we have seen in Broadway or the West End. Set in a bay off the Li Jiang River a little way out of Yangshuo, it involved the local limestone hills being lit up, different coloured lights beamed across the 'lake', a cast of hundreds in different multi-cultural attire, water buffalo, singing, dancing, bamboo boats, fishing and so on; difficult if not impossible to describe, but mightily impressive.

Monday, we arrived at Nanning mid-afternoon, later than we had predicted and tonight we have a banquet with some old friends. The bus trip wasn't too bad as bus trips go with a modern and spacious air-conditioned bus, but the trip took nearly five hours and whilst the countryside was beautiful and fertile, one can only take in so much countryside panoramas. The hotel was the five-star Majestic (Xin Du Hotel in Chinese), with a significant number of westerners wandering around. I find myself in a junior suite on the eleventh out of twelve floors, which overlooks the central People's Park, along with many middle aged looking Western couples together with their newly adopted Chinese babies, all crying and bedlam all around, but a lot of happy new parents; this must be the new baby capital of China I decide, as whilst this is the first time that I have stayed here, it is the second time that I have been to this hotel and witnessed similar parties of new babies and parents.

On the Lijiang River at Guilin with those magnificent hills in the background

28.6 Hainan

w/c 19ᵗʰ November 2005 - The dominating factors though are preparations for the impending board meetings and the main event – our joint venture tenth anniversary celebrations to which we have invited customers from all around China to Hainan Island, along with and entourage from our team.

Wednesday and everything seems to be coming together. Still everything else seems to be on schedule even if there may be some major rows to be had ahead with unknown consequences; the delegate list for our sales conference is about 117 tobacco industry guests and forty-seven others. Life is hectic and my cold is now becoming significant.

Thursday I am in a bad way with a very sore throat, heavily swollen glands in my neck and I am generally out of it. Work wise this is disastrous as I must fly to Hainan tomorrow and give a major speech on Saturday; I feel terrible at present.

The flight to Haikou in Hainan Island, China's most southerly province, took three hours. Hainan is described as the Hawaii of China and is geographically south of Hong Kong and Guangdong province. It is more southerly than Taiwan and located in the South China Sea, being marketed these days as China's main beach/affluent tourist destination. I have heard a lot about it and indeed positive things, although I remain a little skeptical due to everything else that I have seen around China.

This is one of those very well-organized travel agency trips and we are collected by minibus for a one-and-a-half-hour trip to the Sofitel Hotel at Boao, described as a dream destination. After a ride down wonderful highways, we turn off to a private barriered road announcing our arrival at the hotel complex on Dongyu Island. This goes along the side of a very impressive world class golf course, designed apparently by the Aussie Golf Pro, Graham Marsh and looking suitably sadistic with lots of huge bunkers, water, and lakes, along to an impressively large hotel complex and waterway. I find Hainan Island described as China's own version of tropical paradise. Boao was once a small fishing village in this small agricultural island but has become a modern-day phenomenon due to its rapid development in recent years and hosting the Boao Forum for Asia, an Annual Conference attended by the heads of State and government and business leaders from twenty-six countries worldwide. The Sofitel Hotel has a world class convention centre and resort hotel, built to cater for the highest levels of conventions – this is our destination, and we are paying for it! And I still have a cold! It is certainly a classic five-star hotel though with a nice comfy bed to stay the night in.

Dinner tonight was held in the hotel and was relatively sensible with a lot although not all our guests, but I survived it. The hotel seems to have great facilities and a great climate, but there do not appear to be many beaches around, perhaps built for just conferences and golfers and those who wish to hang around pools. I will hopefully get a chance to explore a little more over the coming few days.

w/c 26th November 2005 - Today was the big conference meeting to celebrate the tenth anniversary of our cigarette paper manufacturing joint venture and to launch the new products from newly invested joint venture to supply mainly the Chinese Tobacco industry. This is an official meeting and the excuse for bringing our customers on an all-expenses paid three-day trip to Hainan, China's foremost hot weather tourist destination. So it was downstairs to the main conference hall for our 122 customers from all over China and an entourage of Directors, special guests, joint venture, and joint venture partner employees. Our joint venture partner, UK principal, the CNTC and I gave speeches followed by a short company film and a technical presentation. Mine, as GM was the longest speech and I featured again in the film, although my Scottish colleague took a starring role, looking very dashing in and around the factory, more importantly giving another Western input along with a whole bunch of German engineers. The whole event lasted one and a half hours and went very well, despite me starting to lose my voice as the cold has started to affect my throat, but I managed to avoid any squeaky moments although remained husky in the main. We all went away happy, or at least we were, although I am not sure that our Chinese partners would have been so happy at the heavy UK partner's branding and emphasis, and underneath the united exterior to our customers, we are anything but relaxed with each other and won't be until the board meeting in a couple of days' time; maybe not at all afterwards! Giving the speech reminded me of the other big external one that I did in Grenoble, France, probably ten years ago now to about 500 Europeans; I do try to avoid them, although I am getting more comfortable somewhat in my older age.

The weather is hot and humid, and we are bussed out for lunch to outdoor restaurants alongside a windy beach that looked far too dangerous for the windsurfers close to it. Some good surf and some local dishes to boot, whilst I hosted a table with customers from Guangxi. Then it was off to a river for some rafting. Now we had been worried a little about our shoes and I had worn my trainers. Bit daft really, because what happened next was a one-hour water fight fueled by bai jiu, with those in the know ducking out but the rest of us having a great time. We were handed bicycle pumps upon getting onto the rafts, wondering in a slightly alcoholic haze, why, only to get a burst of water from the raft operators, thereafter world war three let lose water wise and a great excuse for me to soak our principal, and anyone else head to toe, including most of our customers; still they all seemed to have great fun and appreciated me letting my hair down, ably assisted by a customer service assistant unsuccessfully covering my back! Kids' stuff, a wonder that no one fell in the water! Soaked right through – literally!

The area around Boao is wonderful but manicured and I am not sure that it is a place for laying around on beaches, more a golf and conference resort. Hotel seems great; room excellent, large comfy bed, big bath in the middle of it in an unusually French style design and views over waterways, palm trees, lakes, and pools out front and boats going up and down the waterway, *presumably sightseeing. There are palm trees everywhere and that golf course looks scarier by the minute – so much sand and water!*

Sunday, we left the hotel early for what should have been a two-hour bus ride down Hainan's east coast motorway but turned into a three-hour plus trek due to the motorway being closed. The good news is that this took us up into the hills and through villages and towns in the island showing that it is a beautiful island – green and tropical – palm trees everywhere, banana plants etc. Seems that Hainan had a lot of Indonesians running it until the communists took over. Then it was down onto flat and fertile valley bottoms before more hills and the finally the coast. First stop was the Yalong Bay beach area for a boat ride; in fact we went to look at the coral and sea fish through glass bottomed boats. This seems to be a part of China that has been done right, clean and the weather magnificent if not a little too humid. I am informed that the Sheraton Hotel here is great.

After this we were bussed of to the Nanshan Buddhist Culture Park further along the coast where there are several temples, but also a very large, circa 150 metres high Buddha statue built just off the coast and was impressive to all. Tired from the bumpy and long bus ride, sun burnt on the face and sweaty, we headed back to Sanya city centre, everyone happy.

The digs tonight are the Hotel Resort Intime, a nice five-star hotel about fifty metres from the beach. This built-up area seems very pleasant although not as nice as the Yalong Bay area that we visited earlier. My eighth-floor room in the unusually designed three building complexes had a nice view over the bay to the left, but high-rise apartments all around. The rooms here are not to the standard to the hotel at Boao, but then again, not many could compare with that.

Tuesday and most of the guests have gone although a few linger. I awoke early after an early night the prior evening and before it got too hot and humid, I took the opportunity to don shorts and walk down to the beach for a walk along the front. At 06.45 hours this was a very enjoyable and relaxing walk before returning for a breakfast, sat overlooking the swimming pool and the sea a little further beyond. The hotel is quite a good one of the beachfront centre of Sanya. Curiously there have been a very noticeable high number of westerners, who I have now identified as Russian. Indeed this seems to be a huge 'Russian Resort' as looking around all the restaurant names, menus and signs are in Chinese, English and Russian. Anyway it is packed with them, mainly overweight, wearing dark over the top glasses, hairy, Rolex watches and with big gold chains around their necks – men and women! Reflecting, most westerners who visit China go for the culture, e.g. Great Wall, Xian etc, whilst I guess that for many Russians, especially in the east of the country, this is probably one of the nearest warm weather destinations.

After a relaxing morning we flew back to Shanghai meaning that we shouldn't have too late at night in Jiaxing. I note that I have now been to over 75 per cent of the Chinese provinces but conclude that Hainan Island is certainly one of the nicer ones of them; genuine world class tourist facilities starting to develop!

w/c 25th February and 3rd March 2006 – Friday morning we set off to Hangzhou's Xiaoshan airport for the flight to Sanya in southern Hainan Island, but included a touch down stop in Shenzhen, the large city adjacent to Hong Kong. We eventually arrived early evening to temperatures of over twenty degrees centigrade and fading sunlight, taking a thirty-minute taxi ride to the Sheraton Hotel in Yalong Bay, the upmarket resort east of Sanya. I was delighted that there was a room upgrade that overlooked the centre of the hotel, the gardens and sea; wonderful!

A view from my hotel room, Yalong Bay, Sanya on Hainan Island

The weather was a little cloudy and overcast, but the temperature was okay, and we set out to explore this western five-star hotel, that I had come to learn differs from a Chinese five-star hotel. This is the No.1 rated hotel in Sanya and home for the last several years of the 'Miss World' Competition, the walls sporting photos of several Miss Worlds, contestants, the singer Lionel Richie, Mrs. Morley (wife of Michael Morley the ex-Miss world franchise holder) and so on. Tonight we dined in the Asian Spice restaurant at the end of the East Wing enjoying a Chilean sauvignon blanc and some supper Asian food, accompanied by a walking Paraguayan band.

The reception area was open to the elements at both ends reflecting the climate, like other hotels that I have stayed at in Mauritius, Kenya, and Bali. Outside of the reception is parked a black stretch limousine and inside is parked a bright red Ferrari, neither of course are typical here in China. There is plenty going on and the cabaret in the reception bar went on until midnight. Seemed like a great hotel with several restaurants, bars, swimming pools, tropical garden down to the beach and sea, great views, tennis courts, spas, and gym. The hotel had 511 bedrooms and can hold 1,400 folks, but it was large enough for there to be lots of space.

Saturday morning started with breakfast on the balcony followed by a nice early morning walk along the Yalong Bay beach for a couple of miles. It is unfortunately still a little overcast, but the temperature is in the mid twenty degrees centigrade and the climate lovely. The walk along the beach also included viewing other luxury hotels along the bay until we arrived at a foot pier up along the beach, a place that I had been to once before and densely populated by Chinese tourists as this is where the coach parties on the whistle stop tours pull over to sightsee. I decided against going up the road and running the gauntlet of souvenir shops, but I did end up buying some real pearls, both white and pink from a lady attired in traditional Muslim gear, selling walking along the beach.

Sunday there is an excellent world class golf course nearby, but this is not an occasion for me to play and I note the two adjoining hotels are a Marriot and a high-class Holiday Inn as best that we can make out. As I tend to, I read a book about the place and find out that the average age here is eighty-one years old, the oldest average of any province in China, second globally it quotes to Havana in Cuba. An interesting statistic and I am left wondering about the effect of the high rates of hepatitis A will have upon this in future?

A few more facts about Sanya and Hainan:

Miss World was held here in this hotel in 2003, 2004 and the 55th such event in 2005, after previously being held in London in 2002 and Sun City, South Africa in 2001. And it's still not politically correct to show it on major UK channels.

Sanya was only given its name in 1984 and upgraded to a city at the same time at the start of its development as a tourist destination.

Sanya is located on the southernmost point of both Hainan and therefore China, surrounded by the Wuzhi Mountains and is facing the South China Sea.

The annual average temperature is 25.4 degrees centigrade, with the highest monthly average being 28.4 degree C in July and the lowest being 21 degrees C in January. The annual sunshine totals 2,563 hours on average, and annual rainfall is 1,279mm, basically it is like summer all round. The climate is described as tropical monsoon though!

In 1998 the UN Environmental Protection Organization conducted a survey of 158 cities around the world and Sanya ranked second. There are lots of scenic spots making it ideal for tourism.

The population of Sanya itself is 481,000 with the main nationalities being Han Chinese and the Minorities Li, Mao, and Hui, who each have their own languages in addition to Chinese as well as their own brightly coloured attire as a traditional dress.

Since 2002, Sanya has hosted the International Triathlon Race in Yalong and has a host of festivals including Culture, Sailboat racing and a Coconut festival for which the island is famous. It is attracting more events all the time.

A truly great destination, not China as I knew it!

28.7 Heilongjiang

8th November 2003 – I have a trip up north via Pu Dong airport together with our mechanical engineering manager. The first disappointment was when we arrived at the airport to immediately find that the flight to Mudanjiang was delayed, and further investigation suggested that the delay would be 'at least two hours…. but there are mechanical problems with the plane'. We made an instant decision to catch an earlier flight to Harbin that may inconvenience our hosts at the other end as it meant that we simply reverse our travel arrangements for the next couple of days.

The two and a half hours flight to Harbin was quite reasonable. We crossed over land and across the Yellow Sea, then back over Shandong Province before crossing the Bonhai Sea to the three provinces that comprise the Dongbei region, or otherwise the old historic Manchurian region of Northeast China, before landing in Harbin the capital city of Heilongjiang Province, China's northern eastern most province. As we approached, we saw vast flatlands with fields of primarily maize stretching out for mile after mile reminding us of the flatlands of central Canada as one approaches the Rockies. The main difference here being the high number of populated farms on the landscape. Upon arrival we discovered a modern airport some forty kilometres out of the centre of Harbin and cold but crisp weather, about minus ten degrees centigrade, but with sunshine, blue skies, and no real snow evident. Picked up by a local driver in a black Nissan four-wheel drive, we were taken to the modern and impressive five-star Singapore Hotel near to the city centre.

Our room on the twentieth floor allowed us access to the Executive facilities. The hotel's rules and regulations were generally okay but included such translations as '7. Within the hotel the following conduct is prohibited: (a) Get drunk and create a disturbance, come to blows, gambling, go whoring, drug taking, dissemination of reactionary, obscene and superstitious books, pictures of promiscuous drugs, pornographic devices, and other criminal activities'. Well one gets the drift.

Harbin turns out to be a very interesting place although heavily industrialized region in the cold north. The Russians took the place over effectively when they signed the Sino-Russian agreement to build the trans-Siberian railway across the region to Vladivostok, therefore giving them a snow and ice-free trading port in the Pacific. This agreement was signed in 1860 and by the 1890's the place was teaming with Russians. The Japanese spoiled the plan a little in 1904 with the Russo-Japanese war that kicked all the Russians temporarily out of Dalian to the South, but Russia recovered the situation and re-enforcements to the community picked up with the heavy immigration of wealthy Russians fleeing the Bolsheviks in 1917 aiding the development of a huge industrial community. The place was taken over again by the Japanese between 1931 and 1936, but again recovered by Russia before the signing of an agreement between Chiang Kai-Shek and the Russians to give the region back to China in 1945, which may have been fine for the Chinese, but for the fact that the Russians took all the industrial machinery with them upon their departure, leaving somewhat of a void in the economy. Thereafter the region has had its unstable moments both on the Northern border with skirmishes with the Russians as well as an uneasy border with the North Koreans to the South. The region developed as a heavy military production area serving China's mighty, but inefficient army.

Today Harbin is home to some 6.4 million people, has China's premier skiing resorts within 150 kilometres and is the home of Harbin beer, which apparently being established in 1900, was China's first brewery and boasts the country's second largest domestic brand sales.

The town centre has an old street of original Russian buildings that is nearly 100 years old and even an old Russian cathedral, ala the one in Moscow, albeit a little smaller. The driving around town seems infinitely more disciplined than in much of the rest of China and the wide roads are well marked and well controlled, like many western cities. This is a big industrial city set in a big arable area but strikes me that it is the most un-Chinese city that I have visited to date, reminding me of what many eastern European cities may be like, but also similar in terms of climate and autumnal greyness to several Canadian and North American cities, maybe a Chicago, Boston, Cleveland or even New York suburban feel, the perception magnified by the wide roads, cold weather, dying grass and silver birch around.

Traveling out for dinner and a walk afterwards confirmed that Harbin has an amazing amount of Russian heritage. The Russian cathedral abandoned in the 1930's has been restored and is now home to an art gallery and the city is the hub of trade with Russia these days, particularly for leather goods. Other main industries include huge timber forests nearby, rich mineral reserves, the nearby Daqing oil fields, a developing automotive business replacing the old military aerospace buildings, developing tourism (skiing and the internationally famous annual ice festivals with the ice sculptures), huge tracks of farmland and pharmaceutical products.

Tonight we headed out to a zoological restaurant on the outside of town with our host and his company President for what was a particularly disappointing dinner and setting. It's not that it was terrible, just nothing special. Afterwards we got to walk down that famous Russian Street that had unfortunately generally shut down except for a few bars but gave one a sense of grandeur with the gold etched walls and green roof spires and making one imagine that one was in St. Petersburg, before a drive by the cathedral and off for an early night.

Sunday, I headed out across the river for a cold walk around the city's famous National Park of Sunshine Island, which in the summer is packed with locals relaxing and in January and February is host to the 'Ice Lantern Festivals' and those ice sculptures. Unfortunately today was a cold nothingness, with no one around, no water lilies, lake water starting to freeze, measured to a depth of some 2 inches and generally resembling a flipping beach summer camp in winter!

Finally we headed out for the four-hour road trip to Mudanjiang, to the southwest of this northerly province which turned out to be an eventful six hours! This may not have had the panorama of the internationally famous Icefield parkway drive between Jasper and Lake Louise in the Canadian Rockies, but it had all kinds of things to keep one interested, not least the fact that we discovered that the price of petrol was ¥3 (£0.26) per litre! The main road is still under construction, so the speed was limited by the fact that the road was not all dual carriageway and with periodic patches of heavy ice, at one of which we came across a major accident with a car crushed under a lorry, one body almost certainly trapped in there and another corpse lying on the side of the road, marginally covered by a coat, blood everywhere, with as usual in China a whole host of folk watching inquisitively and doing nothing; sobering moment. The countryside was undoubtedly agricultural, rural, and poor, scarred in places by uncontrolled mining and factories belching out fumes into the atmosphere or just abandoned. In between though it was very pretty, with big, wooded hills, although not mountains per say. This region has lots of wooden carts pulled by extremely hardy horses, some of which we also witnessed stood up in the back of an open lorry traveling down the road with low sides.

And if you don't have a horse, it seems one uses cattle to pull the carts, preferably a bull, assisting the harvesting of the maize crops before the winter totally closes in. The houses seem to be grouped into agricultural communities, villages, and are generally one-story red brick with pitched roofs and a small yard around them although periodically large houses exhibited Russian influences, possibly old mill owners' houses.

Lunch was an experience that I will never, ever forget. We arrived at a collection of restaurants either side of the road, which seemed non-too up market and the car was immediately accosted by teenage girls trying to entice us into each of their family hostelries, with the competition being quite fierce. I could see from the conditions that we weren't going to eat much in the way of food here for sanitary reasons and I managed to dissuade our host from ordering frogs and stay to more basic diets. We were ushered into the only private room, which turned out to be the living quarters of the household with heated stone plinth at the side providing the heated bed for the family at night times and a doctor's screen barely disguising the family's basic spare clothes in the corner. When my engineering manager returned from the toilet, I said I wanted to go, and his face turned colour as he said, "but it is terrible'! As usual in China, I laughed it off as they are trying to protect me from any thing that is not 5-star and headed off in the direction which he pointed at. He was right, this was terrible and quite the worst toilet that I have ever seen anywhere, and the only surprise was that I wasn't sick, perhaps just too stunned by events. I find myself compelled to describe this – a brick shack outdoors, with room for one person, no door, two rotting planks of wood some two feet off the ground and about a two feet gap in between with a huge pile of what cannot be described as anything else, but frozen shit! Unbelievable, it would have been easier to find a tree, but relieved myself quickly and escaped, returning to inform my wife that she shouldn't drink too much at lunchtime and only happy that I didn't have any stomach problems. Unbelievable, or perhaps I have just had a sheltered life; unbelievable! I found myself wondering whom the poor person was who had to dig this out as there was no discernable place for it to run and everything was frozen anyway. Surely this was not the main loo, but yes it apparently was, and I look around at the other diners continuing just as normal. Upon departure two waitresses and the lady owner came to say goodbye and seemed transfixed, thanking us for visiting them.

Next it was a detour to one of China's premier ski slopes at Yabuli, which *hosted the Asian Winter games in 1996. It seemed okay, but the hills not big enough, although well-resourced with seven or eight slopes that we could immediately discern as well as other winter sports facilities. I found myself again wondering though what the medical facilities would be like if one had an accident, remembering also the body abandoned back on the road like a piece of meat.*

Then through some more scenic hills, more Russian style houses, rows of beehives alongside the road, past hordes of peasant farmers and down into the city of Mudanjiang, the third largest city in this province. This had been one of the most interesting journeys in my life and a whole geography lesson and too many things to take in; quite an experience, but with residual memories of those abandoned mines and aging and derelict old industrial premises..........
and a dead body.

We entered Mudanjiang from the North and were taken to the grey and very large 'Beishan Hotel' set at the foot of a large hill. This hotel was pure old communist style and more Soviet style in nature with its size and greyness. The good news was that we had a suite, the bad news was that some wallpaper was missing, the paintwork chipped, the bed rock hard and the lighting too bright. The fan above the showerhead in the bathroom had no cover and if it was running and one tried to grab the showerhead, there was a distinct possibility that on may lose at least one finger; the fan remained off. This was eerie and left me wondering if there were bugs in the room, not of the insect variety. There did not appear to be many guests, too many miserable, stout, unattractive and unsmiling employees dressed in military colour and styled uniforms, which did nothing to make me feel welcome. This of course was the main government hotel in the city, visited by Jiang Zemin, Deng Xiao Peng and other Chinese Chairmen and Premiers over the years, but one could not disguise the fact that it was dreadful, with big military square at the front. One can only hope that the much-vaunted President's suite was much better. The only good news about it was the fact that I finally got to go to the loo! This was old communist China with a vengeance and reminded me of the differences that exist in the rapidly developing south and eastern regions of China and the staid and underdeveloped north and west of the country.

We were glad to escape relatively early for a dinner at a nearby hotel, although again with some of the least impressive and blandest food that I have had in China, accompanied by traditional local baijiu.

Looking around at the countryside, the cold, and the lifestyle it is not difficult to understand why it is well reported in China that local girls from this region escape this environment by going into the oldest profession in the world elsewhere around China!

Monday morning and it was back to business, the reason that we have made this important visit! We are visiting a competitor's factory (unsure if my competitors knew about this though) to view a piece of equipment. The factory was very impressive or at least the few bits of it that we were allowed access to! Then it was off to see some of the factories that our host had within his group and was a lesson in the decaying nature of the traditional northern Chinese industrial base, the bit that hasn't modernized that is. First it was an old paper mill making imitation leather and insert moldings for car roof interiors, which was not too bad, but gloomy and unattractive. Then it was a 'new' workshop that he acquired six months ago, which was quite well fitted, but was terribly dark and dingy inside, poorly lit and must be incredibly cold inside during winter, reminding me of what I expected of old traditional inefficient communists engineering plants. This was a building on a huge decaying site, which we discovered was the city's main employer and a state-run factory, employing 60,000 people until it closed a few years ago. Now a few buildings are rented out to budding entrepreneurs who between them only employ 2,700 folk and it still looks to be over manned. Next it was off to his workshop, which was somewhat better and the kit that he is making was quite good. Good meeting and then off for a local trip before lunch. First though our engineering manager and I had to go to the loo, and would you believe it, yes virtually the same again, although there was more of a drop this time to the pile of muck below, maybe four feet; the biggest concern that we didn't fall down the gap between the wood into it!

Again this local trip was one of those experiences! We were told we were going to see some bears, which we assumed would be a zoo, so we were surprised when we headed off into the quite beautiful countryside, through wooded hills and rural agricultural communities on what was becoming a lovely day. Half an hour later we came across another farming community set in a beautiful valley bottom and then into a large walled factory facility. Entering it became apparent, from our increasingly confident English-speaking guide that this was a bear farm producing gall bladder bile extracts for traditional Chinese medicines, which sell for a fortune. Fascinating, albeit entirely unacceptable, facts:

They had over 1,000 bears captured from the region's local countryside.

This was the largest bears gall bladder powder producer in China.

Three species were present; a few Malaysian bears that resembled more a Kuala bear than what I would call a bear with strange faces, but the vast majority being local black bears and brown bears.

They have a laboratory where they are trying to clone a panda bear (as stated)!

Black bears average 200 kilogrammes in weight when fully grown.

Brown bears average 400 kilogrammes in weight when fully grown.

The biggest brown bear that we saw was over 1,000 kilogrammes! Heck, just like a bloody 'grizzly', but smaller than the stuffed Kodiak bear that I had once witnessed in British Columbia! That said it was still very big.

They were kept in small cages that would not be considered humane in the West and would be quite illegal. If the animal rights folk knew about this, they would have a field day! Clean conditions though, must be said, but sad.

The medicinal effects of the gall bladder extract apparently can fix a lot of things – good for the liver, heart, skin, heavy drinkers and just about everything else apparently and we came away from the gift shop with bear's gall bladder wine, antler horn powder, gall bladder powders and even some ginseng as gifts from our hosts. After the white spirit wine the prior night I suddenly feel like I need some, but none of the packets claimed that they could cure headaches!

This farm was also run as an amusement centre for tourist and locals, with a small hotel, entertainment of talented trained bears, factory tours, gift shops.

Our guide claims that he has learnt the English language so that he can emigrate to New Zealand next year with his family.

After this experience, we headed off for dinner in a Korean restaurant back in Mudanjiang, a North Korean restaurant that is. Again this was a 'first' for me and I found that these small spicy dishes were quite pleasant. There was a whole street of these Korean restaurants – apparently girls can get visas to come and work here for three years, but cannot get married and must go back, a policy that is strictly enforced by the North Korean Government. They even sang a few traditional Korean songs to us over lunch, helping to take our mind off the cold.

I discovered few other things, which didn't surprise me – like the fact that there are NO westerners living in this town, although of course they do have the occasional western visitors to the paper mill, mainly German engineers. The population in the city is 720,000, but that increases to 2.8 million when the local countryside folk are included. It is within 100 kilometres or so of the Russian border and a couple hundred kilometres of the North Korean border. Mudanjiang is not a rich city.

After a quick walk along the expansive riverbanks and taking in the new developments along it, we headed off to the small, but new airport for our flight back to Shanghai. The only significant point of note at the new airport being the transparent glass toilet stalls!

What a trip – not out of a travel holiday brochure and not all nice experiences, but interesting experiences in life none the less. But those unbelievable toilets!

28.8 Henan

5th October 2002 - Wednesday is my first visit to Luohe in Henan (not to be confused with Hunan or Hainan) province. Pronounced 'Heurrnaan', or at least is by me. Know nothing about it except that Luohe tobacco factory is a big and important customer of ours. A quick look at the map suggests that it is not too far away, a relatively quick flight from Shanghai over Anhui Province into Luohe, maybe an hour, hour, and a half at most. I am not making much progress on travel arrangements – I still know nothing except that I was being picked up early from my apartment. Would you believe it, my senior colleagues turned up in suits and ties, the first time in a long while I have witnessed this (It's been golf shirts and slacks for the last five months). It was explained that they were wearing jackets because it may get cold, I remained without a jacket. At Hong Qiao airport they have ceased the practice of removing shoes as one goes through security. Our new customer service guy, who is only twenty, accompanied us as my translator and informs us this is his first flight ever. I am impressed by him, his keenness, but he is so young, but I wish he would shave off that silly looking moustache that he is trying to grow – and he's wearing not only jeans, but a denim jacket as well! Not surprisingly, he is a little nervous and thus overly keen to please – runs off after things and like most Chinese very supportive and deferential to their elders, i.e. me. This is something that we westerners probably more associate with the Japanese, but it is genuinely refreshing and encouraging to see a society that has so much respect for one's elders – there must be benefits in this! I can cope with this.

In the event we flew into Zhengzhou, the capital of Henan then had a one-hour taxi trip to our hotel in Luohe. The area was very hot and arid, reminding me of Xian, but flat without hills. The large wide roads, which I am finding are standard almost everywhere now, were lined by newly planted lines of trees that were eight to ten deep. Very attractive and will provide a good screen in time. Apparently, it only rains three times a year, which explained the dust, but there must be good irrigation in place to supply the large flat fields that appeared to yield healthy crops. Small an inadequate tractors and trailers everywhere provide a constant transportation stream of crops away from the fields. My deputy said that he didn't like the area 'because it was dirty'; it certainly seemed poor in places.

Luohe turned out to be a town crossing a river centering around a very long straight road. Very dusty, very dirty, but efforts are obviously being made to upgrade the apartments that lined to road, and the surroundings, like all Chinese cities are a building site development. Very apparent and visible evidence of the Muslim community all around, including the domes on the tops of some buildings. I start to wonder how many Muslims there are in China. Too many tiled exteriors though and large chimneys very visibly belching pollutants into the atmosphere. Apparently, Henan province is the most populated province in China, a situation that was very recognizable in

Luohe. Folk everywhere. The highest tobacco sales in China also I'm told. To look at the people remind me of those in Xian. A country city shall we say.

The hotel was different! A bit of a flea pit despite claims that it was the best in town. Heavily stained carpets, badly chipped and scratched wooden dark varnished surfaces, finger marks on the mirrors and switches, mold around the bath and on the shower curtains, splashes on walls, wallpaper peeling off, sparsely furnished rooms, limited sheets of loo paper (not on a roll), electric wiring a visible nightmare and I hate to think what might be lurking under the plastic matting in the bathroom, what was above it was bad enough. Room overlooking garages at the back and right into employees' lodgings. I start to ponder what I might catch, my worst hotel in China. I now understand why my deputy had made the comment about Henan being dirty, this was a way of preparing me. At least the TV had 30 odd channels and the bed was great. The material in the room was surprisingly well translated, although sparse (But it did remind me that I should not bring LPG or fuel oil cookers into my room), until here-we-go, I notice a piece of paper next to the bed:

'Beautiful hair and face and massotherapy care.

Respect Guests:

After your tried trip and busy work and nervous life, please choose one's own centre provide good service. You will all change and comfortable.

One's own center will take refined skill with you happy life! We welcome you here! Massotherapy ¥88/hour.'

One can draw one's own conclusions!

Day one of the factory visit was a hoot; I went down a storm again with some very positive meetings. This even though my new translator for the occasion, My male translator was now very nervous and on two occasions found himself translating and speaking English to a somewhat startled Chinese purchasing manager and in turn speaking to me in Chinese. Poor lad, but he did okay! I am discomforted though by his way of sitting far too close to me all the time, so that there is contact with my legs and arms. This is typically Chinese (male to male contact), but I do not like it and would appreciate my space; I must talk to him about this. Good guys at the factory though and thoroughly hospitable. Had dinner at the factory's own restaurant facilities, which was excellent. Among the starter selection, there was some form of gelatinized cold meat, which was quite delicious, and as the rotating table had remained motionless for a while, to offset the requisite alcohol consumption, I did a good job of clearing this plate. As I was finishing it and the replacement one was on the way they informed me that this is a local Henan speciality – donkey! The next plate remained untouched. After dinner, after a shed load of Chinese baijiu (55 per cent proof), red wine and beer, my translator and I got dumped back at the hotel whilst the rest went out gallivanting. As we got out of the lift on our floor one couldn't helped noticing the open room door right opposite the lift full of 'painted girls' awaiting beckoning calls from clients – ah this must be the "Massotherapy" department! The Chinese are just so subtle and discreet sometimes! They were there to be noticed!

Thursday started with a breakfast meeting with the director of the cigarette factory. I was glad that my evening the prior night had not gone on any longer; others weren't so lucky judging by the condition of some of the bodies around the breakfast table. Turns out that they had a heavy session until late. Heck. The meeting with the director went quite well and I came away with gifts of packs of their best brands of cigarettes and a nice enough crystal set of cigarette lighter, tray and ashtray. After seeing crystal being cut by hand in the Czech Republic several years ago, this clean-cut modern crystal seems a poor comparison, but it has its own attractiveness, and the gesture is thoroughly appreciated.

At the airport, we were boarded forty-five minutes before departure, truly amazing, as generally they tend to go in for the 'get everybody on with ten minutes to go' routine out here. I had noticed that my boarding pass has no gate number, no date, a hardly legible hand stamped flight number on it, and a scribbled seat number, which to my embarrassment I read incorrectly until I got relocated by a surly and stressed hostess. The Chinese are unbelievable on domestic flights. Long gone are the live chickens and vegetables routines, but these have been replaced by carrying as much hand luggage on board as you can plus all the gifts that one accumulates on trips, and which are inevitably given at the last moment so that they are in separate bags. There are no enforced limits on what you carry on despite all the rules being in place. The result is chaos, not enough luggage space, arguments, stressed stewardesses and so on.

w/c 21ˢᵗ June 2003 - Wednesday I head off to Hongqiao airport with a joint venture sales guy and my translator in tow, where I discover that we are also being greeted by a senior joint venture Sales guy when we arrive. I am a little concerned as many SARS checks remain in place at toll booths and the airport – health declaration forms and temperature checks; although recovering, I still have an intermittent cough and my voice still not recovered. At Shanghai, I relaxed a little as I passed through the first temperature-imaging camera with a loud affirmative buzz and green light. After a one-and-a-half-hour flight we arrived at Xinzheng airport, just outside of Zhengzhou, the six million-population city, which I haven't been into before. It apparently has the largest bus manufacturing plant in China and one of the largest TV screen production facilities.

Zhengzhou was a good experience, meeting the cigarette factory people for the first time and the factory director taking us for dinner at a truly splendid local restaurant, with fantastically tasty local dishes and great company. The only downside being the apparent Henan custom of the guest having to drink three glasses of baijiu in succession before being joined by the host for a fourth; oh heck, especially as there were three of them. My translator was partly exempted this, but the others in a party did not escape and all ended up looking to be in trouble with characteristically red faces. An early night followed at our hotel which claims to be the first International hotel in Zhengzhou, opening in 1981 was also very good, albeit with a frugality in its approach, but I suspect also southern European input upon its unique art deco internal designs. A choice of fifty TV stations and the best air conditioning units I have found in China help me relax, although I spent five minutes trying to remove a full-size wall mirror before I realized that there was no wardrobe behind it. My only curiosity was the sign at the entrance of the modernly appointed hotel declaring, 'No Smoking; Watermelons and Slippers are prohibited in this hotel'; the Chinese mind works in great ways sometimes.

The morning's itinerary was meant to be a brief meeting with the Director of the local Chinese Tobacco Corporation for Henan Province before heading to Luohe to see more customers. However, the very affable Director took a distinct liking to me, a mutual feeling, and as a result we ended up having a truly splendid 'Sharks Fin' banquet at the city's top restaurant. These banquets, as well as 'Abalone', are the pinnacle of Chinese dining. I was intrigued to learn that the pay structure for such meals is that you only pay for the bowl of shark's fin soup and that the huge variety of other dishes that arrive all come included in the price. At £250.00 for seven of us in a provincial city, this was expensive! Apart from the moral issue and debate about eating shark's fin and the associated fishing policies, shark's fin to me is pleasant although not exceptional, although the associated courses often are. Anyway, it was also more baijiu, and it was another excellent meal for me to remember before we took the two-hour trip to Luohe.

After some good meetings and all-important debt collection at Luohe, it was out for dinner in the factory's spartan and aging private dining rooms, which I have dined at before and remember the local food to be excellent. The loos were typically Chinese, and I still cannot get used to walking into these places to find a man squatting with door open and one piece of paper in hand, seemingly indifferent to the world. A poor night's sleep followed in a reasonable three-star hotel, with its introduction in English stating 'Your stay will make our hotel more glorious' telling one all you need to know. Henan, I am told, has a population of some 100 million and is relatively poor, but its arable fields look good for all the recent rain and the country's massive tree planting campaign has developed considerably in Luohe since my last visit here nine months ago. Reminds me how fast China is improving its lifestyle and environmental awareness.

Friday, I discover that the sales guys have changed their travel plan and that as a result we were not able to go and visit the ancient Song Dynasty city nearby to Zhengzhou; this annoys me and I decide to take it personally, although this was not the case; the issue is just the constant changes. Then on the way home in torrential rain, we end up queuing for two hours on the motorway due to routine SARS checks! Just when I think that it cannot get any worse, I get a call from work to inform me that due to SARS our customers now have huge stocks of cigarettes and are shutting for most of July as a result and won't therefore be needing paper from us; no sales!

I reflect upon a comment made by the purchasing d from Zhengzhou who commented upon the changing circumstances in China. He was the same age as me and observed that 'When I was young, we had one shirt to share between five of us, now my sixteen-year-old daughter cannot choose between her fifty shirts and is still not happy that there is enough choice'. The Director of the CNTC in Zhengzhou also demonstrated the changing times and his wealth by driving us in his brand-new Volkswagen Passat, cost a mere ¥285,000, some £26,000, and commenting that his nephew was studying architecture in London for three-years at a cost of ¥260,000 per annum. There is a lot of money in the tobacco industry everywhere I remind myself. There is more money in China than initially meets the eye, not all of it 'over the table' I am led to understand; again this is not a part of Chinese culture that I have any involvement in, but I am regularly reminded that this activity remains rife, despite draconian laws to counter corruption. I remember a phrase used to me a little while ago, 'China is on the take'; just can't help itself.

28.9 Hong Kong and Macao

It is worth noting that Chinese nationals were not able to fly on direct flights into Hong Kong but had to fly to an airport adjacent in Guangdong province and then enter by pre-arranged visa via the land immigration entrances. Indeed for a long while until about 2004, Chinese from elsewhere required special passes even to enter Guangdong.

w/c 20ᵗʰ September 2003 - Monday I head off to Hangzhou for our 1,000 kilometres flight to Shenzhen in Southern China's Guangdong Province, the capital of the backdrop to Hong Kong and one of the three big powerhouses in China, the other two being Beijing and Shanghai. Shenzhen is literally just over the border from Hong Kong's New Territories. I eventually got a snapshot translation of the agenda for the sales conference this week – tonight is a two-hour meeting in the hotel, then it's two days in Hong Kong sight-seeing, one day in Macao sightseeing and travel back to Hangzhou on Friday. My translator is accompanying me and my deputy and our Technical Marketing Manager, are also there along with twenty-seven folks from our State-owned joint venture partner. We have about eight-seven customers in tow on this holiday that we are paying for! I suddenly feel guilty. My secretary is fed up, her mood compounded by the fact that she is fighting with her parents again because she isn't married yet. I have been to Hong Kong three times before, the first time in 1994, the last time two years ago with the family, but I have never been to Macao before or indeed Shenzhen city, so I am a little excited at the prospect. We also have a night out in a Macao casino organized, which doesn't thrill me and may lead to my early return to Jiaxing. I recognize that I may have faults in my make up, but gambling is not one of them.

The flight took just under two hours, and we landed with the ground temperature at an acceptable twenty-four degrees centigrade, but a smog spoiling the surroundings. This was my first look see at Shenzhen and our taxi trip from the airport to our city centre located Panglin Hotel took thirty minutes. I am not sure who is the jinx at present, but our taxi picked up a puncture on the way, the second time that this has happened within two weeks. Shenzhen seems to still be building itself, albeit with many established high-rise flats and corporate buildings. Somehow though on first sight it seems to lack the romance, flare or general impression of style compared to Shanghai. Certainly there was no immediate evidence of any old towns, but there was evidence, plenty of it, that the hills in the city centre areas had been skinned of greenery, resembling the mine dumps of downtown Johannesburg, and were simply and systematically being mined away to level the land to build more buildings.

The view from my twelfth-floor room frontage looked right out over the small triangular central square towards distant hills, the view interrupted by many tall buildings of different and varied designs. The most eye catching being a gold/bronzed-tinted glass covered high-rise building away to the left of my view. Innovative stuff, but it's not Hong Kong! Below, on about the sixth floor are an external extension and a relatively small outdoor swimming pool and sundeck; I am not tempted though. Tonight we have a dinner with all our customers before sitting through 'the Conference', which was two-hours of speeches in Chinese, muggins being the only one who could not understand what is being said and the situation was not conducive to translation either whilst my fluent German colleague sat there smugly taking it all in. At least I was in the front row, whilst he was very publicly relegated to the back row, another Chinese sign; the Chinese snub.

My translator has been slightly moody, unusually, and it took me until Shenzhen to find out why. I have known since I have been here that there is very little confidentiality in China with everyone seeming to know everything, often except for what they need to know. The Chinese are the best gossipers and sharers of information in the world, giving validity and credence to the phrase 'Chinese whispers'. My translator, I also know is well plugged into the system and is a veritable mine of information, priding herself upon her contacts, often amazing me at what she has found out. However, she didn't know about her boyfriend's promotion by me in advance, and it seems also that she was virtually the last to find out. It seems that a lot of other people knew the night before I made the changes as it is suspected that either my deputy or the personnel manager had talked to their mates! How do I get over this concept of confidentiality? Anyway, it takes me some time to explain to her that the changes were between me and her boyfriend and not her direct business, so she shouldn't be upset that I hadn't taken her into my confidence.

The conference dinner was absolute chaos – no table allocations, no name places, and a general jostling for position. I was delighted that although the evening was hospitable, the drinking was moderate, dictated by the fact that arrangements provided that the conference came after dinner. The conference was not too bad, just too long and ended late, enabling me to head off to bed leaving many to relax around town.

Tuesday morning was an early start as we headed across the border into Hong Kong. As a teenager I dreamed about crossing this border into China, the irony being that I am now making this journey in reverse. The border crossing itself was an experience, possibly the worst passport control in the World (on the Chinese side) with the Disney style queuing arrangements being destroyed by a group a little old ladies who decided to destroy the queuing system and head in a straight line, undoing the tapes as they pressed on, leaving me battered, bruised, sweaty and pissed-off. Still one keeps learning in life and the morale of this lesson is to follow the little old ladies, who turned out to be far less frail than their external appearance and had no hesitation in shoving me around to get to the front!

This is my fourth visit to Hong Kong, my last being with the family in 2001 and I look forward to seeing any changes and some alternative venues, but things came to an abrupt halt at the HK immigration desk. My passport expires on 4th February 2004, which is no problem, except that as a British citizen I am automatically given a visa for 180 days, even though I only want one for two days. The problem is that February the fourth is only 154 days away and the computer couldn't handle this, not being able to provide a visa that goes beyond the validity of the passport. The result that I was taken to one side for thirty minutes, holding up the whole travel party and giving everyone a chance to look at me suspiciously and to speculate what I had done wrong, whilst supervisors sought to alter the system to allow me in. I muse at the irony of it all as I should have had the easiest access of the lot.

Once we were in Hong's New Territories, we started to relax and take in a different environment. The bus took us into Kowloon, where we are staying at the Intercontinental, Grand Stanford Hotel, which is just as grand in many respects as its sounds, full of professional Americans, although there was also a share of rich, but south London accented cockney types, making me wonder what profession they may be in, especially as they seemed to be up to no good in terms of Champagne drinking and things hanging off their arms. My room, on the second floor, has a wonderful view of Hong Kong Island. This view provided a classical view of the Island, looking wonderful during the day, but very special at nighttime.

The first venue after a typical Cantonese style lunch was a drive around the rich houses of Hong Kong at Repulse Bay and a visit to a beachside temple and beach before going to Ocean Park. Some were disappointed by this as they saw it as kids' stuff, some got into the mood, others plainly didn't. I encouraged some by leading the way on the Mine Ride Rolla coaster, then the Rapid Rapids water run happily getting soaked, which was also exhilarating and those who joined me also thoroughly enjoyed themselves. The aquarium, dolphin and sea lion displays made for a good afternoon, before we had a dinner at the restaurant at the main entrance of the complex, the only downside of which, was that it was alcohol free, which suited me fine, although the joint venture sales guys managed to produce some bottles of baijiu from somewhere, but not enough to spoil the evening! Then it was a coach trip up to the Victoria Peak of Hong Kong overlooking the city and a chance to get some mandatory photographs with customers before taking the funicular railway down the steep hillside and back to the hotel. The train was built by the British in 1888 and reminds one that we were once a nation of engineers and innovators before abdicating a leadership position. A pint of Guinness with my German friend and a couple of customers finished the evening off well; a pint literally being the case given Hong Kong's high price structure. Along the way I also note that Aberdeen Harbour has been ruined as the city seeks to upgrade its standards. A concrete road bridge now spans the harbour, large buildings and apartments surround it, large boulders at the entrance calm the waters and the famous 'boat people' seem to be declining in numbers and now restricted to a small corner of the harbour. Yep, if you are a westerner and you want to see traditional Chinese culture, you can now go to China to see it, forget Hong

Kong. Signs everywhere reminds one of how important the Hong Kong Jockey Club is towards the funding and running of Hong Kong.

At lunch today I was amused to see that in the restaurant, as in many other public locations, there are 'No Smoking' signs posted, indicating fines of HK$5,000. This does not dissuade our party from the cigarette industry from collectively lighting up, correctly guessing that no one is going to stop them or enforce this by-law. Around the city road names such as Waterloo, Gloucester, Hereford, and the likes reminds one of the British heritages.

Wednesday and the first stop today is the Hong Kong Convention Centre on the waterfront where Chris Patten and Prince Charles sailed away from in the QE2 after the formal handover in 1997 and for photos with the gold Bauhinia sculpture, then to the Wong Tai Sin Temple, which is famous, but I have had my fill of Chinese Temples and all the burning of josh sticks and associated smoke makes me think that ancient Buddhist monks must have died blind and of lung cancer. Next it was Hong Kong's famous gold and jewelry shops, including gold toilets, bathroom décor et al to see, tacky, followed by a watch shop and then off to the glamourous new Pacific Plaza shopping centre, that was very westernized and horrifically overpriced for the party of travelers, the brand names and the prices would not be out of place in Paris, London, New York, or Tokyo. Finally in the day's hectic schedule was dinner and a cabaret on a two-hour boat trip around Hong Kong Harbour, providing an opportunity to view Hong Kong's dramatic nighttime skyline, one of the world's most famous city views and stands comparison only with Paris's Eiffel Tower and Sydney's Opera House in terms of instant recognition. The new World Financial Centre, now the region's tallest building is solid, maybe less attractive, or innovative than some other buildings, but I am sure that it will grow on folk, especially with its 'teeth/claws' design on the roof.

The other big impression of Hong Kong that hit me was the presence of large numbers of westerners, many more than witnessed during our family visit in 2001, and whilst many were obviously tourists, the vast majority seemed to have the confidence and presence of expatriates living and working here. This surprised me, especially as most seem to be Americans, apparently having filled the expatriate boots of the vacuum left by the Brits exodus in the 1990's.

Thursday started early in glorious weather with another breakfast at a local restaurant then onto the ferry port in Kowloon to Macao, which I think may have been the location of the old airport in Hong Kong. The journey on the high-speed ferry took longer than I expected for some reason, as I hadn't realized that it was quite so far away, but the sixty minutes journey was made quite comfortable by the first-class standard leather seats. The journey passed a myriad of islands and hilly coastline silhouetted in the early morning sun and then Macao was there in front of us, certainly not the initial impact of Hong Kong, but created a buzz of excitement among our group and I am pleased as although I have skirted the coastline on a boat trip in 2002, I have never actually visited this special economic region that has so much history.

Macao was run by the Portuguese for about 500 years, and it shows! The contrast to Hong Kong's efficiency couldn't be starker, the buildings plain and drab in the main central areas, the roads narrow and not conducive to traffic, although the historic bits are straight out of Portugal's capital, Lisbon, bringing back memories of my visit there some six years ago. First stop was the old cathedral, which sadly burnt down at some stage, but the facia remains as a famous landmark and the stepped approach up to it from a cobbled square and street road below was pleasant enough, as was our visit to the old fort adjacent which is now a museum, leaving the Chinese what the hell these 'canon things' were?

Then it was back onto the coach for lunch at our Holiday Inn, Macao, hotel before a slightly disappointing afternoon going to the Mazu Temple for a few photos, contrasting a lovely short drive through old traditional style pink Portuguese homes on the hillside, which are unsurprisingly lived in by local Government officials, then it went downhill as we had to visit a clothes shop for an hour, which like the jewellery and watch shops yesterday is an unfortunate factor of Chinese travel agency tours as they seek to boost profits and wages by getting kickbacks and commissions. Finally, in the afternoon's calendar, we headed off to the central square to have photos alongside the Golden Lotus, which is the emblem of Macao, contrasting with Hong Kong's Bauhinia golden flower. Tonight's planned events – dinner, dog racing and then hitting the casino's – there is a buzz of excitement in the air as gambling is forbidden in mainland China.

After a relatively social dinner it we were off to the Greyhound racing, which turned out to be the high spot of our trip to Macao; no seedy stadium his, but instead a very professional, clean, and modern set-up, although it is always sad to my mind at such events to cast around and see the folk who spend their lives at these events, addicted to the lure of betting – same all over the world, but none more so than the Chinese.

Back to the hotel, some headed off to shows, others for karaoke or the casinos, whilst my translator, I and a couple of sales guys walked around a few shops and then headed for the world-renowned Casino Lisboa, which looked great from the outside and was a hive of activity inside, but to me was strangely disappointing. Maybe my enjoyment is affecting that I am dumb enough not to understand how to play the games and lose money! The western prostitutes hanging around outside of the casinos highlight the lure of western girls to Chinese men; mainly Russian and Portuguese girls, but I suspect that you could find all races here if one looked close enough. Reminds me that the Portuguese and Spanish reputedly gave the world syphilis.

Friday was an early dash to the Macao-China border post at Zhuhai. The weather is great and this time the customs clearance was easy and well managed. Then there was a two-hour coach trip up to Guangzhou, the capital of Guangdong province to catch a plane back to Hangzhou, only to discover that a customer from Hubei Province was waiting in Jiaxing, the result of which was a dinner, karaoke and a later night than planned.

It has been a good week, despite a few administrative frailties relating to the conference organization and the disappointment to me of Macao. I feel a little guilty, as this sales conference was a mass holiday, but I console myself that the benefits of massive customer contact outweighed the downsides of being out of the office for a week. This is how things work here in China.

w/c 2*nd* July 2005 – Sunday it was a China Eastern flight to Hong Kong. The airport was chaotic, full of Chinese traveling parties and all that goes with it, compounded by the need for a new customs declaration form system for baggage, more bureaucracy. The emigration queues were also packed, but my acquired knack of taking the extreme left queue, right next to the seldom used Diplomatic and special assistance passport check, ensured that I get through quicker than most as the line invariably divides into two; a proven system and winning formula. Arriving in Hong Kong for what is my fifth trip here, the purpose being to meet a potential British guy who may be able to assist with our new business in China. The new airport in Hong Kong is on the island of

Lantau and is now seven years old. I have only been in and out of this airport once before during a family holiday in 2001 when we managed to escape just before a monsoon/typhoon hit the shores, one of the last flights, if not the last. It is a vast and impressive airport with an underground high speed transfer train from the gate to the main terminal and a huge baggage collection area; All very clean and efficient. I check in at the Regal hotel desk for a transfer bus only to find that despite my booking form in my hand through a travel agency, that I am not booked in, but at least they found some space to accommodate me. I elected to take the transfer bus, which at HK$140 is somewhat cheaper than the limousine cars that I have been known to take, but which here are HK$540. The bus is slow, but the 45 minutes trip gives me a chance to take in the wonderful views.

The islands comprising much of Hong Kong are typical of the southern Chinese coastline, with green fertile hills and small sandy bays, although some of the hills don't seem as fertile as some that I've seen, in fact some of these on the way in are downright barren come to think of it, maybe the results of the roadbuilding projects. I am immediately reminded of Hong Kong's high rise apartment blocks that are very narrow, typifying the architectural style driven by the very high land values because of a lack of space. Travelling over the large suspension bridges that now link the islands, highway No.3 South, I witness the high number of working boats and barges below in evidence approaching and departing from the huge container ports that were on our right-hand side. Hong Kong island and that infamous view lay away in the distance ahead. Then we reach apartment blocks after apartment blocks before suddenly appearing with a close-up view of the main part of Hong Kong island briefly before disappearing down into the Western Tunnel and reappearing minutes later Hong Kong Island itself with the waterways on the left and the World Finance building right ahead. I immediately note the good driving standards, unlike China, of course driving on the left-hand side of the roads, again unlike China, another glimpse of the British legacy, although I am not sure where the design of the red taxis with silver roofs emanated from? We travel along the road towards 'Central', along Harcourt Road with the high and many glass paneled buildings to the right, including that famous Bank of China building and the Ritz Carlton Hotel with the many Bentley's parked outside. Then it was past the famous ferry ports to the left, the International Convention

Centre on the frontage and so on, onto the North Causeway and turning into the entrance of the five-star Regal Hong Kong Hotel.

The hotel is great, I am only here because the four-star Excelsior was full and this is a higher standard and cheaper, although tucked back along the Causeway about ten minutes' walk from the Excelsior. My room is near the top on the twenty-first floor, with one of the biggest beds that I have ever seen, but overlooking a couple of sports stadium, one of which I think they hold the Rugby World 7's tournament in, along with hills and many typical Hong Kong apartment buildings. Looking out the hotel is in a busy location surrounded by roads and the green traditional trams below very much in evidence.

I met my friend early evening and we headed out for a twenty-minute drive to Stanley Bay on the other side of the island for a beer before dinner, reminding me of visits gone by. Tonight was a super evening, eating at a tapas restaurant on an open cold colonial style balcony outdoors in a building that has just been relocated to this area from central Hong Kong, stone by stone, pillar by pillar, thereby keeping this old British building. Great food and Spanish atmosphere with wandering musicians keeping us entertained in the background. Stanley Bay is famous for its clothing and gift markets, but there are also a few bars and many restaurants and the bayfront is currently undergoing a facelift; it would be good to revisit in a couple of years' time.

I am reminded of the comments of a good American friend who observed *'You Brits did a great job with Hong Kong'*! Indeed, and over the next decade or so I had the pleasure of visiting several times, noting the changes, often subtle, sometimes not, with its building developments, as it moved forward towards China and the agreed parity of its legal systems within fifty years.

28.10 Hubei

w/c 5ᵗʰ July 2003 - Tuesday afternoon we fly for my first visit to Wuhan in Hubei province. This is my twenty-seventh different city in China and my eighteenth airport. This visit is way overdue as I had originally cancelled a planned visit in February and subsequently arrangements had got stuffed by the SARS restrictions. Wuhan is set in a very flat area, with many lakes around and made up from three towns (Hankou, Wuchang and another that I can't immediately recall) that grew into each other where the Han Shui River flows into the Yangtse River; hence it has a wealth of history and is a key trading city. These three towns, one on either side of the Yangtse and one in the area between the two rivers intersection are neatly divided into the wealthy Government and University area (Wu Chang), Commercial area (Hankou) and the industrial area. We are staying in a very nice hotel in the commercial area. Apparently, it has a total population of a mere 8 million, apparently the same size as Shanghai was before the Pu Dong area was added within its jurisdiction several years ago. A joint venture between Nissan and a Chinese automotive manufacturer have just set up headquarters here for a billion-dollar investment in China and the French are major investors here in a range of products and services and have been the biggest overseas investor here over the last twenty years, including Citroen, Fiat, Financial services, and many others apparently. All the taxis seem to be Citroen or Volkswagens. There is quite a large western population dominated primarily by the French and with a healthy tourist input. I also discover that the Three Gorges project is only some three or four hours away by car; damn I should have known this in advance and planned for it as this is the last 'main tourist' destination on my list. The downside of Wuhan was that it was pouring down with rain when we arrived and continued to do so for much of our stay; not surprising really when you visit during the rainy season, but I am greeted as a good luck charm by many as it is normally very hot and dry although it is traditionally prone to flooding, some with disastrous consequences in the past at times of high rainfall.

A good visit with the director of the local State Tobacco Monopoly followed in his modern ninth story office, then off for a super seafood meal at a local speciality restaurant with associated, yet relatively conservative quantities of baijiu, before heading back to the hotel to meet another customer and completing the evening's formalities with a collective relaxing foot massage and drinking Chinese green tea.

After a super night's sleep on the nineteenth floor of our twenty-six-story hotel it was off to the very modern and well invested Wuhan cigarette factory. I am no longer intimidated by the opulence and level of investment in these modern factories that I feel privileged to see, but I cannot remember visiting too many of a similar standard, if any, in the West. Lunch at the four-star staff canteen private dining rooms.

Dinner with the Wuhan management team concluded the day's events, but this is where the week's events started to slip away a little from my plans. Doing business in China is all about making friends and a little alcohol over dinner always assists this process. If you get it right, you become 'friends for life' and therefore you get more business. Tonight we went to a splendid grand new gigantic restaurant in Hankou; European colonial styled on the outside formed into a large crescent, greeted by a host of tall girls at the door in traditional bright silk dresses and then up the palatial large and wide marble steps to a private room on the fourth floor. Our hosts were also quite excited as for many this was their first visit to the city's latest glamourous hot spot, and I was the excuse. The food was great, the service lousy, but it didn't spoil the evening for the large turnout – twelve of us – or indeed the steady flow of red wine that helped the evening go with a swing. A good time was had by all, and everyone went home happy that they had made new friends. Nice folk these Hubei types; quite genuine and modest in the main.

Cities never look at their best in the rain and Wuhan's Hankou is no exception. Looking out of my hotel window over a grey skyline, despite new investment, there are a lot of old buildings, which probably only means ten to twenty years, but they do look old, standard communist style five or six story concrete apartment blocks with their roof tops littered with rubbish: row after row of them, with washing all over the place. Shame, but we will be coming back to Wuhan on Friday and Saturday and hopefully will see a different side to the place, which I am a little intrigued about.

Thursday, we set off on a three-hour train trip to Xiangfan, which is in the west of Hubei province. I am interested that we have booked the standard sleeper cabin arrangements; this supports the Chinese preference for sleeping at every opportunity. It is still raining heavily as we leave, but this has only served to enhance the greenery of the flat, but fertile fields on the way to Xiangfan; mile after mile of rice fields and farm workers with coolie hats working energetically, albeit at a steady pace, whilst oxen graze the watery pond sides. This is a comparatively poor area, but given its geographic proximity to the Yangtze, it has a wealth of history, most of it as being a battle ground in Dynasty after Dynasty, the consequence is that it is a real mixture of Chinese indigenous races. My understanding is that we will arrive, go to the hotel, have a rest for a few hours, wander into the factory later in the day, then have dinner with a couple of folks from the factory; couldn't have been more wrong as it turned out.

We arrived at one o'clock, too late for traditional lunch in China, but were picked up at the decrepit train station in Xiangfan to be informed that the Factory Director was awaiting our presence for a late lunch. Okay, we are all hungry despite the heavy meal last night and the hotel breakfasts, so we headed off to our hotel, but no time to check in, straight up to the dining room. Here we are put in a very large private room with a huge circular table, which seemed a little odd, but made more sense after wave after wave of unfamiliar people arrived in our midst. These people it seems are from a large and important meetings between the very modern Ningbo cigarette factory in southern Zhejiang Province and the Xiangfan management team as they have a mutual business arrangement. This was wholly unexpected, but this is typical of what I come to expect in China, with its inherent lack of planning in such arrangements, and the communications are worse than the planning – always expect the unexpected and I have given up getting excited about it. I counted nineteen in all as we sat down for a magnificent banquet lunch, me as the guest of honour accompanied by a sensible quantity of 'baijiu', albeit with the customary 'one by one' toasting arrangement. As things were starting to wind down, things took a bad turn. Egged on by the one very westernized and fluent English speaking handsome young Chinese man from Ningbo, his team were encouraged to drink whole glasses of beer with me. Their mission was clear – to get me drunk. Starting with a young lady opposite me, who reluctantly I suspect, but at least with a smile on her face, drank five consecutive 'one on one' toasts with me. A quick calculation by me reckoned that drinking beer in wine glasses could at least keep me going for a while, but after the baijiu I was maybe not quite so sure. Then it was another guy, then another, then another.................... This situation was out of control, but I had no way out despite my polite repeated protestations to the factory director as 'chairman' of the table to draw events to an end. He didn't, partly humoured by the 'challenge', partly by not wanting to upset his mischievous business customers who were having a whale of a time and partly, like the rest, waiting and watching carefully in comparative silence to see how much the westerner could drink before he gets drunk. BBF! I am in trouble, but have no option now, I have not encountered such a situation before, quite frankly am unsure how to handle it and my brain was starting to fail in having any good ideas, it's a 'face' thing, I am in for the count and must take them on I decide, even though they have totally ambushed me! Hell I'm British after all. Then the Ningbo senior managers started drinking with me. By now I am getting applauded with genuine approval and admiration for each glass that I am drinking. They are impressed and I am making friends, but I am consciously stuffing rice down my gullet in between each toast. When the table's chairman finally called events to a halt, I was still standing, although sweating profusely and too inebriated to be relieved, but have nineteen impressed dining colleagues, including my translator and our sales guy. F**k; the things I do for business. I leave to numerous backslaps and respectful words of encouragement.

They kindly cancelled the afternoon's meetings that were introductory anyway – and we had already done that! Somewhere along the way I remembered that the city's population is 700,000, although the surrounding area incorporated 5.7 million people.

Thursday's dinner was a mere three hours later, at least I had managed an hour's sleep and consumed some headache tablets. We wander down for what I am informed will be a quiet dinner, but my heart sank as we entered the room, oh no, it's that mischievous party from Ningbo again, but at least there were only twelve of us this time and they graciously decided that we should only drink beer. Despite a few playful moments and a little more beer than my body needed, the evening went well with me getting a personal invitation to go to Ningbo's cigarette factory by their purchasing director, the key point here being that they are one of the biggest and most prestigious cigarette factories in China; and they are not currently a customer!

Friday, I go down for breakfast after a comatose night's sleep in my suite and carefully survey the breakfast room to ensure that it is free of Ningbo folk before entering. A good factory visit around a very old communist style factory, but looking relatively well managed, and an excellent lunch in the company's own excellent dining facilities followed before we were taken for a quick look at the city's newly developed riverside walks along the Han Shui Riverbanks and a chance to see the poor living conditions of the city's minority people. I note that the roads in Xiangfan at present are mainly potholes punctuated by short spells of tarmac, but like so many Chinese cities the roads are lined by those mature Parisian style trees that add a certain elegance often to quite *poor surroundings. We took the train back to Wuhan, this time taking the up market sleeping carriages.*

We end the week staying another night in the city of Wuhan, high waters in the two rivers and all. I see I the TV that the annual flooding of central and Eastern China has so far claimed 500 lives and made half a million homeless, reminding one of the importance of the huge water management programmes being introduced near here – the controversial Three Gorges project. It is not about destroying homes, history, and the environment – it is about supplying clean water to the largest population on earth, saving lives through flood avoidance and providing electricity; quite basic and simple really. The news confirms that the situation down river in the neighbouring Anhui Province is deteriorating fast.

Dinner was in the restaurant called the Long Gong, on a large boat parked on the shore of the wide Yangtze overlooking the intersection between the two rivers and the vast Yangtze river bridge. Quite a lovely spot, but certainly not yet the Bund at Shanghai. I am told that the water from the Han Shui is so clean that it is pumped all the way to supply Beijing, whereas the same cannot be said for the Yangtze. Again there were surprises as 'friends' friends appeared from nowhere for dinner taking our dining compliment to seven. As is so common in these situations, these guys appear from nowhere, are not introduced, often say nothing, and then slip away into the night, often to karaoke I suspect. Then it was an early night, which was needed after the food and beverage excesses of the week. We have eaten like kings and had a wonderful, but testing time, all of which has done nothing for my middle.

Saturday after a relaxing start we are picked up by the CNTC car and whisked out to the city's 'East Lake', a few kilometres south of the Yangtse and on the edge of the more up market Wu Chang district. This was a glorious visit on a glorious day. The lake being far larger that Hangzhou's West Lake (Which incidentally I am told is one of thirty-four West Lakes in China, although I remain vague about the precise number of South Lakes, North Lakes, and East Lakes – typically Chinese; keep it simple) and frankly a tad more up market on the day, dissected by a couple of tree lined man-made roads, we headed for the gentle hills of the far shores and to the Moshan Hill Tower looking back over the city. The views from the top of the five story typically Chinese tower were beautiful, spoiled only slightly by the power station and chimneys in the distance away to the south. The statutory cable car also had a minor adverse impact upon the scenery, but the city's Wu Chang skyline on the north shore looked good and I was impressed by the standard of these facilities – the general cleanliness and lacking the general grubbiness of many Chinese tourist spots and set in gentle afforested hills. A traditional Chinese music session, including over seventy bells, by folk in traditional Chinese dress was no less impressive and kept me engrossed for twenty minutes or so. I liked this place and overall I found it on a comparison with Hangzhou's West Lake. Then it was a drive back through the modern and clean Wu Chang district, past the famous Chinese universities attended by quite several foreigners apparently, before we stopped at the historic five-story Yellow Crane Tower on a hill near to the intersection between the Yangtse and the Han Shui rivers. Again this attraction was very well done, having been rebuilt many times over the centuries due to fire – either lightening or destroyed by attacking marauders. The views from the top were impressive, you could see the clarity of the Han Shui water flowing into the yellow waters of the Yangtse and could sense the history of the views from this small hill given its proximity to one of the most famous rivers and one of the more strategically important spots on earth. The adjoining park exhibited a range of traditional poems etched in stone tablets from numerous famous writers and politicians including Mao. Probably the best appointed and most interesting traditional tower that I have been up in China. Yes, I enjoyed this, before going for dinner with yet another CNTC Director and his family, his son almost fluent in English at the age of fourteen and was clearly targeted by his mother to practice on me, much to his extreme embarrassment and obvious shyness.

28.11 Hunan

7th July 2002 - Wednesday and it is an early start. Noodles with the gang for breakfast in a dirty local garage, with dirty local tables, and even dirtier walls, floors, and ceiling, then off to Changsha, the capital of Hunan; this could be interesting.......... a potential disaster! The flight was bumpy and not helped by the fact that we were at the back of the plane and had a planeload of Chinese families who were obviously flying for the first time. Lots of noise and excitement and the woman in front of me threw up over the two people next to her – and that was before we had left the ground! Place was like a cattle market, and I decided that sleep was not an option, especially with a thirteen-year-old boy sat next to me who couldn't sit still.

The taxi from the airport was again unbelievable. I don't know how we pick them. There are very nice taxis out here, but the one at the front of the queue when we got there, wasn't one of them! There was the customary stench of fumes, I am sure that the exhausts are plumbed through the air vents, although this wasn't true because precisely nothing was coming through the air vents, which is not what you need when the external temperature is thirty-eight degrees centigrade and there are five in the car. To start the car the driver used his hands to twist two cables together underneath the steering wheel – he hot-wired it! The interior resembled the interior of a partially full rubbish skip.

This is Hunan Province, the home of Chairman Mao Ze Dong. The countryside is fertile, gentle hills and very green…and very hot. Unfortunately, it is marred by numerous very tall chimneys bellowing black smoke into the air. These are from red brick factories. Changsha is a big and bustling city, and like everywhere else, changing very fast – a mixture of old and very new, but not yet well adjusted. We passed two very interesting buildings – one twenty-five story glass circular building which got wider as it went up and a large building in the shape and colours of a large ship with porthole windows down the side – very French design style!

The cigarette factory was a very modern twenty-six story building with expansive and glamorous reception area. The money in cigarettes is unbelievable – these are big time players! Disaster, we have lost all the business, effectively stolen, as suspected by our own joint venture partners by agreement some six months ago prior to my arrival. So what does one do in these situations – one goes for dinner, makes friends and gets happy! The dinner wasn't too heavy, and I managed to get excused the karaoke bit, to which the young men disappeared to, allowing me to get back and have an early night. Dinner had a few interesting courses and one extraordinary incident. The food in Hunan province is spicier than Zhejiang. Going into the restaurant, which was grubby, we passed animal cages, not just the customary fish tanks, but birds (large and small), ostrich, a deer with antlers, pigs etc – get the picture. A little later we were trying many of these animals. I was not impressed by the pigs' trotters, for which we were issued with one plastic glove to pick up, giving me the feeling of being a doctor of some sort. Birds appear fried and chopped – heads and all, frozen with their tongues hanging out in a moment of terror.

After dinner, the vice technical director produced a packet, which at first glance looked like an up market crisp packet. Inside were several smaller packets that were passed around. My deputy insisted that my translator did not have one; very insistent, although the lady purchasing director said that she has had it in the past and that it was good. The content was a chewy fibrous material with a liquorish taste. I started chewing and thought okay, but nothing special – a minute later it hit me – I haven't felt as strange in a long time. This was a drug, although I know not what and don't wish to; at least I know not to try this again in future. Ten minutes later I had regained my composure enough to notice that the others were having an hilarious time, except my translator who wondered what it was all about – I reflected on the potentially dangerous effects of such things – this was not good, this was silly! I am a big boy and cope with such things; I hate to consider the potential effect and vulnerability on a teenager in the wrong situation.

I also managed to do what has been on the cards for the last eight or nine weeks – I pulled the plate over at the dinner table. After a relaxing few glasses, I stood up to toast the guy opposite me on the table. I did what I have always done traditionally when I stand up at the table – I grabbed my napkin in my lap so that it doesn't fall on the floor. However, the wine had relaxed me a little, and I forgot momentarily that in China the napkin is tucked under your dinner plate. As I am tall the result was inevitable – plate tipped over, soup bowl over, chopsticks and holder flying etc; and everyone thinks I'm drunk! Flipping heck, I wasn't, but I'm not sure they were convinced – in their state the whole room must have seemed pissed!

Thursday was a chance to catch up in the morning before a plane trip back to Hangzhou. I use the time usefully, also practicing my Chinese words, that I must learn in time for my Friday night lesson, so as not to make my teacher "sad, that she is a poor teacher" as she declared after my pitiful efforts on Tuesday! As I leave for the airport, I see my deputy, who has just got out of bed. He informs me that he got to bed at two o'clock and that he had had a lot to drink. The trip to the airport was eventful. Having negotiated a lower rate, the taxi driver decided that he was going to save money by not taking us on the expressway toll road. The result was that we had a bumpy, slow, but extremely interesting ride to the airport – interesting sights along the way. I also found I could buy the 'chewy' stuff at the airport.

On the way home we came across the immediate aftermath of a horrific head on car smash. Shouldn't be surprised given the style of driving, but this was a real shaker – if the two drivers weren't dead, they should have been – both seriously trapped and unconscious – moments like this put life into perspective.

In January 2019, during a fleeting visit to China, I visited Changsha for an overnight stay after looking at a nearby factory. Changsha had developed into one of those mega cities, miles upon miles of high-rise apartment buildings and malls to accommodate the huge migrations from the countryside. This was the plan and I had seen the early days of this development in 2002 and now witnessed firsthand the huge changes. One of my British travelling colleagues was truly shocked by this, so many people living in so many high-rise apartments, and he struggled to get his mind around it all, summarizing in his opinion that *'this just isn't right'*! The city was unrecognizable to me, and I am reminded that this had occurred all over China without exception – a very changing world and at an unbelievable pace!

28.12 Jiangsu

w/c 13ᵗʰ July 2002 - Wednesday and off to the brand-new Nanjing cigarette factory by car – a four-hour drive. These are our second biggest customers, about to become our number one customer. Firstly, there was a new one on me – a fellow selling beer from the gap in the central reservation of the fast lane of the motorway. I note that when we pass Suzhou the sign said to Hunning Speedway, which of course they did not mean (Expressway), but is a more apt description in the dust and road works and reflecting the way people drive around here! Then it was a traffic jam and another fatal accident – a lorry flipped right over and flattened.

The approach to Nanjing is beautiful, very green, and fertile, surrounded by mountains, over a river and through a large ancient city wall. It is the former capital of China and has the tomb of Sun Yat-Sen in the surrounding mountains, who is referred to as the 'father of China,' even by Mao, who's Communist Party overthrew him. It is thirty-eight degrees centigrade outside (part of the heat wave hitting China at present; it is forty-four degrees centigrade in Xian), and a long wide straight tree lined boulevard led to the city centre, past a mixture of new tall buildings and old traditional buildings. Interesting, the road reminds me of the approach to Milan, although oddly in this city folk seem to respect the traffic lights. Then it was to the five-star Jinling Hotel, which turns out to be an added unexpected bonus. It is famous all over China and listed in the top ten of Chinese hotels. It was the tallest hotel in China (thirty-six floors) when it was built in the 1980's with a revolving restaurant on top, but has subsequently been superseded by hotels, in Shanghai. It is part of 'The Leading Hotels of the World' network and I cross another one off the list. The Alfred Dunhill, Versace and other high brand shops on the ground floor say it all. Ominously, the hotel is part of a 'twin tower' complex, albeit twice the height of the otherwise identical adjacent building, which bears the proud sign 'The World Trade Centre'!

The cigarette factory is brand new and quite unbelievable. A grey imposing office block, eight stories high which could be a world class hotel with wonderful artifacts in the reception area, basically the ground floor, a hotel adjacent, which is a world class hotel, all-weather tennis courts outside for employees, fishing lake, private walled garden (Suzhou style), indoor Olympic size swimming pool and large gardens with fountains and two sets of impressive gold deer statues, and including three trees that are all over a hundred years old that were simply relocated here from their old site. The standard pagoda and Chinese summer house sit comfortably in the middle of it all, oh and there is a futuristic greenhouse. The factory is something else for a cigarette manufacturing plant. Robotics, automation, lots of space, not very many people anywhere, hundreds of supervisory cameras – fabulous, all built for US$6 million I am told. How do we compete with this stuff, and everyone is at it! Good meeting and an early and sensible banquet in their hotel, albeit with an arrogant Director, although I conclude that with this lot he is allowed to be. Oh yes, and an Olympic standard complex is being built next door, nothing to do with Beijing, just that the city wants one – an entire *!#king sports complex; to be up within two years. And we in the UK cannot even organize a National Football Stadium. Ah yes, then there was a phenomenal thunder and lightning storm that wiped all the lights out and flooded the restaurant as the waiters forgot to close the windows. Instantaneous road flooding everywhere – I am now getting used to these. Back to the hotel for an early night. I am also not convinced that I was not dumped and that the rest of the gang went out again, but I cannot prove it – only look at their eyes in the *morning. The Chinese certainly can close you out, whether they like you or not at times! I suspect that they went to places considered unsuitable for me.*

Thursday it is off to see the local CNTC folk in their twenty-third story office in the Sheraton hotel complex, then back to Jiaxing. Breakfast was a slightly embarrassing start as I sat down next to my translator going through the normal morning formalities and niceties, only to realise after a while that it was not her – well, at times people do look similar, and this young lady was remarkably similar – and just as miserable at breakfast time. The road works outside detract slightly, but it is explained that the city is building a whole brand-new subway system from scratch. Not a chop stick in sight; this is a western breakfast room with a few Chinese variations – too many western businesspeople for my liking though.

An incredibly positive meeting and lunch with the CNTC cheered me up no end – I finally found a guy talking sense about modernizing the approach to management in China! This has given me confidence to push ahead with my own reforms and curiously my deputy seems to be coming to the party. A terrible trip home followed – five hours by car in pouring rain. Another nasty accident and many near misses witnessed. I conclude that giving the Chinese more cars with the standards that they have is comparable to handing loaded revolvers to four-year-old in a playground. This is a serious point, not a mock. I am genuinely worried that future population control will be by killing their children on the roads as an increasingly affluent China buys more cars. Somebody could make their name as a transport minister, but they have a mammoth challenge ahead to end fundamental practices…or lack of them! Lorry drivers are the worst and the vehicle overloading, overt vehicle pollution, poorly secured loads and poor vehicle maintenance take me back to my childhood; the driving standards I do not recall – only in my worst nightmares!

28.13 Liaoning

10ᵗʰ July 2004 - Monday our flight was to Shenyang in Liaoning province and my onward journey to Liaoyang; this is my first visit here. This province is to the north and right of Beijing as one looks at the map, a place that I understand to be part of the ancient territories of Manchuria. It borders North Korea, Inner Mongolia and on its south coast on the Bohai Sea, above the Yellow Sea, is the port of Dalian, one of China's biggest ports, a massive development opposite Shandong Province. Although in northeast China, this is still over 1,000 kilometres from Mudanjiang in Heilongjiang where I went last year, reminding me of the vast scale of China.

Having left the airport we progressed through miles of flat and very fertile farmland along track roads in the direction of Liaoyang, away from the Province's capital. The greenery is in stark contrast to the baron wastelands that my colleague witnessed in January on his last visit I am informed. This is a poor area, despite the massive crops' growth – tomatoes, maize, rice and so on. Liaoyang is one of those old traditional Chinese communist industrial cities – grey, polluting factories, very evidently polluted atmosphere, presumably polluting all the crops around; somewhat of a nightmare of a place, although the centre of town is starting to show some signs of development, with modernized temples and open recreation areas for its citizens. Our hotel, the Fu Hong Guo Ji Fan Dian, was something of an oasis in amongst all this heavy industry and predominantly single-story housing, a five-star hotel, established by the guy who owns the highly profitable edible oils factory behind. Next to the hotel is a twenty-five-story tower block under construction, still using those horrible grey tiles on the exterior, which is apparently going to be an extension to the hotel. Given that there is virtually no one staying in the hotel and given the fact that the extension is in fact several times bigger than the hotel itself, I can only assume that this place must be a tax write-off for the hugely profitable edible oils factory, or a clever long-term punt!

Anyway, lunch was good and modest followed by a very positive visit to the engineering factory that we are visiting, meeting an affable Austrian fellow, who is the general manager and who has been living here for five years now, following spells in the Czech Republic, Russia, and a host of other places before this. He is in a similar situation to me in many respects I guess, but Liaoyang is nowhere near as modern as Jiaxing, still he seems to be building a good business and enjoys personally driving his brand new 3-series BMW.

After a good session and meeting, we were taken to visit the newly opened Buddhist temples in the city centre, site of the largest indoor erect Buddha in China we were informed, some 21.48 metres of it, due apparently to the fact that we are in the twenty-first century, and Buddha's birthday is on the eighth of April, hence the four and eight. All this helps me to deduct that Buddha was an Aires like me! Anyway the guided tour, which wasn't easy *to translate by our comical translator there but was full of what I define as Chinese twaddle, making absolutely no sense to man nor beast in the English language, but obviously was deeply meaningful to the Chinese around, even if it was all bunkum. I really must read up about the Buddhist religion I decide.*

Outside, in the newly created open square area, the locals were walking and playing like modern China is doing all over the country, enjoying the benefits and relaxation of the new facilities, but it was apparent from all the looks and attention that we were getting that they still are not used to foreigners around here and many cameras turned in our direction.

Then it was out for dinner at another restaurant, mercifully not one of the many Korean style dog restaurants in town, along with a German guy, and some Chinese colleagues. Slow evening, but wonderfully frugal with the alcohol and good food. Sleep was wonderful after the long today; real five-star pillows and bed.

Tuesday and we were off to meet another engineering supplier, this being a bonifide state owned traditional engineering plant, and boy it showed. No sign of presentation or real marketing skills. The introductory video broke down, one of the pictures fell off the wall, in stages, and the whole thing reminded me of some sort of moldy meeting rooms at Fawlty Towers. Terrible and engineering not much better, and although it did remind me of the derelict factories that I had witnessed previously up in Heilongjiang, to be fair, this was somewhat better in standard; could introduce them to a good gardener though. The Europeans were obviously struggling with their joint venture and the prevailing environment. Enough was enough and we escaped for our flight back to Shanghai. The legacy was of grey factories, abandoned factories with belching chimneys – a scene from and industrial nightmare!

28.14 Shaanxi

w/c 28ᵗʰ July 2002 - The China Northwest Airlines flight to Xian from Beijing was quiet and uneventful. I am supposed to be a member of the frequent flyer programme, but my card hasn't arrived yet despite applying two months ago.

Upon arrival at the airport we made friends with a driver who got us two cabs and we also managed to negotiate a good deal to hire him to tomorrow together with an air-conditioned minibus for out trips around the district.

Xian is another very large and ancient city, has its own Muslim quarter, indeed, we are informed, predominantly Muslim. The heat is searing and arid compared to the excessive humidity in Beijing a fact that is making all the news in China at present. A walk down the street to the belltower was followed by a wonderful, air-conditioned shopping trip to cool down, followed by a good meal in the hotel.

Xian is very hot, arid, dusty and like all other Chinese cities, being rebuilt, albeit at a slower rate than many. Features such as power station chimneys belching out heavily polluting smoke, detracted somewhat from its appearance.

On Friday our hired taxi turned up as expected, or should I say planned, which cheered me. What followed was an amazing experience for all of us, except my eldest daughter, who couldn't understand what all the fuss was about. We headed the thirty kilometres outside of the Old City walls to Qin Shi Huang's tomb (The First Emperor of China), the Terracotta Army, some hot springs, and the Banpo Museum. The temperature was hotter and getting even hotter.

Emperor Qin was apparently a bit of a bastard in 200 BC, but he was the guy who unified China, built the Great Wall, standardized the language, and introduced standards (widths of cartwheels, distance, weights and more). He was not a guy to mess with, apparently killing millions, but he knew a beautiful spot when he saw one! The area of his tomb was set in the backdrop of wonderful mountains and fertile fields of fruit, coupled with a gorgeous southern Mediterranean type of climate. Despite the comparative scruffiness of the towns and city, this is the sort of area where you could build a retirement house with swimming pool next to the golf course – reminding me of an Orange County, California, but at this stage it is some way off. That said, Qin upset a lot of people and his Tomb area on a man-made mountain got trashed – still the scenery remains beautiful.

The Terracotta Army is something else, despite my daughter's proclamations that they are 'just bits of old pot and earth'! About 1,000 soldiers have been dug up to date (out of an estimated 8,000 in total), which should keep somebody in a job for a while. They were only discovered in 1974, by a local farmer digging a well, and the site only opened in 1979. I must pinch myself that this was 200 BC – what were we doing at this time in Northern Europe? The sophistication is unbelievable. Too many facts to report but must be seen and has been declared by the local authorities as 'the eighth wonder of the *world'. They are not far off the mark. Sadly on departure there were the normal souvenir touts. What wasn't normal was that my son and I decided to buy a box of five miniature terracotta soldiers for the $1 or ¥5 that they were being offered for. What followed was not nice. I gave the guy ¥10, expecting some change, but he then informed me that the whole box was ¥50, but that he could do it for ¥20. I asked for my money back, but he refused saying that I hadn't given him any money yet, to the disbelief of his female companion as I hovered over him. I won't go into the detail, but eventually I had to pull my son off him, as he was about to deck this fellow, whilst I started shouting for Police whilst my family wondered off and tourists gave us a wide berth. The only reason that I pulled my son off, was that I wanted to smack this fellow first, but I have grown wise, gave the guy another ¥10 and we simply walked away (with our box of five ornaments) despite the guy chasing us claiming that we still owed him money – the worst side of Chinese capitalism! This spoilt the trip here.*

Apparently, in order that secrecy about the army be maintained, Qin Shi Huang, killed all the 720,000 workers who assisted in its creation either by slaying or by being buried alive.

The hot springs at the bottom of a nearby hill were China's equivalent of Bath's Roman Springs and had been visited by all Chinese modern leaders at some time, except for Mao I note. Chiang Kai Shek, former President of the Republic of China, had been shot at here and he had 'resigned' here after a revolt by his own side.

The Banpo archeological museum was just plain odd! The short cut trip to it through the local village back streets with un-metaled roads and rubbish everywhere was even more interesting. This is a site of genuine, but boring archaeological importance. Discovered in 1953, it goes back several thousand years BC. It has been developed though as a series of disjointed and historical exhibition halls including on photo exhibition of black Africa, which seemed to concentrate on bodies and organs, as well as a guy with his mouth on the rear end of a cow! The last exhibition was equally odd room full of vivid sexual reproduction organs and illustrations in all their splendour, including diseases – we concluded that it must be 'educational', but very dated and truly weird. The kids were not sure quite what to make of it! The site reflected the era that it had been discovered – 1950's Maoist architecture – concrete, frugal, together with outdoor basketball court and adjacent concrete residential block.

28. 15 Shandong

W/c 23rd November 2002 Tuesday very early start we shoot off to Pu Dong Airport for our flight to Yantai in Shandong Province, Northern China, to visit yet more customers ahead of the December annual tender for next year's business. I have not been to Shandong before but know that it is a few Provinces to the north of me, just southeast of Beijing. The just bit being several hundred miles, say 500 miles.

Yantai airport is surprisingly close to its city, Yantai, which is quite unusual for many Chinese airports. The bad news for us was that Yantai cigarette Factory was nowhere near the Yantai airport or Yantai city; it was some eighty kilometres away in a one-horse town called Qixia. We were picked up by the Director's driver who whisked us along a brand-new expressway at 160km/hour (100 miles/hour), which is the fastest trip that I have had in China. The land was unusual, arid, and hilly with not a lot growing and the newly planted trees, fir trees, seem to be dying. The houses, which seem sparsely grouped together, were in typical northern China coral format with an integral walled and gated yard to the house. Apparently, apple trees are big in the area, and we later sampled the produce, which was delicious. This region is also the home on Chengyu vineyards, China's largest red wine producer. There was no rest, as we were taken straight to lunch with the factory Director together which had a good mixture of foods, but too much Chinese red and white wine. This was followed by a long tour of the aging, yet apparently well managed and clean factory; nice folk and we supply 95 per cent of their business, so we are all friends and happy. Generally though this is a poor area. During discussions I found out that we were in Northern Shandong Province, 700 km from Beijing, 100 km from the huge port developments at Dalian and 130 km as the crow flies to North Korea. Good day, except the trip back to Yantai took too long and the approach to Yantai was disappointingly old Chinese Industrial until we got to the five-star Golden Gulf Hotel, which was right on the seafront of the Shandong north coast peninsular, not unlike the southwest of England is terms of shape, and I could watch the breakers coming in from the Yellow Sea. Oh yes and its extremely cold up here, with thick layers of frost on the hills and the odd snowflake. Dinner was a splendid feast in the hotel's restaurant with a 'wide screen' window overlooking a pleasantly lit bay front. These customers are happy and happy to see us, and they gave me a gift; just what I have been wanting for a while – A man's handbag, quite typical out here, a sort of clutch bag!! Prestigious Alfred Dunhill brand as well. Like many of the bags out here, the bloody zip is faulty. Perhaps it's just me. I am wondering which event I should exhibit my new handbag; nice colour too! Can't get my mind around carrying a handbag though.

Woke up Wednesday to the beautiful view across the bay to islands silhouetted against the skyline that freshened me up after a dodgy night's sleep.

We then had a three-hour taxi trip, as I decided to skip the bus trip this time, to Qingdao. The roads were largely good, but the countryside remained poor resembling Mediterranean type terrain in Spain, Southern Italy, or the Greek Islands. Baron and uninteresting despite some spectacular hilltop formations standing out against the skyline in places. Water seemed sparse, indeed there was a distinct lack of its evidence, and lots of dirt, dust and not much vegetation was in evidence. The initial entrance to the suburbs of Qingdao, suggested that it was a bit of a dump and after several miles of suburban Industry I hadn't changed my mind. Then we hit the seafront and the scenery changed distinctly allowing me to recognize why the city is often referred to as beautiful and why the 2008 Olympics will stage the sailing events here. The bay was actually very nice and some of the houses on it extremely nice, off set by the jagged hills that surrounded the city. May not be Rio de Janeiro but has potential.

The Haiqing Hotel was well located looking directly out to the sea and they had arranged a room with a front view, which was fine but very exposed and the howling winds would later keep me awake at night. This city is the home of Haida, one of the World's largest white goods manufacturers, Tsingtao beer, which along with Budweiser just about carves up the Chinese market and Chengyu Red Wine. There is also a lot of the English language in evidence along with many new developments in the modern downtown area, although not yet the finished article.

The lunch that preceded the meeting was a wonderful array of genuinely delightful and tasty Shandong specialities – spicy and highly edible, including some delicious Kebabs, which I mused was a bit like the Chinese equivalent of Mediterranean food. Thereafter the meetings were fragmented, and dinner was a low-key selection of delicious seafoods that was very pleasant and nothing horrible included, even the squid was good.

Thursday turned out to be a day of sightseeing, awaiting the return to town of the deputy factory director, who never materialized. Saw a far better side of Qingdao today, which turned out to be very impressive and modern, albeit with a contrast of some old European style tradition and areas where poor and rich live next to each other. Firstly, we headed off to Laoshan, which was along the coast to the east and to its Taoqing temple. Pleasant drive along the coastline and another good look at more traditional Chinese Temples, which are becoming a little monotonous, but this one had enough to maintain my interest. One of the temples stood for fertility; facing me was a temple for male energy, the one on the right was for boys to pray for wives and the one on the left was for women to pray for a husband. My translator felt strongly enough to spend ¥100 on Chinese sparklers (scented josh sticks) to wish for the last option. The sales guy and I stood back in due deference. The complex was also inter-dispersed by several 1,000-year-old trees that were mightily impressive and was surrounded by hills and the sea, as indeed is the whole of Qingdao. The temple had been re-opened by Premier Ronglu is 1997.

The afternoon was fun. Firstly after lunch it was the main seafront square, which bore a strange large red sculpture, which dominated a large part of the seafront and the park it was set it. A distinctive landmark and a focal point for the city; this will appear in photos if it lasts and will be a reference point for the 2008 Olympics. Then it was a walk along the promenade avoiding the large waves breaking over the sea wall and via various seafront gift shops until we reached the Music Park that was suitably relaxing. Then it was a visit to the main shopping street, briefly, given my distaste for shopping. The city turned out to be enormous and was a German colony until 1914, when the Chinese demanded its release, which the Germans duly did – they gave it to the Japanese, which really upset the Chinese at the time. Still many old German style buildings remain, large churches, mansions, and other such places, unlike I had experienced elsewhere.

Contrasting this is the modern seafront houses, large glamourous apartment blocks and superb tennis courts that grace the seafront, apparently dominated by Korean, Hong Kong, and Taiwanese owners, a playground of the wealthy. The city centre is growing an impressive array of modern and large buildings on its skyline that will number a lot more by 2008.

The trip home from Qingdao to Shanghai was fine, but I was tired by the time I returned to my cold apartment to find the stench of the first coat of varnish on my newly laid floor. Just as I was settling in for the night my

German friend phones me desperate for a beer, a fluent Chinese speaker who understands the culture and a long-term resident. He is depressed, he is finding it hard and our Chinese partners like me and don't like him apparently. He is on a downer, and I am not sure where it is going. He speaks Chinese fluently and claims that 'You are in a much stronger position Jeremy as you do not have a clue what is going on and just do your own thing, which they respect'. I am not sure where this is going, and I quickly left him in a bar getting drunk; he was on a mission, and I was not in the mood. An interesting take on life though by him.

w/c 23ʳᵈ April 2005 - Friday is the day of the annual company trip to Tai Shan in Shandong province, but first there is a full day's work to be done.

All thirty-three of us departed via a not so good quality coach to Shanghai's central train station at 17.00 hours, only to hit heavy traffic, but we got there on time with two or three very traffic sick folk, especially my translator, who is quite pathetic in these situations and does not command much sympathy.

Shanghai's train station was chaotic, so many people and so busy, a mess of crushed humanity, no wonder SARS could have spread so quickly. We set off at 20.00 hours on our trip by sleeper train. There is no chance of sleep as these folks are in party mood! After ten hours or so on the overnight train north from Shanghai, our delegation of employees plus tour guide arrived at Yengzhou Station at six o'clock in Shandong Province, before being whisked away for a quick and very Chinese breakfast in Qufu City near to our destination.

This was followed by a day of 'Confucius'. Qufu is the hometown of Confucius located in southwest Shandong at an intersection between a mountainous area in central Shandong and the plains in the west of the province. Qufu, it seems was the capital of the Lu Kingdom in the Zhou Dynasty (1046 BC-256 BC). Today in Qufu we are here to visit the ancient Confucian Temple, Confucian Mansion, and Confucian Family Cemetery. This I discover is an official world cultural and natural heritage site, although I had never heard of it before. All my Scottish colleague and I know about it is that fact that David Carradine used to say things like 'glass hopper' and 'Confucius he say' when we were kids watching the US TV programme. Apparently, there are seventy-seven generations of Confucius descendants buried among the 1,000 or so graves that were all destroyed during the Cultural Revolution and have had to be repaired and restored.

By the end of the day, my Scottish colleague and I had had enough of bloody Confucius. All Confucius' ed out! This was a very Chinese day and Confucius was obviously very deep seated in the psyche of the Chinese culture, but I think that a lot of the stuff was over the head of even my colleagues although the day was enjoyed by all.

Then a bus trip to Tai An, a city of some seven million people, also in Shandong and I can honestly say that I had never heard of it before. We checked into the three-star Oriental Hotel for a brief and much needed rest before going out to a nearby up market restaurant for a fantastic dinner enjoyed by all, including hiring the disco room for everyone afterwards. Late, but sensible night, at least for some of us although there were one or two bodies lying around come the end, by which time a few others had been carried away!

Sunday was correspondingly a slow start for many as our main objective was to climb the nearby Tai Shan Mountain. This was magnificent, a coach trip most of the way up, took the cable car to the very top then spent several hours wandering around the kilometre or so of mountain top walks before descending for a late lunch at a local restaurant. Great chance for photographs and a wonderful place reminding me that there are many effectively undiscovered tourist places by the West yet.

Immediately after lunch a colleague and I took a taxi for the trip to the city of Jinan where we have business over the coming few days thanks to a request from our leader, more time away from the factory, but at least it gets us out of the twelve-hour train trip back to Shanghai and subsequent coach trip!

When we got there, it was a nice opportunity to walk around the city's central although not overly impressive lake before a nice Sichuan style dinner followed by a foot massage and then receiving a phone call from a mayor, a friend, who is coming down to pick up an old American friend from the airport…. now (22.30 hours). The result was a very late night or early morning catching up on life and eating various barbeque foods from a late-night Korean style barbeque restaurant. The American guy was interesting. A Harvard trained lawyer who had become an entrepreneur, made a lot of money it seems and whose brother is the governor of Nebraska. He now lives in Boise, Idaho or somewhere like that and has two young kids by his Chinese wife.

This was not the start that was planned for Monday morning and our *early meeting at an old state-owned paper factory in central Jinan. Although I have landed at Jinan airport several times, this was the first time that I have visited the city. It is pleasant, but nothing too special at first look, but it does benefit from having many hills surrounding it.*

A meeting followed in a depressing derelict and shut typical Chinese state-owned factory before a 6-hour coach trip to the coastal city of Qingdao that I first visited shortly after my arrival two and a half years ago. We are staying at the Qingdao Hotel not far from the seafront and have an excellent seafood dinner in a food street opposite with all sorts of crustations, the likes of which I have never seen or eaten before along with a pint of local draft beer, which tasted significantly better than the bottled stuff that we must tolerate normally. Qingdao is also the venue for the water sports events at the 2008 Beijing Olympics and it is being developed fast with the seafront Marina and Olympic Village being built nearby in a prominent position. This is quite a sophisticated city given its long term, but mainly German heritage and more recent investments. It is the home of the annual Qingdao Beer festival, akin to the Munich beer festivals, which attracts visitors from all around the globe and the HQ of much of China's wine production as well as the home of Haier, the largest white goods supplier in China, maybe globally now!

In between I find myself pondering some facts from an article sent to me that confirmed my fears for road safety in China. China has 2 per cent of the world's car population and 15 per cent of the world's road accidents. The black market for illegal driving licenses is huge and the result is that 680 fatalities are being reported each day; I can believe this, and the situation is getting crazier and crazier each day. No one seems to be able to drive and certainly no one has any driving discipline! Each day I see more and more police at traffic light junctions, and more are wearing seat belts, but persistent offenders seem to be ignored by the law. It is quite simple – no one knows any better!

Tuesday morning we had a meeting at another paper factory on the outskirts of Qingdao and were pleased to see that this factory was at least running. The meeting went well precipitating the need to have an impromptu lunch at another excellent seafood restaurant, followed by a lovely walk along the Qingdao seafront and a photo opportunity with our host. Because of developments at Jinan we decide to stay tonight and head back over there tomorrow morning on the way back to Shanghai. This left room for another seafood dinner, leaving me wondering whether I can eat any more oysters, clams, or other shellfish types. At least I avoided the sea slugs and if you could see them so would you!

Wednesday morning was a very early start heading out on the forty-five-minute taxi ride along new highways to a new airport. It was full of foreigners reminding me of the extent of western investment here.

Over the years 2004-2012, I was to be a regular visitor to the city of Binzhou in Shandong as our company created a joint venture business there. Binzhou was 350 miles southeast of Beijing. Most of the trips were mundane in the early years, although that did not adequately describe the immense business challenges that developed there over time. Below are a few extracts from initial visits there only.

w/c 24th April 2004 -Tonight's dinner was in a large local restaurant with the new management team in northwestern Shandong, or at least they soon will be the new team as we are all here for tomorrow's official signing ceremony for another one of our parent company's deals – buying 80 per cent of a paper company here in a business that I understand quite well. We join our company principal and CEO as well as a close friend from Jiaxing who is proving additional translation backup over the two or three days of serious negotiations periodically interrupted by socializing. This was a decent meal, and we have good friends here I conclude albeit with reservations, although in balance the food is not so great up here; maybe they just haven't discovered what we foreigners like yet, but its 'not so delicious' as translators tend to say. This was unfortunately followed by an unexpected karaoke session for most of the party, whilst our principal concluded the deal, at four o'clock in the Morning surrounded by an army of translators and lawyers!

The big issue of the night upon my arrival was not only the fact that the weather has got colder so no one is planning on wearing open neck shirts or golf shirts, but also tomorrow's big ceremony is going to be a very formal occasion; re: I need a shirt jacket and tie, and it is getting late in the day. As I was travelling for a casual weekend away with colleagues when called at short notice to attend, I didn't have anything beyond light trousers and open short sleeved casual shirts. Panic on, as I am dashed off to buy the largest white shirt that they can find in the city in the five minutes before dinner, I end up borrowing a tie from a Brit colleague and getting our principal to empty all his pockets of the considerable number of digital cameras, wallets, passports, cash, pens, and miscellaneous other junk from his largest Jaeger jacket to borrow it. It smells I'm told, but I have no sense of smell. All kitted out, I look fine I decide, and our principal's nephew even jokingly mentioned that I make the jacket look respectable after all the years of his uncle wearing it.

Monday morning we were up early again as planned and whisked off to a new hotel for the official signing ceremony accompanied by the cameras from three TV stations and numerous still cameras officially at 08.58 hours, the five and the eight numbers being very lucky ones in China, just a shame that it is raining. Local dignitaries were all there – mayors, party secretary and other government aficionados, before we set off for a visit to the older factory of the operations; not the reason that our company has invested in this business, but still contributing a profit. Later we had a formal lunch together planned with returning government officials and local industrialists and we knew what to expect!

Lunch was one of those lunches! Moutai, top drawer baijiu, 52 per cent proof, was the order of the day as a beverage and everyone got into the swing of things, the Chinese elated that they have resolved their financial problems with a creditable partner, whilst our principal was thrilled by his latest deal, although a few of the rest of us were a little more reserved on the day for a combination of reasons. I feel as flat as a pancake for some reason, cumulatively tired by events perhaps, but flat and not so certain about the deal. Anyway, our Jiaxing translator got drunk, like dead drunk, the mayor and Party secretary ended up drunker that he was it seemed, giving me the two biggest bear hugs, and kissing me on both sides of my face upon their departure and everyone was happy. I am not sure that I have ever been held so tightly by a man before in my life and certainly not kissed in such an intimate manner on both cheeks. I suspect he was happy and that they will both have enormous flipping hangovers when they eventually come around.

Afterwards, having time to kill before we to go to the airport and having checked out of our rooms, we all ended up in our principal's hotel suite in our various guises and respective conditions of sobriety and relaxation – the overseas team plus two or three guys from Binzhou and at different times our lawyers from Jiaxing....and a shed load of luggage. It was only a matter of time before the Moutai took affect with our translator collapsing on bed, comatose and *didn't move for a whole two hours other than to roll over and put his arm around our principal, who was by now flat out and snoring very loudly. This is not a typical corporate occasion, and I could see that the 'new foreigners' weren't particularly comfortable with the circumstances, whilst the local folk wondered perhaps what they have got into, whilst I am increasingly getting used to this approach. If I had been up all night doing the deal he had done and washed away my lunch with as much Moutai, then I would be snoring as loudly as he was. Probably counting the extra millions of value that he has added to his empire.*

2ⁿᵈ July 2005 - The trip this afternoon was a good one, the smooth one and a half-hour flight from Shanghai, both on time and into Jinan, Shandong Province and along the new motorway which now goes all the way to Binzhou, reducing the car trip to one and a half hours at the other end. This time we are staying at the four-Star Yin Mao Hotel, the alternative good hotel in the city and the first time that I have stayed here, although I have visited for an opening ceremony before.

Dinner with the joint venture management team and a couple of government friends was a pleasant one and sensible. Bed was early, but unfortunately sleep was not despite good rooms and temperature inside – a car alarm going off outside every fifteen minutes all night, significant heavy lorry movements all night along the main road outside, no sound proofing in the hotel, combined with the fact that the room foyer light kept coming on every so often due to it being automatic on movement detection and the fact that this sensor kept picking up the movement of my feet at the bottom of an otherwise very comfortable bed. Outside I am told the temperatures are dropping to minus 8 tonight, which I can believe given the ice and residual drifted snow that I witnessed on the way in, along with the iced-over rivers locally. The other main thing that I noticed was the incredibly changed landscape when I drove into the city on arrival, with new buildings appearing rapidly and the vista considerably different to that of my last visit at the end of September last year. This is now officially the fastest developing city in Shandong I am informed.

In most of the hotels that I stay in these days, the English is generally quite good, but this one, although not bad, was not great either, including such headed phrases in the printed materials as:

> *'Olbby Service' (Lobby Service)*

> *'Hall pair is paid attention to' (?)*

> *'Accept the Silver Place' (Presumably reference to the safe in reception)*

> *'The disabled person serves car'*

> *'Visits and hire car to serve in the city'*

> *'Live continuously' (something to do with late check-outs, but a nice thought)*

> *'The flavored drawing room'*

Other examples of phrases included:

> *'Such as needing and put up a guest for the night and get platforms handle and enter and stop and continue' (?)*

Thursday morning was a good meeting at our factory with the general manager, who had been quite frustrated and de-motivated before my visit, which turned out to be my first in an official direct capacity.

In the afternoon, despite my protestations, it was a visit to Sun Tzu's birthplace, some forty kilometres away. Sun Tzu, it turns out, is very famous philosopher, general, military strategist, the author of The Art of War, akin to Confucius in terms of fame and folklore and was the Father of War, writing the thirteen Strategies of War, that appear all over China and makes a lot of sense, given when he developed them. This tourist spot has been recently built-in traditional houses set out in similar fashion to the Forbidden City in Beijing in grounds 999 metres long and 88 metres wide, all walled in. Very interesting stuff, although not enough of the descriptive signs in English and it is bloody cold reminding me how far 999 metres is (one kilometre) when walking slowly and making small talk with local government officials from Hiumin County. Interesting and enlightening background about this historical figure.

Tonight we had dinner with the deputy governor from Huimin County and then treated to a full works of a massage tonight – open showers, saunas, dip pool, body scrubs and back massages. All very Roman and all a bit different.

This was an interesting trip. Professionally I have now been officially appointed as a director of our filter company up there, an investment that I am unsure about, but I am here on the ground in China and hence the appointment. A colleague has spontaneously bought two apartments as an investment that may turn out to be a good one. The city is booming and has got these at rock bottom prices.

w/c 15*th* May 2006 - Wednesday morning I was up reasonably early, and I left for a trip to Binzhou that is much overdue on my behalf as I missed the last board meeting due to my broken toe. That city is incredible, changing in scenery every time I go back; the pace of change being unbelievable and outstripping that of Jiaxing. The general manager gave us a tour of the city, viewing new lakes, luxury villas, wide highways, universities, schools, technical schools, factories, hotels, government buildings, apartments and so on that all seem to be happening simultaneously. Mind boggling!

The hotel that we are in is nothing special, but the bed is comfortable, and the air conditioning works well which is just as well as the temperature is very hot and conditions dry. The tour takes in our host's new house, a villa, in a private residential area, which is quite nice or at least will be I suspect when it is finished; now why can't I find anything like that in Jiaxing? After that we went and had a look around the new factory which is coming along nicely with the new five story office block opening this August, the paper machine running, and ancillary processes starting in July.

Afterwards we had a large banquet at a new seafood restaurant, with my old friend, the government member for Taiwan Affairs hosting the dinner and despite the absence of the mayor who is spending a lot of time in Thailand these days, it was still a wipe out on bai jiu, followed by a full session of KTV where I was at my best singing Beatles songs.

Thursday morning we had a meeting at the old factory before departing *to look around another possible business opportunity with an old state-owned paper mill becoming available. An absolute nightmare, environmental disaster, terrible equipment, poor quality and 2,000 employees all looking as if they didn't have a care in the world, certainly no interest in housekeeping or the whiffs of suspected chlorine gas or other emissions. I really don't want to be doing this deal, but we are taken to see another opportunity, a straw pulp mill some forty kilometres away from the city, which is better, but still a step too far I suspect.*

Dinner this evening was just us, in a local farmhouse restaurant in separate grey brick buildings alongside the city reservoir. This was quite pleasant, except during the dinner I took a call from our principal and went outside to talk privately and walking through the gardens, suddenly aware that I was in the middle of a cabbage patch along with just about every mosquito in town. I find myself chuckling as I had phoned him at 10.00 hours this morning as I had been told that he was in America, so I thought that I would catch him just before he went to bed. His response had been a bit testy, but I had thought nothing of it. This evening he informed me that he was back in the UK and that I had awoken him at 03.00 hours in the middle of the night!

This has been a positive visit, but I am fed up and 'all Chinerred out' for want of a better way of putting it. I am uncertain about the long term, not particularly fit, missing home and not enjoying work here anymore as the frustrations and exasperations are outweighing the novelties of which there are few left these days. This could be a reflective weekend.

28.16 Yunnan

w/c 4th December 2004 - My trip is to Kunming in Yunnan Province. This is my first time to Kunming, or indeed Yunnan province in the far southwest corner of China, bordering the Vietnam. I am however not as excited by this event as I normally am in these circumstances.

Arriving a little late after a delayed flight, I was disappointed by the weather, which I had understood to be consistent all year round down here but turned out to be wet and as cold, if not colder than Jiaxing, allowing me to sport my new suede Boss jacket. The traffic also turned out to be terrible, suggesting that there is a congestion problem beyond just a rainy-day affect, taking an hour to get to our city centre New Era Hotel, occupying twenty-eight floors of which my room turned out to be on the nineteenth with great views of the city centre area. Many parts of the city remain old and poor. Cities are never at their best in rain, and Kunming wasn't, not helped by the extensive blue fencing screens masking massive road works, but I did notice impressively built walls along the way, well decorated, although little else of note. Not a good first impression and disappointing after what I had heard so many good things about the place and the province. Kunming is known as the garden city and Yunnan borders Vietnam, Laos and Burma with Thailand also not being too far away. Yes, I should be more excited by all of this than I am.

This is my colleague's old patch and who still has several very good contacts here materializing in a good meeting at the Kunming cigarette factory where currently we haven't ever had any business.

Dinner was good food, although a disappointing setting in the hotel's seventh floor restaurant, enabling me to get an early night whilst my deputy headed out with customers and translator caught up with some senior old contacts.

Wednesday morning and we go off to the International Tobacco Exhibition in the city, the primary reason for us being here. The exhibition was relatively small but gave us the opportunity to a few competitors from Europe and add to their worries. We left at lunchtime, mission accomplished and went off for the hour and a half drive along yet another new highway through the green and vegetated countryside, reminding me of nearby Guangxi Province with the fertile orange soil and gentle hills to the famous 'Stone Forest' at the Shillin Yi Autonomous County, which I had never heard of before. This scenic area of karst geomorphology was under sea water about 300 million years ago, but about 270 million years ago the crust uplifted and the water drained away, whereby over time the remaining limestone eroded forming thousands of stone peaks, pillars, varying shapes, and stalagmites resembling a huge forest; hence the name the 'stone forest'. Many of these stones have been given names fueled by traditional Chinese imagination. Fascinating place, but still not that many foreigners here, highlighting the tourism potential that is yet untapped.

After lunch it was off to another place, that even my translator didn't know about, but was casually mentioned by the lady taxi driver that we had hired for the day and involved a 100-kilometre detour along windy and hilly, but newly asphalt roads to Jiu Xiang in the Hui Autonomous township. This place was unbelievable and again difficult to described, but included walking through very large prehistoric caves, underground valleys, rivers and minority presences with huge stalactites and stalagmites et al. Amazing place, a wonderful surprise and not a foreigner in site, indeed not so many Chinese for that matter. Maybe I should be investing in the tourist industry.

Later, back in Kunming, we went for dinner at an amazing minority restaurant, which was built in the fashion of an old minority village with stone slabbed floors, wooden buildings etc overlooking a live minority floor show with rituals, dancing and the likes which kept everyone entertained in a market type atmosphere. Great food and great experience with much of the singing and dancing reminding me of First Nations culture in North America.

w/c 3ʳᵈ and 10ᵗʰ June 2006 – The trip to Kunming was two hours and fifty minutes flight before a short transit stop and the forty minutes second stage flight to Li Jiang, which I have heard lots of good things about.

Li Jiang is 350 kilometres northwest of the provincial capital of Kunming in Yunnan province, this being the province that has the highest numbers of minority peoples in the whole of China (about twenty-three different groups, or tribes). Yunnan borders Vietnam and Laos to the south, Burma (Myanmar) to the southwest, Tibet to the west and northwest, Sichuan province to the north and Guizhou province to the east. Its location leaves it well exposed to drug running from neighbouring countries and the import of counterfeit goods such as cigarettes and the likes I am advised. I gather that this is where Michael Palin dropped into, via Shangri-La to the north, when he completed a trip over the Himalayas, and is the start of the great Yangtze River which runs through here from the mountains. Indeed four great rivers start off in this region, including the Mekong, and set off in different directions. I understand that we are about one hundred kilometres from the Tibetan border. The main minority here is the 'Naxi' people who were nomadic tribes who reportedly migrated here from Tibet a long time ago from the tenth century onwards.

The houses are set out largely as enclosed courtyards and the matriarchal traditional system ensures that the women are very much the head of the house! In every sense I understand.

The taxi drive to Li Jiang from its small, but functional airport, took about twenty-five minutes to cover the twenty kilometres to the four-star *Wangfu Hotel* set near the edge of the ancient town, which was my third-choice hotel as the place was busy, but fine if not a little short of atmosphere and was certainly quiet. Peaceful. The old town of Li Jiang was something else though and one of those moments in life when one struggles to describe what is all around and to remember everything, but certainly a magnificent experience.

Li Jiang is nestled amongst the green rice paddy fields, large hills and pine forests and is the capital of the Naxi kingdom. It has large scale, centuries old maze-like winding cobbled lanes and clean freshwater streams running everywhere amongst the traditional one-or two-story houses and shops. Culturally it is fascinating with shops everywhere, but still somehow not overly commercialized and more pleasantly not overly busy either. Apparently, a devastating earthquake destroyed one third of the town in 1996 and before that the town suffered an even more devastating one in 1966, but the traditional old structures remained, whilst the newer buildings collapsed, so now the new buildings are constructed in the traditional design; the result is something of beauty. The shops include the brightly coloured minority fabrics, silverware, copperware, leather, musical instruments, wood carvings, arts, and crafts and so on. This is the largest old town that I have seen in China, far better and less commercialized that Yangshuo in nearby Guangxi and I can see why it is something of a mecca for adventurous backpackers, which explains the development, very tastefully, of a host of bars and restaurants around the town, especially the central square. That said, there weren't many foreign visits in evidence at all.

Nearby or at least within a day's trip, there are all sorts of potentially exciting outward bounds type trips, but we opt for a relaxing weekend staying in the town. These options included a two-day hike through the Tiger Leaping Gorge, a snow-covered mountain, the first turn of the Yangtze river or up to Shangri-La right on the border with Tibet but takes six hours to get there.

Upon arrival at the hotel I was taken to the second-floor suite before a planned short walk which took two hours and we got lost in the maze of lanes despite the excellent sign-postings and regular lane side maps, but allowed the sampling of a 'baba', a traditional fried bread pancake thingy. Dinner was in the Sifang Square which was an amazing atmosphere.

We ate in front of the large and rustic Sakura bar, alongside a stream just off the central square and with bars and restaurants all around lining *the lanes. Noisy, but pleasantly so with a few westerners, Japanese, Koreans, Taiwanese, but mainly upmarket Chinese tourists and the evening atmosphere was infectious including mass dancing in the square which was like a Chinese equivalent of line dancing and minority women singing traditional songs, as well of course as modern western music blasting out of the bars.*

Friday, we went for a walk up the hill from Sifang Square to the Li Jiang Lion Hill Park and the Wang Lou Pagoda, apparently a World Heritage site since 1997, which had five stories, sixteen main pillars of twenty-two metres in length and claims to be the highest wooden building at thirty-three metres high, in China, although for some reason I am a little sceptical about this claim; maybe. All sorts of other facts emerge, typically Chinese in detail, such as the fact that the tower has 9,999 dragons carved into it bringing long longevity, which I suppose in an earthquake zone is highly appropriate. The views out over the old town and silhouetted surrounding mountains from here though were exceptional despite the slight haze. From here we descended into the Wu Residence, a rebuilt old town museum that had previously been destroyed by earthquakes and is now the home of Naxi musicians. This was a walking day and after that we discovered the other end of the old town bordering the new town, even discovering a lonesome English bar run by a Yorkshire man the bar called the 'Frosty Morning'.

Minority women in traditional costumes singing in Li Jiang, Yunnan province

Suitably refreshed, then it was more walking, following the river flows upstream and northwards into the old town until we reached the Black Dragon Pool Garden and park, containing the Dragon God Temple amongst other attractions. This was quite pleasant and peaceful, firstly finding a medium

sized ornamental lake, Naxi musicians, small waterfalls, bridges, Chinese humped backed bridges and more. After that dose of culture we traipsed back to a small 'Bu Bu' bar/restaurant on a back lane owned by a French Aussie, where we reviewed digital photos enjoying a glass local red wine.

On the kilometre walk back to the hotel from the central square we purchased a photo book of the town, unable to do justice to what we had witnessed with our own photos. It was difficult to describe accurately and reflect its beauty, this wonderful place with traditional minority-coloured costumes in the main worn naturally by the older folk much like the old ladies in Brittany, France and in areas around the Mediterranean wearing their long black dresses and lace bonnets, but these are far more colourful in nature.

Today was a rainy afternoon which continued with increasing force throughout the evening, still we set out for dinner later this evening enjoying the busier and more convivial atmosphere despite the rain. We dined at the same Sakura bar, but not sampling the fatty Naxi dishes on this occasion. A very special place!

On the face of it the place is much commercialized being all shops in the old town, but no one here is too pushy and, or in your face, and nowhere seems too busy. We are informed that the nearby Shu He is much more natural and undertake to wander the four kilometres over there tomorrow.

Saturday was wet and murky to start, but as the rain abated, we decided as one does that, we should walk the few kilometres to She He, or so we thought, dressed in shorts, and armed with backpack and umbrellas and a slightly dodgy map we set off. Two hours later we were still walking at a good pace but still hadn't found our destination, other than the fact that we were aware that we had made some errors in navigation, confused by the fact that newly constructed housing areas had changed the roadways since the map had been printed. In all we walked at pace for three hours and fifteen minutes, but never did find She He, an estimated ten to twelve miles. Dinner was at a restaurant sat at a second-floor open window overlooking the dancers in the square below, sampling more Naxi dishes, amusing ourselves at some of the less talented translations on the menu, the worst of which was 'Fuck the plum to boil the chicken', no kidding, which we decided not to try. Our best guess that it was probably meant to say something like 'stuffed plums and chicken', but we will never know!

w/c 13ᵗʰ August 2011 - Thursday and I was awake early at three o'clock. It has been several years since I had a chance to explore a bit of China due to increased international business commitments and today, I was heading off to a place called Xi Shuang Banna and its airport in its main city of Jing Hong in Yunnan province. I left Jiaxing heading to Shanghai's airport and then a three-hour flight to Kunming and then a one hour stop over before a fifty-minute flight on to Xi Shuang Banna.

We arrived re-invigorated by the climatic conditions, which was beautiful, warm, indeed hot and greenery everywhere! Like some form of paradise and we were greeted by our host at the contact company and taken out for lunch, which included a dish of fried grubs and large bees! A local speciality dish, we are informed and which my colleagues only tried one each, whilst I nonchalantly ate more. Then a chance to check in to the hotel and to our rooms on the eighth floor out of nine. The hotel externally is in the impressive style for this region with red/orange sloped roofs and looks like something one would see in Thailand.

The area is remarkably close, less than one hundred kilometres, from the Laos border and everything we see seems to reflect that with all signs in Chinese, English and a language that looks like Thai writing, the local dialect of this region that includes Thailand, Myanmar, Laos, and Vietnam. The architectural style reflects these influences and there are statues of elephants everywhere and we are informed that there are elephants out in the forests nearby.

We are here to discuss fibre for potential use, this being a large banana growing area and tomorrow we will visit the plantations and factory.

This evening our host took us out to a local minority restaurant where we saw a show in the bright local costumes. I looked on the internet for information about this place.

Xishuangbanna (or Sipsongpanna), is an autonomous prefecture in Yunnan Province, in South West China. The capital city is Jinghong, the largest settlement in the area and one that straddles the Mekong River, called the Lancang River in Chinese.

The Six famous tea mountains region, (literally, 'Six major tea mountain') located in the prefecture produce some of the most highly regarded Pu-erh tea in the 20th century.

Xishuangbanna is rich in nature, historical and cultural resources, noted for its folklore, rain forests, rare plants, and wildlife. Its major tourist attractions include Menglun Tropical Botanical Garden, Manfeilong Pagodas (Tanuozhuanglong), Jingzhen Pavilion, Wild Elephant Gully, Dai people's village at Ganlanba.

The well-known traditional festival is the ethnic Dai's Water-Splashing Festival. It lasts for three days from April 13 to 15. Besides the water festival event it also consists of some other events such as Dragon boat races, firing of indigenous missiles, flying Kongming Lamps.

Since the opening of the Xishuangbanna Gasa Airport (formerly 'Jinghong International Airport') in 1990, traveling to Xishuangbanna by air has become more popular and convenient and there are daily flights connecting Xishuangbanna with Kunming City. The area also has air connections with Dali, Chengdu and Bangkok. The Xishuangbanna Airport is six kilometres south of Jinghong City.

In October 2010, plans were announced for a 530 km railway linking Xishuangbanna to Vientiane in Laos; connections to Thailand are also possible.

Its local commanders were the Dao family during the Ming Dynasty and Qing Dynasty.

The prefecture has an area of 19,700 km². Xishuangbanna is the home of the Dai people. The region sits at a lower altitude than most of Yunnan and has a tropical climate. It is fast becoming a sought-after tourist destination.

Xishuangbanna harbours much of the biodiversity of Yunnan Province, which harbours much of the biodiversity of China. Its tropical climate and its remoteness until recent times accounts for this. In addition to an abundance of plants, Xishuangbanna is home to the last few Asian elephants still in China; the species roamed over a large part of the country even as late as a few hundred years ago. The elephants are protected in a reserve, but the plant diversity is threatened by, and has for five decades been threatened by, the proliferation of rubber plantations which completely destroy the rainforest and replace it with a monoculture of trees originally from Brazil.

Passiflora xishuangbannaensis is a recently discovered passionflower species that is endemic to Xishuangbanna.

With censuses in the year 2000 Xishuangbanna had 993,397 inhabitants with a population density of 50.43 inhabitants per km². This is not densely populated therefore by Chinese standards.

In the early 1950s, the Han population of Sipsongpanna was less than 10 per cent of the total; today the Han population may soon overtake the local Dai people. Most of the businesses had been bought by the Han, and commercial signs, which were earlier Dai/Chinese bilingual, are now solely in Mandarin. However, the Dai villagers have also prospered as property owners, often renting out their livestock quarters to Han migrants as the area undergoes rapid urbanization.

The native Thai name Sípsóng means "twelve" and Pănnă means "thousand rice fields". So Sípsắŋpănnă = "twelve thousand rice fields".

Dinner tonight was with our host at an ethnic Dai restaurant with a small stage show. Afterwards we went back to the hotel and a large show at the auditorium over the road. The place was packed and the show, two hours in length and a mixture of old, modern, and most remembered for the stunning clothes on show, but the dancing, music and gymnastics were all mightily impressive. Another privilege to see such things and a demonstration of the capabilities of the local Minority peoples in China.

Friday was different, a meeting with our contact who we had met yesterday and his boss, who had hurriedly shot over from Nanning late last night, *deciding we are important possible contacts, something that had not made clear when setting up these meetings.*

We set off for an hour's drive into a local Dai community, driving through those wonderfully wooded hills – mainly new plantations with rubber trees on the hills and banana plantations in the flat valley bottoms. We eventually arrived at our destination, an old factory, in a flat area with hills silhouetted all around. Truly beautiful naturally. I had to stifle a laugh when they said that this was world famous and lots of foreign visitors. Yes, there may be some overseas visitors, especially those in Asia and 'in the know', but this is not a global destination as indicated and despite the re-assertions that foreigners are here everywhere, in the three days here we only saw three other foreigners, two who were on the plane, and the bars and restaurants, whilst developed, were not westernized, although there was an obvious Asian-Thai influence, as opposed to Chinese!

There is a potential business opportunity here though and we had a good meeting and discussions, before decamping to a local village and a local lunch, at which we enjoyed baijiu. This afternoon it was back to the hotel for a rest and then this evening, my colleagues and I entertained ourselves at a hot pot restaurant on the banks of the Mekong River, a name synonymous to me with the Vietnam War and the troubles in the Mekong delta area lower down.

28.17 Xinjiang

W/c 29th May 2004 - I was invited by a friend, a bank president, to take me and a few others over to Xinjiang the coming weekend, for a long weekend. This, although the timing is not good, is quite exciting for me as it is very different from the rest of China. Xinjiang is the northwestern province that borders Pakistan, Afghanistan, Mongolia, Kazakhstan, Kyrgyzstan, Tadzhikistan, and very, very close to Uzbekistan, mostly former Soviet states, and close to India. It is a vast area and a long way away, north of the Indian border, Nepal and directly north of Tibet. I am told that life over here is very different, that 'security is not as good as in the rest of China', which I took as typical understatement, but that the holiday places are fine.

First was our trip to Shanghai and the flight to Urumqi, capital of

Xinjiang, an autonomously run region. I am excited about this, as it is new and different, looking up a few background facts about Xinjiang, I discover that:

> *The population of Urumqi, the capital, was circa one million people, 80 per cent of which are of 'Han' descent (i.e. traditional Chinese blood, but this may have been because they have been 'bussed in' to dilute the locals, ala Stalin's people's migrations in the USSR).*
>
> *The provincial population is circa 20 million people.*
>
> *The land area is 1,660,400 square kilometres.*
>
> *It is the largest autonomously managed region in China.*
>
> *It has the world's largest inland basin (Tarim Basin)*
>
> *It has the world's 2ⁿᵈ largest desert (Takle Makan desert).*
>
> *It has a diversity of ethnic groups of which the Uyghur's are the largest (47 per cent), followed by Han's at 39 per cent. There are also significant minorities of Tatars, Hui, Kazaks, Xibes, Kugiz, Mongols, Tajiks, Uzbeks, and Russians.*
>
> *It is China largest producer of cotton at 33 per cent of the country's output and produces 80 per cent of its hops.*
>
> *It is a major sheep farming area.*
>
> *It is rich in natural energy materials, with the largest reserves in China of oil, natural gas, and coal.*
>
> *It is also rich in minerals such as beryllium, mica, and multi-coloured granite. There is also the largest copper mine in China here.*

Basically though, this is a Muslim state run by China, a melting pot of nations existing in a mountainous and desert area that once was a key part of the old silk road. I am intrigued but suspect that we won't have enough time to do it justice due to its vastness.

The flight was five hours and I discover that the time difference in the capital city of Urumqi is four-hours, or at least that it is meant to be, given its location, but is not! Suddenly I am excited and start to appreciate the size and scale of this country. On the plane there are discernible differences, such as the fact that the food comes with Muslim stickers on it and many of the passengers are distinctly, well, to my mind Pakistani or Afghan looking, many of the men wearing brightly coloured skull caps, larger than the Jewish equivalent and a little squarer in shape together with a bit more depth. Even the Han Chinese look more rugged, due to a few generations of cross breeding. Meanwhile, below the scenery is wonderful – contoured hills, snow covered mountains, winding rivers, deserts with large sand mountains, winding roads and so on. Yep, this is something new for me.

We arrived on time at early afternoon and were told that we were heading off to the hills, before returning for an evening flight to Yili (Also shown on maps as Yilin and Yining) about forty kilometres from the Kazakhstan border. The trip to the mountains was about one and a half hours by bus on the bumpiest roads that I have experienced since Kenya. When we got there, we found beautiful grassy hills, snow covered mountain tops and were greeted by horsemen, Mongolian looking types, who immediately told to us to get on a covered cart pulled by two horses and taken up a windy wooded road to a waterfall. Lovely landscapes and lots of photo opportunities; then it was a dash back to the airport for our on flight to Yili, noting the dry stony riverbeds, strangely contoured reddish green hills, and the fertile flat valley bottoms as we approached Urumqi again. Here again, like so much of China, I notice that there is a massive tree-planting programme being undertaken.

Upon arrival at the airport in Yili, which is a small ex-Military airport like one I had once witnessed on the south coast in Beihai, I totted up that this was my twenty-second airport in China, which matches the twenty-two airports that I have been to in the USA. There were military helicopters everywhere, required for monitoring the extensive borders around this area. We went out for a nice dinner at a local restaurant – lamb, lamb, and lamb. The meal was washed down with a little baijiu; I leave the other men to relax over a beer and get an early night.

Xinjiang province comprises one sixth of the land area of the whole of

471

China I am informed. Big! I discover that minorities up here can have two children and that most girls have a boyfriend or are married by the time that they are eighteen, unlike traditional Han Chinese who settle down later.

Saturday, after the tiring prior day's travel, started at a sensible time as we set out for three hours' drive along straight motorway roads into the mountains. To the left was a long snow topped mountain range, which is in Kazakhstan I am told, to the right were desert type hills that reminded me somewhat of the hills in Nevada and inland California, but in between there were open and fertile flat fields, full of fruits and others crops. After two hours or so we hit the greenish foothills and then climbed into the mountains, which reminded me of the Alps, before arriving high up at Lake Sayram, all 457 square kilometres of it. Here there was another opportunity for horse riding, which I managed to avoid, and of course for several wonderful photo opportunities with the backdrop of snow-covered mountains, the lake and green tree lined hills, as well as the traditional circular tented villages of the nomadic sheep grazers and horsemen. The weather is glorious, hot with clear blue skies. I kept telling myself that this is not really China, but I pinch myself and of course it is. Along the way I had noticed lots of sheep herds, and shepherds, cattle grazing, round white yurts of the nomads, fresh fruit growing in abundance and many horses and carts in operation by the locals. There is a distinct absence of a major tourist industry, two other small buses seen the whole way.

Back in the bus, it was back down the mountain to a small town, where we had lunch on the side of the road at one of many restaurants of a similar nature all in a line. The downside evident from the start with was the loos, just like the ones that I had experienced in Dongbei, northeast China, last November, nightmare. The next mistake was to see the food being prepared – lady pulling the meat off the sheep's head, rubbery looking stomach lining and so on. The meal was quite disappointing in the event, with the lamb tough.

Then it was another one of 'those experiences' when we went to an annual horse-riding event, a sort of country fair, on the outskirts of the same town. There must have been tens of thousands of the 'Turkish' Muslims here – riding horses, singing competitions, horse racing, eating, sheep picking (carrying a beheaded full-size sheep around a large area on horseback, whilst others try to wrestle it off you – quite aggressive and some excellent horsemanship displayed) picnicking and so on. I must confess that without feeling threatened, I did feel exposed as we received considerable attention, or I did, looking American I guess, and more than once heard someone say in English 'Bush no good.' With no other westerners even vaguely in evidence apart from us, or indeed any other Han Chinese for that matter, the Chinese in our party wanted out of there quickly as a result. I wanted to have stayed much longer and take in this minority event, which we were privileged to have been a part of. The horse riders were magnificent, taking off at speed and leaning over to pick up things off the ground and many other circus type tricks in evidence.

This area intrigues me and in talking to our guide I get to learn a bit of the history and background. Yili and its surrounding area have a population of two million people covering an area of 50,000 square kilometres in the Yili Kazak Autonomous Prefecture, adjoining Kazakhstan. The main population here is generically known as the 'Turks' and are relatives of the ancestors of the folk living in Turkey these days, the consequence of a large migration in the 13th century. The result is that many of the dress codes, and traditions are similar, and the language commonly understood, albeit a quite different dialect. The food is mutton and lamb, although there is also beef, but no pork and there is also a plentiful supply of fresh vegetables and fruit – peaches and strawberries etc.

The population is virtually all Muslim, but I note that the military around at the borders and other places are all Han Chinese, as are many of the government officials in the area I am informed. The dress code is variable, but most of the women seem to wear a headscarf, but not the younger generation so much. I really cannot readily identify these people as Chinese, indeed they are not Han Chinese, but they just live in Chinese territory. This place is the backdrop of the world, about as isolated from seas and oceans as one can imagine or geographically possible; indeed, until the borders opened recently, this place was isolated. During the Cultural Revolution, many of the Kazaks slipped back over the mountains to Kazakhstan, but in recent years the increased trade opportunities has brought many of them back; and more!

The Chinese have been bringing in Han Chinese to the area for the last forty years to dilute the local population, initially as military outposts, but as a result the Han's are detested, although in the main it remains under the surface. Many of the people are nomadic, living in circular yurts and their modern-day equivalent, grazers of the foothills and there are many great horsemen around. Houses are often virtually without exception; one story high outside of the towns, built of bricks, but often lined with cement.

Most of the signs that I see are both in Chinese and what I would describe as 'Arabic' type in style, with little English in evidence. I understand the minorities, of which I am told there is forty-one varieties in the area, speak a Turkish language written in Perso-Arabic, and speak and learn Chinese only under duress. These are not Chinese, and the area is more what I would expect to see in Pakistan or Turkey, although I have been to neither.

The time is standard Beijing time, even though in reality, Xinjiang should be four hours' time difference. The net effect is that they have adjusted very well; they go to work at ten o'clock, eat lunch from two o'clock and eat dinner late at night. Thereby, China is all on the same time zone, unlike the USA, which has a three-hour time difference from east to west, or the Soviet Union, which I think has six separate time zones. This works without confusion and folk seem quite well adjusted. On world time zone maps, this is the bit where the straight lines go decidedly wiggly!

Afterwards we set off for the Kazakhstan border crossing point for some photographs. This was a hot and remote spot in a wide flat scrub valley bottom, with snow topped mountains in the background, looking not unalike the Rockies from a distance. The border opens at four o'clock daily we were informed, and this border post was opened in 1997 to encourage trade. I note a few Russians around and a crowd of western backpackers ready to cross and scale those mountains.

On the way back to the airport, we had a while at the bridge over the river in Yili. This is a wide river that needs some serious dredging, like so many of China's rivers, however, unlike most of China's rivers it flowed to the west. There seems much confusion about where it flows to, but appears that it ends up in Lake Ural, well documented now as one of the world's great ecological disasters as it has, dried up!

The day ended on a most disappointing and upsetting way when we arrived at the airport only to find our flight delayed by two hours. A colleague decided to check the digital camera's photos of the last two days, only to discover that somehow all the photos, not only of the last two days, but also from previous trips, have been deleted somehow! BBF, this is upsetting, as there have been some wonderfully personalised photos as well as group ones in some of the most stunning scenery possible. Dam it again! Flipping modern technology; never had this problem with the old type.

Tonight, after the flight back to Urumqi, we stayed at the five-Star Yin

Du Hotel, which has also been awarded the five-star diamond awards from the American academy of hospitality sciences and is the best hotel in Xinjiang. First though it was a late dinner at a speciality regional restaurant, which involved eating more mutton, all sorts of bits – cut joints, one style fried, one style boiled, stomach lining, lung, and face meat; I consoled myself that there were no hooves or eyes in evidence. As an alternative to mutton, there is of course lamb; even the fish looked like a sheep! Not the tastiest meal that I have had, although not terrible.

Sunday morning, we are traveling again. I am honestly extremely excited. This is all a very new experience for me having never been to Turkey, the Middle East, Afghanistan, or Pakistan. I am discovering a whole new world and it is a refreshing change. It is also encouraging to see a Muslim community that is not being torn apart by any form of major conflict and seems to be existing in peace, although my Han colleagues seem less certain, distinctly uncomfortable at times.

This morning we head out east and south towards Turpan, although I see other translated English spellings having it as Turfan. The drive is three hours and takes us out along the western front of what becomes the Gobi Desert, which is a grey pebble desert, horrible nothingness for the next 1,200 kilometres to the east of us. There are mountains to the sides though which are beautifully silhouetted. Soon we pass a massive wind farm, with 297 windmills, then its past a large Salt Lake with associated salt factory, 150 metres below sea level I am told. In the main though the wide valley bottoms are stony nothingness. In time we come to a ravine in some hills and then out into an open desert area, barren stuff, although with mountains set back to our left. Eventually we arrive at 'Turfan,' which is an oasis in a desert, albeit a man-made one. In my geographical ignorance I knew nothing of this place's existence, but it is quite amazing; stunning!

It is differentiated from the surrounding desert due to the availability of water; it is as simple as that. The place started here some 2,000 years ago and was on the infamous 'Silk Road', the northern route, the major trading route between Eurasia and Asia proper. It was formed at a problematic area on the route as the area is all desert and there was no water, so somebody formed the town and brought water to it – from the mountains some seventy kilometres away. To do this they started digging underground tunnels flowing down to the town, some as deep as 150 metres in parts, but ten metres deep closer to the town and with maintenance holes to the waterway every two hundred metres or so. There are 1,500 of these channels.

This is an amazing piece of engineering and is classed as one of China's three great man made works along with the Great Wall and the Grand Canal. The result is a beautifully green oasis in the desert, in a city, which has 50,000-60,000 people in its centre, but the area homes 500,000 folk, still small by Chinese standards, but I remind myself that this is not the normal China, merely Chinese territory in name only for all intents and purposes. The people are virtually one hundred per cent Uyghur's.

The town specializes in growing vines and therefore grape production, although it is rapidly striving to develop its tourism, but not really reaching overseas visitors in a big way due to its remoteness. Most of the buildings are single story, made from brick with flat wooden roofs and vines growing everywhere proving leafy shade and respite from the extreme heat from the baking sun. The beds are outside of the houses, set off the floor and on which they place 'Turkish carpets' at night-time to sleep on. I like this place and the skyline is only disturbed a little in the centre by a few higher buildings, which are not of a brilliant design, but do not overly detract. The school looks like a mosque to me, as does the adjacent hospital. There seems to be fresh drying fruit everywhere, raisins in great abundance. Everywhere there are buildings which look like they have every other brick missing and it turns out that these are used primarily for grape drying, but some folks have adapted them as bedrooms; I went into one and found it very cool and refreshing respite from the heat. I like this place but have never seen the likes of this before. I keep reminding myself how remote this area is, but what great opportunities there will be for specialist holidays in the future as the tourist industry gets established here.

We visited a number of touristy sites, often under vines, bought some fresh raisins and few souvenirs before having lunch, the best that I have had in the region so far – kebabs – decent meat on skewers. Even had a little rice, the first time that I have seen this over the last few days, as this is not a rice area though, potatoes being prevalent.

After lunch it was off to one of the many sets of old ruins around at Gaochang, a city that was formed and developed over 1,400 years but is now very ruined buildings in the arid desert made of mud bricks and has been since 1383 following a lengthy battle. Large area and must have been some place in its heyday. Then it was a few photos with camels in front of the 'Fire

Mountain' (or Flaming Mountain depending upon the translation) and then a cooling off period under yet more vines.

In a remote corner of Gaocheng, we were approached by three young girls selling bells, dressed in traditional local minority red flowery dresses and skull caps. They spoke a little English and I engaged this as they were not 'hard selling,' I even decided to have a photo with them and without enquiring I offered them some money, ¥20 (about £1.30) as it was the smallest note that I had. They said no, but I assumed this to be modesty and they duly posed with me and others and eventually took the money. A few minutes later they came up and simply gave me two bells that they had been trying to sell. Seems that they had talked among themselves and decided that they should do this as they were only trying to sell them for ¥5 each anyway. I was touched by this kindness and innocence in the harsh reality of a commercial world. They were good an honest kids, which left me feeling guilty as I just realised that I had introduced them to a new commercial concept – demanding money from future customers for photographs; Darn it, I had just taken away some of their commercial innocence!

This area is so vast that I just wish that I had taken another couple of days off work for this business trip to cover more of this diverse region. Everything is so far away from everything else.

Tonight, we check into the Grand Turpan Hotel, which is not particularly grand, but fine, a three-star affair. Dinner tonight was at an open-air food market off the main square, the square design of which was very Chinese, I hope not a sign of things to come as this city modernizes; it really should keep its own cultural identity. The food and service though were vastly different, in what were hot conditions, with school type tables laid out and many traditional hot food stalls around from which you chose what you wanted and paid later. A little chaotic, not particularly hygienic, and very Chinese-Muslim, but fun and the skewered kebabs and spicy chicken dishes were good, as was the local version of naan bread. We even managed to engage some of the old Uyghur boys drinking baijiu on the adjoining table and get a few photos to boot. Pleasant cultural experience, although watching the 'pop' singers and dancers in another open-air square was not so much fun. Still the atmosphere was good and the outdoor lifestyle proving once again that it has its merits.

Tourist picture in Turfan, Xinjiang, in and around the most wonderful grape vines.

Xinjiang province at the Flaming (or Fire) Mountain near Turpan.

Monday, we had the long journey back to Urumqi and an extra hour up into the Tianshan Mountains to the beautiful lake, called the Tianchi or Heavenly Lake. This is incredibly beautiful, but I realise that I have been spoiled by seeing some others that stand comparison in Europe, but especially in Canada, although it does merit some comparison with Lake Louise I Canada it must be said, but without the same degree of trees.

No getting away from it, this is special.....and busy, being within easy reach of Urumqi; there were even a party of retired Americans here. It is developing fast, and a Tao Temple is currently under construction at a quiet part of the Lake. As always in China, there is not much walking to be done, just turn up, take the photographs, and move on.

In all my time in China I have been noticing the tiled communal trough public toilets and thanked my lucky stars that I had no stomach problems. Today however, was that day; shall we say, a 'Chinese first' as I had to go, without going into any more detail!

Next it was into Urumqi past herds of camels and a visit to the newly developed Grand Bazaar, which contains an exceptionally large an attractive mosque, together will a very tall ornamental 'calling tower' and lots of bronze life size camels. Though this has been commercially developed and the new centre of city and they have done it quite well, despite the presence of the KFC and a Carrefour. We ate in a large eating food hall, designed in a pseudo-American style food hall, with several places serving and where you chose what you want and eat in a communal dining area. Not the best setting, but the Muslim food was excellent; though, this was an indoor version of what we had done outdoors last night. For once I prefer the atmosphere of the original, not the sanitized version.

There was just enough time for a short look around the Bazaar's markets, which seemed to have everything that you would expect from the 'Silk Road's' history – wooden carvings from Pakistan, Pots from Pakistan, indeed lots of things from Pakistan and lots of Pakistanis come to think of it with many sporting the long chin beards and traditional garb; for all intents and purposes resembling Bin Laden in attire, but very nice people, fluent in English and very happy to engage in conversation, with one thing in common – they all hate Bush! There were also lots of jade and Persian-Turkish style carpets, all of which I am reminded originated here.

We arrive at the airport in suitable time and check in, keen to get on the way home and back to our own beds. Then we heard that the flight was delayed, albeit with no concrete information, then suddenly after a casual enquiring question, we find that the flight has been cancelled! This will guarantee a late-night getting home.

The rest was all very Chinese orchestrated chaos, the first option being to stay the night, the second option being to take a later flight on a different airline at additional costs, which we took, unsure of whether our already checked in bags would materialise in Shanghai with us. On the flight I also noted lots and lots of very, very muscular men of varying sizes, reminding me that I had seen many in Urumqi; there have been a major body building, wrestling or weightlifting competition there over the weekend.

w/c 11th September 2004 - The flight to Urumqi (Alternatively written in English and pronounced in Chinese as Wulumuqi), from Lanzhou was three hours, ensuring that we arrive early afternoon in bright sunshine, but slightly cooler and very acceptable conditions. The flight provided a wonderful array of views of the dry hills, desert, open flatlands, and snow-covered mountains below; a wonderful assortment of scenes.

The city was pretty much how I remembered it, but taxi drivers being as they are everywhere taking us all over the shop to run up his meter. Anyway, we eventually arrived at the five-star Hongfu Hotel, which was impressive as was my room on the twenty-fourth floor, with en-suite computer, fax machine et al, recently redecorated in a modern art deco type design in the guest tower block. I am happy, although it is more expensive than I like to pay, but I am reminded that this is the busy time of the year as these summer months are the height of the tourist season. The views out over the city to arid, but increasingly vegetated hills show a city of contrasts and very much in a development phase, although judging by this hotel, its clientele and the one I stayed at on my last visit, there is certainly a developed side to it. I can tell that my translator and the sales guy are plotting to keep us all here to see more over the next few days after our visit to the Xinjiang cigarette factory tomorrow, which I am informed is some 280 kilometres away.

Unable to see the customers until tomorrow, we took some time out in the late afternoon and early evening to look around the Grand Bazaar, the new mosque, and its smaller predecessor across the road. The surprise though was a friend of my translator who she 'knows' from the Internet coming to meet us and show us around the place, which was a nice plus, including being taken out to a local speciality restaurant nearby to our hotel. Shopping was a must of course, but as usual I managed to largely resist temptation, more interested in the array of gifts, the live camels, the women on horseback resembling erstwhile Canadian Mounties in their red tunics, taking in the cultural scenes and the people who come in all shapes and forms of Turks, ethnic Muslims, veiled women and so on. They are more intrigued by me it seems, some managing to do so in an apparently menacing way, perhaps thinking that I am an American.

The restaurant turned out to be quite something special, an up-market place, but certainly different. Set in a big old house, the restaurant had a ground floor in the centre of which were three traditional Turkish-Muslim-Arabic type musicians playing pleasant music as entertainment, supported periodically by what I would in my ignorance call 'Belly dancers', although I am not sure that is the politically correct definition these days and the last time, I saw something like this was either in a James Bond scene or in one of the Carry-On films. This though was the local culture. Surrounding the floor was a balcony on which we had one of the tables and off these ran private dining rooms, all very elegantly appointed, with a mosque dome above the food preparation area; even a reference to Istanbul was noted. Unsurprisingly, we had lamb, and lamb and lamb; it's a wonder that there are any sheep left in this part of the world as that seems to be all that anyone eats. That said, it was delicious, whether it was the skewered kebabs, the kidneys or the meat variety, the lamb chops or the braised lamb in rice accompanied by mixed spices, peppers, and natural local yogurt......oh yes and tea, no alcohol, making it four out of five days without alcohol. A brilliant cultural experience and again the sort of thing that I would have expected to experience somewhere like the more exotic spots of Turkey (as per photos of Istanbul), Egypt or one of the other Middle Eastern countries. An interesting feature is the pay up front and self-service type approach, even in this high-quality restaurant, presumably typical and a development of the street market approaches to food service with the communal tables in the streets and squares of the area that I have witnessed before. Also notable was the fact that we did not sit down for dinner until nine o'clock reminding me that everyone eats later here, and that the day starts later and ends later than other parts of China.

Thursday morning we are up and off to the cigarette factory at Kui Tun by taxi. At breakfast I try yet again one of those nice-looking Danish pastries that all good Chinese hotels seem to have, looking for all the world like the delicious ones that we have back in Europe and yet again I find myself disappointed by the dryness and taste which are so different to the originals. Indeed these are often so dry and so tasteless that I find that these are one of the comparatively few things in China that I don't eat.

The journey to the west was primarily along a wonderful new dual carriageway toll highway, the journey taking three hours. All along our journey we have the Tianshan snow covered Mountains to our left with the dry looking foothills in front of them. The weather is sunny and wonderful and the skies clear blue assisting our appreciation of the surrounds, which apart from the mountains is flat. The plains, whilst not looking overly fertile, are certainly being well harvested and I guess have been reclaimed over recent years of plain scrubland that we later witness. Maize is in evidence as are some vines and other crops, but the main one seems to be cotton, with maybe over 100 kilometres of cotton fields being harvested by thousands upon thousands of brightly dressed women with large baskets on their backs, reminding me of pictures of slave cotton pickers in the southern States of the USA in years gone by. Like in Lanzhou, Gansu, there are a high percentage of large four-wheel drive country vehicles reminding me that this is the big open countryside.... and that there is money around somewhere! Just before we reach Kui Tun, the ground rises a little into grasslands where were see flocks of sheep and goats being tended to by their shepherds, the bigger flocks having shepherds on horseback.

Then we reached Kui Tun City, notable by its industrial approach – power stations and factories etc. My initial reaction is that most of the people are Han Chinese and therefore have been bussed in here at some stage in the past. I also get the impression that this is some form of new town, constructed twenty to thirty years ago in the middle of nowhere, but a maybe wrong.

The hotel, the Grand International Oriental Hotel, is the largest three-star hotel in Xinjiang, but reputedly the best around. No problem I say, I have stayed in some excellent three-star hotels in China; unfortunately, this evidently was not one of them despite its prominent twenty-four-story tower!

My room is on the eighteenth floor and has stunning views over the city below stretching away from the mountains down towards a large reservoir and flatness thereafter as far as the eye can see. This is a vast expanse and reminds me of the plains in Canada and US Mid-West. I discover that I am right that this is mainly a Han Chinese population, primarily because it originated some forty years ago as a Chinese Military outpost to control the locals and it still has a significant military presence, perhaps explaining the orderliness of the layout of the city's blocks of tenement apartments, wide roads, and good cleanliness. The population is small, a mere 120,000 - insignificant in Chinese terms.

We arrive at one o'clock, and I am informed that we will be going to the factory at five o'clock, and then going for dinner thereafter. I was forewarned that they drink a lot in this part of the world. This was fine until having settled into my hotel room I get a call that we are now having lunch with the deputy factory director, a job like vice chancellors at British universities, they seem to run the show. Lunch was very pleasant, just six of us, but with too much baijiu for my liking and at the end of the meal I find myself staring at the ugliest fish that I have ever seen. I am informed that this is a rare species in China and that I couldn't get it anywhere else for legal reasons (protected species), suddenly making me feel a little guilty over this thing. It was removed to let me have the tastiest bit, which I had foolishly assumed would be the large white meat but turned out to be something resembling a long thick white noodle, which my translator informs me is the backbone; good for men's health apparently and suddenly I am pleased that I have drank plenty of baijiu and I chewed through this thing. Anything that is good for my health though, I am game for. Otherwise the food was delicious with plenty of lamb of course.

Then it was back to the hotel for a quick sleep reminding why so many senior Chinese businessmen have beds in their offices, and then off to the factory, which in keeping with every other one in China is being rebuilt. Dinner was in my hotel and came with the warning that the venue was here as if we drank too much it would be easy to get us to bed. BBF. What is worse is that they turned up with three female employees, nearly always the most dangerous sign from a drinking viewpoint, which was worrying as was the fact that there was eleven of us. Didn't seem like a silly evening, but perhaps numbed by the lunchtime activity I guess I consumed my fair share of local baijiu in response to their very hospitable welcome. They were delighted to welcome a foreigner, a rarity, and I really liked the deputy factory manager *who puts on a good show. As I made my way up to bed, I realized that I had had enough though; silly me!*

I hardly noticed that the room was a tip – damp on the walls, stains on the carpets, poor wiring, appalling tiling in the bathroom, barely enough room for the toilet behind the bath and the bathroom phone was on the opposite wall, some ten feet away from the loo, defeating the objective really and just where it can get drenched in water from the bath's shower. The bed was comfy though and there I rested fully clothed until next morning.

Friday, I awoke feeling like death warmed up and sick as a parrot. I have done a good job of alcohol management this week but failed miserably yesterday. My only consolation is that I made some very good friends of our customers who were delighted to see me. The plan was for an early start for a drive to the mountains and then back to Urumqi tonight, but I am very aware at breakfast that I am in no state to do anything, unable to eat or drink and hoping frankly to get out of here and back to Urumqi. However, they decide to let me rest until midday and then head off to the Tian Shan Mountains near the Kazakhstan border, some one hour to the south, this range dividing north and south Xinjiang. I am unsure what to expect but had thought that we would have a quick look around and return, especially as I have never felt less like wanting to do something in my life, given my condition.

We set off towards the mountains with me feeling sicker and sicker as we went along good roads to start with, but bumpier ones as we ascended the mountains. Soon we passed through a new town nearby to an oil refinery and I am informed that this is 'oil town', the original drill site nearby being the third oldest in China. Then it was across vast grassy flatlands hosting large herds of sheep, cattle, horses, and camels, towards some pretty impressive, styled foothills, the likes of which I haven't seen elsewhere. I am informed that there are lots of wolves out here and even black bears and that the numerous small caves were dug by gold miners. They tell me that there are also ski slopes developing here, but that they aren't busy and there aren't any ski lifts (!), skiers being taken up by four-wheel drive vehicles. I am told that the snow in the city can get up to 1 metre depth in winter and progressively deeper as one approaches the mountains, such yet untapped potential here in this wider area.

Anyway we didn't make the snowline, stopping below the tree line in grassy mountains by a Kazak minority circular tent, a yurt of sorts, where I am informed, we are having lunch; heck I am feeling terrible, worse and I now have this dropped on me. Feeling awful, I go for a walk across a mountain stream and into the woods and make myself sick, feeling somewhat better afterwards. Then I discover many of the people who I had dinner with last night and more, including two other visitors, have turned up and assisting the preparations totaling thirteen of us. I get my bit in first getting my translator to tell the deputy factory director that I am feeling very sick, can't drink baijiu under any circumstances, maybe nothing for that matter and probably wouldn't be able to eat. He was surprisingly understanding about me not drinking, albeit slightly begrudging in his acceptance of this position.

Then I discovered more – they had just killed a sheep in my honour and were preparing it whilst we watched upon its dissection and making skewer kebabs from the meat and fat among other dishes. I have this strange feeling in my stomach as we entered the large round circular tent with ventilation hole on top, low tables in the centre and where we removed shoes to sit cross-legged on bedding. This was a nice atmosphere and one of those special experiences in life, which would have been more so had I been feeling at all well. The local tea is a black tea, not Chinese green tea and served with cow's milk, which was quite welcoming. Then the others started on the baijiu, and I watched at the madness that followed over the next three hours, the host pouring baijiu into only three quite large communal glasses that were passed around on a regular basis. Apart from some nice spicy vegetables, including some potato dishes the lamb came, and kept coming and kept coming – kebabs, stewed, fried, and finally the head, where the host cuts off meat from the face and puts it directly into everyone else's mouth and then did the same with the sheep's brains. Having experienced this only three days before I was quite prepared for what was coming and managed it well; happy though that I didn't have to eat a slice of ear, BUT I DID GET A WHOLE EYEBALL GOUGED OUT AND PUT INTO MY MOUTH, which wasn't the testiest thing that I have ever had and amused myself as a diversion, by trying to imagine the faces of certain members of my family and friends had they been there. An hour into proceedings our sales guy just keeled over and slept like a baby along the inside of the tent, an hour later two other guests were sleeping also like babies and one women employee very, very loud and talking nonsense, which even I realized was rubbish. My translator was unhappy as she was getting caught for toasts and drinking stuff she didn't like. I was just stone cold sober, feeling better with every minute and every piece of *food that I consumed, eyeballs apart, all washed down by copious quantities of fresh tea! Yes, this was a special occurrence.*

Saturday morning in Kui Tun (Pronounced 'Kway Twun') the weather was lovely, very much appreciated. Last night, unable to get off to sleep I had ventured up to the twenty-second-floor western style snack hall, which was small and empty, the views of the city hindered somewhat by the fact that the windows probably hadn't been cleaned since the hotel was built. Having not eaten much in the way of food yesterday, I had suddenly felt hungry, but found no way of ordering food as there were no English menus anywhere in the place. Looking at a map of Xinjiang, I realize that we have traveled about halfway from Urumqi to Yili, the city near the Kazak border that I flew to early this year, but that there is the huge mountain range in between. I am informed that Kui Tun itself is still some thirty kilometres from the Kazak border.

As we left Kui Tun I discover that the deputy factory manager has given me a gift of two bottles of local baijiu; I will have to think of someone to give these to. I do though have happy memories of the place and the area and the hangover of two days ago will fade in the memory.

We arrive at lunchtime back in Urumqi, to the five-star Hoi Tak Hotel in the downtown area, where my room is on the thirty-first floor of this thirty-story block, seemingly the current tallest building in the city and overlooking a new People's Square below and looking out onto the surrounding light brown contoured hills on the skyline. There are too many old factories and a power station discernibly too close to the city, but these probably emanate from eras gone by. We had entered the city on a new highway the connecting road off which cuts through an old and very poor part of the city. Give it three years and I am confident that this will have all changed I am sure of that, with these poorly brick built one story houses being demolished to be replaced by tree lined boulevards and high-rise apartments set back from it; that is the way out here and one certainly can't have this type of entrance to any self-respecting city in China.

Tonight we head out into the city again, unable to get a plane back to Shanghai either this afternoon or tomorrow morning, which frustrates me slightly and I find my translator and I disagreeing on the need to plan to avoid such events, she contesting that given the nature of Chinese business that one cannot plan. Whilst I sympathize with her sentiment, this could have been avoided and means that I will get home late tomorrow night and with a shed load of things to do ahead of the coming week's visits. This does not help my mood and is dead time. Dinner was a normal Chinese one tonight, i.e. no lamb and comprised of an assorted mixture of vegetables and three large fish heads; when will these folks learn? An interesting development was me doing what I often do with a rice bowl, which was adding a spicy sauce from one of the dishes to add flavour. Upon seeing this both my colleagues ordered rice bowls and started doing the same, concluding that it was delicious and stating that 'They are learning from me all of the time; this was a good idea'! It is evident from being around the modern city centre and People's Square that the city centre is dominated by middle class Han Chinese, not minorities, which I find unusual having seen so many Uyghur minorities here in other parts of the city. It is also apparent that I am not so much of a novelty here; perhaps the locals just think that I am "Russian". The hotel meanwhile seems to be dominated by a group of middle-aged Scandinavian Ladies, Taiwanese and Hong Kong folk.

The plane trip back was late and a long four and a half hours back. I read on the plane that 16 million Chinese travelled overseas in the first seven months of 2004; that's a whacking 64 per cent up on the same period last year.

w/c 8th October 2005 - Sunday morning I go to Shanghai with my translator and the salesman for Xinjiang, as usual not sure what I am going to apart from the fact that it is their 45th Anniversary celebrations; this will be my third to Xinjiang. The flight was delayed, so they served us lunch there before starting the 3,454 kilometres trip to Urumqi. I later discover that the earthquake in adjacent Afghanistan and Pakistan has killed 40,000 people and that extreme weather conditions are making things worse.

At the airport we were greeted by extremely tall glamourous models who ushered us onto a bus for our journey along a motorway to Kui Tun. We are booked into the Kui Tun Grand Railway hotel late in the evening and are immediately summoned for dinner by the purchasing team from Kui Tun cigarette factory for what was a lively dinner accompanied by bai jiu, but at least I managed to survive it, only I suspect because many had been drinking for some time prior to my arrival. My seventh-floor suite in this hotel is spacious and far better than the hotel I stayed in last time; I am informed that there are now four decent hotels for a city that they are starting to dub as the Shanghai of

Xinjiang, which just goes to show how much bai jiu they must be drinking as it is absolutely nothing like Shanghai, not even with the wildest of imaginations. These guys should get out more. Anyway, met the production director whose daughter has just started studying an English degree at Newcastle University back in the UK, reminding me of their lust for overseas education.

Monday morning and the weather started to change fast which was a shame as it was a ceremony to celebrate the factory's 45th anniversary and a good chance to show off all their new investment which was reasonable impressive for this bland old ex-military outpost. We were collected in another police convoy of buses and taken to the factory to be welcomed by TV cameras, banks of photographers, tall glamourous and un-Chinese looking models, fireworks, band, dancing lions and all the pomp that goes with one of these events before freezing for an hour listening to speech after speech by various dignitaries, including the governor of Xinjiang. The strange part was that everywhere I go in China I attract attention work wise and usually the cameras end up on me or other westerners. At this event, although I got a lot of attention from the employees and other visitors, it was as if I was invisible to the cameras which were even switched off as they got to me, strange as I was the only westerner present in an audience of over a 1,000 folk! Just shows how things vary from region to region, but I haven't been blanked like this by the media elsewhere, but then remind myself that this is the land of the Kazak and Turk minorities and that there are also a lot of Russians and oil folk in the region, so presumably no novelty value, maybe even the opposite.

My hotel suite has a large bay window, very large as I have the end of the building and both sides in my room. However, the views are not wonderful, notwithstanding the fact that I directly look out onto hills several miles away and snow-covered mountains behind them. The problem is what is in between, scruffy, and stark buildings associated with the railway station, several rows of parked railway carriages in the station sidings, the main railway line, presumably between Yili and Urumqi, an open-air coal store, large water tower and then plains for miles and miles until its hits the hills. About a mile away is the main highway, with what looks like a power station to the left of the panorama in the distance and what looks like some sort of oil or gas refineries away to the right, with odd large building dotted in between.

After lunch we had the afternoon to relax before tonight's activities and I take the opportunity to sleep as the temperature drops and the rain comes in, making the place miserable. At dinner I was quite happy with life, delighted that I had escaped the need to drink any bai jiu when I discovered that tonight's concert entertainment was indeed outdoors; hell! A cold one! In stark contrast to the rest of the day the deputy factory director and factory director, both appear independently to greet me and feel most welcome, singling me out a little bit embarrassingly in a dining hall containing about 200 people and reminding me how warm the welcome was last year. The factory director is really pleased telling me that he has been to over twenty countries and how wonderful it was to have a westerner present at this special day for them and all heads turned!

We are herded onto the bus convoy and taken to the local football stadium, re concrete stadium Chinese style, where they have set up a large outdoor and uncovered stage on the football pitch. Luckily it has just stopped raining but is freezing and as all the guests have special plastic seats left for them in the open air that are nice and wet, and as an afterthought the organizers raided the local army stores and issued those large green military overcoats that I see periodically although sadly there were not enough to go around. Anyway the concert was excellent and televised, being hosted by a stunning young CCTV lady from Shanghai and a local TV celebrity who is big in Xinjiang and well known nationally. Indeed there were many nationally recognized stars to entertain a very excited audience and left my translator very excited also; maybe six or seven big stars as well as the local factory team providing dance entertainment at the start and end and the factory director summoned up to do a duet with a young female star; thank God for his karaoke training! By the end of the day I had also met most of the people that I had met last year and felt that the trip was worthwhile, although I was frozen and returned to my room to find it frozen and the air conditioning not working.

This was as I felt next morning when I awoke, I remain frozen and tired. We depart for Urumqi airport bearing gifts including a nice suitcase, a cigarette set including glass lighters and ashtray (plain crystal) and a Chinese glass something that is difficult to describe. I seem fated with Xinjiang, having been there three times and three times I have left with an upset stomach and plane delays, this time by two hours.

Xinjiang today is very much in the eyes of the world's media and is the focus of much speculation and reporting of human rights abuses relative primarily to the Uyghur people. These though were my experiences and observations from the region, certainly a place where cultures met, and my Han Chinese friends were very weary of their personal security there.

28.18 Chong Qing

w/c 19ᵗʰ December 2009 - Tuesday we are all up early and off with to Pudong for our flight to Chong Qing. It is also my first time to visit the municipality and province of Chongqing. The views of the hills and mountains below as we approached Chongqing were breath-taking, with mists hanging into the hillsides like those in ancient paintings.

Upon arrival the initial reaction was how misty the city was and the trip to our Hilton Chong Qing Hotel was about forty minutes by taxi. This five-star hotel is set in the city centre, near to the river and a five-minute walk from Renmin (People's) Square. This really is a western standard hotel, and I am delighted at the cheap rates that I have got for this trip, albeit the area next to it all demolished, being prepared for new construction. Our room was on the fifteenth floor of this thirty odd story hotel; I note the 'earthquake warnings and procedures in the room.' This evening we dined in the hotel at the international restaurant. The food was international, albeit all the western dishes were German, I suspect reflecting a German chef or demand for German clientele in the area, although the hotel is absent of foreigners, who have disappeared home for Christmas.

Chongqing is a major modern city in central-western China, one of China's four Provincial level municipalities and the only municipality in western China, created in 1997 when it was separated from Sichuan Province. In 2005 it has a registered population of over thirty-one million people. It was the wartime capital during the Sino-Japanese war (1937-1945) before the government disappeared en masse to Taiwan and is set on the Jialing River which feeds the Yangtze River with its intersection here and hence many foreigners come here for the start of the 'Three Gorges' River trip down the Yangtze. It has a long and varied history and quite westernized. The mayor of Chong Qing has the same status in Beijing as that of a provincial governor, very senior. It is very hilly here and the only major metropolitan area in China without significant numbers of bicycles as a result. It reminds me of a European city with its windy and random tree lines hillside roads, with the deep gorge of the river Yangtze.

I am glad to note that the average temperature for December is about ten degrees centigrade but has one of the lowest sunshine levels annually in China and is damp in winter. Chongqing is though well known for its fogs in winter and autumn times and associated heavy pollution that is in evidence when we arrived. The government has put an extremely high profile on reducing pollution levels here and it has national emphasis and targets. This was the place that was raided big style by the central government a couple of months ago with a view to reducing ongoing high-level corruption with 4,893 gangsters being arrested formally, the city being traditionally renowned for its organized crime in China.

The area around the city out in the countryside rural and agricultural, but the city is a major industrial city and is rapidly urbanizing. Due to its inland geographic location, built on the largest river in China, Chongqing has historically developed as a major armaments producer, but unlike the major eastern and south cities, its overall exports are low, and its markets China orientated. It is a though major automotive producer. For some reason unknown to man, it is a twin city with Leicester in the UK amongst others!

My first impression is that it is very hilly and fertile, which at first sight gives some similarities to Hong Kong given all the hills and high-rise apartments. This though is scruffier and still evidently in a development phase given all the new high-rise buildings under construction, not all of them attractive. This must be viewed as more like a Shanghai and the use of English in this city is immediately very evident everywhere, as are its Christmas decorations which are an entire industry on its own.

Wednesday did not go quite as planned. We lunched at a nice restaurant of the edge of the Yangtze River on a steep embankment of eleven floors that has been very well done with a variety of restaurants, pirate ships, bronze statues, and Chinese gift shops. This was a lovely area, but very misty before departing back to the hotel and to buy some dried fruits and spices to take back.

Tonight, one of my wife's relatives took us out to a lovely traditional Sichuan restaurant set on the deep banks of the Yangtze River for a lovely dinner. He is well educated, having studied Law at University and now a household designer specializing in shopping malls and supermarkets. He is doing quite well in life despite being quite young at twenty years old.

Thursday 24th December 2009 and we are up at five o'clock for the trip by hotel car northwest and about ten kilometres from the Sichuan border to the nearest town to my wife's home in the 'mountains'. This though turned out to be a successful day and one of the most truly fascinating days of my life, not only in China, but anywhere.

Firstly, we had a long four hours' drive along wonderfully empty highways through the Chongqing's hilly and mountainous countryside. Consequently, there were many extremely new road tunnels. The hotel driver incredibly careful in his black Ford limousine car with impressive all tan leather interior; it was at least a comfortable ride; our progress only slowed a little at times by the morning fogs in the area.

We arrived in the city of Kai Xian and then drove up along a wide dammed river towards my wife's local hometown, a small rural town. It is set back on a wide river that I guess to be part reservoir and part food source for the locals surrounded by hill and 'mountains' that as always are beautiful, especially given these winter months, but difficult to appreciate fully in the early morning mists.

The village elder from her hometown is assisting us today and he advised that we could get everything done back in the city of Kai Xian.

The next few hours were all good news. In between this we took our friends to lunch at the best restaurant along with the driver who it seems is also impressed with me and kept wanting photos together. These folks are not wealthy, although they do not need much money to live around these parts, but I was surprised therefore when the uncle removed a wad of money and counted it under the table and then checked successively by the other two of ¥22,400 (£2,400). It turns out that this is the electricity bill money to pay for the mountainside area and which he had collected from houses and was going to pay to the authorities later.

Then we went to go and meet my wife's parents. We are informed that the roads are a little uneven, but the hotel limousine driver is keen to try and take us, viewing a large tip at the end of it all, but also apparently wanting a job in the more lucrative Yangtze delta area with me in Jiaxing.

Anyway, what happened next was one of the more fascinating moments of my life, an insight, beauty, emotion and well so much! The initial drive back was uneventful, but then we turned to the local ferry, a haphazard affair crossing the river reminding me of the one in Dawson City, Yukon, but not that professional and certainly not overly safe and I note that we are the only car, although several folks on foot and a few motorbikes. I had assumed that we did not have far to go once we had crossed. This temporary situation I assume was due to work related to the Three Gorges damming and effect upon the area. The sun was out, and I looked around at the surrounding countryside, the beauty of the outline of the mountains, the skyline in the sunshine, the greenery, the terraces, and white houses that exist.

The trip started well enough along the river side on a new concrete one lane road that has been dug up again periodically for design repairs ensuring that the car bottomed out too often much to the disturbance of the driver, and me, although this was nothing compared to what was to come. As we turned off the concrete road onto a track, I thought that we would not take long, but not realizing that my wife's parents farm was up at the top of the mountain.

Then after one and a half hours after crossing the river, having driven up and up past countless houses and through farmyards and fields, we arrived at her parent's place. Chinese mountains are vegetated by and large and not as sheer at the larger global ranges of the Alps or the Rockies. This one is very fertile, and I note quickly that her parent's patch included orange trees, walnuts, peanuts, rice paddy fields as we tracked down alongside of the paddy field terraces on mud banks around the basic brick house and yard. The place was spotless, something her father has always insisted upon, with a satellite dish on the roof. Then there was the pig in the sty, two cats, a dog, geese, and ducks running around, with a tied-up cow and donkey not too far away. My eldest daughter was terrified of the geese and wanted to be on my shoulders. She was though as good as gold with her grandparents and behaved well. Sadly, as the light was about to disappear, we could only stay for about an hour before going back down the mountain for a trip back to Chongqing city that took us over six hours, arriving at about midnight. The limousine had had a battering and you can be sure that they have never seen a car like that up there, nor a foreigner apparently!

My wife had not been home for several years, although had seen both of her parents in Zhejiang at the birth of both daughters. There had therefore been much excitement all around with all the neighbours and many relatives coming to witness her return, to see the half-blood kids that are adored and treasured in China and her foreigner husband. Everyone seemed thrilled for my wife with many of her former childhood female friends and neighbours in genuine tears of happiness.

I did take a moment though to stop in amongst all the photos, look around and reflect. This is one of the most beautiful spots on earth, fresh air, high altitude and peaceful. I felt extremely privileged to be experiencing this in my life. It was great to see the place where she was born and brought up. The views down to the dammed river were magnificent and I could only imagine what it would all be like in summer when things were really growing! The mountain air was just so fresh and could imagine that in ten years' time that this will be a different place again as at present the younger generations are leaving for the cities, but that means more money is being sent back for the older generation, many of whom are migrating to local towns and cities. This place could be a paradise.

As we departed to waves, tears, wide smiles and shouts I am thrilled for my wife and her parents; this was long overdue and unfinished business and we vow to go back and see them in a few months when we come back, although we will stay in Kai Xian and let her parents come down and stay with us for a few days. I am also thrilled that our elder daughter has seen her grandparents again and vice versa and indeed they saw our baby at a more developed stage. This is important in life, and I suspect that the many photos taken will be precious. So much of this reminded me of my days as a child visiting the mining village of St. Denis in Cornwall – not developed, vegetables and the likes in abundance, a calmness about life and relative innocence.

We arrived home late and tired after over eighteen hours traveling; nearly Christmas Day. My wife is suddenly ecstatic after keeping her emotions in check and is thrilled in all respects and so proud of the kids. What a day!

Friday, Christmas Day, and who would ever have thought that I would have been in Chongqing, China for such an occasion! I explain that this year we are not exchanging gifts but have had a 'holiday' coming to Chong Qing and going to grandparents.

Chongqing weather, whilst warmer is certainly greyer and it is very noticeable how late the light comes up here each day, between seven-thirty and eight o'clock; quite different to Jiaxing. This morning we relax a little reflecting upon yesterday – yesterday we made a lot of people happy.

w/c 26th December 2009 – Reflecting I note that about two thirds of China *lived in the countryside until only a few years ago prior to the urbanization and migration processes starting, so my wife's family was no different to how most of the China lived and more than 50 per cent of China still does, i.e., more than 650 million people. The habitat of the mountain, although a little chilly at night, but no extreme cold and an affable all-round temperature and climate and is far better than much of China, fertile, clean air and plenty of exercise and no damaging health environmental issues such as mines, factories (although the main nearby factory was submerged by the recent creation of a lake) or the likes. The diet up there is also a healthy one although not diverse, in a community that is close knit. That is now all changing of course at a mindboggling speed as witnessed again in Chongqing, its houses, and its huge and modern shopping centres et al. There is always a refreshing innocence to my wife and having been to her home and surrounds I now have a much better appreciation of what has contributed to that. Her parents are kind and good people!*

I finally got to Chongqing! The land of the Three Gorges and the Yangtze River. So much history and this unfortunately was not the sort of trip to find out and explore more. I have been impressed with the city, not sure about the heavy mists though, a little depressing at times. I must still do the Three Gorges Trip sometime, a trip that takes four days, although not with the views that one used to get due to the dam project that submerged them.

I also note the wisdom and strength of character of my wife's parents, who refused to let her, or her brothers work on the farm, but insisted that they study at school and work hard, unlike many others around who let their kids skip school and worked. That has benefited her and demonstrates the value of education to anyone; education is not everything but goes a long way in life.

I was to visit Chong Qing many times over the coming years (2009-2016) and was amazed to witness the improvements made everywhere across the board as the rural provinces modernized and the progress and development of Kaixian in particular. Simply incredible.

28.19 Sichuan

w/c 27ʰ August 2011 - Wednesday started with a trip to Pudong airport along with three colleagues for the three hours long flight to Chengdu in western China's Sichuan Province; my first trip there to see a paper mill that has closed.

The Hotel in Chengdu was a Chinese four-star hotel, but was not one of the best examples, in fact it was lousy in many respects and the host has made a mistake in putting us here, reflecting their lack of funds. Additionally, our fourteenth-floor bedrooms looked out of the back onto a vacant building plot that had been levelled in central Chengdu.

It was a pleasant dinner with our hosts though, some traditional spicy Sichuan dishes, but it was the variety of tastes that impressed me. I even enjoyed the 'sea slug' delicacy and the abalone was decidedly edible. Afterwards the driver got lost getting back to the hotel and after that my British colleague and I went out to a very pleasant bar area along the riverside, although I only stayed under an hour before leaving him to it all.

The host was a good one, sixty-three years old and spoke a little English claiming that he was from an 'international family' given the fact that his daughter and wife have lived in Los Angeles in the States for the last six years, his younger sister in Canada and his younger brother in the UK for the last twenty years. Such is the modern world! This is not an untypical situation.

Chengdu is a big city with 6.7m people living in the city itself and another 7.1m including the nine districts that comprise its immediate suburbs, thereby totalling 14m in the 2010 census. An ancient city, it is one of the leading cities for investment with 133 of the Global Fortune 500 companies invested here and even has Consulates of the USA and Germany here.

The city has been around since the fourth century and was sacked by the Mongols in 1279 who killed 1.4m people. Sichuan became the war time refuge of the Kuomintang, Chang Kai Shek's government headquarters before he disappeared to Taiwan in 1949. Accordingly, he brought a lot of industrialists, intellectuals, academics, skilled workers, and professionals to Sichuan, which lay the foundation for its development and industry today. American bombers were based here in 1944 as a part of the war against Japan. It is also famous as a panda bear breeding centre with so many fertile hills around. In 2008 it was remarkably close to the centre of the devastating magnitude 8.0 earthquake that killed 80,000 although Chengdu itself was unaffected directly.

The climate is monsoon influenced humid sub-tropical and is mild and humid as a result. It is famous for its food – its variety and its spiciness. It is not uncommon to rain all year round and its sunshine is affected as a result, although the environment is regarded as good for health.

Thursday and unfortunately, I hardly slept all night in aver uncomfortable bed. Still despite an elevator failure, we headed out for the factory about forty-five kilometres to the northeast of Chengdu in the direction of the centre of the Sichuan earthquake that dominated in 2008. I was whacked but stayed in reasonable form for the meeting and factory visit, the factory very impressive, but closed due to lack of working capital due to a loss of sales orders.

Then it was a lunch with the Chairwoman and the team in a large banquet. Luckily, it was only beer and sensible, but too long. The food though was delicious and afterwards we drove through the local city and into the centre of Chengdu for some site seeing, although at thirty-eight degrees centigrade it was too hot to get out of the car. This and the associated cities here created another one of China's new mega cities.

We left Chengdu at early evening and were back home just prior to midnight. This was my first trip to Sichuan in western China, a famous province and just to the west of my wife's home province, Chong Qing, which was once part of Sichuan, and many folks still refer to it in the same context. I have now visited 69 per cent of China! It is quite pleasant to be traveling in China again after a break effectively of several years except for Chong Qing. This is a vastly different country to the one that I arrived in approaching ten years ago now, far more developed, and affluent and all that goes with it including too much flipping traffic.

28.20 Hebei

w/c 4ᵗʰ February 2012 - Wednesday I was up early and collecting my British deputy and then to Shanghai for our flight up to Shi Jia Zhuang, in Hebei province near to Beijing. This is my first visit to this province and the city. We are going to look at a flax and speciality pulp mill there and are being collected by a fellow from Hong Kong who owns it. This will be my twenty-fourth province-SAR is China (71per cent of China's provinces), leaving nine more to visit and I am left wondering if I ever will get the chance?

My colleague was good company on the flight from Shanghai to Shijiazhuang Hengfeng International Airport, which suffered a lot of turbulence before landing at the new airport or has one new terminal with another bigger terminal being built, some 320 kilometres or so to the southwest of Beijing.

Having been collected we had a positive meeting at an old decrepit speciality pulp mill an hour out of town, with a Hong Kong national and his wife, a former University Professor in Hong Kong who studied for his master's at Imperial College, London and his wife who was a trained medical doctor. There were all sorts of issues in this traditional papermaking city, and I recall that many mills were closed in this area on environmental grounds ahead of the Beijing Olympics, which was the right call, although it is also apparent that some have re-opened again since. This was followed by a hot pot dinner and then back to Shijiazhuang, to check into the newly opened Intercontinental Hotel there, which was a real Intercontinental.

Shijiazhuang is the capital city of northeast China's largest province, Hebei and had a population of 10.81m in 2010. It is a newly industrialized city and is home of a large garrison of troops ready to shoot off to protect Beijing and accordingly has many People's Liberation Army Colleges and Universities in the city. During WW2 it was a large railway town and is a commercial centre for products coming in by train including grain, tobacco, and cotton. Until 1948 it was known as Shimen. It is twin towns with many places including Des Moines, Iowa; Saskatoon, Saskatchewan, Canada; Parma, Emilia-Romagna, Italy; Bielsko-Biala, Poland; Cheonan, Chungcheongnam-do, South Korea; Soria, Castilla y León, Spain; Falkenberg, Sweden; Edison, New Jersey, United States; and Nagykanizsa, Hungary. No British counterpart listed though!!

Thursday morning, I look out of the Intercontinental Hotel window to see my sixteenth-floor room that it looks right out over a nine-hole golf course/park right in the middle of town along with frozen lakes and river/canal; almost New York Central Park like, or even the park in Boston, the name of which that I cannot immediately recall!

These were real time snapshots of some of my travels around China, too many experiences to document here. I consider myself privileged to have enjoyed these moments at an incredible time in China's emergence and development, an historically pivotal period. Incredible is the size of the country, its scale, ambition, organization, and desire to succeed in everything that it does. No westerner can totally understand the sheer pace of changes and developments that had taken place during my time in China and indeed that continues despite the challenges of coronavirus pandemics, global changes related to Russia's invasion of Ukraine and the uncertainties that prevail.

Epilogue

As I conclude on my nearly fifteen years in China I reflect upon the experiences and impact to date. There were far more experiences and emotions that I could begin to have included in this book alone.

China has transformed itself from a developing country into a modern and dynamic society that probably is to be the largest economy in the world. It has developed its wealth initially through becoming the factory of the World and its associated trade exports and increasingly through the internal developing middle-class markets and the rich as it modernizes, exporting its skills and financial backing. This incredibly fast paced society is unlikely to slow down much anytime soon, and its wealth is contributing globally.

It has built relationships worldwide, including many that are off radar to much of the West, and its people have spread around the world, in the most adding to societies through trade, hard work, huge investment and drive. They are welcome tourists in most countries given their penchant for buying expensive products and gifts. Just as welcome, often more so to many, are the overseas investments in infrastructural projects, perceived by some as investment traps, maybe, but enable through cooperation with China, those countries to benefit and develop, and it will be interesting to see what happens in Afghanistan going forward, particularly given what is already happening in neighbouring Pakistan and its proximity to the old silk road.

At the time of completing this book China has been celebrating, with considerable national fanfare, the notable 100th anniversary of the 1921 birth of the Chinese Communist Party there with light shows across the country and demonstrations of its successes in improving the lives of its people. It is proud and, on a roll, assisted by a somewhat naive western world at times! It now has a wide-ranging capability, an unbelievable thirst for improvement and is pushing the traditional boundaries as we know them.

Its ambitions are demonstrable at many levels, including as an example the medal successes at the 2020 Olympic Games in Tokyo whereby China finished second only to the USA in the medal table for both gold and total medals.

On a personal viewpoint, I remarried and have two wonderful children, a sign of the changing world with increased movement whereby opposites attract. China though damaged me with the dice permanently loaded against foreign companies. China was hard work and despite the welcome and often personal friendliness, within the set of circumstances that I was dealt business wise, it was never easy, not from day one and continued to get harder, much harder. I conclude that foreign investment is there to be taken advantage of, if not correctly positioned, that is the way. Frustration abounded. I damaged my career by staying far too long, many factors influencing that decision. Personally though I treasure the experiences and the privilege to live where I did during historic times.

A few points to reflect upon perhaps:

> Chinese society through its controls and rules has an orderliness that is absent is many parts of the western world. Any modern and developed society must have appropriate management control of its people; one can't have anarchy.

> There is respect for many parts of society that is admirable, especially in for instance its elders, for education and the teaching profession.

> China recognizes the value to its society of an excellent education and installs hard work from a young age. Its policies and focus have this as a high priority to fuel its drive, support its ambitions and improve the lot of its people.

> There aren't the overt drug problems and abuse, at least not like in the West, with largely an absence of the crime and wastage of lives that goes with it.

> One doesn't generally see folk sleeping or camped on the streets in China's cities, thus no spoiling of the cities, one can cynically comment why this may be, but this needs social reflection.

Generally there is good law and order, at least from a personal safety and security viewpoint, a stark contrast to some of the global rebellions that we have seen in recent years elsewhere, not least in the USA as parts of cities were annexed unfettered by radical extremists; a slippery slope indeed.

I didn't feel my freedom was restricted or controlled, nor was what I said. Likewise the bureaucracy that I initially found tiring and boring initially has now been applied to much of the western world in what are now seen as sensible measures of society control.

There is no gun crime in China – there are no guns outside of the military or security forces.

The country, whilst at times having differences of opinions internally, is not divided as so much of the West is, not overtly, except for obvious areas as Xinjiang and Hong Kong. The West remain divided and distracted, caught up in politics and not focused on addressing the issues, often politically afraid of doing the right thing.

Immigration is strictly controlled, unapologetically.

China is very resourceful at many levels and generally 'finds a way' to get things done – there always seems to be a route around barriers – when it suits!

ID Cards, when the irrationality is removed from consideration, is not a bad idea. It is clear and becomes an integral part of society.

China has a strength and stubbornness and is playing the long game and with that it has patience. A patience sorely tested by the protesters in Hong Kong. Whatever the validity of the reasons to protest or not, and it is quite possible that China had been pushing the boundaries on its agreements, the protestors weren't going to win that situation, there was no obvious solution with no one realistically prepared to go to war to protect the protestors and

Hong Kong. The clock can't be turned back, and Hong Kong is a part of China. China was publicly taunted and had no option to impose itself it that situation and unfortunately the situation in Hong Kong may have changed more quickly, therefore.

Contracts and agreements once based and supported upon trust and relationships by much of China are increasingly legalistic.

Whilst there is now some incredible wealth around and being a socialist society, there aren't the financial safety nets in society that one sees in some economies elsewhere, such as a free national health service or handouts for being unemployed. Economic hardship is still very real and a motivation to work and improve one's life.

China has modernized incredibly, has developed some leading positions and controls more and more of the globe.

Globally Chinese expatriate communities have developed extensive networking communications systems, benchmarking, sharing, and comparing all aspects of life and they seek to improve their lot in life.

In the West folk talk about freedom and that should rightly be protected, but it would be wise to be open minded and learn the good things about China and perhaps apply the best of those things, albeit in modified forms perhaps to our own societies. China is coming – it is coming, harder and harder, and faster and faster! And it's very big and very strong and armed with the skills and resources necessary including its military might! We must get used to this fact.

In my diary extracts I made various comments regarding certain USA tourists in China. These reflected my instinctive observations at that time these were written, and based on the overt confidence of its citizens. These comments though should not be taken as me being anti American! To me America is a wonderful country that I have had the pleasure to have visited many times and observed its more recent progress and issues via a range international and domestic media of various bias. If one has money there it is a wonderful place to be with the best of everything.

However and pertinent to this book and its leadership race with China, it is obvious that the US has a substantial number of current challenges that have been and continue to deflect its attention away from global leadership and the lack of demonstratable competency of its country's management. I include a range of examples relevant:

Leaking national borders with associated uncontrolled and unregulated immigration, a problem, but something that will trouble internal political balances for generations to come, in what is already in a sensitive and unstable position, as well as potential security implications.

High crime rates, particularly high-profile crime, with the overlapping challenges of racial division and all those guns in circulation throughout society, legally or illegally.

Troubles policing many of its own cities and the control of societies within. Whatever spin one may want to put on it the situation is not great.

A deeply divided country at many levels, frighteningly so. As one elderly citizen said to me 'I don't know how this is going to end up, but maybe another civil war.' It is a divided team and in my spirting experiences, and business ones, divided teams are rarely the winning ones.

A seeming lack of clear, coordinated leadership, lacking a consistent strategic policy. Of course, I could be wrong, but that is not what its leading news channels are telling the world across the political spectrum, nor most other media channels in my experience. There is a nastiness in it all as well that does not set good examples.

It seems apparent that considerable energy and efforts used up 'playing politics' and justifying positions, rather than focussing on problem solving solutions and reducing divisions. As a non-US citizen, it seems to default to its constitution, guns, and abortion and that is where things get stuck.

The US is exposed as the leader of many global themes and social systemic development that transgress to the rest of the following western world. These themes have obvious effects on behavioural practices, a current example being the application of 'wokeness,' again a divisive situation given opinions expressed. Social media only exacerbates this situation.

There is a major issue distilling the truth and the facts of situations, in high up positions, that has spread across society like a cancer with fact checking and podcasts proliferating 'fake news.' In my life I have always tried to establish the true facts as the basis for control, progress and development, a reference point that everyone believes in, or at least understands, with credibility. It is apparent that this is not the case in the US and elsewhere and when we get into 'Your truths' then it is apparent that facts are not likely entirely on firm foundations.

The West, led by the US, is losing its way through its decadent lifestyles, the culture of celebrity and division.

I highlight these examples, not to pick on America, but to highlight some of its constitutional challenges that are in stark contrast to that of its main global competitor, China. Indeed China obviously has its own set of challenges, but has a very coordinated strategic approach, is developing through education, social stability, improved lifestyles, seems universally 'hungry' and therefore less distracted by the challenges listed above.

The USA's global leadership strife's have been highlighted in recent years by apparent conflicts with its Allies and culminating with the manner of its exit from Afghanistan, a military defeat with the world watching through global media from a front seat position. Demotivational for its military, its citizens, and its western allies.

How to compete with this? That is the question.

Firstly China's wealth was initially built upon the West's willingness to surrender its manufacturing to China and comply with its own strategic plan. History cannot be rewritten, and this cannot be easily reversed, but questions, especially with carbon net zero and goods and raw materials being shipped all around the world, are, can some of this manufacturing sensibly be relocated to proximities closer to home, in low environmental impact modern factories? It now will not have so much impact upon China as it has grown its internal markets, but it would claim back some control of its own supply chains for western countries and create jobs.

These supply lines are now more likely to be re-assessed anyway, both politically given Russia's invasion of Ukraine and Western concerns regarding China's intents, but also commercially given the escalating costs of fuel and delivery delays of goods from China affected by coronavirus lockdowns. A time for strategic review.

A major step would be to define the playing field that the competition is taking place on. Is it clearly understood and are the rules and objectives, especially long term, fully understood? How to compete on an equal basis? Be incredibly careful in catering for the interpretation of those contractual rules.

Be strong but fair, with a high degree of diplomacy required and absolute positions will not work unless there is a position of significant strength.

Strategically, do countries need or are they truly dependent upon what China has to offer, noting that its low costs base has risen and that many are now tired of the traditionally low-quality products that could be built closer to home and without adverse green consequences. Given environmental footprints it does not make so much sense to be moving non-speciality products all around the globe, including disposable ones or ones that quickly break and require routine replacement, a macro environmental issue.

Yes, protect the intelligence and security systems, be strong, but war will not be the answer. Talking to an American soldier in Seoul's Incheon airport once, where there is a huge and visible American presence guarding the border between North and South Korea, who said that they could not pick a fight with China 'there just are not enough bullets'! A joke, but.......... China will undoubtedly though continue to build its military might to what it sees as a competitive situation with the USA as a part of its negotiating positioning and spreads its might geographically.

Investment in foreign countries may have to be considered and reviewed to protect its culture, key assets and certain industries and ensure stability. An issue is that China has already bought up or invested in a lot of the world whether it being through industry, energy, software, microchips, precious metals, media, infrastructure, and assisting the developing countries of the world or individuals investing in housing. Things may be slowed down, but the ball has been rolling and seems to me to be gaining speed.

As an eminent social scientist recently said regarding left wing individuals criticizing right wing leaning government discussions and actions, "in my experience people should put their own house in order before trying to re-organize the world." This is a valid point that I consider should also apply to the western economies; there is a lot to put right, and leaders should be stronger at implementing corrective actions that would strengthen their own countries positions.

The West would benefit from increasing ambition, education, incentivizing work, and incentivizing marriage, understanding and social stability, developing adequate infrastructures and of course applying some degree of common sense that at this moment of time seems to have escaped some, and of course ensuring good law and order. Thereby avoiding the social breakdown in society.

Hand in hand with this must be the re-establishment of respect for authority and the discipline that goes with it, stepping away from the personal attacks and divisiveness that currently seems to exist fuelled by social media

Be prepared to enforce the rules agreed and not to be bullied.

'Asian hate' is not the answer at any level! We live in a multicultural society and must find ways to coexist peacefully and without fear.

Along the way also recognize the positives of the dynamics at play, noting as a random example, that Emma Raducanu, whilst very British, is the product of a Chinese mother.

There is no one answer. Whatever the challenges, I would expect China to continue to consolidate and develop its power platforms over the coming decades growing towards global leadership. China continues to ride the wave of self-created opportunity and ambition that the West actively played ball with. It is now a question of finding the balance.

An overt indicator of this rise was that several of the main pitch-side sponsors at matches at Football's 'Euros 2021' were Chinese – Hisense (White goods and electronics), Tik Tok (Video-sharing social media networking), Vivo (Smart-phones development, software, and online services), Alipay (a PayPal type equivalent) and AntChain (the largest productivity blockchain platform).

It is happening!

In this book, I sought not to criticize and judge, but to critically observe and try to understand and compare. To keep things in context, as China has opened, especially over the past fifteen years, being a westerner there today does not carry the novelty value that it did at the time that I arrived upon those shores twenty years ago. There are many more foreigners these days with many more having passed through. At the time I started there much of China had still not really had contact with foreigners and my diary entries reflect that in terms of attention and reaction to me at times.

All the information quoted in my diary extracts about China was from the English language China Daily newspaper or broadcast on CCTV's English language channels unless stated otherwise.

In closing I wish to point out that whilst my personal diary extracts provide insight into primarily my travel times, that business was all consuming, no sense of nine to five working, but almost twenty-four-hour, seven-day a week situation given events and circumstances. This was hard and challenging work.

Finally, but not last in my thoughts, I wish to take the opportunity to thank all my friends and colleagues in China for supporting me during my time there, and being there as a friend as best one could despite life's challenges, and of course to my wonderful family.